The

# TRIUMPH OF GRACE
in the Theology of
# KARL BARTH

G. C. BERKOUWER

---

THE

# TRIUMPH OF GRACE

IN THE THEOLOGY OF

# KARL BARTH

1956

WM. B. EERDMANS PUBLISHING COMPANY

Grand Rapids, Michigan

*First published May* 1956
*Second edition November* 1956

LIBRARY OF CONGRESS NUMBER 56-9380

———————

Translated from the Dutch
DE TRIOMF DER GENADE IN DE THEOLOGIE VAN KARL BARTH
by HARRY R. BOER

This American Edition is published by special arrangement
with the Dutch publisher
J. H. KOK, KAMPEN, THE NETHERLANDS

PHOTOLITHOPRINTED BY CUSHING - MALLOY, INC.
ANN ARBOR, MICHIGAN, UNITED STATES OF AMERICA
1956

# TRANSLATOR'S PREFACE

Perhaps no contemporary theologian is so well known by name in the English speaking world, and so little in terms of his thought, as the Swiss theologian, Karl Barth. Unlike Emil Brunner, he has not, with the exception of a few books, had the good fortune of seeing his works translated into English. The reason for this is doubtless the massive productivity of his pen. His *Kirchliche Dogmatik* alone in its present unfinished state numbers nine volumes, each having from 700 to 1100 pages, the greater part of which is in small print.

No one in our generation has so profoundly influenced European theological thought as Karl Barth. It would seem altogether desirable that understanding of the basic motifs of his theology should increase in the non-European world. Since many who are interested in Barth's thought are unable to read German, the only avenue open to them for becoming acquainted with it consists of books and articles written about his theology. Works in English that deal comprehensively with this subject are, however, surprisingly few. For this reason no apology need be made for the appearance in English, albeit in translation, of an authoritative work which attempts to penetrate to the heart of Barth's theological conception.

Dr. G. C. Berkouwer, Professor of Dogmatic Theology at the Free University in Amsterdam, is undoubtedly one of the most qualified men in Europe to express an evaluation of Barth's theology. He has not only carefully followed the writings of that theologian since he became a figure of stature in the early 1920's, but he has written extensively about Barth in books and periodicals. The volume here presented in translation has, because of its fairness to Barth and its loyalty to the author's Reformed theological commitment, had a highly favorable reception in theological circles in the Netherlands and in other countries. A German translation is at present in preparation.

Professor Berkouwer brings to bear on his study of Barth a fine understanding of both Protestant and Roman Catholic thought, an

iii

understanding which has been shaped by the rich tradition of Dutch theology in its impact upon him, as also by an intimate acquaintance with continental theology as a whole.

The present work should be of interest to all who desire a better understanding of Karl Barth. Professor Berkouwer presents him as the contender for a theology of triumphant grace which is moving in its imposing effort to restore to its due place in Christian thought and in the life of the Church the sovereign grace of God revealed in Jesus Christ. Has Barth, in his endeavor to do this, done justice to the grace which the Scriptures proclaim? Has he in all his massive appeal to Scripture and to the history of theology set forth this grace in a manner that correctly reflects the good news of God's redemption in Christ? This is the central question to which Professor Berkouwer addresses himself as he pursues the one theme of Barth's thinking in crucial areas of his theology.

A few comments must be made on the translation itself. I have endeavored to set forth accurately the thought of the author, to do so in good English, and to adhere as closely to the original word as the first two aims permitted. Berkouwer's Dutch is clear, but it is also fluid and suggestive. To capture and convey his style of writing has been difficult and I cannot hope to have wholly succeeded. I do cherish the hope, however, that shortcomings in this respect have not in an appreciable degree obscured the message of the author.

Characteristic of Berkouwer's writing is his technique of italicizing. This is a not uncommon manner of writing in Dutch and in German. Barth himself is much given to it. In general, the translation italicizes where the author does, but in many instances the formulation of the English carried its own emphasis and where this was the case I omitted the italics.

The translation is unabridged save in some minor respects of which I wish here to take note. Phrases and sentences in the body of the book have upon infrequent occasion been omitted when their incorporation in the English text, in contrast to the Dutch, would have created the impression of redundancy. The translation of the footnotes presented a far greater problem than did the body of the book. Professor Berkouwer wrote for a Dutch public and very many of his references are to the opinions of Dutch authorities. Very few readers of this book will be able to consult them. The references to these authorities are so interwoven with instructive comment, however, that in the interest of retaining the latter I have seen little alternative to translating them almost in toto. A few references that would have little or no meaning to a non-Dutch reader I have omitted. In view of the abundance of footnote material I have here and there omitted or translated only in part when there could be no question of prejudicing the fulness and clarity of the argument. Biblical references which in the Dutch edition all appeared in the footnotes have for the larger part been incorporated in the body of the text.

The several extensive footnotes on Dr. C. Van Til's criticism of Barth the author has reworked and gathered into a whole which is now presented in the form of an appendix at the end of the book.

Finally, I wish to call attention to the footnote indicated by an asterisk on page 62. It concerns the translation of the important expression, "das Nichtige," whereby Barth indicates a concept basic to his understanding of evil.

HARRY R. BOER

## Publisher's Note

This second edition of the English translation of *The Triumph of Grace in the Theology of Karl Barth* is in every respect the same as the first edition, except for the addition of the Translator's Preface and one more entry in the bibliography found on page 402, and the correction of a few typographical errors.

# CONTENTS

I. BARTH'S CONTINUING SIGNIFICANCE    9

II. THEOLOGY OF CRISIS?    23

III. THE TRIUMPH OF GRACE IN CREATION    52

IV. THE TRIUMPH OF ELECTION    89

V. THE TRIUMPH OF RECONCILIATION    123

VI. THE ESCHATOLOGICAL TRIUMPH    151

VII. THE TRIUMPH OF GRACE IN ITS ANTITHESIS TO ROME    166

VIII. AMBIGUOUS TRIUMPHS OF GRACE IN THE HISTORY OF THEOLOGY    196

IX. THE NATURE OF THE TRIUMPH    215

X. THE UNIVERSALITY OF THE TRIUMPH    262

XI. THE DIVINE TRIUMPH    297

XII. THE TRIUMPH OF THE END    328

XIII. THE TRIUMPH OF GRACE AND THE KINGDOM OF GOD    347

APPENDIX: The Problem of Interpretation    384

BIBLIOGRAPHIES    395

INDEXES    404

The
Triumph of Grace in the Theology of
KARL BARTH

# I

## BARTH'S CONTINUING SIGNIFICANCE

A**T HOME** and abroad the theology of Karl Barth continues to be a subject of vital interest. The judgment expressed at various times that its influence has passed the high-water mark is unmistakably being contradicted by the present theological situation.

As Schleiermacher placed his stamp on the theology of the nineteenth century, so Barth has now for about thirty years dominated the theological debate of our century as it comes to expression in terms of thesis and antithesis. Only recently it was suggested that the influence of Barth was gradually yielding to that of the New Testament scholar, Rudolph Bultmann, whose "demythologizing" of the New Testament has occasioned so much discussion. It would doubtless be a serious error to underestimate the response that Bultmann has found, and problems associated with the interpretation of the New Testament continue to stand in the forefront of theological interest. But it cannot be denied that the many questions and problems posed by Barth determine the whole of the contemporary theological situation more decisively than Bultmann's views do. The discussion centering around the (important!) question whether Bultmann's "demythologizing" conception still leaves room for a trustworthy kerugma is overshadowed by the comprehensive theological problems posed by Barth. In the polemics loosed by the theology of Barth almost every aspect of Reformed theology, especially its dogmatic aspect, has been subjected to review. In one way or another, the views of Barth in their exegetical, confessional and dogmatic expression, as they are set forth in his extensive dogmatic works, touch both the foundation and the superstructure of the whole of theology.

The proclamation of the Church, her dogma, the authority of Scripture and its proper interpretation, election, the image of

God, creation and redemption — all of these subjects have come to stand in the center of intense theological discussion.

In addition to his impact on the theological world, Barth's views have had powerful repercussions in non-theological spheres. Both he and his disciples have drawn conclusions from the fundamental positions of his "dialectical" theology that lead to a confrontation of his views in other than theological areas of thought and action. Political problems, especially the problem of Christian political action, relations between "East" and "West," the re-arming of Germany, were drawn into the discussion that centered around the name of Barth. It became evident that Barth was not simply a theoretical theologian, a "scholastic," but the author of a concrete, self-applying theology with all manner of implications for ethics and the pressing practical problems of the contemporary world.

For these reasons the search for the basic motif of his colossal dogmatic structure remains vitally relevant. This search is no doubt a difficult one, and many who undertake it will be conscious of having left the main path now and again. Still, considerering the importance of the problems involved, the urgency of determining the central theme of Barth's thought cannot be disputed.

It cannot be disputed either that the longer one concerns himself with Barth's theology, the more the conviction takes root that one meets here a consistent development of a central thought, that there is discernible in it a clearly recognizable theme amid all the variations of the whole. The search for the central motif has now been pursued for some thirty years, and the results have been very varied. All manner of motifs and themes have been suggested. Some have subsequently been revised, others have been maintained up to the latest phases in the development of Barth's thought.

An important question in the discussion has been the problem whether there is a *disjunction,* a fundamental *break,* between Barth's *Römerbrief* and his later dogmatic expositions, or whether there is *one* central theme — with unimportant modifications — that controls the development of his whole theological vision. In general, it can be said that the impression of an undeniable continuity is becoming more and more settled among students of Barth. The nature of this continuity is not easy to determine and, in view of Barth's own strictures on views he has expressed in earlier stages of his development, care must be taken not to mistake continuity for identity.

In the search for the dominant motif in Barth's theology, connections have been laid between him and the most varied streams of thought in earlier and later times. His theology has been described as neo-Marcionism,[1] neo-Manicheism,[2] Occamism,[3] and new-Modernism,[4] to mention only a few of the more prominent characterizations.

1. In a review of the first edition of the *Römerbrief* A. Jülicher already spoke of neo-Marcionism. Cf. A. Hein, "Moderner Marcionitismus und practische Theologie," *Theol. Blätter,* Vol. 1, 1922 pp. 124ff. and 145ff.
In the foreword of the second edition Barth replied to this criticism. He calls for carefulness in criticism, although he acknowledges that Harnack's book about Marcion showed him "certain striking parallels" to his own thought. But, "in the decisive points there is no correspondence," *Römerbrief,* 2nd edition, 1923, p. xvii. Cf. G. C. Berkouwer, *Karl Barth en de Kinderdoop,* 1947, p. 123ff.
2. K. Schilder, *De Heidelbergsche Catechismus,* Vol. III, 1950, p. 357ff. Concerning the accusation of neo-Manicheism made against the Calvinists in the 16th century (because of their doctrine of predestination) cf. Vol. I, p. 198.
3. The subject of Occamism was raised especially in connection with Barth's view of God's freedom in His revelation. We find the parallel Barth-Occam pointed to already by D. Tromp, *Nieuwe Theologie,* 1926, p. 15; cf. G. C. Berkouwer, *Geloof en Openbaring in de nieuwere Duitsche theologie,* 1932, p. 215ff., and *Karl Barth,* 1936, p. 1936, p. 76ff.; H. Van Oyen, "Over wijsgerige affiniteit van Barth's theologie," *Onder Eigen Vaandel,* 1938, pp. 274ff. and 286ff. Van Oyen is of the opinion that the accusation of Occamism is not justified, but that there are passages in Barth in connection with contingency and accidence, arbitrariness and alienation, which point dangerously in this direction, p. 286. E. Brunner spoke of Barth's "unheard of theological nominalism," *Natur und Gnade,* 2nd edition, 1935, p. 39. Cf. also Jerome Hamer, *Karl Barth. L'occasionalisme théologique de Karl Barth,* 1949, p. 260.
It is clear, it seems to me, that in his later development Barth showed himself to be increasingly aware of these dangers and that opposition to the idea of "arbitrariness" ("Laune") occupies an important place in his dogmatics. We think here of his conception of the "Deus revelatus," his sharp criticism of the "potentia inordinata" as endangering the assurance of salvation, and his Christological interpretation of God's omnipotence. We shall discuss these questions in the course of the argument.
4. C. Van Til, *The New Modernism, An appraisal of the theology of Barth and Brunner,* 2nd ed., 1947; J. Severijn, *Vragen van tijd en eeuwigheid. Bezwaren tegen het nieuw-modernisme,* 1947. S. U. Zuidema considers Van Til's argument successful: "Het nieuw modernisme," in *Mededeelingen v. d. Vereeniging voor Calv. Wijsbegeerte,* Dec., 1946. Wholly different is the judgment of H. U. von Balthasar, *Karl Barth. Darstellung und Deutung seiner Theologie,* 1951, who describes Van Til's analysis as "fully grotesque" (p. 68), because Van Til sees the whole of Barth's theology in the light of "the philosophic presuppositions which are alleged to constitute its basis." Cf. also Th. L. Haitjema, "Een Amerikaanse aanval of de dialectische theologie," in *Pro Regno pro Sanctuario,* 1950, pp. 211-227, in which he speaks of a "horrible misunderstanding" (p. 217).

On the other hand, Roman Catholic theologians have time and again stressed that in Barth can be seen the consistent development of the Reformation, and therefore they have thought, via criticism of Barth, to launch a central assault on the Reformation.

It is therefore not an easy matter to expose clearly and responsibly the central thought of Barth's theology. An added complication in crystallizing its basic thrust arises from the new and strange elements upon which one comes again and again, and which are far removed from "traditional" theological thought patterns. Indeed, so marked is this feature in Barth that one may ask whether it is possible to enter sufficiently into the new mode of theological thinking, really to understand Barth and to do justice to him.[5] With respect to Brunner, the situation is wholly different. Brunner's theology can be grasped without experiencing much difficulty in the way of complicating conceptions. The difficulties that meet us in the theology of Barth, on the other hand, arise not so much out of his form of expression as out of his *mode of thinking*. Finally, we wish to note that Barth has on more than one occasion distanced himself from characterizations that have been made of his theology as, for instance, his rejection of the characterization of it as "monistic."[6]

---

5. As examples we may point to Barth's view of the relationship between creation and Jesus Christ (not as the Logos *asarkos* but as the Logos *ensarkos*), to his doctrine of the image of God, of the chaos, of angels and demons, his exegesis of chapters 1 and 2 of Genesis, and his conception of the "ontological impossibility" of sin.

6. In his KD III/4, p. x, Barth refers to his being accused of "monism." Brunner, for instance, spoke of a "monistic framework" in which he sees the elimination of the "tension of life grounded in the dialectic between God's holiness and His love." *Dogmatik*, II, p. 366. Brunner thinks to direct such a framework in Barth's doctrine of double predestination and in the "granting of salvation to all" which he believes Barth to teach. From "monism" the expression "Christo-monism" must be distinguished. The later expression has in its reference to Barth been used by Brunner, Althaus, myself, and others. It is, according to Barth, "hardly a beautiful term" when it is used polemically, KD III/3, p. v. He asks "whether a Christian theologian can with good conscience and a joyful heart do anything else than put 'Christ only' first and last in all his thinking?" It is clear that this question does not answer the question put by the expression "Christo-monism" because this did not intend in any way to detract from the "solo Christo" but only to reflect on the validity of the Christological foundation of Barth's dogmatics, and on his criticism of general revelation and of Art. II of the Belgic Confession. In 1938 Barth himself spoke of the "Christological concentration" of his thinking which from 1932 on found expression in his *Kirchliche Dogmatik*: K. Barth, "Parergon. Karl Barth über sichselbst," "*Evang. Theologie*, 1949/1950. Also H. Berkhof spoke of Barth's "Christocentrism" in "De betekenis van Karl Barth voor theologie, kerk en wereld," *Wending*, 1947, p. 14.

Over against these difficulties that stand in the way of interpreting Barth is the growing volume of his writings wherein he has expressed himself on many dogmatic questions concerning which students could for a long time do no more than entertain suppositions as to what his views on them were. It is therefore reasonable to assume that the fundamental tendency of Barth's thinking will increasingly present itself more clearly[7], even though the problem of true interpretation will continue to cast its shadow over every analysis.[8]

*    *    *

By the increasing clarity of motif of which we speak here, we certainly do not refer to a clarity that flows forth from a "system" constructed on the basis of one fundamental principle. Barth himself has often declared that his dogmatic development has not been one that followed a course of purely logical deduction. He is conscious of having come to walk in unexpected paths. It is therefore necessary to exercise care in characterizing his theology, lest we fall into the danger of over-simplifying the course of its development. A few examples will illustrate what is meant here.

As far as I am aware, no one had before 1940 concluded from Barth's writings that he would *necessarily* have to come to his subsequent rejection of infant baptism, even though he had already treated the sacraments.[9] Among the surprises of which Barth himself speaks is his new insight into the doctrine of creation of which, in connection with his exegesis of Genesis 1 and 2, he writes, "I myself am not unaware of its unusual character. I had certainly not expected that closer study of the text and of the problem [of creation] would finally lead to this result."[10] Precisely here, he writes, he has found it necessary to abandon much of the theological tradition. He then continues, "in the doctrine of predes-

7. We think here of the digest given of several volumes of the KD by Otto Weber in his *K. Barth's Kirchliche Dogmatik*, (1950 from I/1 to III/2; the 2nd edition, 1952, has been extended to include III/3 and III/4), and of Barth's introduction to it in which he speaks of those who have read the KD "entirely" before they judged him and in their reading "desired to understand and did understand" what the KD wished to say (p. 6).

8. An instance of this is the interpretation of Barth given by von Balthasar, *op. cit.* We shall return to this question later.

9. K. Barth, "Die Lehre von den Sakramenten," *Zwischen den Zeiten*, 1929.

10. KD III/1, Introduction, p. 1.

tination as such I would much rather have remained with Calvin,
instead of distancing myself so far from him. Also in laying down
the main lines of Christian ethics, I would have preferred to follow more accustomed ways. But I was quite unable to do this.
The longer I allowed the Bible to speak to me about these things,
and the longer I reflected on what I understood its speaking to convey to me, the more the new conceptions pressed themselves upon
me."[11]

Barth's development, therefore, presents us with a characteristic structure of growth and expansion of earlier thoughts in terms
of continuing confrontation with Scripture and confession. Barth
is clearly aware of the fact that his theological effort is a human
undertaking, but that in this undertaking the irresistible and overpowering testimony of the Scriptures propelled him forward on this
path of unexpected developments.

It was, in view of these considerations, natural for Barth to concern himself with the question of the extent to which it is possible
to speak of his agreement with the theology of the Reformation.
Whoever reads up to and including his treatment of the doctrine
of reconciliation[12] is continually struck by a very close association
with, and recurring appeal to, Luther and Calvin and the confessions of the Reformation. This is especially noticeable in Barth's
continuing polemic against Roman Catholicism.[13]

At the same time, according to Barth's expressed declaration,
it is not his intention simply to restate Reformation theology. He
acknowledges explicitly that on fundamental points he departs
from the Reformers. He considers it necessary to do this consciously and freely, in order that orthodoxy be not confused with ortho-
doxism, and in order to prevent the denial of the confession of the
Reformation that the Word of God should always stand *above* the

---

11. KD II/2, p. vii. This would not seem to mean, however, that Barth came
to these "new conceptions" exclusively in direct connection with his preparation
of II/2 (1942). The trend of his thinking about election was clearly evident
already in his lectures in Hungary (1936) and in the questions which he answered there in connection with them. Cf. K. Barth "Gottes Gnadenwahl" in
*Theol. Existenz heute*, Vol. 47, 1936. Moreover, there are undeniable points of
contact between Barth's present views on election and the *Römerbrief*.
12. KD IV/1 (Die Lehre von der Versöhnung), 1953.
13. Cf. Barth on the relationship between original Paulinism and the Paulinism
of the Reformation, KD IV/1, p. 695ff. See also at the conclusion of section 61
his references to questions 60-64 of the Heidelberg Catechism, pp. 717, 718.

Church and her teachers as *the* critical norm that validates the entire Church and her teachings. This does not mean for Barth a break with the Reformation, but rather its necessary further development, and includes a critical reproduction of the confessions of the Reformation.[14]

Barth feels that only in this way can he remain true to the fundamental principle of the Reformation, namely the normativity of the Word of God.[15] Thus, in the doctrine of election he finds it necessary to depart from Calvin, but he wishes fully to honor certain scriptural conceptions of Calvin. The question remains, however, whether this manner of treating the Reformation preserves continuity with it. In Protestant circles this had been denied more than once, while many a Roman Catholic has thought to find in Barth the consistent development of the Reformation.[16]

If Barth's relationship to the Reformation was dynamic and mobile, it was in its concrete expression one that contained many surprises for the student of his thought. Some of these we have already noted. We note further here his strong emphasis on the ontological goodness of human nature which even led Brunner to speak of the "new Barth."[17] Barth also drew attention to his views by time and again defending dogmas that had for long been regarded as antiquated by the liberal Protestant theology of the nineteenth and twentieth centuries. From 1927[18] to his latest volume of the *Dogmatik* published in 1953[19] he defended the doctrine of

---

14. Cf. K. Barth, *Gotteserkenntnis und Gottesdienst nach reformatorischer Lehre*, 1938 (treating of the Scottish Confession of 1560), in which Barth states that he is not concerned to present an historical analysis "but a theological paraphrase, that is, a critically-productive repetition of the original text," (p. 6).
15. Barth has also defended himself against the charge that the new theological orientation means a return to the orthodoxy of the 17th century. More than that, it is not possible to be a theologian "without constantly having to oppose also Luther and Calvin": "Die Neuoriëntierung der Prot. Theol. in den letzten dreiszig Jahren," Radio address published in *Kirchenblatt für die ref. Schweiz*, 1940, Vol. 7.
16. Cf. among others H. U. von Balthasar, *op. cit.*, p. 31: "We must enter into discussion with Barth because in him real Protestantism finds a — finds its — fully consistent statement." Also C. J. De Vogel has spoken of a restatement of "the fundamental motifs of the Reformation," Ecclesia Catholica, 1946 p. 31. Cf. my *Conflict met Rome*, 3rd ed., 1955, p. 305ff.
17. E. Brunner, "Der neue Barth," *Zeitschrift für Theol. und Kirche*, Vol. 48. (In English, "The new Barth," *Scottish Journal of Theology*, June 1951.)
18. In Barth's *Prolegomena*, 1927.
19. KD IV/1, p. 226.

the virgin birth, especially against Brunner who has, also since 1927, launched sharp attacks against it.[20]   Alongside of this defense of the virgin birth stands his incisive attack on Bultmann's "demythologizing" conception, wherein Barth especially maintains the historicity of the resurrection of Jesus Christ.[21] And — to mention no more — he defended against liberal Protestant theology the traditional Christological dogma of the deity and the humanity of Christ by rejecting the criticism of the "vere Deus et vere homo" as a speaking beside the point.

Small wonder that the question has been asked again and again whether it is possible to fit Barth into one or other of the traditional theological patterns. What must one think, for instance, of a characterization of Barth's theology as "new-Modernism" when in that theology are taught the virgin birth, incarnation, resurrection, and ascension to heaven?   Does Barth's theology present us, perhaps, with a new mode of theological thinking?   Does it constitute a theological category unique in itself, born in a critical period of human history and pursuing its development in the increasing apocalyptic tensions of our time?

Still other questions obtrude themselves.   What was the background of the tension that became noticeable within the ranks of the dialectical theologians in the course of the years?   What occasioned the shipwreck of the common program known as Zwischen den Zeiten (Between the Times)?   Why do we see Barth taking position, in varying contexts, against his former colleagues Brunner, Gogarten and Bultmann?   And why do *Barth* and *Thurneysen* still stand together?   How was it possible that a conflict should arise

---

20. E. Brunner, *Der Mittler*, 1927. Concerning the conflict between Barth and Brunner, cf. my *Het werk van Christus*, 1953, chapter V.

21. KD III/2, p. 531 ff., particularly against Bultmann's conception of resurrection-*belief*. Further, Barth's *R. Bultmann. Ein Versuch ihn zu verstehen* in *Theol. Studien*, Heft 34, 1952. It is impossible to understand how Brunner can write that this brochure against Bultmann means "not a clarifying advance in the discussion but only a beclouding of it," *Das Ewige als Zukunft und Gegenwart*, 1953, p. 157. Especially the questions which Barth put to Bultmann about Heidegger and the New Testament are very important and certainly constitute an "advance." On the other hand, it is difficult to understand how Barth — with the example of Bultmann and that of many others before him — is willing to speak about the danger of a given philosophical method only when "it is changed from being an instrument into something wholly different," *R. Bultmann*, p. 45. The problem lies in "the instrument" as such. Cf. Barth himself : "His association with Existentialism, however, has for Bultmann *fundamental* significance," *ibid.*, p. 45.

within the circle of the theologians of the Word that had leveled veritable solar-plexus blows against subjectivism, psychologism and historicism? Whence the shadows that began to fall over the regained insight that the gospel of the Old and New Testaments places the righteousness of God over against *our* righteousness, over against all anthropocentric experimental theology and mysticism?

Looking back on thirty years of theological development, one can continue to ask questions in this vein. It is not our intention, however, to seek an answer to these historical questions. Our concern is with the theology of Karl Barth, and in particular with that theology as it bears on the proclamation of the Church in the congregation of God's people and to the entire world. That it does indeed have this bearing is evident from the fact that Barth's dogmatic works are flanked by a sizeable number of sermons which it is not possible to regard as standing dualistically alongside his dogmatics without doing injustice to the deepest thrust and intent of Barth's theology. That his views of law and gospel, of gospel and law, of election and reprobation, of the knowledge of sin, and of the work that Christ is yet to do, must have profound effect on the proclamation of the Church is, therefore, hardly subject to question.

\* \* \*

Not only for its own sake, therefore, but also because of the close bearing of Barth's theology on the proclamation of the Church, the analysis of his dogmatic visions remains an exciting and necessary task. Although his *Dogmatik* is as yet far from finished, the direction in which his thought has moved since the appearance of the first volume of the *K. D.* in 1932 can be clearly discerned. This direction can be characterized in various ways, but Barth will certainly be done no injustice when one characterizes his dogmatics as unambiguously Christocentric. This does not mean, however, that Barth can be classified with other theologians who have pleaded for a Christocentrically oriented theology. It is more than plain that the Christological, Christocentric accent in Barth serves another or, at all events, a differently oriented function than one finds, for instance, in the various ethical theologies in the Netherlands or in the writings of Barth's one-time teacher, Wilhelm Herrmann.[22] This is evident particularly from the fact that Barth underscores with increasing emphasis that *all* knowledge of God is *exclusively* determined by and is dependent upon the knowledge of Jesus Christ, and that this is not simply a matter of our epistemology, but that it is directly related to the *nature of the revelation of God in Jesus Christ* who is the dominant and all-controlling central factor in the doctrines of election, creation and reconciliation. Only in Jesus Christ do we meet the true and decisive revelation of God. Therefore Barth polemicizes against any and every denial of a Christological dogmatics. He turns himself sharply against every abstract God-concept and against an independent theology of the first article of the Apostles' Creed (God as Creator). He will not acknowledge the legitimacy of a relatively independent knowledge of God which would *precede* the revelation of God in Christ. The absolute revelation in Christ alone forms the full content of the gospel. On the basis of this revelation, which is the revelation of *reconciliation,* of "God with us," the good tidings of the gospel must be preached in the world. And on the basis of the revelation the whole of dogmatics, through its reflection on the content of the gospel, must subserve the interests of the Church and of her proclamation.

It is in connection with the content of the gospel regarded from *this* point of view that Barth's theology bears a pronouncedly *triumphant* character and, in its service to the Church and her proclamation, shares in the joy and the gladness of the gospel.

We are aware that this characterization requires qualification, if only because Barth has more than once trained his theological artillery on a too triumphant Christianity and on a correspondingly triumphant Church and theology.[23] We think here of the issue that he has taken with the Church's easy intercourse with God, with her pretentions and manner of speaking, with her absence of respect for the Word of God, as causes of a pseudo-

---

22. Cf. K. Barth, "Die dogmatische Prinzipiënlehre von W. Herrmann," *Zwischen den Zeiten,* 1925.

23. Cf. Barth on the use of the word "Christian" "in our all too victorious modern Christianity," *Der Heilige Geist und das christliche Leben,* 1930, p. 92. For his criticism relative to the Church: "Quousque tandem?" *Zwischen den Zeiten,* 1930, and "Die Not der evangelische Kirche," *Ibid.,* 1931, and relative to theology: "Unerledigte Anfragen an die heutige Theologie" in: *Die Theol. und die Kirche,* II, 1920.

triumphant attitude. Barth wishes to emphasize above all the triumph of God's grace. It is his conviction that only in this way a barrier can be erected against every triumph whose essence is not *grace* alone. From countless explicit statements — as we shall later see — as also from the whole structure of his dogmatics, it appears that this theme has become the dominant motif in the theology of Barth. In one way or another all the discussion centering around Barth is related to this emphasis on the triumph of grace.

It is therefore important to understand the nature of this triumph in Barth's theology.

The old debate with respect to the "theology of glory" and the corresponding defense of the "theology of the cross" is by no means made irrelevant by this emphasis. Such a break with an important aspect of past theological discussion is nowhere discernible in the development of Barth's thinking. On the contrary, it is his purpose to show that the triumph of grace is most intimately related to the cross and therefore to the *theologia crucis.*[24]

\*       \*       \*

In the nature of the case, no judgment as to its validity is implied in so characterizing Barth's theology. We shall later have occasion to demonstrate at some length that the nature of the triumph of grace is decisively determined by the *components* that are taken up into the structure of that triumph. This does not alter the fact, however, that it is wholly fair to Barth, and that it is theologically warranted, to place this motif central in our analysis and to allow Barth to express himself fully in terms of it. For it is through *this* emphasis that he wishes to serve the Church and her witness in the world.

On the other hand, the positing of this central motif does not exclude our meeting with elements and presuppositions in Barth's theology that call for scrutiny. In the history of theology we time and again discover clearly evident presuppositions that have decisively influenced theological thought. Consciously or unconsciously they have played an important role in molding theological conceptions. Barth has always been conscious of this insofar

---

24. To be treated more extensively later.

as theology is a human undertaking. He has, in fact, years after the writing of it, clearly indicated certain philosophic presuppositions in his *Römerbrief*. It has become plain, however, that while not denying the *danger* of presuppositions in the construction of a theology, especially philosophical ones, Barth does *relativize* this danger. Philosophical elements, he holds, can be employed in the service of theological activity. This use does not in itself constitute a danger. Only then, in his opinion, does a real danger come into being, when a certain philosophy is made the foundation of theology. We see this clearly in his polemic against Bultmann. Barth has no objection against the use of the terminology of a given philosophical system. "Augustine spoke in neo-Platonic, Thomas in Aristotelian, F. C. Bauer and Beidermann in Hegelian terminology, as Bultmann is now speaking in the language of Heidegger."[25] This is not in itself a point against him. But the danger becomes very real when basic significance is attached to the philosophical system from which one draws. "His association with Existentialism, however, has for Bultmann *fundamental* significance."[26] It is *this* that makes his theology questionable. Barth, then, distinguishes between a neutral use of philosophical conceptions and a use of them which involves acceptance of the ideas which they represent. When this happens philosophy "instead of being an instrument becomes something wholly other."[27]

It seems to me that in making this distinction Barth underestimates the material influence of neutral philosophical elements in theological activity. It is not possible here — as is evident from the history of theology — to distinguish between form and content, as Barth himself indicates in his reference to the examples of Augustine, Thomas, and the theological thinking of the nineteenth century as it was influenced by Hegel. One need only note the philosophical motifs operative in Thomas' doctrine of the sacraments, and the consequences of Hegelian thinking for the doctrine of the Trinity and for Christology, to become convinced of this. There is clearly a difference between the use of philosophic material, on the one hand (Augustine and

---

25. K. Barth, *R. Bultmann*, 1952, p. 45.
26. *Ibid.*
27. *Ibid.*

Thomas), and the acceptance of a philosophy as the foundation of a theology, on the other (Bultmann), but this does not alter the fact that philosophic presuppositions in the construction of a theology always take their toll.[28] The problem of the conscious or unconscious use of philosophical categories therefore always plays an important role in theological thought. Even Barth's later self-criticism did not involve simply *formal* modification of his earlier theological thinking, but it had consequences for the manner in which he had thought to serve the Church with this theology. The full light of the gospel which he had wanted to transmit through it was — when one takes Barth's self-criticism seriously — obscured by this "form."[29]

The inter-relationship between philosophical presuppositions and the content of a given theology is much too complicated to permit an understanding of it simply in terms of a form-content distinction. For this reason the problem of the use of conceptions which are not congruent with revelation constitutes an important problem for every theology. This does not mean, in the nature of the case, that the discovery of certain philosophical presuppositions in a theology warrants thrusting upon it by way of logical deduction conceptions or ideas which that theology itself explicitly rejects. It is precisely one of the engrossing and fascinating aspects of the history of theology that the overpowering influence of the Word of God time and again breaks through existing presuppositions at decisive points. This is the case with Augustine as well as with Thomas, and clearly excludes an analysis in which philosophical supremacy leaves no room for the possibility of such a break-through. On the one hand, it must be fully

---

28. Consider the neo-platonic influences in the theology of Augustine.
29. As early as 1935 Barth observed about his *Römerbrief*: "I had at that time no other desire than simply to set forth the meaning of Paul's letter to the Romans. This I did partly in a remarkable wrapping of Kantian and Platonic conceptions" *Grundfragen*, 1935, p. 24. This corresponds to the fact that in the foreword of the second edition of the *Römerbrief* Barth speaks about "the better understanding of the real orientation of the ideas of Plato and Kant for which I am indebted to the writings of my brother, Heinrich Barth," p. vii. Cf. also the self-criticism in later volumes of the KD. We shall allude to this later. Note also E. G. Van Teylingen, "Over de wijsgerige achtergrond der dialectische theologie," *Philos. Reform.*, 1945, p. 2ff, and H. van Oyen, "Over wijsgerige affiniteit van Barth's theologie," *Onder Eigen Vaandel*, 1938. S. U. Zuidema has been warranted in continually pointing out the influence that philosophy can have upon theology so that it cannot be used without peril as a "form" for theological thinking.

acknowledged that all manner of presuppositions in a given theology can darken the light of the gospel; on the other hand, it is not legitimate to *reconstruct* a theology — in this case, Barth's — in the light of such presuppositions. In this manner it is possible and legitimate fully to come to an understanding of Barth's theological views, while at the same time fully recognizing that these views hang together intimately with fundamental presuppositions. This approach to Barth gives us the right to undertake an analysis of what Barth unquestionably wishes to place central in theology and in proclamation, namely the *triumph of grace.* To illustrate the centrality of this theme in the theology of Barth we shall quote him extensively and endeavor to trace the manner in which it functions in the whole of his dogmatic system. This will immediately confront us with the question whether this triumph is identical with the biblical conception of the triumph of grace. Unquestionably: the tremendous debate centering around the theology of Barth touches a central concept of the Scriptures, namely, *grace.* It is a deeply moving struggle in which the issue is none other than the *euangelion,* the good, the joyful message of salvation.

\*　　\*　　\*

Before entering upon our inquiry into the several aspects of the one triumph of grace in the theology of Karl Barth, the question arises whether the position of this theme is not directly contrary to the manner in which the dialectical theology was represented when it first appeared on the scene, namely, as a theology of *crisis.* Does the theme of the triumph of grace imply that there has been a radical turning in the course of Barth's theological development, a turning from crisis to triumph, from judgment to grace? Was the *crisis*-motif initially the decisive motif in Barth's theology?

# II

## THEOLOGY OF CRISIS?

D URING the first phase of its development we constantly heard dialectical theology characterized as a "theology of crisis." This description frequently had critical import. It regarded dialectical theology as a sort of desperation-theology which had its origin in the depressed mood of Western Europe during and after World War I. Dialectical theology, it was supposed, reflected the disillusionment which began to take the place of evolutionistic optimism. It was the *theological* expression of Spengler's historical and cultural pessimism as he had set this forth in his *Decline of the West*. The theology of crisis, it was said, arose out of a crisis in human history, the crisis caused by loss of confidence in man, in his ideals and in his achievements. It was regarded as nothing less than the exposé of the desperate human situation occasioned by the catastrophic events of that time.

Represented as taking its rise from these historical factors, dialectical theology was viewed as the theology of the absolute No, the theology of *crisis* and of *judgment*. It was recognized that this description did not do full justice to the nature of the new theology, for the crisis could not be separated from the majesty and justice of God, from the judgment that was *His* judgment, and from the No that was *His* No. Nevertheless, the center of gravity in it was regarded as lying in the negative, judging, irrevocable and implacable No which was pronounced over every righteousness of men.

At the very beginning of the new theological development Paul Althaus took issue with the crisis as it found expression in the theology of Barth. He saw in it a complete denial of the sense and purpose of history, a skeptical flight from the concrete action of God in history, and feared that this crisis-thinking would mean a real impoverishment of theology in that the crisis was seen not only as the judgment of God over human *guilt,* but also

23

as the divine judgment over all creatureliness *as such*. In contrast
with this emphasis Althaus posited that we must speak not only of
judgment, but also of grace, not only of the divine No but also of
the Divine Yes to man and to history.[1] Althaus saw the "No" of
Barth as the formal handling of a concept by means of which it
was possible to judge in a pronouncedly pessimistic manner of history, of the Church and of religion, of piety and morality, of culture and of human development. The theology of crisis was in this
manner interpreted as a pessimistic form of thinking in which No
triumphs over Yes, and judgment over grace. It was against this
everything but triumphant theology that he lifted his warning
voice. He desired to complement the No with a divine Yes.

In studying the literature of the early period of dialectical theology — roughly between 1920 and 1930 — one does not get the
impression that Barth was deeply affected by this criticism. It is
certainly not going too far to say that he was plainly of the opinion
that Althaus had misinterpreted the relationship existing between
the Yes and the No, and that consequently he had misunderstood
the thrust of the "theology of crisis."[2]

This brings us to the important question of what we must understand by the word "crisis" in the theology of crisis. In this
connection it is necessary to consider that the name "theology of
crisis" was used not only by critics of this theology, but that
Brunner wrote a book bearing this title, and that the "crisis"
idea unquestionably played a large role in the theology of Barth.
The simple *word* "crisis" which, for that matter, also appears in
the New Testament does not make plain what we must understand by the "theology of crisis." In any case, it must be said that
it was plain from the beginning that this crisis did not find its
center in doubt and despair. It was evident in the writings of
both Barth and Brunner that their concern was not to interpret

---

1. Cf. especially P. Althaus, "Theologie und Geschichte. Zur Auseinandersetzung
mit der dialektischen Theologie," in *Zeitschrift für systematische Theologie* Vol.
I, 1923. Also my *Wereld Oorlog en Theologie*, 1945, p. 14ff.
2. Cf. Karl Barth. "Polemisches Nachwort," (supplementary to an article
about Ludwig Feuerbach) *Zw. d. Zeiten*, 1927, p. 38, in which Barth directs sharp
criticism against W. Bruhn's interpretation of his theology (in Bruhn's *Vom Gott
und Menschen*) with particular reference to the charge that Barth allows the
knowledge of judgment to "turn over" into knowledge of grace. To this Barth
replies, "No!... Bruhn knows and cites the places in which I long ago expressed
and gave basis to this No."

a deplorable historical situation, but that in one way or another crisis was related to *salvation,* that it pointed to *grace.*

ᐱThe idea of crisis, therefore, while ever so profound a theme in this theology, is an idea which stands in a context that certainly does not intend to exclude grace. On the contrary, emphasis is placed on the fact that the central issue is the proper view of salvation. This is qualified, however, by the consideration that salvation appears as salvation only when all *human* escapes have been *cut off.* Salvation must be seen exclusively as *God's* salvation and as unmerited grace.ᐱ The Yes and the No do not limit or compensate each other, but they are interdependent in such a manner that the No that is pronounced over all human righteousness points, as *God's* No, to the righteousness of God *with a view to salvation.* For this reason the concept of crisis in this theology may not be regarded as an independent theme, but can be rightly understood only when it is seen in indissoluble relationship with the grace and light of God. This makes clear why Barth has always been opposed to every interpretation of his theology which represented it as stemming from the mood inspired by World War I. He has been unwilling to acknowledge the legitimacy of the view which identified him with the No of cultural and historical pessimism rather than with the saying Yes of God.[3]

These protestations notwithstanding, Barth has again and again been interpreted on the basis of his accent on No and on judgment. It was particularly Gogarten who in the year 1937 characterized Barth's theology as a *skeptical* theology in a publication that caused considerable stir, entitled *Judgment or Skepticism.*[4] According to Gogarten, the central thrust in Barth was not the actual judgment of God, but the skepticism occasioned by

---

3.Cf. K. Barth, *Kirchenblatt für die ref. Schweiz,* 1940, p. 100. "Does the theological renascence of today take its rise from the great disillusionment of the recent World War and its consequences? Answer: During this period it had in any case its inception. During that time we were not asleep but were taught some things by the events that took place. I neither can nor want to prove that without the World War we would be standing where we are standing today. But who can prove that we have been brought to our present positions by the World War?" Barth does not deny (as little as Thurneysen did later) that a given situation can exercise influence on theology, but this is still not an "explanation" of theology so influenced, since all depends how in such a time the Word of God exercises its power over the mind.

4. F. Gogarten, *Gericht oder Skepsis. Eine Streitschrift gegen Karl Barth,* 1937.

the crisis which allegedly controlled his thinking. It is not surprising that after rejecting the criticism of Bruhn, Althaus and others, Barth did not, so far as I know, react to this criticism of Gogarten.[5] It is also plain, it seems to me, that Gogarten (who was himself everything but skeptical with respect to the political developments in Germany from 1933 on) did not do justice to Barth's conception of crisis and judgment, and that his dilemma: judgment or skepticism? did not materially contribute to an understanding of Barth's theology.[6]

The center of debate during the first phase of the development of the dialectical theology was, in the nature of the case, Barth's *Römerbrief*. In this commentary the thought of crisis played an important role. This crisis is discussed not only in the two sections whose titles include the word, but everywhere the thought of crisis recurs as an indication of the crisis of "eternity" over "time," as the judgment of God over every effort of man to find, in one manner or another, a way to God that shall begin with himself. In the foreword of the second edition Barth speaks of his true purpose, namely, "to keep constantly before us in its negative and positive meaning" the qualitative-infinite difference between God and man.[7] He wanted to emphasize, against every overstepping of the boundaries, that *God* is in the heavens and that *we* are men upon the earth. The "crisis" of the reality of God is the radical, universal, and permanent crisis, it is the judgment of God over all human righteousness. Never, never, is man able to obliterate this distinction or to cross this dividing line.

In connection with Romans 1, Barth points to the righteousness of man which meets its condemnation in the judgment of God. This means not simply the pronouncement of judgment over

---

5. Barth did engage in a polemic against Gogarten in his KD I/1, p. 128ff. in connection with his judgment of Barth's *Prolegomena*, 1927, a polemic which is of importance in connection with the transition from the *Prolegomena* to the KD. Cf. F. Gogarten, "K. Barth's Dogmatik," in *Theol. Rundschau*, 1929, p. 70ff.

6. This becomes even plainer when we remember that Gogarten, associated as he was with *Zw. den Zeiten*, was in the nature of the case well acquainted with the fundamental motifs of dialectical theology. Van Teylingen correctly observes that Gogarten's book was "evidently written with resentment," *Philos. Ref.*, Vol. 10, p. 6. In this connection it is of importance to note that in 1923 Gogarten himself wrote about religion with special reference to the antithesis between religion and revelation. Cf. his *Von Glauben und Offenbarung*, 1923, especially pp. 5ff. and 17ff.

7. K. Barth, *Der Römerbrief*, 2nd ed., 1932, p. xiv.

atheism and humanism, over autonomous morality and human pride, over culture and other towers of Babel, but this judgment directs itself especially to man as via *religion* he seeks to make his way to God. It is *precisely* in *religion* that Barth detects the most refined and cunning human effort to reach beyond himself. Here, even more than in other areas, man attempts to establish his *own* righteousness, and to secure himself against the divine judgment.⟩

This righteousness is the human righteousness of religion, of the *pious* man, of phariseeism, the man-made righteousness which is nothing other than "irreverence and insubordination."[8]

Also this way — however frequently entered — runs dead in the fiery barrier of the unspeakable holiness and majesty of God. It is precisely here that man must die in the judgment because it has pleased God to put an end to all human righteousness and — at that barrier — to reveal *His* righteousness. At this boundary all illusions, moral and religious, are exposed *as* illusions, because they were the point of departure for the supposition that God and man are partners, that they walk together on a plane of equality, which is nothing less than "the worst perversion of the truth."[9] The crisis consists in this, that man in *all* his endeavors stands under the condemnation of the radical No of the true and living God, the No of His holy judgment in the presence of which man cannot live, but can only *die.* ⟩Faith, therefore, is not another and new endeavor, it is not a new possibility to bridge from man's side the chasm between God and man. On the contrary, faith — and this is the miracle of faith — is the radical acknowledgment that our own ways are labyrinths and dead-end roads, it is the acknowledgment and the acceptance of the divine judgment. Faith is not a human way, it is not merit or achievement. It is the hearing of God's No. But this hearing does not plunge us into despair. The divine No proclaims that all *our* ways are futile, and thereby *His* way, the way of life, is opened to us. It is therefore necessary that man "becomes conscious of this situation, that he becomes aware of the crisis, that

---

8. K. Barth, *Der Römerbrief,* p. 36. Cf. also Brunner's views of that time in his *Erlebnis, Erkenntnis und Glaube,* 1923, in which he writes against "religion as experience," p. 6ff.; further, his *Die Grenzen der Humanität,* 1922, p. 3, and *Die Mystick und das Wort,* 1924.

9. *Der Römerbrief,* p. 58.

he acknowledges it as a divine crisis, and that in this crisis he chooses for the fear of the Lord. He must hear and understand the No of God as a divine Yes, because it is *God's* No."[10]

This does not mean that it is possible to change God's No "dialectically" into a Yes by human fiat. The hearing of God's Yes is not an easy matter. Barth therefore emphasizes that nowhere so much as here does the unwillingness and impossibility of man to live by the righteousness of God *alone* become manifest.

Man prefers to go his own way, the way of the autonomous human spirit, which is particularly the way of religion, the way of human righteousness, as he elaborately sets forth in the chapter on "the boundary of religion."[11] But this religion nowhere and never transcends the judgment. As an *immanent* human possibility it does not have the power to survive the judgment. It does not have the positive power to escape the fatal sentence of the divine tribunal. On the contrary, "man is completely delivered to the whole of the problematic situation that his religious capacity brings into being."[12] In another place Barth puts the matter even more strongly: "Among all human capabilities it is exactly the capacity for religion which is the most significant factor in describing the dualism between time and eternity."[13] Religion does not survive the crisis but is rather the *focal point* of the crisis. The crisis is the boundary which no religion can transcend. And what is true of religion in general is true of the *Church* as "organized religion."[14] In the Church and in all religion man seeks to justify and maintain himself. The existence of religion is an incontrovertible fact,[15] but "in every comprehensible and historical sense it must be viewed and surrendered as a phenomenon in the world of men (which is the world of sin and death)."[16] "All the regard and admiration in which religion in this world may be held may not hinder us from recognizing that every claim of religion to absoluteness, transcendence, and directness is null and void."[17] In religion the world of mankind achieves the deep-

---

10. *Ibid.*, p. 99.
11. *Ibid.*, p. 211ff.
12. *Ibid.*, p. 213.
13. *Ibid.*
14. *Ibid.*, p. 325.
15. *Ibid.*, p. 162.
16. *Ibid.*, p. 163.
17. *Ibid.*

est expression of her falling away from God. How is it then possible that precisely *here* the divine halt! should not sound and the divine judgment not become manifest?[18] We can speak of *grace* only "when the religious possibility, having been taken in all its seriousness and seen in all its power and development, is sacrificed."[19]

\* \* \*

It is evident, therefore, how central is the place of the crisis-motif in the *Römerbrief*. It indicates distance, it signalizes the judgment in all its ominous and limiting character, it indicates the infinite distance between God and man, and the radical condemnation of every synthesis between the two that is effected from man's side. There is no possibility of a way of salvation that is of man's making. When an attempt — in religion — is made in this direction, then it is precisely there that religion "as the pinnacle of human possibility stands revealed as the catastrophe of human possibility, so far as God is concerned."[20] The ease and the pride that constitute this way are unmasked in the judgment. In religion man does not transcend himself but is rather struck down by the judgment. The illusory character of such religion is here radically judged: "The religious man is the sinner in the most evident sense of the word."[21] This, however, raises the question anew and acutely, whether on the basis of this conception Barth's theology may be called a "theology of crisis," that is, a theology which, if not exclusively, is nevertheless dominantly characterized by the *crisis* motif.

As a tentative answer to this question we shall have to say again that it is plain from the *Römerbrief* and from other writings of Barth's early period that this "crisis" does not have an independent function as an *isolated* motif occasioned by the negativism and disillusionment obtaining in Europe after World War I. We do not meet here a desperation-theology which is hardly distinguishable from a pessimistic attitude to life, but rather a sharply antithetical accentuation of that crisis which is directed against the pride of man who does not know the reality

18. *Ibid.*, p. 164.
19. *Ibid.*, p. 165.
20. *Ibid.*, p. 235.
21. *Ibid.*, p. 152.

of God and yet thinks to approach Him without difficulty or danger. The emphasis on the crisis in this connection intends an underscoring of the word of the New Testament that God dwells in light *unapproachable* (I Tim. 6:16), and that He is a *consuming* fire (Heb. 12:29). The crisis is not intended as a self-evident and automatic negation of man and of all things human, it does not indicate an ontological disposition of the creature as such. Rather, it functions in Barth's theology as a means of unmasking man's own righteousness, the unmasking of the pharisee and his way of salvation.

That the crisis is not simply the form in which a reigning sense of catastrophe is cast appears especially from the fact that the absolute No of God is not the *last* and *only* Word of God. The crisis stands rather — regarded from God's point of view — in direct connection with the *Yes* of God, with *redemption*, with *grace*, the great *miracle* of God. This divine Yes does not arise from the heart of man, nor is it heard and understood by means of a logical dialectic which can turn the No into a Yes. It comes to us *exclusively* from God Himself and is heard at *that* point where, in the acknowledgment of the judgment that is pronounced over all human righteousness, the divine forgiveness and justification by faith are appropriated. The crisis, therefore, does not indicate the final doubt and despair characterizing human life as it stands in the shadow of catastrophe and the last trump, but it finds its central significance in its pointing to the saving, exclusively divine action of God's righteousness as it stands *over against* and *opposed to* the righteousness of men. In this connection Barth speaks of the new man, the new world of God, the resurrection and the light of God that arises out of the darkness. It is not religion, but *faith* — as miracle, beginning, creation — which is directed to these things and gratefully accepts this righteousness of God as an "aliena justitia." This faith is not a new human religious possibility, but it is the exclusion of human possibilities and the acknowledgment of the forgiving action of God, the Yes of His grace, the justification not of the religious man, but of the godless. The proclamation of the absolute crisis is not a theme of despair, but it opens the only possible way to salvation by shutting off all others. Therefore the crisis, seen from God's point of view, is the reverse side of grace. Barth was certainly not concerned to play a game of paradoxical dialectics,[22] nor to compensate for the No by the speaking of a reassuring and moderating Yes. He was concerned to expose the exclusiveness of the salvation that is in *God's* hand alone, and which can only in *that* exclusiveness be salvation for us. The preaching of the absolute crisis is the reverse side — by the grace of God not *more* than the reverse side — of the divine testimony that God will Himself change the shadow of death into the dawn of a new day. The proclamation of the crisis points to the Word of reconciliation and forgiveness which oversteps the death-boundary for us. When the dark crisis sections in Barth's *Römerbrief* are isolated from *the light that shines in the darkness* it is not possible to understand Barth's theology either in its beginning or in its further development. Undoubtedly some philosophic, especially Platonic, thoughts have placed their stamp on Barth's *Römerbrief* and this has not infrequently created the impression that he was more concerned with the crisis of "eternity" over time than with the judgment of the living God. Biblical thoughts are constantly obscured by a transcendental *boundary*-idea, which reminds one more of philosophical idealism than of the gospel.

The more is it understandable that this stamp played a role in the judgments that have been expressed about the *Römerbrief* when

---

22. This appears plainly in Barth's lecture on "The problem of ethics in our time," *Das Wort Gottes und die Theologie,* 1924, p. 147. "Because God says Yes to us, therefore we stand so radically, so inextricably in the No." "So there appears *in* the judgment that which is above the judgment, namely, God's love, forgiveness *in* the acknowledgment of sin, the beginning of the new, the original life *in* death and the end of all things," p. 147. And even plainer in: "'God has waited only for that humility which again gives Him His honor which He cannot give to any other; He has waited only for that repentance by which man yields himself to His captivity for favor or disfavor, for that comforted despair in which man acknowledges himself joyfully to be lost because he has understood the meaning of this being lost. For these things God has waited, if indeed we can speak at all of a waiting of God. Now, and now fully, God realizes in them their relationship to him in its positive significance as love, forgiveness, life, mercy, as *grace,*" p. 147. (Eng. tr: *The Word of God and The Word of Man,* 1928).

To this corresponds what Barth says in another place: "There is no way from us to God, no via negativa, no via dialectica, no via paradoxa." If there were a way from God to us it could well be described "after the manner of Feuerbach," p. 153, but it would be a fata morgana *in our* dialectic. Cf. also p. 171 about the dialectical way, and K. Leese, *Die Prinzipienlehre der neueren systematische Theologie im Lichte der Kritik L. Feuerbachs,* 1912.

it is considered that it is hardly feasible to separate form and content in Barth's discussion, and that the content of his message was
affected by the philosophic mold in which it was cast.[23] This became plain to Barth himself, as we may learn from the material
correction which he himself later effected.[24] He speaks then about
the eternity of God and declares that in the beginning he accentuated too strongly the "divine future" as a *boundary* and as the divine No that is pronounced against all piety and culture. He became aware that this emphasis might create the impression that
he was only concerned to effect an "upheaval in the soul of the European man" after the first world conflict. Barth speaks of his *reaction* which, it seems to me, came to expression in this, that any
Christianity which was not entirely eschatological was criticized
by him in such a manner that there was nothing of (real) Christianity left in it. By his emphasis on *boundary* and on *distance* he
did not escape the misunderstanding that he was concerned about
these for their own sakes. But, at the same time, Barth says that
*this was in no sense his intention.* The result of his study was dangerously one-sided, but this result was in reality in conflict with
his deepest intentions. "And above all, one notes with amazement
that in my commentary precisely that one-sided super-temporal understanding of God remained visible as the only concrete result of
my work, *which to combat I went out to do battle.*"[25] This was
caused by a "self-misunderstanding out of which many of our expressions during those years arose," and it took quite an exertion,
according to Barth, "to pilot our theology out of the narrow straits
of the suspicion that it was really no more than a 'theology of crisis.' "[26] It is plain that more was involved in the inter-relationship

---

23. We have already alluded to Barth's self-criticism in 1935 respecting the
Kant-Plato influence in his theology. It is remarkable, however, that in connection with his use of these (philosophic) concepts he adds, "I ventured then to use
these concepts, but if someone were to say to me today: you must use them, I
would decidedly say No," *Grundfragen*, 1935, p. 24. This remark was made in
answer to the complaint "that I no longer use the language of the *Römerbrief.*"
He writes of those who complain, "They should on the contrary be thankful
that I no longer burden them with expressions like 'Hohlraum' and 'Todeslinie' !"

24. KD II/1, p. 715ff.

25. *Ibid.*, p. 716 (my italics).

26. *Ibid.*, p. 717. Cf. same page, "Theology of crisis it could not and indeed
might not be for more than a moment."

between "form" and "content" than the mere use of a temporarily employed formal manner of expression.[27]

This does not change the fact, however, that in the *Römerbrief* as well as in the later self-correction it appears clearly that Barth was least of all concerned to speak a despairing and negative message of crisis. We believe that Barth could later say with good reason that in the one-sidedness of the reaction, which he himself admitted was not without danger, *this* was not the burden of his speaking.

His deepest intention was to point to the crisis *for the sake of* pointing to the grace of God, to speak the No *for the sake of* making the divine Yes heard. In this crisis all human ways are exposed as dead-end roads *in order that* the one Way might be revealed. The divine Yes is the background of the radical crisis which is suspended over the whole of life. For this reason the proclamation of the crisis has never been for Barth the symptom of a negative and pessimistic view of life. It is rather the testimony concerning the exclusion of human righteousness, and in this exclusion it points to God's incomprehensible forgiveness as "the fundamental change underlying the relationship between God and man."[28] Faith has nothing to do with an abstract No as an *ontology* of the fallen creature, but *in* the No it finds the Yes of forgiveness. "We can hear the No under which we stand in no other way than in terms of the divine Yes, we can hear the voice of human irreverence and insubordination in no other way than as borne by the deeper voice of the divine forgiveness. We cannot hear the cry of human pride other than as superseded by the restful harmony of the overcoming grace of God."[29]

We must therefore not see here a strange and peculiar dialectical "balance" between Yes and No, but a conquest of the Yes *in* and *through* the No because the triumph of the Yes becomes manifest exactly at that point where judgment is pronounced over man's

---

27. *Ibid.*, p. 717. We think here particularly about Barth's views concerning our lost "immediacy" of access to God and about the unity with God in connection with the constantly recurring "remembering," e .g., *Römerbrief*, p. 147. It is indeed not a construction when von Balthasar connects these views with the dangers of an identity-mysticism, *op. cit.* p. 75ff. Cf. also Barth's observations about "the timeless, the transcendental disposition of the world of men," *Römerbrief*, p. 149, which he relates to supralapsarianism, p. 150.

28. *Der Römerbrief*, p. 69.

29. *Ibid.*

*own* righteousness. *In* the crisis grace is the issue, in judgment forgiveness. It is in the desert that a highway is made straight and the mountains and the hills are leveled in order that the glory of the Lord may be revealed (Isa. 40:33). Therefore the crisis is not relativized by the forgiveness, but *in* the acceptance of forgiveness the crisis is acknowledged in repentance and sorrow.

\* \* \*

If the relationship between nature and grace is not the dialecticism of a logical balance but one that touches God's righteousness and man's unrighteousness, it is not difficult to see that the crisis-concept could be employed as a simple criticism of all manner of phenomena in which one thought to discern human pride, the "hubris" of the *religious* and especially the *Christian* individual. Not infrequently the crisis-concept was used in a conflict in which one could see only one enemy, namely the pharisee. The divine judgment on the "righteousness" of man of which Paul speaks in Romans 1 presented itself as a ready instrument for a merciless criticism on all kinds of manifestations of "Christianity" and "churchianity." It cannot be denied that Barth himself, during his first period of theological reflection, directed his sharpest barbs not only at subjectivism and consciousness-theology, but that he saw the function of the "crisis" no less as a scoring of the "age of the Church" and the romanticizing and crystallizing of the "hubris" of the religious individual in the broad area of the whole of human activity. This criticism of refined religiosity, of Christianity and churchianity, and of the "Church of Esau," became an occasion for many to engage, in various theological contexts, in what was often an unmerciful criticism through which a crusade was launched against all religious and ecclesiastical pride. In the course of this crusading the thesis was posited that God's glory could only then appear when our religious and churchly life was radically placed "in the crisis" and permanently surrendered. The divine "crisis" became an all too easy weapon to handle and, once discovered in the treasure chamber of God's mysteries (the unapproachable light!), the crisis could be employed in the struggle against all "short-circuiting" and "anticipation," against overweening self-esteem and phariseeism. Moreover, in connection with the fact that it is precisely the gospel of Jesus Christ that stands diametrically opposed to all these "hubris"-phenomena, crisis-thinking and the program of "casting-into-the-crisis" seemed apriorily legitimized by the gospel. It is plain, however, that every critical approach can — in a simplistic manner — make use of this weapon and that it is possible in this way to turn crisis-thinking into a *negative* and *unfruitful* criticism.

It became an easy matter to concentrate all opposition against the one enemy, the *beati possidentes* (the blessed possessors) who simply because of their "possessing" bore the sign of rejection on their foreheads. When we survey the history of the past thirty years it will not be possible to deny that Barth's theology was often used in this fashion. It was frequently forgotten that it is possible to operate with the "crisis" and the surrender and the "hubris" in an irresponsible manner, and that all this could be brought together in an accusation so fantastic, so sure of itself and so delivered from the heights of righteousness, that it became difficult in the extreme still to detect in it the voice of the *humble witness* and to discern *God's* glory. It was also forgotten again and again that the general criticism of all "possessing" as in itself a manifestation of human righteousness could easily lead to an unfair analysis of Christianity and of the Church, and that a situation could be created in which it is hardly possible to keep an open eye for the fact that the living Lord Himself can say to the Church, "I come speedily: hold fast what thou *hast* that no man take thy crown" (Rev. 3:11). Although we will want to remember that in the same chapter the Church at Laodicea is rebuked because she said, "I am rich, and increased with goods, and have need of nothing" while she did not know that she was wretched and miserable and poor and blind and naked (Rev. 3:17), nevertheless, the many-sidedness of the gospel which never generalizes makes it plain that there is an essential difference between the self-sufficient riches of the Laodiceans and the riches that we meet in Psalm 23: The Lord is my shepherd, I shall not want. There is a great danger that crisis-thinking will be employed as an uncritical weapon[30] and that one will for-

---

30. See the warnings of Barth already in the *Römerbrief*, p. 112, in which he speaks of "temple-building *and* temple-destruction." "Martensen *and* Kierkegaard." and about the danger of the *new* phariseeism "which manages not only to be 'self-justifying' but humble to boot!" p. 84.

get that there is also such a thing as an unbelieving "casting-into-the-crisis" which plays lightly with God's grace and the riches of His gifts. The whole of Scripture warns against pride in the use of God's benefits — "what hast thou that thou hast not received?" — but *never* is this warning presented in the form of a crisis which has no regard for distinctions.

Unquestionably it is necessary to beware of every form of crisis-thinking which bears a negativistic character, because such thinking readily breeds a new form of pride — "judge not that ye be not judged, for with what judgment ye judge ye shall be judged"[31] — and because human criticism is so easily identified with the judgment of God. Nevertheless, it must be remembered — especially in this connection — that in Barth's view the crisis was indissolubly united with the positive reverse side of it, namely *salvation,* and that already in the first phase of his development Barth had an eye for the emphasis that he was later to place over against Pelagianism, semi-Pelagianism, and modern-Protestant and Roman Catholic theology, namely *forensic* righteousness, the justification of the *godless.* This was also Barth's concern in the crisis-situation of sharp and excessive expressions as becomes evident when we see that this justification is viewed in connection with *faith*, faith not as a human contribution to salvation, nor as co-operation with God, but as "Hohlraum," as "empty" faith which has nothing in itself but is directed to and rests upon the "extra nos." It is this *faith* that gives to God the glory in the *same* action in which it abandons all human righteousness.[32]

*          *          *

---

31. Cf. Barth himself later about "the responsible and dangerous matter" of "criticizing the Church," KD IV/1, p. 772ff.
32. For faith and "justitia aliena" cf. *Römerbrief,* p. 131, 134ff. Since then dialectical theology has frequently appealed to *Calvin* who has indeed continually spoken of faith in relationship to its content. Cf., among others, P. Brunner, *Vom Glauben bei Calvin,* 1925, in which the concept "crisis" comes strongly to the fore: the crisis of man, the No of faith, the emptiness of faith (chapters 1 and 2). In the light of Barth's treatment of the doctrine of justification by faith alone (KD IV/1, 1953) it becomes plain how Barth could see the line of his *intention* being continued up to 1953 when he again uses the expression "Hohlraum" (the "emptiness" of faith) and does not find it "new, strange, or horrible," although he does ask why he found it necessary earlier to speak so *negatively,* VI/1, p. 701. Cf. p. 847 in which Barth speaks of faith as "recognition, acknowledgment, confession." This squares with the strong expressions which Barth now uses to indicate the *positive* aspect of truly-human faith, KD IV/1, passim.

Only when we fix our full attention on the dominant place of God's Yes can we obtain an insight into the large *continuity* that exists between the first phase of Barth's theological reflection and its later expansion and elaboration. When the prevalence of the Yes over the No, or rather, the merciful dealing of God in crisis and in judgment, is not fully recognized and understood it might be thought that Barth has in the course of his development exchanged a pessimistic for an optimistic, a desperation-theology for a theology of triumph. That which is later more clearly unfolded in Barth's dogmatic writings is, notwithstanding all manner of variations and surprises, an underscoring of this *grace-accent* or, to put it more sharply, a more emphatic and persistent pointing to the decisive grace and love of God which could already in the *Römerbrief* be discerned as standing in intimate connection with the crisis-motif. Not without justification does von Balthasar speak of Barth's later development as "a paradoxical rehabilitation of the *Römerbrief*."[33] But then the accent may not be allowed to fall — as is still done from time to time — on the *crisis* and on the *No,* which we also meet in Barth's later works, but much rather on the *triumphant character* of grace, which theme pursues its way with increasing clarity from the first via the second edition of the *Römerbrief* through the most recent volume of his *Dogmatik.*

Barth's theology must *from its inception* be characterized as triumphant theology which aims to testify to the overcoming power of grace. We do not find in it a transition from crisis to grace, or from disjunction between God and man to fellowship between them, but rather a relationship between these polarities which Barth was concerned to set forth in varying emphases and accents.

This accounts for the fact that Barth does not — as is the case with so much of triumphant theology — minimize or deny the judgment. The triumphant note in Barth's theology, as we shall later see more fully, stands in direct connection with both God's *judging* and His *gracious* action in Jesus Christ. Barth's theology is an exposition of this *Christologically* determined and *Christologically* filled Yes of God to His creation. We do not find in Barth a dogmatic vision which fascinates by its pessimism, but a testimony

33. H. U. von Balthasar, *op. cit.,* p. 93.

to the *radical* and *universal*[34] grace in which the triumph of God is revealed.[35]

\*   \*   \*

We shall later examine more closely various aspects of this one triumphant and definitive Yes of God. At this point we wish further to emphasize that there are many indications that already in Barth's earliest writings he regarded this triumph as the light surrounding the crisis clouds which he discerned.

At times, it is true, the light appears to be obscured by the clouds, and the thunders of the judgment frighten by well-nigh drowning out the notes of mercy and grace. Often, when the shadows of the *irrevocable* No, the *barrier* of God's unapproachable majesty, confront us, the divine Yes seems to recede into the distance and we have difficulty in clearly and comfortingly discerning the thesis as it comes to expression *in* and *through* the antithesis. Again and again, however, the judgment and the crisis are interpreted *in terms of* and *in connection with* grace, and light breaks through when it seemed that only darkness remained.

That this representation is not unfaithful to the motif that controlled dialectical theology in its first phase becomes even clearer when we consider the sermons that flanked Barth's theology. It is not possible to separate them as the pastoral part of his work from his "real" theology. Barth's observation that the sermons of Schleiermacher must be taken into account to gain a true insight into his theology [36] is applicable to himself. It is necessary to see the connection between the *Römerbrief* and Barth's sermons. They reveal, even more than the *Römerbrief,* that the crisis-motif did not serve an *independent* and *isolated* function (as part of a *desperation-*theology), but that the crisis could be understood *as* judgment only

---

34. We do not intend hereby to anticipate decisively the question of the apokatastasis which will be discussed more fully later. Cf. chapters IV and X.

35. Cf. my *Conflict met Rome;* M. P. van Dijk, *Existentie en Genade;* H. U. von Balthasar, *op. cit.* In connection with this triumphant character of grace, the nature of which we shall analyze later, note Barth's view of the "joyfulness" of theology, and in his doctrine of the attributes of God his conception of the glory of God, KD II /1, p. 722ff., and in relation to this his observation about theology as a "peculiarly *beautiful* discipline," p. 740. "It is always a sign of degeneration when science becomes dull for a man. But what a particular degeneration is required to make theology dull." Concerning the pulchritudo Dei cf. p. 741ff. This beauty of God is not an abstract conception but is immediately related to Jesus Christ, p. 753, and specifically to the incarnation, p. 746: it reveals "in a special and intensified manner the beauty of God."

36. K. Barth, *Die Protestantische Theologie im* 19. *Jahrhundert,* 1947.

when the divine voice of *forgiveness* was heard. It is *this* that makes the crisis understandable at the point where the boundary between God's holiness and man's self-made righteousness becomes visible. The No and the Yes of God cannot be assigned to the *Römerbrief* and to the sermons respectively. In the sermons the No and the Yes — in the same mutual relationship as in the *Römerbrief* — come equally to the fore. In fact, we see even more plainly — not in theology, but in the *Church* — how emphatically God's Yes resounds *in* and *through* the judgment. This makes plain why the sermons of Barth's first period are so clearly marked by the triumphant grace-accent.

This triumph is the triumph of the grace of God which we shall later see come so clearly to the fore in Barth's expositions on creation and redemption. We think here of the book of sermons which Barth and Thurneysen published together in 1924, "Komm, Schöpfer-Geist" (Come, Creator-Spirit). In the same year Barth wrote his book on the first epistle of St. Paul to the Corinthians (The Resurrection of the Dead), in which he also assigns important roles to the conceptions of *boundary* and *judgment*. But this is not a crisis which threatens grace, nor is Barth concerned about a grace that takes the place of judgment or that relativizes it. The Yes of God is preached to the congregation in the same breath in which the heavily accented crisis and judgment are declared. This is the same emphasis as that found in the *Römerbrief*, namely, that of the Righteousness of God and the New World that is found in the Bible.[37] The sermons also show the antithetical character that is so distinctive of all of Barth's theology, but clearly with the purpose of following in the path of Isaiah who summons men to see the way of God that has been prepared in the *wilderness* that they may discover in it the glory of God, and to learn that all flesh is as grass and its beauty as the flower of the field (Isa. 40:1-6). The message of joy resounds here against the background of faded beauty (Isa. 40:9ff.) and the Word of God stands when the breath of the Almighty has withered the flower and the grass (Isa. 40:7-8).

Continually Barth's sermons connect the No with the Yes and the Yes with the No as they point to Him who did not come to call

---

37. Cf. *Das Wort Gottes und die Theologie*, 1924. (Eng. tr.: *The Word of God and The Word of Man*, 1928).

the righteous but *sinners* to repentance. The message that is heard
is medicine for the sick and life for the dead. We do not find here
a humanly constructed balance between the Yes and the No of
God, but the triumphant Yes which is revealed *in* the crisis when
God in holy self-defense blocks our *many* ways and reveals His *one*
way.

In a sermon in which Barth speaks of the Yes and the No, he
writes: "In God the Yes and the No exist only for the sake of the
Yes. People who have heard this divine 'however' no longer wonder about this Yes and this No. They go about, they labor, they
pray, as prisoners they carry about with them something of the
freedom of the coming world. Alarmed, yet steadfast in spirit,
they are already now God's witnesses and way-preparers. Let no
one say, I cannot bear to hear this. Jesus has said, also in its significance for us, 'I am the resurrection and life.' "[38] In another
place, in connection with Isaiah 54:7-10, Barth speaks of forsakenness and mercy. He complains that the tragedy of our time is that
we do not hear God's Word as His word of grace. But the prophet
declares: Thus saith the Lord your Redeemer who has had mercy
on you. "We may doubt their [the prophets'] witness, and we do
it continually. We are also able to believe it, however, and to allow
our 'No' to be overcome by their Yes. Praise be to God, who has
according to his great mercy begotten us again unto a living hope
through the resurrection of Jesus Christ from the dead."[39]

The sermons which Barth preached even before 1924 are everything but pessimistic "sermons of the time." We hear in them,
rather, the invitation of Jesus to those that labor and are heavy
laden to find rest in Him,[40] and the call not to be anxious for the
morrow because God cares for the birds of the heavens and for the
lilies that grow in the field. In these sermons there is held before
us the unspeakable mercy of God which surpasses understanding.
In them the crisis in which "religion" finds itself is exposed, but
this crisis is set forth in terms of Jesus' conversation with Nico-
demus. Religious discourse cannot lead to any fruitful result and

---

38. *Komm, Schöpfer-Geist*, 1924, 2nd ed., p. 23.
39. *Ibid.*, p. 55.
40. *Ibid.*, p. 65ff.

therefore Jesus does not enter upon it "because on such a basis God cannot be seen."[41] In all *our* religious seeking and asking we stand under a roof that hides heaven from our eyes and therefore Jesus speaks of being *born again.* "We must obtain eyes for His, for God's, concern. Then our concerns will shrivel up."[42] Jesus does not give recipes that show the way to God as other teachers of religion do. He is Himself the way. "There is no place in Jesus' thinking for religious dreaming about God, as though there are ways to God without God. He Himself has said, I am the Way. Who has ears to hear, let him hear."[43]

All these sermons from the "crisis"-time are full of exhortations not to fear, as in the sermon on Revelation 1:17-18 (Fear not! I am the first and the last) which bears the title "Good Friday."[44] Jesus Christ is preached as the Conqueror[45] and we are presented with the *peace* of God.[46] There is a boundary surrounding the life of man, but "on the other side of the boundary we find rest."[47] Barth also speaks of doubt and despair in his sermons, but as "comforted despair." This is not a *combination,* a *synthesis,* of comfort and despair, and there is no question of uncertainty or tension as to whether comfort or despair will emerge the victor. The "comforted despair" rather coincides with the groaning of which Paul speaks in II Corinthians 2:5, and it is permeated with the comfort that meets us from the coming aeon. Death is not the last word and we may not resign ourselves to the No that hangs suspended over our life because "we know the Yes," though for a while "we must suffer because it has not yet broken into our life as the last, the final, word."[48]

In all of Barth's writings — and not least in his sermons — it is evident that the light of God's grace and of His Yes breaks through the shadows of His judgment over human self-righteousness. Only *in* the acknowledgment and acceptance of this judg-

---

41. *Ibid.,* p. 103.
42. *Ibid.,* p. 105.
43. *Ibid.*
44. *Ibid.,* p. 129.
45. *Ibid.,* p. 137.
46. *Ibid.,* p. 180.
47. *Ibid.,* p. 187.
48. *Ibid.,* p. 253.

ment, and *in* the exclusion of all self-vindication, can the grace of God truly be acknowledged and received.

It is also clear that in placing God's righteousness over against human righteousness Barth was not concerned about an abstract antithesis between "time" and "eternity" as an automatic judgment of eternity over all things temporal. This explains why Barth is aware of a development in his thinking, but not of a radical *break* with his earlier thought. There was in his earlier period a strong reactionary strain, but later Barth declares that this reaction was *too* strong, "too arbitrary and self-willed."[49] This does not mean for Barth that he has broken with his earlier emphasis, however, but only that he sees more plainly what he now can say and must say in a new form which, according to him, is less philosophical and more biblical. Barth therefore speaks of a "deepening" in his thinking, and this is related to the transition from his *Prolegomena* of 1927 to his *Kirchliche Dogmatik* which he has been writing since 1932.

Barth sees progress and deepening in his thought because he opines that in the "new" beginning he has cut himself loose once and for all from the philosophical foundation of Christian doctrine. Barth is amazed — as in 1938 he looks back over the years — that he did not at a much earlier date arrive at the "Christological concentration" of his theology, according to which the whole Christian doctrine is concentrated in Jesus Christ[50] and may therefore not be made to depend on one or another anthropo-

---

49. KD II/1, p. 715ff., where Barth states that he had at that time (i. e., in the *Römerbrief*) not yet reflected sufficiently on the biblical idea of eternity. For this reason he had not made plain that he wished to speak about *God* "and not about a general conception of boundary or crisis," p. 716.

50. "Parergon," *ibid.*, p. 272. Barth regards his book on Anselm as the decisive turning point in his development, *Fides quaerens intellectum. Anselms Beweis der Existenz Gottes,* 1931. This book, appearing between the *Prolegomena* of 1927 and the KD from 1932 on, is not an insignificant dogmatic-historical intermezzo. It signifies the Christological concentration taking place in his thought as over against the "natural" way to the knowledge of God and the way of the analogia entis which in 1932 he called an invention of the antichrist. This does not mean that he accuses Anselm of this fault. Rather the contrary is true, so far as Barth's distinctively own interpretation of Anselm's proof for the existence of God is concerned, namely, that it rests upon the following order: revelation, faith, and *then* "ut intellegam" : "*fides* quaerens intellectum." Note especially Barth's conclusion, pp. 198-199.

logical (in his case existential) analysis of human nature as the basis of theology.[51]

In its further development this Christological concentration runs wholly parallel with the emphasis on the "sola fide" and the "sola gratia."

According to Barth's own view, this is a development which makes it possible for him to show more plainly what was *from the beginning* intended by him when he spoke of the triumphant Yes of God. It will have to be acknowledged that this view of Barth is not in conflict with the earlier phase of his thinking. It is true that already in that first period there were shiftings in emphasis. The differences between the first and the second editions of the *Römerbrief* show this clearly.[52] But however incisive the differences between the two editions may be, it is not possible to view them simplistically as "optimistic" over against "pessimistic" theology.[53] Much less would it be justified, after this first shift in emphasis, to see Barth at present in the light of a second shifting of ground which now brings him to a triumphant theology! The new world of God — the triumph of the Kingdom of God's grace — which in the first edition of the *Römerbrief* came so prominently to the fore — continues via warning and continuing reflection to dominate in the second, albeit in different form, and in Barth's further thought this has remained and is increasingly being accentuated as the dominant motif in all his theology. Only in this way is it possible, without resorting to forced constructions,

---

51. Of importance here is Barth's reply to Gogarten to which we referred earlier in the discussion. In reviewing Barth's *Prolegomena* Gogarten had criticized Barth for not developing an anthropology. Barth replies that he regrets having been on the way to such an anthropology in 1927, KD I/1, p. 130ff. Gogarten's criticism (too little anthropology!) comforts him in that "the damage did not become as extensive as it might have become," p. 131. The danger of the *Prolegomena* was that an "existential philosophy" would provide the basis for dogmatics, p. 129. Cf. F. Gogarten, "Karl Barth's Dogmatik," *Theol. Rundschau,* 1929, p. 70ff.

52. Cf. Foreword, *Römerbrief,* 2nd ed. in which Barth speaks about the revision, "in which, so to speak, not one stone was left upon the other," p. vii.

53. Concerning the first and second editions of the *Römerbrief,* see especially the Foreword of the second edition in which the factors involved in the revision are indicated. Further: Th. L. Haitjema, *Karl Barth,* 1926; H. U. von Balthasar, *op. cit.,* and Karl Barth, "Unerledigte Anfragen an die heutige Theologie" in *Die Theol. und die Kirche, Gesammelte Vorträge,* Vol. II, pp. 1-25.

to understand the fundamental themes of Barth's theological labors.

*        *        *

Viewed in this light it is not surprising that in the moving history of dialectical theology estrangement took place between Barth, on the one hand, and Brunner, Gogarten and Bultmann, on the other, and that the intimate bond between the *two writers* of the *Römerbrief,* Barth and Thurneysen, has remained unsevered to the present day.[54]

Thurneysen is plainly a wholly different figure than Barth. He was not a systematic theologian but a pastor, a man deeply concerned with the care of souls. But notwithstanding the differing structures in which their theological activity came to expression, their relationship to each other has remained unchanged up to the present. It was to Thurneysen that Barth dedicated his K. D. III/2 with the words "Dein Alter sei wie deine Jugend!" [May your old age be as your youth!] Although Thurneysen is but seldom referred to in Barth's *Dogmatik*,[55] it is remarkable how close they still stand together. This relationship is not accidental. Their companionship began when both of them saw their religious and social ideals collapse in the post-war years. Thurneysen himself shed some light on the rise of dialectical theology when in 1927 he commented on the time that preceded the writing of the *Römerbrief.* He spoke of the war in which Barth and he could see nothing else than "judgment pronounced over all too bourgeois Christianity."[56] The religious-social ideology in terms of which they had lived as preachers in Safenwil (Barth) and Leutwil (Thurneysen) lay in ruins about them. A vacuum appeared in their thinking which till then had had norms to guide them. "It was a time in which almost all teachers of earlier times failed us." In that desperate situation, says Thurneysen, both he and Barth had learned something decisive from Kutter who again and again emphasized the action of God over against all human effort. But ultimately and most importantly,

---

54. They wrote the Römerbrief *together!*

55. Cf. KD II/2, p. 766, concerning Thurneysen's "illuminating treatise, *Die Bergpredigt,* and several other shorter references (cf. index of authors in KD II/2).

56. E. Thurneysen, "Zum rel. sozialen Problem," *Zw. d. Zeiten,* 1927, p. 515.

it was the *Bible* which saved them from utter despair. "We read the Bible anew, with far fewer presuppositions than before."[57] They heard again the message concerning the forgiveness of sins and the proclamation of the kingdom which is not of men but which comes from God Himself. "From this meeting and confrontation with the Bible in the midst of the need of-the time Karl Barth's *Römerbrief* was born." They found again actual answers to the problems with which the times confronted them.[58] They did not find an answer that remained distant from the reality in which they found themselves, but they discovered a *message* of God that was close as life to them.[59]

In this connection Thurneysen reflects on the Reformation and "on that which in our own time had been said and done by both of the Blumhardts to whom we looked up."[60] "Certain it is, that in the meeting of these two factors the forward movement of our time, if it is to be granted us, must proceed." The Reformation and the Blumhardts, one can also say: sola fide, sola gratia, and therein the triumph of grace — in these things Barth and Thurneysen saw the hope of the future. Seen in this light, it is not surprising that in his history of 19th century Protestant theology Barth gives a place to J. Chr. Blumhardt, the pastoral fighter against the demonic possession of Gottliebin Dittus, who began and ended his defense of the truth with the triumphant cry: Christus Victor![61]

Blumhardt, according to Barth, was the theologian of hope. It was Blumhardt's conviction that Christ provided not only an inner salvation, but power, might, the help and the kingship of the real Jesus. Concerning this conviction of Blumhardt Barth writes, "Is it in reality possible to evade the insight of Blumhardt?"[62] This conception of the power of Jesus makes Blumhardt for Barth a pastoral figure and this constitutes for him the break with the entire consciousness-theology of the 19th century. For this reason Blumhardt finds a place in the history of the new theology. In connection with this we must finally note

---

57. *Ibid.*, p. 517.
58. *Ibid.*, p. 517. Cf. also A. J. Bronkhorst, *K. Barth,* 1953.
59. E. Thurneysen, *op. cit.*, p. 520.
60. *Ibid.*.
61. K. Barth, *Die Prot. Theol. im 19. Jahrhundert,* 1947, p. 590.
62. *Ibid.*, p. 594.

Blumhardt's eschatological expectation: the return of Jesus Christ. Blumhardt broke through the boundaries of both liberal and pietistic theology and again put real *questions*: "the theodicy question, the problem of the universality of revelation and of faith, the problem of the practical significance of New Testament miracles, the problem of the unity of soul and body, the actual power of reconciliation, the nature and presence of the Holy Spirit, the reality of the Christian hope."[63] Academic theology erred in not heeding these questions simply because Blumhardt put them and answered them pastorally and not theologically. "The moment had to come and has come in which the insight would break through that something decisive was to be learned here, precisely for academic theology."[64]

It is not difficult to see the connections here: Thurneysen, Barth, and Blumhardt, the relationship between the care of souls and theology which is found in the triumph of grace,[65] in God's Yes that comes to expression in His judgment over all the ways of men. It is therefore more than a wish for peacefulness in declining years when Barth dedicates his volume on anthropology to Thurneysen with the words, "Dein Alter sei wie deine Jugend."

\* \* \*

We should not conclude this chapter in which we sought to penetrate to the nature of the "crisis" concept in the theology of Barth without devoting some attention to another theologian who is mentioned by Barth with unusual appreciation, namely Frederick Kohlbrugge. Let us not, to begin with, posit an antithesis between the "systematic" Barth and the "unsystematic" Kohlbrugge. Our concern is with the systematic construction of the one theme, of the one melody that is heard in all its variations. As early as 1927 Kohlbrugge had significance for Barth. In that

---

63. *Ibid.*, p. 597.
64. *Ibid.*
65. Note especially Barth's observations about J. Chr. Blumhardt in his KD III/4, p. 42ff. Barth posits that about which Blumhardt was centrally concerned, namely, "the name of Jesus": "in this name not only a spiritual but a world-historical, cosmic decision has been taken. It poses not only the question of one's disposition to it, but it poses the question of authority. With respect to this, those who confess Him must take position," p. 422. Here Barth wants to learn not from Mrs. Baker Eddy (Christian Science), but from Blumhardt, "or better, there where Blumhardt himself was taught," p. 422.

year he refers to Kohlbrugge among others in whose theological company he felt at home, and then writes about him, "his name I could justly give a double underscoring."[66]

It is plain from the beginning of Barth's acquaintance with Kohlbrugge that his appreciation for Kohlbrugge's "theology" is indissolubly associated with his *doctrine of justification* for which Abraham Kuyper also had so great admiration. Kohlbrugge was concerned to preach the justification not of the *moral* or the *religious* man, but of the *godless* man. This confession is defended by him over against every synthesis theology of the 19th century as the comfort of the "extra nos," of the "aliena justitia," in which the deepest ground for the certainty of salvation must be found.

We are therefore continually struck by the emphasis which both Barth *and* Kohlbrugge lay on the sola fide-sola gratia in opposition to every attempt to view justification *analytically* as a conclusion which God, as it were, draws from what — in sanctification — is already present in the believer.[67]

We can unmistakably see the point of contact between both theologians in their conceptions of religion and faith, of hidden pride and phariseeism and, in connection with these, of the grace of God which absolutely precedes all human piety.[68] From this point of view it is understandable why Barth in his polemic against the subjectivism of the 19th century consciously avoids criticising Kohlbrugge but rather singles him out as a witness to the glory of triumphant prevenient grace.

At a later time Barth was to subject Kohlbrugge's thought to a critical correction, when he pointed out that Calvin saw the relationship between God and man more clearly than Kohlbrugge did because Calvin did *not* permit sanctification to be swallowed up by justification, just as he did not permit obedience to coincide

---

66. *Prolegomena*, p. vi.
67. For Barth's appreciation of Kohlbrugge see: "Ludwig Feuerbach," *Zw. d. Zeiten*, 1927, p. 29, in which he characterizes *Vilmar* and *Kohlbrugge* as "upright guardians" of 19th century theology. Also, K. Barth, "Rechtfertigung and Heiligung," *Zw. w. Zeiten*, 1927, p. 298, where he refers to the "tremendous preaching" of Kohlbrugge about *justification.*
68. According to Kohlbrugge the synod of Dordt should have attacked the Remonstrants in terms of the doctrine of justification by faith, by which he evidently meant that the Remonstrants with their views of "praevisa fides" had an incorrect conception of faith.

with faith, or law with gospel.[69]   But this may not obscure the
fact that Barth's sympathy is plainly directed to Kohlbrugge.   At
one point he had certainly "reached the profundity of Calvin,"
and in a certain sense he had surpassed it, namely in "the inex-
orable understanding of grace as sovereign and as remaining sovereign."[70]

In Kohlbrugge Barth hears a hymn of praise for the grace of
God: "here we listen to a note which from Hegel to Vilmar, no,
from the time of Leibnitz to his day, had not been heard."[71]   It
was the voice of the Reformation, the confession of sovereign
grace, and that not only at the beginning of the way of salvation
but to its very end.[72]   In this Kohlbrugge has been "the teacher
of the Church."[73]   Barth's criticism of Kohlbrugge's onesidedness
does not touch the heart of his theology.   It has been a streaming
light in the midst of much darkness by its acknowledging of the
"simul peccator et justus," and of the *synthetic, forensic* judgment
of God.   Barth's appreciation of Kohlbrugge, therefore, does not
rest in the first place on his criticism of the religious-moral man
as such,[74] but is occasioned rather by the "whence" of his criticism: the message of full salvation in Christ.

This all-out emphasis on the sovereignty of grace Barth has
never regarded as an alien body that did not fit into a theology of
crisis.   Barth's early sympathy for Kohlbrugge illustrates — besides the connections with *Thurneysen* and *Blumhardt* — the
underlying theological strains which from the beginning played a
decisive role in his thinking.

---

69. Barth's remarkable words — in connection with the whole of his development — are as follows: "For Calvin nature does not disappear when grace
appears ... for him obedience is not swallowed up in faith, or the grace of
sanctification in the grace of justification ... Where in Kohlbrugge we hear only
one or almost only one word, in Calvin we regularly hear two," *Die Prot. Theol.
im. 19 Jahrhundert,* p. 586.
70. *Ibid.*
71. *Ibid.,* p. 585.
72. *Ibid.,* p. 583.
73. Cf. also Barth's "Der römische Katholizismus als Frage an die protestantische Kirche," in *Zw. d. Zeiten,* 1928, p. 297 in which Barth, in connection with
the problems of forgiveness and faith, asks, "What other leading figure in the new
Protestantism can on *this* point be called as redoubtable and as trustworthy as the
one Kohlbrugge?" Barth's concern is evident: "Where then has the view been
considered adequate that there is no other grace than grace for thieves, grace in
judgment?"
74. This does not take away the fact that there are also points of contact between
Barth and Kohlbrugge in their critical polemic against various manifestations of
the life of the Church. Cf. my *Kohlbrugge In Onze Tijd,* 1948, p. 17

To a certain extent we can agree with Vogel that in the first phase of Barth's theological development the emphasis falls on grace *in the judgment* while the later development showed that he was more concerned to manifest *grace* in the judgment.[75]   It would be improper, however, to speak of an essential modification. It is not distance and judgment that constitute the central motifs in Barth's theology, but the preaching of that grace which assumes distance and judgment, and which can be understood only in the acknowledgment of the judgment as a merited judgment.[76]

\*     \*     \*

On the basis of all the foregoing we feel warranted in characterizing Barth's theology as a form of theological thinking in which, in ever broadening reflection and in consciously Christological concentrations, the triumph of grace stands central.   Barth wants to stimulate the preaching of the gospel in the somberness of a catastrophic and depressing period of human history and to infuse new life into the witness to Jesus Christ as Victor.   He wishes to do this in sharp antithesis to every kind of triumph that can be found in man or in the world.   The "sola gratia" and the "soli Deo gloria" flow together for Barth from the one mighty glad tidings of the gospel as the only hope for our time.

75. Cf. H. Vogel, *Verkündigung und Forschung,* 1951, p. 122. What Barth writes in the Foreword of his KD III/4, 1951, in connection with his earlier development (*Römerbrief* and *Prolegomena*), is worthy of note. He writes that "saying no" is not the "highest art," as little as "the destruction of all kinds of false gods" is. If one is to see a "turning point" in Barth's development, it must, in his own judgment, be seen as follows: "Some are seeking to discover the alleged or actual turning point in my thinking which presumably took place some time between 1932 and 1938 — according to other learned investigators somewhat later. As far as I am concerned, the situation is simply as follows: gradually (for the rest, as eager as ever for battle!) I came to have more and more appreciation for *affirmations* from which and by which a man can live and die," p. ix.

76. Cf. H. Vogel, *op. cit.* "For one who recognized that already then (*Römerbrief*, 2nd ed.) the message of the free grace of God in Jesus Christ was the *one* theme of the theological thinking of Karl Barth, it was clear that his theology was not a theology of distance (diastase)," p. 121. Cf. M. P. Van Dijk, *op. cit.,* p. 67, who opposes the idea that Barth was one-sidedly concerned about the distance between God and man and about God's transcendence. Only, I believe van Dijk is *not* correct in what he writes about Barth's elimination of the idea of crisis, p. 69. The relationship judgment-grace remains dominant in Barth's dogmatics. This relationship is not, however, dialectical. The triumph lies in in the Yes of forgiveness and justification.

Precisely for this reason it is understandable that Barth's theology everywhere became a subject of discussion and asserted its influence also in the proclamation of the Church. In addition to this it sounded forth the deep strains of triumph in a time in which the struggle for the freedom of the sovereignty of grace flamed anew in confrontation with the theology of Rome.[77]

In this complex situation it is more than ever necessary to avoid one-sided reaction but to approach in terms of responsible analysis the profound questions that center around the triumph of grace. When it is supposed that Barth's theology can be approached from the isolated aspect of *crisis,* or of the *distance-*concept, or of the *hiddenness* of God, it will not be possible to understand the emphasis on grace, on communion, and on the certainty of salvation in his theology.

For these reasons — and also because of the defense of the sola gratia which is the common calling of sons of the Reformation — Barth's theology continues to interest us deeply. For it desires to put questions to us that arise from the gospel, especially the question whether we have really understood what unmerited grace is. Such questions always call not for a one-sided reaction, but for an answer. They are questions which are directly related to Barth's appreciation for Thurneysen and Kohlbrugge, and as such they are concerned with the ultimate certainty of salvation.

When in 1927 Barth recalls an earlier word of Overbeck, "Other than through audacity it is not possible to establish a basis for theology," Barth replies that this audacity consists in the fact that at the beginning of theology that remains standing which *stands* there. Thereupon he gives expression to this "beginning" by citing from Kohlbrugge what is undoubtedly one of his most triumphant utterances:

"When I die — I do not die anymore, however — and someone finds my skull, let this skull still preach to him and say: I have no eyes, nevertheless I see Him; I have neither brains nor mind, nevertheless I comprehend Him; though I have no lips, I kiss Him; I have no tongue, yet I sing praise to Him with all who call upon His name. I am a hard skull, yet I am wholly

---

77. Cf. also M. P. van Dijk, *op. cit.,* p. 20.

softened and melted in His love; I lay here exposed on God's Acre, yet I am there in Paradise! All suffering is forgotten! His great love has done this for us when for us He carried His cross and went out to Golgotha."[78]

What is the meaning of triumph of grace in the theology of Karl Barth?

78. *Prolegomena,* p. 110.

# III

## THE TRIUMPH OF GRACE IN CREATION

WITH this chapter we begin the analysis of the theme of the triumph of grace which dominates the whole of Barth's dogmatic thinking. It is not only possible but necessary to elucidate this triumph from several aspects. In doing so, however, it must be remembered that all the various aspects shall be considered to set forth one and the same triumph of the grace of God. This one theme comes to the fore throughout the length and breadth of Barth's dogmatics in countless exegetical, dogmatic, and doctrinal-historical connections. It is the theme of the sovereign and decisive grace of God revealed in Jesus Christ. In order to set forth this theme we shall discuss the triumph of grace in the theology of Karl Barth as it comes to expression in *creation,* in *election,* in *reconciliation,* and in *eschatology.* In this chapter we shall discuss the triumph of grace in *creation.*

\* \* \*

The question might be raised whether from a methodological and practical point of view it would not be preferable first to discuss Barth's conception of the triumph of grace as he gives expression to it in his doctrine of election. Considering the decisive place which election occupies in Barth's dogmatics it would be wholly warranted to do this. It is better to begin with a treatment of creation, however, because in this way we can most readily come to an understanding of Barth's conception of the triumph of grace. Moreover, the intimate connection which Barth posits between election and "history," between God and man in Christ Jesus, makes it desirable to treat election and reconciliation in immediate conjunction with each other.[1] For these reasons it is preferable first to discuss creation.

---

1. This is also evident from Barth's view of the identity of predestination and the election of Jesus Christ, KD II/2, p. 213. Concerning this history between God and man Barth writes, "This history is a unique triumph of grace and therefore of God's sovereignty," p. 219.

It may properly be asked how it is possible to speak of a triumph of grace in connection with *creation*. Does not the conception of "triumph" assume the existence of a hostile power or, at least, an opposition, which must be "overcome." Orthodoxy, with her confession of creation, fall, and redemption, regards the triumph as first coming to expression in the enmity which God placed between the seed of the woman and the seed of the serpent (Gen. 3). The establishing of this enmity was God's answer to man's fall into sin. It is clear, however, that for Barth creation itself manifests this triumph. This emphasis is intimately connected with his conception of the relationship existing between creation and the covenant of grace.

It is therefore necessary first of all to set forth the component elements of Barth's doctrine of creation.

\*     \*     \*

When Barth speaks of creation he does not have in mind an act of God which can in and by itself be a subject of theological reflection. The reason for this is that in his view creation is indissolubly related to the covenant of grace in Jesus Christ. It is not possible to speak of a natural theology with an independent cosmological interest in "God as Creator." The witness of the Scriptures is differently oriented. It does not witness to an abstract highest being as *prima causa* of all things, but it witnesses to the Lord of history, the God of Israel. In the history of creation we are concerned with the history of *salvation*. It is not possible to say anything that is meaningful about creation outside of Jesus Christ. Only in *Him* can we understand creation. And when Barth says "only in *Him*" he does not mean the creation of all things through the second Person of the trinity, but through Jesus of Nazareth. In creation we are exclusively concerned with the relationship of creation to Jesus Christ. By Him and with a view to Him and to His grace the world was created so that it is never possible to regard or understand creation "as such." The biblical message concerning creation does not present us with cosmological or ontological truths of which everyone who is not wholly blind can take note (through the natural light of reason), but it witnesses to an act of God's grace.[2] It is not possible first to come to a knowledge of creation in itself, and then advance to a knowledge of redemption in Christ. Creation can be seen only in Jesus Christ and in connection with the incarnation of the Word.[3]

Creation, it is true, is the external ground of the covenant but, conversely, the covenant is the internal ground of creation.[4] This specific connection between *creation* and *covenant*, between creation and Jesus of Nazareth, draws attention. In order to understand Barth properly here, it must be remembered that he is not concerned simply about a *noetic* problem (namely that *knowledge* of creation is possible only in terms of the revelation in Christ)[5], but also about an *ontic* problem which touches the whole *being* of creation. This world has been created "through the child that was born at Bethlehem, through the man who died on the cross at Golgotha and rose again the third day. *He* is the creating Word through which all things became. From *Him* creation derives its meaning."[6]

Barth has called this conception "a remarkable turn-about in the whole of our thinking."[7] But such thinking is necessary. It alone can prevent us from abstracting creation from the gracious and reconciling work of God and from seeing the history of creation as a "pre-history" which has meaning in itself. When creation is seen as meaningful in itself it is forgotten that God's action in creation is related to Jesus of Nazareth. All that happens in creation happens *in* Jesus Christ "who is the primordial image, the model or system, underlying and giving direction to all things."[8]

2. KD III/1, p. 378.
3. *Ibid.*, p. 54.
4. *Ibid.*, p. 262. Cf. II/1, p. 576.
5. "What it means that God is Creator and what the work of creation means is no less hidden for us human beings than all else that the confession of faith includes. It is not so that the truth about God the Creator is directly accessible to us and that only the truth of the second article requires a revelation," *Dogmatik im Grundrisz*, 1947, p. 57. Cf. also Barth's *De Apostolische Geloofsbelijdenis*, 1935, p. 45 where he speaks about the significance of the fact that "credo" stands *before* "creator of heaven and earth."
6. *Grundrisz*, p. 66.
7. *Ibid.*
8. KD II/2, p. 7.

Creation does not precede the covenant, but the covenant precedes creation.[9] Creation without grace is an abstraction. The history of the covenant is the foundation of the whole of the history of God's relationship to creation and to man.[10] For this reason the emphasis on the triumph of grace comes to the fore in the doctrine of creation. There is no "pre-history" which as history of creation stands in a *neutral* relationship to the covenant that was revealed later. Before the world was created there was already God's decision "with a view to this event in which God desired to have communion with man, the incomprehensible communion in Jesus Christ."[11] Creation cannot be seen *in abstracto,* but only in the light of the covenant which is the inner ground of creation. For this reason it is possible to speak of a *prefiguration* of the covenant of grace in the created world. There is an inner *unity* between creation and covenant. Creation does not, it is true, constitute the whole of God's works.[12] It is possible to speak of a later *new* element which in God's relationship to man transcends His earlier creational activity[13] and which can therefore be distinguished from creation. But this distinction does not involve a disjunction.

Creation as the *first* work of God[14] precedes the second work of God's grace within the sphere of created reality. But the relationship between God's first and second work may not be so construed that the latter comes to be viewed as "an afterthought which can be ignored in regarding God's first, His foundation-laying act of creation."[15] It is precisely the first, the creative act of God, which makes it impossible to disregard the second, the action of God in Jesus Christ and in His covenant of grace. Creation *as* the first work of God bears "the character of a model. It is the shell of the second (namely the covenant), and is therefore

9. *Grundriss,* p. 73.
10. KD II/2, p. 7.
11. *Grundriss,* p. 73  cf. KD III/2, p. 11.
12. KD III/1, p. 51.
13. *Ibid.*
14. *Ibid.,* p. 48.
15. *Ibid.,* p. 49.

its outer form in outline."[16] When we define creation as the "cause" of the world's existence we say something which from the viewpoint of the Christian faith is "wholly meaningless."[17]

The prefiguration of the covenant is the *mystery* of creation. The eye of faith must discern this significance of creation. For the prefiguration is not simply symbolic, it is not merely a pointer. The history of creation is the "exemplary visible beginning" of the history of the covenant.[18] Because it is this, it is full of analogies of the covenant of grace in Jesus Christ. "God has permitted the creation to take place in this analogical fashion *because* in creation He, so to speak, thought of redemption."[19]

Prenter rightly speaks of the "significative" meaning of the history of creation in Barth's theology. It provides a "sign-language prepared to do service for the history of redemption."[20]

It is clear, therefore, that already in Barth's doctrine of creation the *triumph of grace* is prominent. It becomes evident in the prefigurative and sacramental character of creation.

*       *       *

At the beginning of all things stands the Will of God[22] which, in Jesus Christ and with a view to Him, desired the coming into being of the cosmos and, in that cosmos, man in communion with God. When we see in which way Barth develops this thought we come immediately upon a conception which occupies a decisive place throughout the whole of his dogmatic exposition. We come upon the conception that the divine will as expressed in

---

16. *Ibid.*, p. 46. Note especially p. 262: "Creation does not *promise, announce, prophesy,* the covenant but, without being identical with it, *prefigures* and to that extent *anticipates* it; it not only prepares the way for the covenant but, in doing so, it is itself a unique sign of the covenant, a true *sacrament.* Jesus Christ is not the end, He is the beginning of creation." Cf. also p. 265, and the sharp formulation in the *Grundrisz*: the covenant is "older" than creation, p. 73. Also, on p. 73, the covenant is not "something secondary, something supplementary."

17. *Ibid.*, p. 47.

18. *Ibid.*, p. 265.

19. R. Prenter, "Die Einheit von Schöpfung und Erlösung. Zur Schöpfungslehre Karl Barth's," *Theol. Zeitschrift,* Vol. II, 1946, p. 170. Prenter's expression, "in a certain sense," is, it seems to me, too weak.

20. *Ibid.*, pp. 171, 175.

21. Cf. K. H. Miskotte, "Schepping en Verbond," *Kerk en Theologie,* Vol. II, p. 195: "Therefore creation (rather, the work of the Creator) prefigures reconciliation (the act of reconciliation) and reconciliation *surpasses* creation in that it at the same time *fulfills* and confirms it."

22. KD III/1, p. 108.

creation excludes "the other" because "anything else which could have happened became, with that happening (i.e. creation), a matter of the past."[23]

When through the divine will time began, *all* other things "i.e. everything which with respect to the divine purpose was neutral or stood opposed to it" became *past*. All neutral or opposed possibilities "were through the divine will and deed contradicted," they became the chaos, the radically excluded, the in itself impossible world. It might at first glance appear that Barth here in a purely formal manner places the "being" of creation over against that which is "non-being" in the sense of the *reality* of creation as opposed to that which is *not real*. It is not Barth's purpose, however, to present *this* antithesis. He is not concerned with a conception of "non-being" in the sense of Romans 4:17 which speaks of God's calling into being the things that are not as though they were, a *creatio ex nihilo*. In Barth's view, on the contrary, the excluded possibility receives, through God's creative action, a deeply pregnant meaning. The excluded possibility (the chaos and the darkness) is, *because* it is excluded, *a reality* existing at the *boundary*, the outer limit, of that which God did create.[24]

It is, according to Barth, the purpose of the creation account, concerned as it is to set forth *covenantal* history, to give expression to this truth. The creature does not in itself have the power to protect itself against the threat of chaos and darkness but needs the help of God for this. "*He* saw the threatening curse and the threatening misery. He rejected the reality of a creature that would be opposed to or that would be neutral with respect

---

23. *Ibid.*, p. 109.
24. KD III/1, p. 112, and very markedly on p. 378 about the antithesis between creation and "the angry bent of non-reality through the retroactive power of the divine No." Here we must remember that creation is not unrelated to this non-reality because it exists by virtue of its being separated from creation. Cf. Barth's *Grundrisz*, p. 65, in which he speaks about the reality of evil as "the reality of this excluded and contradicted (entity)," as the reality that lies behind God's back and which in creating He passed by. What is *not* good has *not* been created, "but if we are to attribute being to it at all, rather than say that it is not-being, we must say that it is only the power of *that* being which arises from the force of the divine No," p. 65. Finally, with respect to this idea which plays so significant a role in the whole of Barth's thinking, cf. KD III/1, p. 112: "Only as that which in God's decision and action has been rejected and is past, only as the boundary of that which according to God's decision and action is and will be, can this ungodly and anti-godly reality exist."

to Him."[25]    God Himself has driven this threat back to the farthermost limit of creation, to the very *boundary* of the created
world.    This He did in His divine mercy.    The reality of the
creature and the boundary which becomes visible in and by the
act of creation Barth sees coming to expression in the creation
account, notably in Genesis 1:2. Here we read of the "tohu wabohu" (without form and void) and of the antithesis between *light*
and *darkness*.    Barth rejects the interpretation that Genesis 1:2
teaches a state of chaos which preceded the act of creation, as also
the view that it teaches the existence of an as yet unformed material mass which God fashioned into an harmonious cosmos.    He
believes a *third* interpretation is possible, namely that the *"tohu
wabohu"* speaks of the earth as chaos and darkness, abyss, utter
desert, nothingness, vanity, "a situation without hope."    The darkness which was on the face of the deep means *danger*.    This does
not imply a dualistic cosmogony, but points precisely to the *victory*
of God, to the *triumphant Yes* which becomes evident in this, that
God *overcomes* the danger that threatens His creation.

That the Spirit of God moved upon the face of the waters does
not mean that the *Holy* Spirit fashioned the unformed mass into an
ordered cosmos, but refers to a *caricature* of God's truly creative
action which the writer was concerned to depict.    God Himself,
the God of Israel, is not recognizable here.    When we note what
*God* does we see that He *excludes* and *passes by* every other possibility.    The first verses of Genesis 1 speak of *that* possibility "which
God, in that He undertook to create, passed by.    It is a possibility
which He scorned to realize, much as an artist, in choosing to execute a particular project, does not choose others but rejects them,
passes them by, leaves them unexecuted behind him."[26]    Genesis
1:2 does *not* speak of a world which God created, but precisely of a
world which God did *not* create and which, in fact, he *passed by in
disdain*.[27]

*In* the act of creation God excluded this other, this dark possibility.    This does not mean, however, that this other, this rejected
world does not have reality.    Also this rejected possibility is *reality*.
Also *this* world, albeit "in its own absurd manner," *has reality*.    It

25. *Ibid.*
26. *Ibid.*, p. 119.
27. *Ibid.*

was in its reality — though rejected — active as "a shadow which also lay on the world which God willed and created."[28]  God passed it by, but the shadow is real and becomes an actuality when the true choice is forgotten and neglected.[29]  Man can in his folly look back to the possibility which God rejected, he can become enamored of the chaos, and then the "tohu wabohu" can become an acute *danger*.  This is the "undeniable risk" which God "took upon Himself when He hazarded creation, but to which, since He is the Creator, He is fully equal and therefore did not have to fear."  He spoke His creative word which was directed "against that rejected reality," against the reality of "a creature that was strange and hostile to Him."  The Genesis account witnesses to the triumph of His mercy in the creation and in the rejection which accompanied it.

Barth comes to the same view in connection with the creation of light.  God made *separation* between the light and the darkness.  The creation of light was the first of God's works and this fact has placed a stamp on all His other works.  He passed by the night, and He separated it from the light.  From the beginning the whole of created reality partakes of *this* definitive separation.[30]  The entire creation exists in the light that is from God.  Even the night cannot change this because God has designated it as night in order to indicate the *boundary* of the day.  The night is not a counter-day, it has no time of its own.  The victory of night over day would be possible only "if light were not ever and again light, victorious truth, by virtue of the same Power through which it came into being."[31]  The *day* is the time of salvation, the good day of God, not the time of evil.  Light is the *sign* of the divine covenant of grace, and God's goodness brought it into being.  The light shines in the darkness, and therefore nature is not left to itself but it stands in the light of the grace of God.  The creation of light as the first of the works of God is His "Yes to the creature."

Everywhere we meet the same prefiguration of the triumph.  A striking example is Genesis 1:31, namely, that God saw all that He had made and, behold, it was very good.  This "goodness" of the

---

28. *Ibid.*, p. 120.
29. *Ibid.*, p. 119.
30. *Ibid.*, p. 120.
31. The "plunge" into the chaos, against which the cosmos in and by itself is not protected, Barth refers to as "the plunge into that non-existence, non-reality, and non-goodness," KD III/1, p. 121.

creature has no reference whatever to an original condition in which creation and man found themselves. It refers to a unique "being-good" of the *room* which God had made for the development of the history of His covenant of grace. This "being-good" expresses His Yes, His grace and mercy in Jesus Christ, the triumph of grace, all of which become sacramentally and prefiguratively visible in the creation.[32] For this reason it cannot be denied that the triumph of *creation* is of one piece with the triumph of *election*. The relationship between the two, one could properly say their identity, becomes plain when Barth himself draws a parallel between the relationship "light-darkness" and the relationship *elect-reprobate*. Barth admits that the "analogy" between the two is incomplete because election and reprobation are concerned with creatures of God, while the darkness is not a creature.[33] Nevertheless, he insists that there is a true analogy here because of the nature of election and reprobation, which is akin to God's relationship to light and darkness and which becomes manifest in the action of His sovereign love.

The witness of Scripture respecting God the Creator is the witness to Jesus Christ who is the ground and meaning of creation. Genesis 1 points to *Him* — also in the creation of the light — as the great Light that floods the whole of creation.[34]

Darkness and chaos have a place in this witness, but only as *scorned* and *rejected* realities. That is how they appear in God's first work which can only be understood in terms of Christ. Therefore Barth can speak of the *triumph of creation*.

\*     \*     \*

This prefiguration, however, occasions all kinds of questions. Even though chaos and darkness have been passed by and rejected — *in* God's creative deed — nevertheless, they are in a certain sense "real." It is precisely at this point that we meet a central

---

32. About the "goodness" of creation cf. my *Karl Barth en de Kinderdoop,* 1947, and *De Voorzienigheid Gods,* 1950 (Eng. tr.: *The Providence of God.*) Further, in Barth, in addition to his KD III/1, his *Grundrisz,* p. 67, dealing with the words, "and behold, it was very good." Whatever the objections that may be made against the world, "its goodness incontrovertibly consists in this that it is the place where the glory of God and man as the witness to this glory may be found."
33. KD III/1, p. 137.
34. *Ibid.*

thought which receives emphasis in various places in Barth's theology. For him the triumph of God's Yes by no means justifies the conclusion that this is a sinless and exclusively light-filled world.

The rejected darkness may be described as having no being and as non-existence, [35] but, for all that, Barth discusses it as a (not-created) reality. He makes this plain when he emphatically opposes the idea that in creating man God created also the "possibility" of his *fall*. He rejects the idea that man was created with the "possibility" of sinning, of choosing between good and evil, the possibility of the *liberum arbitrium*. That is how Barth regards the section in the Genesis account which is usually referred to as the "probationary command." But why then this command which seems, after all, to open an entree into a direction which man was forbidden to enter?[36]

According to Barth a question is indeed posed in this command which man must answer with his whole being. In giving this command God gives man room in which to be *free*. For Barth everything turns on this: the freedom that is given to man is not "freedom of choice between obedience and disobedience." Precisely *that* freedom is *denied* him, for he hears that God is judge over good and evil.[37] Freedom is not "a place in the middle between obedience and disobedience," it is not "room for movement at the edge of the abyss."

It does *not* lie in the nature of man that he can choose between left and right, between good and evil. For this reason the command of Genesis does not tempt man,[38] and Barth rejects the representation that "God, in giving man freedom to choose for obedience, subjected him to a testing."[39] When God gives man freedom He gives him freedom *exclusively* for the purpose of being *truly obedient*. Man has not been created with a neutral *liberum arbitrium*, but

---

35. See especially III/1, p. 121, where Barth speaks of the judgment referred to in Genesis 1:2 as the judgment that becomes a reality "at only one place in the cosmos which He created," namely at Golgotha. *Here* is the small moment of God's wrath (Isa. 54:7) and, "in spite of all analogies of other darkness on earth, there is *no* other moment." That which is passed by in the reconciliation (namely the chaos) did not really become past only by virtue of the new creation, but "regarded already from the viewpoint of the first creation" it is the "being of this world" which was then passed by.

36. *Ibid.*, p. 299.

37. *Ibid.*, p. 200.

38. *Ibid.*, p. 299ff.

39. *Ibid.*, p. 301.

God created him with "the competence to keep and execute his obedience, to make his own decision to obey."[40]

And yet, in the same connection Barth states that man, in this respect, is *not invulnerable.* It cannot be said that sin could, "according to God's will, take place." But man *was* vulnerable and things *have come* to the actuality of threat from the side of chaos.* Sin *has become* reality, horrible reality. But the choice which man made was *irrational, absurd,* it was *the impossible possibility of sin.*[41]

Sin can only be described as absurd, irrational. A real ground for it there *is not.* It has no possibility other than the possibility of the impossible:[42] it is the "absurd ability" of man to surrender himself to the influence of the "chaos-beast" of Genesis 3.[43] Everything that exists participates in some manner in the right to realize itself, everything that exists has a true potentiality, but "sin nowhere has a rightful place, it is without true potential, it has not the slightest right to find realization. It is only wrong."[44]

Although Barth does not consider an explanation of sin possible, he does come to a circumscription of it. He refers to sin as "the sowing of the enemy in the good ground, the invasion of chaos, the revolution of nihilism, at the end of which only the nihilization of all created being can remain."[45] But none of this is deducible

---

40. *Ibid.,* p. 301. Cf. also "It does not say that God set before man as a Hercules standing at the separation of the ways the choice between obedience and disobedience," p. 301. The same reference to the Hercules figure appears also in the *Grundrisz,* p. 65: "Man has not been created to be a Hercules standing at the separation of the ways. Evil does not lie within the possibilities of the creature that God made." Cf. also KD IV/1, p. 454.

* The Dutch expression that is used here is "het nietige," a proper Dutch translation of the characteristic expression of Barth, "das Nichtige." It does not mean "nothingness" but connotes active, destructive power of a wholly negative character, as is suggested by the corresponding German and Dutch verbs "vernichten," "vernietigen," which mean: to annihilate, utterly to destroy. The concept "das Nichtige" is a powerful one in Barth's theology and particularly so in his doctrine of creation. It is intended to designate the non-created chaos reality which God in creation "passed by in disdain." It is the ever-threatening foe of man and constitutes the enemy over which grace triumphs. I have been unable to find an equally expressive English word in which to render the term and have therefore consistently translated "das Nichtige" and "het nietige" as "chaos." Translator.

41. KD IV/1, p. 454.
42. *Ibid.*
43. *Ibid.,* p. 534.
44. *Ibid.,* p. 455.
45. *Ibid.,* p. 456.

from the world which God created nor from the freedom which
He gave to man.

The freedom which God gave to man is a *good* freedom, it is a
freedom which can never lead him to destruction.[46]  It is the freedom of decision which gives him room "to be obedient voluntarily
in accordance with his creation."[47]  For this reason it is also impossible to trace sin back to what God willed with this freedom which
He gave to man.[48]  Sin confronts us as an inexplicable mystery, as a
phenomenon which is not to be explained in terms of man's creation.  It is solely *chaos, darkness.*[49]

*     *     *

Also here we see that in this "nothingness" which was excluded
by God's creative act we do not come in contact at all with a formal
"non-being."  It has not been *created,* but it *confronts* us.  Therefore Barth speaks not only in his treatment of creation of that which
God rejected, of the chaos and of the darkness that were passed
by, but in his doctrine of providence he discusses the subject extensively again, warns against misunderstanding of it and further
speaks of the *knowledge* and *reality* of this chaos.[50]

Barth is deeply concerned to say something other and something
more than that God, in creating, excluded other possibilities.  He is
concerned with *the reality-aspect of the chaos which God rejected.*
The line which Barth draws in the doctrine of creation is continued
in the doctrine of providence and particularly in connection with
his conception of chaos.  Again he asserts emphatically that the rejected chaos does not belong to the essence of creation and is not

---

46. KD III/1, p. 302.

47. *Ibid.,* p. 303

48. *Ibid.,* p. 313

49. Already in his *De apostolische Geloofsbelijdenis* (ed. K. H. Miskotte),
1935, Barth spoke, in connection with belief in the Creator, about questions of
faith "which cannot, at least not unambiguously and fully, be answered in terms
of the doctrine of creation.  Among these questions he includes those of the possibility of sin, of evil, and of death, all of which are summarized in the question
of the possibility of the devil to be the devil, p. 52.  We can say, Barth writes,
that God is the conqueror of "this absurd, this impossible possibility," but *not*
that these possibilities have been *willed* or *created* by God, p. 52.  Here dogmatics
must be "logically inconsistent."  We may not extend the line of creation
at this point but must consciously refrain from seeking a ground for the existence
of these possibilities, p. 53.  These ideas Barth later develops broadly in his doctrine of the chaos.

50. KD III/3, pp. 327-425.

itself a creature. It is not true "that chaos belongs to the essence of created reality and may in one way or another be conceived of as a mark of its being and perfection."[51]

It is important to note the connection in which Barth wrote these words. He warns against a misunderstanding of the chaos which lies in this, that one may look for it where it does *not* exist. One may think to find it, for instance, in the fact that we live in an imperfect world in which not only light but also darkness is to be found. One may then be tempted to identify this shadow-side with the threatening chaos. Barth, however, emphatically rejects such a view. He acknowledges the existence of this shadow-side and admits that creation "in a certain sense borders upon and has affinity for the chaos."[52] But it is not possible to speak of an identification, because the shadow-side belongs to the nature of the creature, it is even part of the *perfection* of the creature to have this shadow-side. No creature is "nothing," every creature is "something, but something at the edge of chaos, secure but also endangered."[53] This *belongs* to the creature which, precisely in this way, stands revealed as not independent, not autonomous, but as "needy." In *this* way the creature is *good* and *perfect.* Creaturely being is *"good being."*[54] This is not a human self-evaluation but can be understood only in the light of the divine good pleasure which has been pronounced over the creature,[55] the "very good" of Genesis 1:31. In this light Barth can speak of a justification of creation [56] which includes reference to the shadow-side. For it lay in the intention of the Creator that the creature should have a double destiny: an in the sight of God valid "weight and dignity" *and* an equally "in the sight of God existing need and peril of the creature."[57]   In this way the joy but also the misery of existence have their ground in the will of God.[58] This meaning of creation becomes manifest in the fact that God in Jesus Christ makes Himself "the subject of both aspects of existence."[59]   In *this* streaming light it becomes plain

---

51. *Ibid.*, p. 335.
52. *Ibid.*
53. *Ibid.*
54. KD III/1, p. 420.
55. *Ibid.*, p. 422.
56. *Ibid.*, p. 418-476.
57. *Ibid.*, p. 430.
58. *Ibid.*, p. 431.
59. *Ibid.*, p. 432.

that God has justified His creation in its *totality*, that it is *good*, yes, that it is the *best possible creation*[60] because the Creator Himself "willed to endure the contradiction of created existence."[61]

Through the everlasting mercy of God, joy and suffering, light and darkness, life and death, became the portion of His Son.[62]  In Him participation in the negative aspect of creation was the means of attaining a higher end.[63]  The negative and the positive aspects of creation do not stand next to each other with an equal ultimacy, for *life* has conquered.  Therefore one can — in Jesus Christ — see creaturely reality as the theater, the workshop, the object of God's action and discern its character as the "best of all conceivable worlds."[64] That the world should be better than it now is, is excluded because it stands in the light and under the power of this *reconciling* action of God.

Because this is the biblical conception of the goodness of creation we cannot, says Barth, take as our point of departure an aprioristic, metaphysical and formal goodness concept.  Our concern is with the goodness that is goodness according to God's election and creation: the incarnation of the Son of God.  When we see *Him* we can no longer see the shadow-side of created reality as being identical with the threatening chaos.

The creature is subject to the antithesis which exists between the two aspects of creatureliness.  But this does not mean that it partakes of chaos.  It is — with a view to Jesus Christ — precisely in this subjection that creation took place.  The shadow-side of creation may serve to *remind*[65] us of the chaos at the boundary of which we live, but it is not itself that.  In the shadow-side of creation we see weeping alongside of laughing, failure next to success, becoming older as well as being young, death no less than birth.  All this has been distributed over this life according to a pattern of righteousness which is hidden from us.  It does no prejudice to the fact that the *good* creation praises God — in which it is the opposite of chaos — and to the fact that this hymn of praise is also heard on the shadow-side, also in the negative aspect of cre-

---

60. *Ibid.*, p. 433.
61. *Ibid.*, p. 436.
62. *Ibid.*, p. 437.
63. *Ibid.*, p. 440.
64. *Ibid.*, p. 441.
65. KD III/3, p. 336.

ation, through which aspect it *borders* on chaos[66] Therefore the world which God has made is also according to its negative aspect "His good creation."[67]

Before Barth begins his discussion of the actual chaos[68] he points, by way of setting its limits, to the *goodness* of creation. What he means by the goodness of creation is illustrated by the manner in which he time and again speaks of *Mozart.* Barth relates his music to the *two* aspects of creation. He calls Mozart's music incomparable and cannot find words enough to praise it. It provides not only enjoyment, it is food and drink. Mozart should really be adopted by theology, particularly by the theology of creation and eschatology, for he has seen and heard things in connection with the *totally good* creation that orthodoxy and the Reformers have not seen and heard.

Mozart composed in a century in which the earthquake of Lisbon took place (1755) which led many to ask, where is God? while others undertook to "defend" Him. Mozart, however, transcended both the optimists and the pessimists. He heard the Yes *and* the No and he gave form to what he heard in *total* music.

Mozart served God in his life for he knew of the good creation of God to which also belongs the end, the boundary of man. He knew that side of the creature which — without itself being chaos — bordered on it, and he knew that this side could not be evil. The strains of his music reflect also this aspect of creation and bring praise to God so that the whole of creation is a hymn to the Creator who made *all* things well.

In this emphasis of Mozart — the harmony of creation — lies Barth's theological appreciation for him. The harmony includes the negative aspect which lies at the boundary of life. The lamps have been lighted and the shadows may not be interpreted as being the chaos. To do this can only lead to gnosticism which identifies the shadows of creation with the threatening chaos and by so doing surrenders the good creation to radical evil.

We see clearly here that Barth's concern is to reveal the triumphant light of Christ in the world which in both of its aspects is

---

66. *Ibid.*
67. *Ibid.*, p. 337.
68. *Ibid.*, p. 338.

directed Christward. He says of Mozart that he knew the sorrow which the realization that we live at the boundary of evil creates. In his doctrines of creation and providence Barth wants to show the way through this sorrow and lead us to a "Christian" optimism that shall guide us in the present and in the future. This optimism does not rest upon a superficial empirical analysis of the creature, but it is the joy which is *in Christ* who saves *this* creature in *this* border situation, in its non-autonomous and needy character. It is the joy of the divine triumph revealed in the salvation of the world by the first of the works of God — the calling into being of the light, which in the fulness of its symbolism discloses to us the Light of the world.[69]

\*    \*    \*

In addition to Barth's references to Mozart, we can also illustrate the delimitation of chaos by alluding to Leibnitz. In view of the foregoing it is understandable that Barth should concern himself with Leibnitz, the philosopher who is particularly known for his view of this world as the "best possible" world. The question is whether the harmony which Leibnitz discerned in this world is the same as the justification of creation of which Barth speaks. In an earlier writing I discussed the Barth-Leibnitz relationship,[70] but since the publication of this book Barth has returned to the subject anew in his discussion of providence,[71] and particularly in connection with the problem of the ever-threatening "nothingness" of chaos. Earlier Barth had said that Leibnitz's conception of the best-possible world would be a right conception if it could be Christologically understood. Now, however, his criticism, so far as I can

---

69. Barth treated of Mozart in his doctrine of creation, KD III/1, p. 465, in connection with the optimism of the 18th century which "produced the best music of all time." Also extensively in III/3. pp. 337-339. and in *Die Protestantische Theologie im* 19. *Jahrhundert*, pp. 50, 53, 239, and 514, about Strauss's love for the music of Mozart. ". . . whoever understands *that* will be spared a great deal of worthless and infantile critical theological activity." In connection with the *limitation* of our life cf. KD III/4, p. 676 where Barth cites Mozart on the subject of death. We shall return extensively to the question of this limitation in chapters VI and XII.

70. Cf. my *De Voorzienigheid Gods*, 1950, p. 292ff. (Eng. tr.: *The Providence of God*, p. 263ff.), and *Karl Barth en de Kinderdoop*, p. 121ff.

71. After KD III/1 again in KD III/3, p. 360ff.

see, goes farther. In Leibnitz's philosophy, says Barth, there is no room for the reality of chaos. In the final analysis evil, in all its forms is, in the view of Leibnitz, to be explained in terms of the one metaphysical evil, namely imperfection. Evil is *privatio*. It has only a negative qualification: it is the *absence* of something.

Barth directs his criticism of Leibnitz against the conception that the harmony of creation should be evidenced in these terms. Leibnitz had no appreciation for the fact that there is *more* to say about the creature than that it has two aspects, the positive and the negative. Leibnitz constructed his harmonious creation on basis of these two, but he failed to see that the chaos which threatens man is not the same as the negative side of creation (which can be resolved in the harmony). He did not understand that it is *that which God rejected*, that it is the radical danger that threatens always, the horror of chaos.

For Leibnitz, the wolf — to use the figure of Isaiah 11:6 — does not dwell with the lamb, but the wolves have themselves become lambs.[72] The Leibnitzian chaos becomes innocent and harmless and "can therefore not have the character of an energetic and active power."[73] It cannot break loose and offend the Most High. It *belongs* to the created order of things and therefore cannot be a real *triumph* of God over it. "It is in the nature of the case not possible [on Leibnitz's basis] to conceive of the chaos as having any real power and therefore he cannot conceive of a *struggle* of God with it, and a victory of God over it!"[74] It is not possible and it is not necessary "to do away with it and to resolve it." In Leibnitz the chaos becomes something positive[75] — even though it be *privatio* — and over against this view Barth posits emphatically the reality of the chaos as *a power that can take initiative*, as but *ruinous power*, as *destruction*.

The chaos that threatens the good creation is not a necessary negative or positive reality belonging to the imperfection of crea-

---

72. KD III/3, p. 363.
73. *Ibid.*, p. 364.
74. *Ibid.*
75. *Ibid.*, p. 365

tion; it is an alien power which must and will be overcome.  **Only** on this basis can its reality be rightly understood.[76]

*       *       *

We have now, via Barth's appreciation of Mozart and his criticism of Leibnitz, come to a better understanding of the *distinction* between the negative aspect of creation and the true character of the ever threatening chaos.  Yet this does not answer the question what precisely this chaos is.  This question poses one of the most difficult and involved problems for the student of Barth's theology.  The triumph of God is indeed *related to* the shadow-side of creation, but its deepest significance lies in its being a triumph over the reality of the chaos.  It would be possible to describe this triumph as the triumph of reconciliation, but we shall discuss it now in connection with the prefigurative triumph of *creation* because here the *separation* of light from darkness comes emphatically to the fore.  Already at this early point the chaos that God rejected and passed by appears to view.  That we can treat this subject at this point is evident, moreover, from the fact that in discussing providence Barth again and again refers back to the discussion of chaos in his treatment of the doctrine of creation.

In viewing the relationship between chaos and God's government of creation, Barth underscores that *preservation* (as an aspect of God's providence) *means more than simply keeping-in-existence*.  Barth regards the divine "conservatio" as an action of God which is directed against the threat to His creation which is ever posed by the chaos which hovers at the edge of all created

---

76. The importance which the doctrine of the chaos has for Barth appears, among other things, from his observations about Schleiermacher.  Barth writes about him that "he contributed something to the understanding of sin and the chaos," to which he adds "after whom one looks in vain — also in the circles of orthodox theology—for another; still, to see this, especially in connection with the doctrine of providence, is simply essential," KD III/3, p. 375.  The element which Barth appreciates in Schleiermacher is his emphasis on God's saying No to sin.  Here Barth discerns some understanding for what he describes with "some unSchleiermacherian expressions" as "not chosen, not willed, but passed over, rejected, excluded, judged," KD III/3, pp. 375-376.  According to Barth, this idea of God's "saying No" to the chaos can be fruitfully used only in terms of *Christology*.  Schleiermacher did *not* develop his doctrine of sin Christologically, however, and therefore his idea of the "saying No" remained unfruitful.

reality. God's "conservatio" is "His protection against the over-whelming of His creation by this hostile power."[77]

Is it true, then, that created reality is threatened from the side of chaos? Here we come face to face with the problem of the *reality* of non-existence. To this problem Barth gives his own re-markable answer. The chaos that threatens creation is that which God, according to Genesis 1:2, left behind Him and rejected "with out giving it being or existence."[78] Barth's definition of chaos is "that which is real only in this negativity which through God's decision has been given to it, it is real only in its being denied created being. It is a reality which exists only at God's left hand. But in this sense it is, in its own characteristic way, really relevant and active."[79]

The reality of the chaos can only be circumscribed in this way, then, that it points to the possibility which God in His creative word *rejected* and *excluded*.

It is a possibility which in His counsel He put from Him, it is a possibility which He does *not* will and never shall will, it is a reality which stands under the mighty wrathful No of God and "in this way undoubtedly is and has reality." Barth speaks of a negative reality over which God has from eternity pronounced judgment. Man as creature has no power in the face of this danger but is rather threatened by it. The *victory* over the threat that comes to us from the area of chaos is not of our achieving, it does not belong to our task. The creature can only exist in terms of God's *grace*. And the situation in which the creature remains de-pendent upon grace, God maintains by means of the divine preser-vation which consists in this, that God goes *no farther* than to separate light from darkness.[80] Therefore the doctrine concern-

---

77. KD III/3, p. 84.
78. *Ibid.*
79. *Ibid.*, We meet an illuminating comment on this in KD III/3, p. 376. in connection with a discussion of Schleiermacher's doctrine of sin. Here Barth states that sin must be understood "as the work of a mighty divine denial," namely, "a reality — not created, but placed — which exists by reason of the fact that God opposes Himself to it." It is — because of Jesus Christ — "that which has been *excluded* by God's almighty grace and which, having no ground in itself, acquires and for awhile retains its dark basis in this antithesis. It is that which as the ground, origin, and epitome of all contradictoriness lives itself out. Only, in its purely contradictory being and existence as sheer chaos, it has from the beginning been overcome by the almighty grace of God," p. 376.
80. *Ibid.*, p. 84.

ing divine preservation does not teach a metaphysical, neutral "conservatio" or "sustentatio," but a *servatio, a rescue from* and *out of* the danger by which the creature would be overwhelmed and turned into a chaos-element if only its *own* power *existed* to protect it. Preservation as *salvation* — that is the theme around which Barth's doctrine of providence is concentrated. The function of the (impossible) chaos becomes evident in the light of the divine *servatio.* The *servatio* is directed against the overwhelming power of the threatening chaos. In this connection Barth discusses the older theology which (in the doctrine of preservation) regarded man only as an "ens participativum."[81] He considers this conception too cheap because in it preservation means no more than the *dependence* of the creature upon Him who is of Himself the Independent One.

To speak like this is to speak too metaphysically. It does no more than distinguish between human relativity and divine absoluteness. In his doctrine of providence Barth is concerned about far more than a dependence-relationship of man to God. The problem is one of rescue from threatening destruction, it is one of *salvation.* "Is that the whole predicament of man, that the creature is only an ens participativum?"[82] Does our deepest need arise only from the fact that we are *dependent?*

Augustine and Thomas at least sensed that the "nihil" is something more than "non-being in its formal antithesis to existing being."[83] The antithesis in this form does not state the decisive issue. The decisive issue is the *threat* confronting all being which meets it from the realm of menacing non-being. Therefore the older Christian theology with its conception of "nihil" did not penetrate to the heart of the matter.[84] The threat comes from that over which God has pronounced His rejecting and scorning No! Salvation is salvation from chaos, from the abyss which borders upon all creaturely reality. Preservation means that if God were to turn away from the creature for but *one moment* the offensive of chaos would break loose with deadly power against the crea-

81. *Ibid.,* p. 85.
82. *Ibid.*
84. *Ibid.*
84. *Ibid.*

ture.[85] The chaos, as natural neighbor of the creature,[86] is *real* because at the same time that God spoke His Yes to creation He spoke His wrathful No of eternal rejection against the power of non-being.

The chaos that threatens has reality *in terms of this wrath.*

The chaos which borders upon creation is not an "opposite number" for God, but it is the shadow of His work which His wrath *brought into being* and *banished.* But for the *creature* the threat of it is real. He is not its equal. His only salvation lies in God's preservation of the world over against the chaos for the sake and through the power of Jesus Christ. He "preserves" His creature by divine *mercy and compassion, not by a metaphysical sustentatio.*

\*　　\*　　\*

This exposition about the nature of the chaos casts light on the nature of *redemption.* God has in His mercy rejected and driven back the chaotic threat to His creature. He towers above this threat.[87] What we could not do, He has done in Jesus Christ. Through His triumphant grace the world is sustained. The works of God's right hand triumph over the works of His left hand.

The chaos exists only at God's *left hand.* It is not God's creature, but it is subject to His power. It has a being which finds its ground of existence in God's wrath and judgment[88] as the reverse side of His eternal Yes. The chaos exists precisely in the fact that it is *not* God's creature.[89] It is there from the beginning as certainly as from the beginning His Yes implies His No. "Along with God and His creature, the chaos is there from the beginning. Therefore it has always played a role in the history of God's relationship to His creature."[90] Again, this does not mean a creation of good *and* evil. The chaos is not a creature and still it has reality. Barth endeavors to clarify the complication involved in this conception by saying, "not created, but placed,"

85. *Ibid.,* p. 87.
86. *Ibid.*
87. *Ibid.,* p. 343.
88. *Ibid.,* p. 405.
89. *Ibid.,* p. 406.
90. *Ibid.*

and by referring to sin as the *work* of divine denial.[91]   The chaos
has not been created.  The *ground* of its existence is "only God's
not-willing it."[92]   The chaos is not God's *proper* work, it is not
His *real* work.  It is not His "opus proprium" as are His creation
and election, His grace and condescension.  These are His work,
His true work.  But over against them stands the negation, the
antithesis to His "opus proprium," namely, His "opus alienum,"
His alien, His strange work, i.e., the work of His judgment, of His
exclusion, of His rejection, the work of His not-willing.

Because the chaos is the "work" of God's rejection and exclusion the chaos has no cosmic reality.  It is an *impossible* and *intolerable*[93] reality which stands directly *opposed* to His *creation*.[94]
It is the abnormal and incalculable factor which, in the form of
sin, endeavors to bar man's way to grace.  It cannot be categorized
or subsumed under any norm or rational concept.  It is the "contradiction" which can exist only on basis of the "opus alienum,"
and on this basis does in fact exist.  Therefore the chaos cannot
be an object of analysis in and by itself.  We can know it "only in
terms of the mighty counterblow of the sovereign grace of God,"
as the reality which by this blow is shattered and rejected.

This is the triumph over chaos which God achieves in Jesus
Christ.  In Him God took the contradiction and the threat upon
His own shoulders and made its defeat His own concern.  This
is His faithfulness to the creature.  At the moment when God
spoke His Yes, His triumphant No also resounded and the elimination of the threatening evil became fully achieved *fact*.  That is the
meaning of: Let there be light!

Therefore the chaos has no *true* reality.  It is, but it is not *really*.
It "exists" as the object of rejection at God's left hand.

In God's true work the chaos is passed by, rejected.  It could
not stand in the face of the Yes of His self-abnegation.  "It could

---

91. *Ibid.,* p. 376.
92. *Ibid.,* p. 407.
93. *Ibid.,* p. 408.
94. On p. 417 of KD III/3, we read, "The chaos has no existence, as certainly
as it has indeed been created by God (wohl von Gott geschaffen), as certainly
as there is no covenant of God with the chaos." Many will have been surprised
to read this "indeed been created by God" because Barth *denied this* again and
again. The difficulty is resolved in the Foreword of IV/1 where Barth writes that
this contradiction was caused by a printer's error. The "wohl" (indeed) must be
a "nicht" (not) : "a 'not' became an every sense-destroying 'indeed.' "

not bear, it could not endure, the presence of God in the flesh."[95] The incarnation showed that the chaos in its confrontation with the Incarnate One could not maintain itself, and that therefore it would one day as a fleeing shadow and a receding boundary cease to be.[96] The purpose of God's *proper* work is to make an end to His *alien* work. God has shown His wrath and pronounced His No, and He will not have to do this again. In the completeness of this victory it is not even proper to speak of a "permission" of sin, for in the ascension of Christ to the right hand of God the victory has been fully realized. Barth is aware that this is speaking "very audaciously," but "with an eye to Jesus Christ it is not possible to say that the chaos still has objective reality in any sense, that it has any existence other than that which our as yet covered sight ascribes to it, that it is really to be feared, that it is still a danger or can still do damage."[97]

Jesus is the Conqueror! That is the gospel which Barth preaches when he speaks of the chaos. When we think in the obedience of faith we cannot do otherwise than regard the chaos as overcome and disposed of.[98] We have no reason to respect the chaos any longer or to call upon the world to have respect for it. "It is no longer permissible to regard release and redemption from chaos as a matter of the future, as an event that is still to take place."[99] Fear and melancholy may still lead us to think in this way, but this is thinking outside the Christian faith.[100] Therefore Barth sharply criticizes non-triumphant Christianity. Throughout the centuries Christianity has erred precisely in this, that it was not obedient to this vision and therefore its preaching to the world was not born from obedience. The Church has too little known the *joyful* apostolate.

Christianity has in many respects become a sad affair because it has not penetrated to the full seriousness of its confession, the

---

95. KD III/3, p. 419.
96. *Ibid.*
97. *Ibid.*
98. *Ibid.*, p. 421.
99. *Ibid.*, p. 420.
100. *Ibid.*, p. 421.

seriousness of joy, the serious realization that Jesus is Conqueror, He alone, but He fully and absolutely.[1]

*          *          *

The chaos has therefore been rejected in Jesus Christ and through this rejection it has been "emptied."[2]  One can now think of the chaos only in an a-posteriori fashion, one can think of it only by way of "glancing back" to it.  The only role which the chaos can still play is the role of a *defeated* enemy.

How is it possible that it is all past — in Christ — and that at the same time the chaos can still play a role in the affairs of men? This is possible only because we must assume that the power of the chaos of which we are still aware is not a true power.  We can ascribe to it "only the force of a dangerous appearance."[3]  In reality, i.e., in Jesus Christ, the power of the chaos has been broken, emptied, judged.  This holds true for the significance of the chaos for the entire cosmos, and even though we do not see this, it is nevertheless *true*, for the victory has taken place and is in need neither of improvement nor of repetition.  The kingdom of chaos is a shadow-kingdom[4] which has been "objectively put away."  That it still "does" anything in the world is only "because of the blindness of our eyes."  God permits that we can not yet see His kingdom[5] and that we "to that extent still find ourselves pressed by the chaos."  He permits the chaos to be an "apparently effective force."  But it is *not a dangerous* force.  "In this no longer dangerous form of a reminiscence and shadow of its former power it is an instrument of God's willing and doing."[6] God considers it good that we live "as though" the kingdom of chaos has not yet come to an end.  But, actually, through the triumph of grace the chaos is no more.

---

1. Cf. K. Barth, *Christliche Gemeinde im Wechsel der Staatsordungen*, 1948, p. 31: "That is the great exchange which gives life to the world. The old is gone. Satan has fallen from heaven like lightning. The kingdom of God has come near. 'It is finished': what had to happen for the reconciliation, salvation, and peace of men, has really, radically, and fully been fulfilled."
2. KD III/3, p. 423.
3. *Ibid., p.* 424.
4. *Ibid.*
5. *Ibid.*, p. 425.
6. *Ibid.*

In the merciful and gracious action of God in Jesus Christ the triumph of creation, as it is revealed in the separation of light from darkness, is *maintained* and *affirmed*. The *meaning* of creation permeated and filled the act of creation: the reconciliation in Christ. Creation is not a fore-portal of the holy place, it is a prefiguration, a sacrament of the real triumph and therefore the beginning of it. The work which God began at creation in the rejection of chaos and of darkness and in the choosing of the good world is in principle the manifestation of the "emptying" of the chaos. The Genesis account relates this triumph of the creation history. Creation means that "God does not permit the darkness finally to bewitch and demonize the cosmos. He does not consent to an actual realization of the sinister possibility of Genesis 1:2, He does not permit the disintegration of His creation."[7] He has demonstrated that "from the beginning He has once and for all passed by" this world of horror and malevolence.[8]

*       *       *

In direct connection with his treatment of the chaos Barth speaks of the demons, "God's adversaries." It is necessary "to cast at least a glance" at the demons.[9] We should not concern ourselves long with this "chaotic business" because an extensive treatment might be just the thing the demons would like. They enjoy being found interesting and are gladly considered as a subject of independent importance in theology. "A short, sharp look at them is not only enough, but it is the only proper way to treat them."[10] Barth emphasizes that angels and demons are not to be treated under one heading. They stand antithetically over against each other. The older theology spoke of the good and the bad angels as though they were both to be subsumed under the one genus "angel." As little, however, as *nonsense* is a kind of

---

7. KD III/1, p. 121.
8. KD III/1, p. 121. Concerning the relationship between or rather the *identity* of the triumph of creation and the triumph of reconciliation, note the remarkable words: "Genesis 1:2 speaks of the old which, according to II Cor. 5:7, has been radically eliminated by the death and resurrection of Jesus Christ. It tells us that the chaos did not first become the old, the past, the passed over, being of this world in the new creation but was that already as seen from the viewpoint of the first creation."
9. KD III/3, p. 609.
10. *Ibid.*

*sense,* so little is a demon a kind of angel. As nonsense is the negation of sense, so the demon is the negation of the angel in a radical antithesis. Angels and demons are related to each other as the good creation of God is related to the chaos.[11] Here again we stand before the peculiar "reality" of the chaos which one can only regard with horror and revulsion in radical unbelief. The true Christian faith is a demythologizing faith.[12] This does not mean that we must deny the existence of demons, but it does mean that we must engage in an act of unbelief which is founded in faith in Jesus Christ. The old demonology thought about the demons when it should have manifested only anger and disdain.[13] It did not appreciate as it should have that the Bible speaks of the demons only in the sense of struggle against them and rejection of them, and that it calls us — in our own interest — away from them and admonishes us to turn our backs to them. This, says Barth, is something other than placing a "demonology" next to an angelology. When this is done we make the demons a substantial part of the Christian message with the result that Christianity, even when it does not get so far as witch trials, comes to stand in a demoniacal shadow with all the accompanying phenomena of anxiety, fear, and melancholy. It was the fault of orthodoxy that later, in the time of the Enlightenment, the whole conception was thrown overboard and the existence of demons simply denied.

Instead of this we must see that the devil *is essentially the chaos.* He is that element of "contradiction," of opposition and darkness which continues to exist under God's *left hand.* He is "nothingness" but is not *nothing.* The demons are not a creation stemming from the hand of God and therefore they are not to be counted among the creatures of God. Barth repeats with respect to the demons what he has earlier said about the chaos: "They exist only in the fact that God, in saying Yes to Himself and to His creature necessarily says No to them." The demons exist by virtue of the fact that God's election includes rejection, that His grace involves judgment.[14] The identification of the demons with

11. *Ibid.,* p. 610.
12. *Ibid.,* p. 611.
13. *Ibid.,* p. 612.
14. *Ibid.,* p. 613.

the chaos Barth makes plain when he writes, "They are not something other than the chaos, they are not something in addition to it, but they are of it. They are chaos itself."[15] They are the chaos in its dynamic manifestation, in its tendency to power and activity. The chaos is therefore a kingdom of unreality,[16] a kingdom with which God has concerned Himself but which from the beginning He has branded as "nothing and not-dangerous."

The demons do not have a reality which can be placed on the same level with the being, the reality, of the angels. This has been done again and again, but such confusion is impossible for him who believes. Men have believed too much in an independent kingdom of evil with actual power and it was not realized that this power was only a shadow-power. The chaos *presents* itself as a factor that must be taken seriously. Precisely therein it manifests itself as the kingdom of the lie! "It lies in that, in its chaos-character, it represents itself to God and to the creature as a relevant factor worthy to be taken seriously. It lies in that it pretends it can interpose itself between God's grace and the salvation of the creature, that it can weaken and make God's grace of none effect, that it can arrest or hinder the salvation of the creature."[17] The demons lie when with their "kingdom" and their "hierarchy" they create the impression that they have come from heaven to earth and have some business here. In this way — in this lie — the chaos seeks to secure a triumph for itself on earth. The *reality* of the chaos lies in its being respected and in being regarded for what it is *not*. According to Barth, therefore, it is not correct to say that the chaos is only *appearance,* for in the attempt to establish a power of its own the kingdom of chaos *is a reality* among the nations and in the physical and psychical life of man. But even though the chaos is in this sense a reality, it is this only in its quality as lie.[18] It is no more than an imitation of the kingdom of heaven with its angels.[19]

The New Testament shows us this even more plainly than the Old Testament because in the New Testament the Light has dawned, the Light of creation, election and grace, through which

15. *Ibid.*, p. 614.
16. *Ibid.*
17. *Ibid.*, p. 616.
18. *Ibid.*, p. 617.
19. *Ibid.*, p. 618.

the chaos and the darkness have been excluded. Here the kingdom of the chaos is radically unmasked as impotent and revealed
as a defeated army in flight.[20] The New Testament gives us to
rest in a world which no longer lies under the spell of demonic
power and compels us to *disbelieve* in the demons and their
danger. And in this disbelief we are brought to belief in the
victory of truth over the lie.

At the end of his brief discussion of the demons Barth asks
whether it is possible to regard the demons as fallen angels.[21] He
takes account of the fact that this impression seems, at least at
first glance, to be created by the New Testament. In Jude we
read of angels who did not keep their own position but left their
proper dwelling, and II Peter 2:4 speaks of angels who sinned.
Barth does not give an exegesis of these verses because he feels
that they are too vague and obscure to conclude from them to the
conception of demons as fallen angels. He considers it an "intolerable artificiality" to explain the existence of demons in terms of
a fall of angels on basis of these verses. Somewhat plaintively he
observes that such a supposition would make all the results
to which he had come in his angelology and demonology incorrect. He views the doctrine concerning the fall of the angels as
a bad dogmatic dream. This "teaching" arose out of a need that
was felt to give a metaphysical foundation for the fall of man
into sin, a kind of pre-temporal prelude to the sin of man on
earth. In this way the attempt was made to explain chaos, after
all. It was made rational and was systematized or, at all events,
the "possibility" of it was suggested. In all this he sees a terrible
misunderstanding of the kingdom of heaven, namely that also the
angels, in order to be free, had to possess a "liberum arbitrium."
What is untrue of man — the possession of freedom in the sense
of a liberum arbitrium — is even less true of the angels. Their
freedom is a freedom *for God,* and angels with such a freedom
have never stood at the crossroads of right and wrong. This fatal
conception of freedom is the background against which the doctrine of a fall of the angels was constructed. The angels cannot
sin. "A proper angel doesn't do such a thing," and the demons
have never been in heaven even though they like to create the

20. *Ibid.,* p. 620.
21. *Ibid.,* p. 622.

impression that they have been. "The devil was never an angel." He was a murderer from the beginning and he speaks according to his own nature as one who does the lie and is the father of lies: John 8.

The conclusion of Barth's doctrine of providence confronts us in a most remarkable manner with his conception of the chaos when he loads with meaning the words: *according to his own nature* (John 8:44). There is no room for a conception of chaos as creatureliness here. The expression "according to his own nature" may not be stretched to imply a dualism as though the chaos were a "counter-pole" to the good creation, for it owes its existence solely to God's election which involves rejection. Therefore, although John 8:44 stops short of teaching an independent existence of the chaos it is *the text* about the demons, and Barth points to it with emphasis. It is not made clear why the texts in Jude and Peter about the fall of the angels are vague and obscure, but John 8:44 *is* plain to Barth as an illustration of the *non-deducible,* the absurd, character of the chaos which can never be systematized as a component element of creation. It has a "place" only *in* the rejection as an object of God's wrath and because of the triumph of grace. This triumph discloses that the chaos is only impotent, only lie.

Barth concludes his discussion of the demons by pointing to what comes *from God:* solely *good* gifts. After the fashion of James, Barth would not have us be deceived that every good and perfect gift comes to us other than from above. We must not be deceived either with respect to the nature of the chaos, lest we believe that it has "power" and forget that it is a conquered power, a power which through the mighty Yes of God's grace in Christ has *radically* and *forever* been "emptied."

\*     \*     \*

We must conclude this part of the discussion of the nature of the chaos by speaking a further word about the divine triumph over it which is prefigured in creation. We can speak of a real triumph only when there is a reality, a power, an enemy to be overcome. If sin has no created being it must have some kind of reality which is distinct from the cosmos and the mankind which creation brought into being.

According to Barth, it is unwarranted to weaken this "reality" in any way. To minimize the reality of the chaos means only to hurt oneself and to obscure the actuality of the triumph of God over it. Sin is so terrible that sinful man does not of himself have the ability even to understand its awfulness. Sin can only be known *in terms of the triumph of God over it,* that is, it can be known only in terms of the cross of Christ. Outside of the cross it is not possible to learn what the true nature of the rebelliousness of sin is.[22] "The utter seriousness of sin, the enormity of human perversity, the depth of the abyss into which man plunged himself, can be measured by the fact that God's love could respond to this happening and was willing to respond to it only by giving Himself in Christ Jesus for its defeat and thereby for the salvation of men. Even this is not all. He gave Himself in Christ in such a manner that in the judgment over sin the Judge permitted Himself to be judged and allowed the old man of sin to be put to death in His own Person."[23] Only when we see what sin cost God, can we see the dreadful seriousness of sin. If we would know the "reality" of sin we must look at *this* triumph which "emptied" sin of its being, we must contemplate God's eternal decree in Jesus Christ, we must see the creation of the light, the rejection of the darkness, and the reality of *reconciliation.*

These great acts of God reveal the terribleness of the chaos-threat, but also the conquest of this threat and its consignment to utter shame. Therefore an undersanding of the seriousness of sin is not a surrender to pessimism but is involved in and arises from the confession of the love of God and the power of the divine self-abnegation. *The chaos is not the eternal antagonist of the divine power.* Such a dualism is excluded by God's Yes and we must therefore hold to the belief that "the door to a dualistic representation in connection with evil has clearly been closed by God's eternal counsel which on Golgotha became historical reality and we may not reopen it."[24] The cross leaves not a single reason for continuing doubt or despair. It may therefore not be supposed that man

---

22. KD IV/1. p. 456.
23. *Ibid.*
24. Ibid., p. 453.

by his sin falls out of the hand of God. He can undo the work of God no more than Israel, with its desire for a king, could cast itself into a God-forsaken existence. On the contrary: precisely in the way of man's rebellion God reveals sin to be so completely His instrument that no one can resist His will. Because of this man does not by his fall into sin cease to be God's partner.[25] Right through man's No God's Yes continues to resound as the eternal grace-given a priori which preceded it.

The seed of evil *has been sown* and the chaos *did penetrate* into the good creation of God. It did so as the impossible possibility of the absurd rebellion against God's grace. No one can free himself from it and achieve victory over it other than through the light which the decisive divine act of creation has shed over the threatening chaos. In creation this is all a *prefiguration*. The *act of reconciliation* had still to follow. But in the prefiguration of the triumph (the separation of light from darkness), the triumph lies apriorily enclosed. The "impossibility" of the presence of sin in the good creation does not destroy the *inner side* of creation: *the covenant of God*. There is no answer to the problem of the origin of evil; there *is* an answer to the problem of the conquest of evil. This answer — the content of the triumph of election and creation — has a *name*: the Name of Jesus Christ.

*        *        *

In all this it becomes plain that sin can be known only in the light of reconciliation and of the covenant of grace which is the inner ground of creation. Barth's doctrine of sin is treated within the framework of reconciliation.[26] It is impossible to understand the predicament of man apart from the saving work of God. Without the Word of God man is hopelessly surrendered to the tragedy of human existence.[27] Even the strongest emphasis on the majesty and holiness of God cannot lead to a confession of guilt and to the knowledge of sin.[28] The doctrine of sin can never precede the doctrine of Christ.[29]

---

25. *Ibid.*, p. 534.
26. *Ibid.*, p. 395ff.
27. *Ibid.*, p. 399.
28. *Ibid.*, p. 401.
29. *Ibid.*, pp. 403, 433.

Progress in grace does not consist in a "step-wise" advance from a conception of creation as such (the good world), via knowledge of sin to the knowledge of the forgiveness of sin. In this way creation and reconciliation would become disjoined and the prefiguration of the triumph of grace would be lost.

As the prodigal son comes to his confession of sin through the welcome which his father extends to him, and Peter, standing in the presence of Christ, cries out "Depart from me for I am a sinful man,"[30] so there can be knowledge of sin only in the light of the cross. Jesus Christ is the mirror of sin.[31]

In order to expose the nature of the knowledge of sin Barth speaks in this connection about the fall of man. Man falls and dies precisely at the point where his pride induces him to stand.[32]

What is then the relationship between *creation* and *fall*? Does Genesis 3 describe man's "entrance upon the state of corruption"?[33] Can we, *in terms of creation and fall alone,* know anything at all about sin, and does the triumph of grace take place *after* the fall into sin? This is for Barth an unacceptable interpretation because "in the matter of human disobedience and depravity there is no 'earlier' in which man was not yet a transgressor and as such innocent."[34] Sin is *radical* and *total.* At this point Barth begins to treat of original sin.[35] It is not the perpetuation of sin. Barth does speak of a "peccatum originale," but as "the original and therefore comprehensively radical and total deed of man."[36] It is the "Ursünde,"[37] the primordial sin, and it stands "in a certain relationship to Adam."[38] In the Scriptures all men stand under the shadow of this one superscription: Adam.[39] The biblical saga says that "the history of the world began with the pride and fall of man."[40] "There was never a golden age. It makes no sense to look back

---

30. *Ibid.,* p. 433.
31. Cf. IV/1, p. 404, about "this neglect" of the theology of the Reformation as a result of not doing justice to Christology. In the mirror of the cross the reality of God's wrathful judgment against sin becomes visible, p. 455. Cf. pp. 459 and 460.
32. *Ibid.,* p. 532.
33. *Ibid.*
34. *Ibid.,* p. 551.
35. *Ibid.,* p. 556ff.
36. *Ibid.,* p. 558.
37. *Ibid.*
38. *Ibid.*
39. *Ibid.,* p. 566.
40. *Ibid.*

longingly to one. Primordial man was a sinner 'from the beginning.' "[41] Adam means: the truth about us. In Adam we are concerned with a relationship which *God* has determined.[42] This relationship enables us to see the meaning of the triumph of creation and comes to its sharpest expression in the parallel between *Adam* and *Christ*.[43]

It was to be expected that Barth's attention would in this connection be particularly drawn to Romans 5. He has treated this chapter not only in his discussion of reconciliation but also in a separate publication.[44] This is the *locus classicus* of Paul's treatment of sin as brought into the world by one man, and through it death to which all men have become subject.

Since Paul contrasts sharply the deed of the one man, Adam, with the gift of God in Jesus Christ, and the disobedience of Adam with the obedience of Christ, the question of the nature of God's triumph comes very prominently to the fore here. According to Barth the fall has nothing to do with a transition from a "status integritatis" to a "status corruptionis." He also rejects the idea of an "inherited sin which, deriving from Adam, has been transmitted to men."[45] Original sin does not involve a transfer (in time) from integrity to corruption, but Adam is *exemplarily* the representative of all who followed him.[46] In Adam we must learn to recognize ourselves and to hear the truth which through him is addressed to us.[47]

Wherein, then, lies the relationship between Adam and us? Wherein does the imputation of sin lie? To say that it is due to a sovereign dispensation of God does not, in Barth's opinion, penetrate to the heart of the matter. This we find in Romans 5 and

41. *Ibid.*, p. 567.
42. *Ibid.*, p. 569.
43. *Ibid.*, p. 571.
44. K. Barth, *Christus und Adam nach Römer 5, Theologische Studien,* Heft 35, 1952.
45. KD IV/1, p. 557.
46. What Genesis tells us is "biblical saga." "Precisely in this area of the biblical saga Adam also became and existed. And precisely in this area also the fall into sin took place, the fall into sin of the first man. The biblical saga tells us that world history began with the pride and fall of man," KD IV/1, p. 566.
47. For the relationship between Adam and us Barth points to Calvin's ordinatio concept, IV/1, p. 570. Later the idea of "imputatio" was mentioned. Theologians did not, however, dare to draw the consequences. "Was it really only a question of mera imputatio and not at all one of an infection of some sort? Here certain concessions were made to the traditional conception," p. 570.

consists in this: "Also in this respect the word of divine judgment finds its origin in the word of God's grace."[48] For Paul, Adam is the superscription written above all human existence, the name Adam sets forth the condition under which all human beings live, but *in* this typical sinner who stands representatively at the head of the entire human race Paul recognized another who is also a "representative," namely, Jesus Christ who effected the justification. For Paul the deepest message of Romans 5 is Jesus Christ in whom he sees a "primordial Image" and, in connection with Him, Adam is introduced as the type of the Coming One.[49] It is more proper, in Barth's view, to speak of the *Christ*-Adam parallel than of the *Adam*-Christ parallel. There *is* a parallel between the two but the line of Adam and his descendants is not an independent line. It is "really only the reflex of the other," the reflex, namely, of the obedience of Christ rendered for many. All that is said of the typical Adam stands in *this* light. "Is it not clear who and what is here the Prius and who and what is here the Posterius?"

Adam was the *posterius,* Christ the *prius*.

It is true that in I Corinthians 15:45 Paul designates Christ the *last* Adam but this means "that He Himself is the *real,* the *first* Adam whom the other Adam only exemplarily pointed to." The "anonymous one" of the Genesis saga has existence for Paul only in terms of *Christ*. And *in* Christ he hears what is said about Adam and is true of all.[50] In Christ, Paul hears the judgment over the man of sin "which is what every man *was* and which *no one* any longer is since God has had mercy in the universality of His compassion, as before He had included them all in the universality of disobedience."[51]

Scripture may not be so construed that we first see a historical "Adam-reality" which can then be historically compared with the Christ-reality. On the contrary, the human Adam-reality "is superseded, illuminated by and included in the Christ-reality"[52] The history of Adam and his descendants is not the historical point of departure for a comparison. Mankind has no independent signifi-

---

48. *Ibid.,* p. 571.
50. *Ibid.*
50. *Ibid.*
51. *Ibid.,* p. 573.
52. *Christus und Adam nach Römer* 5, p. 52.

cance. It derives its significance from Christ.[53] It is only the type of, the shadow which falls before, the true history of Christ and those who are His.[54] The order of the one history (Adam and his descendants) is the reflection of the other order and *witnesses* to it. Our participation in the history of Adam has no independent meaning but is indirectly a witness to the reality of Christ.[55]

The relationship which obtains between Adam and us does not reveal the primary anthropological reality, for *that* lies in the relationship between *Christ* and us.[56] Already in our fatal past we stood *in the order of grace*.[57] The relationship between Adam and us does not indicate an *originally existing* reality[58] to which then later our relationship to Christ was added. What our *real* and *original* condition was "we must not derive from the figure of Adam, but from the figure of Christ."[59] Our being in Adam stands "from the beginning" in the light of the fact that we are in Christ.[60] There are not two realms having equal standing but there is priority, preponderance, of the one over the other.[61] Adam's sin and Christ's work do not balance each other. Adam is only the type of Him who is to come. He himself is not primary but secondary, dependent.[62] Adam is our Head only in *appearance*. In the provisionality of "Adam and we" human wrong stands over against divine right.[63] In this powerlessness and in this wrong man "can only be an image of the sovereignty of grace and of life."[64] Grace is more than sin! It stands revealed as *triumphant!* It is no longer possible to see the reality of Adam as an independent self-enclosed complex,[65] for grace has penetrated into this "Adam-realm." In the light of the truth that is in Christ we can no longer see the reality of Adam as "purely light-less."[66] For *it stands in the light which triumphs* over this darkness. This triumphant grace comes particularly to the fore in what Paul writes in Romans 5:13: "Sin indeed was in the world before the law was given, but sin is not counted where there is no law." Between Adam and Christ stands Moses the revelation of God's will to Israel. Here it is revealed who Is

53. *Ibid.*, p. 11.
54. *Ibid.*, p. 12.
55. *Ibid.*
56. *Ibid.*, p. 11.
57. *Ibid.*, p. 10.
58. *Ibid.*, p. 11.
59. *Ibid.*

60. *Ibid.*
61. *Ibid.*, p. 14.
62. *Ibid.*, p. 15.
63. *Ibid.*, p. 16.
64. *Ibid.*
65. *Ibid.*, p. 23.
66. *Ibid.*, p. 24.

rael's Lord is.[67] Here also sin is revealed, sin in the likeness of Adam's transgression (Rom. 5:14). Precisely where God is close to man sin is reckoned, i.e. "established as such, registered and put on the account."[68]  In the time before Israel mankind also sinned: sin was in the world and therefore death reigned from Adam to Moses. But in Israel the antithesis becomes manifest, namely, that *God* is gracious and that *man* is sinful.[69] That theme is now played in Israel's history. For in Israel transgressions increase (Rom. 5:20). In Israel we see the resistance of man[70] against grace in all its nakedness. Therefore the law had to come in! The wound had to remain open in order that healing might take place.

Adam had to remain Adam in order to be reconciled.[71]

The miracle which now amazes us is that the increased transgression does not annul the gracious relationship between God and man. On the contrary: where sin increased grace did much more increase (Rom. 5:20). From *this* nation Christ is born.[72] History continues. When grace became more abundant Israel resisted the more in the rejection of the Messiah.[73] But exactly *then* and *in that way* it was — in its most ultimate character — made plain that man was radically unworthy of grace and that God took *everything* upon Himself. "Although they acted the way they did, they were absolved of the guilt and punishment of this action in that God became guilty and was punished for them."[74]  In this act of self-surrender and self-glorification [75] His salvation is extended not only to Israel but to the whole of mankind. In God's covenant — the outpouring of the Holy Spirit upon all flesh — all men are involved.[76] "God's grace was and is valid for all men." Not only Israel's sin but the sin of all men became manifest in the rejection of Christ.[77] Also the gentiles entered upon the "greater abundance" of grace. They — the gentiles — crucified Christ and so participated in the superabundance of Israel's sin for they were Christ's "immediate murderers."[78] But precisely in this way there is also

---

67. *Ibid.*, p. 32.  
68. *Ibid.*, p. 33.  
69. *Ibid.*, p. 34.  
70. *Ibid.*, p. 38.  
71. *Ibid.*  
72. *Ibid.*, p. 40.  

73. *Ibid.*, p. 42.  
74. *Ibid.*, p. 44.  
75. *Ibid.*, p. 45.  
76. *Ibid.*  
77. *Ibid.*, p. 46.  
78. *Ibid.*, p. 47.  The creed mentions Pilate!

now no longer for them either accusation or condemnation."[79] God crossed the boundary to man when man could not cross the boundary to God.

Adam excludes Christ, but Christ does not exclude Adam. The prefiguration of the triumph in creation is fulfilled and confirmed in the history of Christ as the triumph of reconciliation. This triumph is an a priori triumph. Because it is the a priori triumph of grace it reveals that man cannot wholly and really fall from grace. The triumph of grace is correlative to the ontological impossibility of sin! This impossibility is placed beyond any question of doubt by the prefiguration of the triumph of grace in creation. Sin is a horrible reality, but it *cannot* break through the limits set by the boundary of grace. It is exactly in the manifestation of the reality of sin that the irresistibility of grace is revealed, as in Israel's rebellion, in Judas' betrayal, in Pilate's sentence. Not Adam but Christ is primary. Sin is not an abstraction. At the moment of its "impossible" origin it was overtaken and outstripped as a concrete reality. This message is the message of the triumph of grace.

In the creation light and darkness are *separated*. This prefiguration is not a powerless symbol, but an *act* of God which in the abundance of the grace of Christ is revealed as *historical reality*. Sin is *ontologically impossible*. This is not a weakening of its seriousness and horribleness, nor is it a denial of its "reality." It is rather the miracle of the "God-for-us," the abiding miracle of the whole of history. Precisely where sin culminates and seems to celebrate its highest "triumph" the triumph of grace is unmistakably revealed. There is an absolute unity and harmony between the triumph of creation and the triumph of reconciliation. Therefore Barth constantly refers back to the triumph of creation in his treatment of the triumph of reconciliation. "God has placed Himself in the right over against man, just as already in creation He placed Himself in the right over against the chaos."[80] Through the great redemptive event in Jesus Christ — the "God-with-us" — we can see as through a transparency the *ground* and the *beginning* of all things, as also the *original destiny* of man for salvation as the meaning and ground of the will of the Creator.

---

79. *Ibid.*
80. KD IV/1, p. 100.

# IV

## THE TRIUMPH OF ELECTION

THE CENTRAL theme of Barth's theology comes to expression in his triumphant and joyful doctrine of election no less than in the doctrine of creation. Already in 1936[1] this was evident in his lectures on predestination in Hungary, but it has come to particularly clear and extensive expression in II/2 of the *Kirchliche Dogmatik*, published in 1942. Since then Barth's conception of election has been the subject of much discussion.[2]

The importance which Barth attaches to the doctrine of election is apparent from the fact that he places it "at the beginning, indeed, before the beginning of everything that is to be said about God's dealings with His creatures."[3] It becomes clear, too, that the triumph of election is not an isolated given for the theologian to reflect on, but that there is a very close connection between it and the triumph of grace as it finds expression in creation and reconciliation. Dogmatic theology cannot concern itself with any subject more ineffable than the reconciliation that has been effected through Christ.[4] This act of God stands at the center of all theological interest. It is *in* this act that it becomes clear *who* God is in His relationship to the creature. The doctrine of reconciliation in Christ can be treated only in terms of the *mystery* of this doctrine, in terms of God's *decisive* word, namely, the divine *election*. From eternity God has decided upon "this form of His existence in

---

1. K. Barth, *Gottes Gnadenwahl*, 1936.

2. From the extensive literature in which Barth's doctrine of election is discussed we mention the following: G. C. van Niftrik, *Een Beroerder Israels*, 1949, 2nd ed., chapter V; M. P. van Dijk, *Existentie en Genade*, 1952 chapter V; various articles in the *Scottish Journal of Theology*: J. K. S. Reid, "The Office of Christ in Predestination," Vol. I, numbers 1 and 2; J. G. Riddell, "God's eternal decrees," Vol. II, number 4.

3. KD II/2, p. 96.

4. *Ibid.*, p. 95.

Christ."[5] The triumph of election must be seen in the light of this decisive divine action. It must be preached and witnessed to as "the good, the best, the exclusively redemptive message, namely that God has from eternity decided to be God in the form of this, and no other, condescension to men."[6]

By virtue of God's "primal decision"[7] and the "divine self-determination,"[8] therefore, grace is the beginning of all of the works of God, and Jesus Christ is — from the very beginning[9] — the reality and the revelation of this *first* act of God.[10] The doctrine of election tells us about this *gracious* God and that there is no creature which does not have its origin and existence in this grace.[11] In the beginning, in the "primal decision," God is "merciful and not unmerciful."[12] Therefore all the "victories"[13] of His work as Creator, Reconciler and Redeemer find their concentration point in election. "The doctrine of election is, therefore, the fundamental witness to God as a gracious God and the point of departure for all the divine ways and works."[14] This constitutes the *function* of the doctrine of election.

\*      \*      \*

It becomes clear from the relationship obtaining between election and reconciliation why Barth sharply opposes every theological construction which makes election the *obscure* and *hidden* background of the dispensation of grace revealed in history. In Barth's opinion, theology has often fallen into this error, with the result that the doctrine of election came to constitute a serious threat to the certainty of salvation and became the occasion for

---

5. *Ibid.*, p. 98. Cf. p. 96: the doctrine of election is "the decisive word, the mystery of the doctrine of reconciliation." It is not possible to speak about creation and sin *apart from* and *prior to* the treatment of this mystery. When this is done creation as a "realm of nature" receives a relatively independent character with respect to reconciliation, p. 97, and sin becomes "an unforeseen episode," p. 97. Over against this conception Barth posits that God's work in its entirety constitutes "one unique act of divine government. This act is indeed a very differentiated and animated one, but it is not an interrupted, a piecemeal or a broken act. From step to step it realizes itself in each successive stage," p. 97.

6. KD II/2, p. 98.  
7. *Ibid.*  
8. *Ibid.*, p. 96.  
9. *Ibid.*, p. 98.  
10. *Ibid.* p. 99.  
11. *Ibid.*  
12. *Ibid.*  
13. *Ibid.*, p. 100.  
14. *Ibid.*

anxiety, doubt, and fearful self-analysis. In diametrical opposition to this, he posits that election is *in no wise* concerned with the fearful depths of a *hidden* God but with the *revealed gospel*, the *joyful* message. It is not true that there is some mysterious background of election which creates a message of bad news next to the message of good news. On the contrary, election is the *content* of the gospel,[15] it is "a good report, a happy, useful, comforting, helpful message."[16] It is in every respect improper and unwarranted to think that this doctrine announces "in the same breath, good and evil, help and destruction, life and death. It does indeed cast a shadow. We shall not want to disregard this aspect of it. But the doctrine itself is light and not darkness."[17]

The doctrine of election is in essence the announcement of a Yes and not of a No. Never, nowhere, is election threatened or made relative by some deep and final mystery of God. It is precisely the *revelation* of God's true and deep mystery, the mystery of His love and grace for sinners. The traditional doctrine of election has forgotten this altogether too much and in so doing has come to place election in a "twilight." It is therefore necessary, according to Barth, to exercise the greatest critical reserve here;[18] in fact it is necessary energetically to contradict the traditional conception. The fact that election is *gospel* belongs to the deepest things that must be confessed. It is the "sum and substance of good tidings." In Jesus Christ God has from eternity turned His face *graciously* to men in the act of election. There is a book of life, and we stray from the truth when we assume "that it also has room for death, that there is a divine election and a divine rejection in the sense of two equally ultimate divine acts, or that they are to be regarded as two species of the same genus."[19] Election is light and comfort, not

15. *Ibid.*, pp. 13, 98.
16. *Ibid.*, p. 11.
17. *Ibid.*, p. 12.
18. *Ibid.*, p. 13. Manfred Metzger calls the traditional doctrine of election "somewhat unfruitful. It cannot be proclaimed as gospel. So, at least, it would seem. Paul clearly thought differently about the matter. How else could he make the doctrine of election the heart of his message? And he does not conclude the discussion of it with a sigh about its heaviness; he calls it the depths of the riches. With this conception Barth begins." *Gottes Gnadenwahl. Verkündigung und Forschung*, 1949/50, p. 89.
19. KD II/2, p. 15. Cr. his *Gottes Gnadenwahl*, p. 19, where he criticizes the "equal weight" of election and reprobation. Barth does speak, as we shall see later, about election and reprobation, but not in terms of a "too architectonic symmetry."

darkness and horror. In Jesus Christ, God is not against, but *for* us, and *for* the world. We need not and we may not fear that the good news of the gospel has any dark backgrounds that come to us from God's unapproachable light in which the *deepest* decision of God's *real* and *hidden* election has supposedly fallen.

Election does *not* consist of a fear-inspiring and uncertainty-creating decree. On the contrary, it is the absolute counter-pole of the "decretum horribile," and comes to us in the streaming light of Christ's substitutionary work which is to be preached as the gospel of comfort. The electing God is not a God in general, a "summus imperator," but the *true* God, the Father of Jesus Christ. When He is replaced by a "summus imperator,"[20] and His election is understood as "an act of ostensibly naked sovereignty of a divine being,"[21] one must inevitably end in a labyrinth full of uncertainty. When we understand election as God's *gracious* election, we shall not dare to be silent about it. Particularly shall we not be silent about it out of *pastoral considerations,* for election is precisely the shining center of the whole message of salvation. It does not point to an unapproachable *deus absconditus* but to the fulness of grace in the *deus revelatus.*[22]

*         *         *

Election in Christ: that is the joyful message, the miracle which God has worked among men, among all men. This message does

---

20. *Ibid.,* 51.
21. *Ibid.*
22. In this connection it is important to note what Barth writes about the "Deus absconditus." He points out that Luther "occasionally" spoke of the "Deus absconditus" in a manner which leaves the impression of a "potestas inordinata," an arbitrary power, which stands *apart from* and *behind* the act of his revelation on earth, II/1, p. 608. "Understood in this sense, the whole distinction (between ordinary and extraordinary divine power) becomes utterly unbearable," p. 609, for this means that besides the divine willing, ability, and doing that have been revealed, there stands also "another ability, and therefore, another possibility of God to reveal Himself and to act in a wholly different work as a 'wholly Other,'" p. 608. This idea of the "wholly Other" constitutes, according to Barth, a radical violation of the *reliability* of the revelation. God is indeed *free* in His power, His absolute power, *only in terms of His revelation* and we must therefore distance ourselves from a wholly different conception of His "ability" (können). Luther correctly saw that the nominalistically understood "potestas absoluta" destroyed the certainty of salvation by means of its understanding of God's actual "ability" which, "somewhere in the heights or in the depths, can be wholly other than, and can contradict, the ability which we have learned to know on the basis of his works," p. 609. The error of Luther was that he nevertheless held to the idea of a Deus absconditus — as another existence of God — although he summoned men to hold to the Deus revelatus, p. 60.

not take its rise from an optimistic view of man, nor from a weakening of the seriousness and the reality of God's wrath. Barth sharply criticizes Ritschl's conception of the wrath of God as being a human misunderstanding from which Christ, as the revelation of God's love, came to free us.

Over against this view, Barth wishes to testify to the reality of the wrath of God. His wrath is the wrath of the majesty and holiness of God which was provoked by the no less real guilt of man. Continually Barth reminds his readers of the word of Anselm about the seriousness of sin.[23] The doctrine of the electing grace of God does not obviate the confession of our guilt and the recognition of the wrath of God. Barth makes this very plain when he places God's election over against all autonomous humanism and every form of Pelagianism or semi-Pelagianism in which, in an optimistic or semi-optimistic fashion, a favorable judgment of man's capabilities becomes determinative in molding our conception of election. The optimism and joy of salvation find their source exclusively in electing grace itself, in the unwearied sovereign act of compassion and mercy which no ear has heard, no eye has seen, and which entered not into the heart of man. "Quintessence of the gospel," and that without arbitrariness: *that* is the election of God in Jesus Christ. God is no longer against us, but for us: *Deus revelatus.*[24]

\* \* \*

This can be understood only when it is considered that election is the election of God *in Christ*. The doctrine of election is not simply an aspect of theology. It points, rather, to the most concrete reality that can be preached and apprehended: election in the man Jesus Christ. For this reason it truly is the gospel of God and makes possible our speaking of the *comfort* of election.

23. "nondum considerasti, quanti ponderis sit peccatum."
24. KD II/2, p. 11. Cf. Barth on "Immanuel," KD IV/1, p. 3ff. What is at issue here is the "execution of God's saving will," which is something entirely different than "the blind paradox of an arbitrary act of divine grace-power, KD IV/1, p. 11. The "factum purum" of God's salvation stands over against the "factum brutum" of man's sin, p. 10. On the subject of arbitrariness cf. KD II/2, p. 25, and on "the influence of a non-Christian God-concept in the history of the doctrine of predestination," p. 25. God's free election in Christ stands over against "abstract freedom as such," p. 26. Cf. also KD II/2, pp. 120 and 212, and Barth's *Gotteserkenntnis und Gottesdienst nach reform. Lehre*, 1938, p. 97: "Grace is not arbitrariness. The depth of God's goodness is not the strange abyss of a so-called paradox. The divine freedom is not a tyranny which can arbitrarily move also in another direction."

Barth observes that also Reformed theology has appreciated the deep connection between election and Christ, and particularly has it done this in connection with Ephesians 1:4 which speaks about our election *in Christ*. John Calvin spoke of Christ as the "mirror of election." It is this that had led pastoral practice again and again to urge believers to seek refuge in Jesus Christ in order to come to the certainty of salvation and of election. This is a marked emphasis especially in Calvin.

While fully appreciating this emphasis, Barth nevertheless has a serious question to ask in this connection. He asks whether this urgent pastoral reference to Christ as the mirror of election has really been made with full seriousness. As early as 1938 he had observed in his Hungarian lectures that in this conception it was not made plain "what was meant when one regarded the New Testament as saying that we are elect 'in Him' and that we are therefore to know our election only 'in Him.' "[25] What is the *ground* of the fact that *noetically* (i.e. for the knowledge and certainty of salvation) we must look to Jesus Christ alone?[26] Is the pointing to Christ as the mirror of salvation merely a pastoral method in dealing with doubt and temptation, or does this mirror legitimately reflect the *whole* of the reality of election? On *this* point Barth is not satisfied with the deepest tendencies of the Reformation doctrine of election. Does this care of souls, does this pastoral exhortation and comfort, have ground *in the doctrine of election* itself? Or does it perhaps function as a *protection* against the "truth in the background" which stands and remains standing *behind* the revelation in Christ?

Must we look to Jesus Christ because this "truth in the background,"[27] i.e., the fact of the "deus absconditus," is hidden to us? Is there a decision of God which *precedes* the election in Christ in the sense that it is to be distinguished from election as the real, the deepest, and the hidden decision of God?[28]

---

25. K. Barth, *Gottes Gnadenwahl*, p. 3.
26. KD II/2, p. 68.          27. *Ibid.*
28. In discussing the Confessio Scoticana Barth writes that the relationship between the doctrine of predestination and the deity and humanity of Christ must be seen more closely than occurs here, *Gotteserkenntnis und Gottesdienst*, p. 102. The mystery of predestination does not lie in a divine determination "which was actualized in some empty eternity before and without Christ." According to the New Testament it is undoubtedly rather so that "before the foundation of the world," Eph. 1:4, "is identical with that which happened in the stable at Bethlehem and on the cross of Golgotha."

Is there a *prior* decree of election which is afterward brought to realization in the work of Christ in the sense that Christ becomes the *means* for its effectuation? Is there a decree of election and reprobation which, in the final analysis, precedes the revelation in Christ and is *independent* from it? When Calvin says that we must *not* seek the certainty of our salvation in God the Father "if in so doing we have regard for Him alone and apart from the Son," is he speaking *only* pastorally, and is there then, after all — in a preceding decree — a decision of God the Father alone and quite apart from the Son? Is the decision respecting the saving work of Christ subordinate to a pre-temporal decision of God's sovereignty which is meaningful as such? If *this* is the case, says Barth, we can, out of practical and pastoral considerations, continue to comfort believers by pointing them to Christ as the "mirror" of election. But then we must realize that the "background" of the *real* decision of the sovereign God Himself will remain an imponderable on our spiritual horizon, and it will not be possible to prevent doubt and uncertainty from again entering the souls of men. The tension between the mirror of election and the electing God Himself will remain. God Himself then becomes — as the *deus absconditus* — the sovereignly electing and determining God and in this way the idea of Christ as mirror of election is "threatened in the most serious manner."[29] If this be true, there comes to stand behind the *revealed* will of God in Jesus Christ the *final,* deepest, and hidden will which constitutes the real decision. It is then also no longer possible to escape Calvin's "decretum horribile." Is it really possible to comfort pastorally when "in that hidden place the really decisive word with respect to our salvation has been spoken?"[30]

For Barth the real problem of the Reformation doctrine of predestination culminates in *this* question. In the view of the Re-

---

29. KD II/2, p. 68, in connection with the mirror of election in the theology of the reformers. The motif underlying their conception of the pastoral office was not founded in Jesus Christ as the electing God and . . . "what does this information help us in the face of the doubts that assail us in the question which is not born from mere scrupulosity but which is for us the decisive question: whether we ourselves belong to those who will be benefited by that which God has decided to give to His elect through this elect Means which He first chose, whether we ourselves belong to these elect?" p. 118.

30. *Ibid.,* p. 69.

formers, he feels, the absoluteness of the revelation is lost and the shadow of the *deus absconditus* is cast over the *deus revelatus*.[31]

Over against this threatening shadow Barth posits that we may not think of an independent decree of God as standing behind the revelation in Jesus Christ, but that in the most literal sense of the word we may and must view election *exclusively in Jesus Christ as the incarnate Word.*

*At this point* — i.e., in Christ — God's election must be found. It is election which can no longer be relativized by any hidden depths of eternity. Here the labyrinth becomes an open highway, Jesus Christ. In Him we have the first and the last word concerning our election. On this (only possible) reality of election, *the legitimacy of pastoral comfort is founded.*

These questions obviously confront us with deep problems which are involved in the doctrine of election. They do so not only in the area of theoretical theology which has little bearing on the practical life of the Church, but as questions which are *indissolubly* associated with the problem of the certainty of salvation. What Barth points to as the *non-ontic* foundation of pastoral care (the *speculum electionis* as understood by the Reformers) seems to have its disturbing parallel in all kinds of uncertainty on the score of election which are found among believers. In this uncertainty the mirror of election is not truly seen and

---

31. Barth's opposition is constantly directed to the "darkness" in the doctrine of election of many theologians. The theories of the most prominent of them stand "under the shadow of this double darkness," KD II/2, p. 158, namely, that neither the electing God nor elect man are known. The entire history of the doctrine of predestination reveals an effort to see the central meaning of the mystery of election as being one of light, not of darkness, p. 158. But it was not possible to come to certainty here so long as it was not seen that the issue centering in the ideas of the electing God and elect man was one of "known" and not unknown entities." Election is "in both directions" concerned with the *same* Name and the *same* person, namely, Jesus Christ, p. 158. As long as this is not understood the last word about election will always be a word about this darkness. "We can no longer go along with this game," p. 159. He cannot allow himself to be persuaded "that we be silent in the face of this mystery," because in order to be silent we must know with whom we have to do. The result of unfounded silence lay in the fatal development to the right and to the left or in finally ignoring the doctrine of election as a sort of skandalon, p. 159. We may not make of election a mystery game about the *unknown* God and the unknown man. *The* decision lies in the acceptance or non-acceptance of the relationship between predestination and Christology, p. 161. Cf. also *Götteserkenntnis und Gottesdienst*, p. 102.

the comfort of the pastorate remains less than fully effective because it stands under the shadow of the "deus absconditus" and the *hidden* decree. How often has not the power of the proclamation of the gospel been weakened by the doctrine of election and the impression been created that the mirror of election is not in all respects a *clear* mirror?

Too often the impression has been left that a final uncertainty remained — even after the preaching of salvation in Christ — and this has not infrequently led to a *passive* Christianity that was numbed by staring into the dizzying abyss of the divine majesty in its inscrutable and unrevealed ultimate decision.

It is important to see in which manner Barth undertakes to find a way to the solution of these problems of the theologian and the pastor. In his estimation, these problems pose *the* crisis of the Reformation doctrine of election. We shall see that his solution places us squarely before the triumph of grace: the triumph of election.

\*       \*       \*

It is of decisive importance to notice how, in the discussion of this question, Barth views Christ as the *foundation* of election. Barth takes note of the fact that at the synod of Dordt the Remonstrants spoke of election in this manner. They taught that Christ is not only the *executor* of election but also its *foundation*.[32] Barth rejoices over this word, not because of the manner in which the Remonstrants used it, but because it opens perspectives which might have led to a truer construction of the doctrine. He is of the opinion that it "would have been well if the orthodox majority at Dordt, if for no other reason than the striking character of the word, had at least allowed themselves to be reminded of the problem to which not only the Calvinists but the whole of Reformation theology had, in its formulation of the doctrine, given so unsatisfactory an answer."[33]

In the use which the Remonstrants made of the word, it referred only to the salvation which in Christ is *offered* to all and that man had then, on the basis of this offer, freely to decide

---

32. "Christus mediator non est solum executor electionis, sed ipsius decreti electionis fundamentum," KD II/2, p. 72.
33. *Ibid.*, p. 72. On the following page Barth speaks again of the "in itself so remarkable matter of Christ as the fundamentum electionis."

whether he would accept it or not. But the words "foundation of election" can also be understood in a wholly different manner. They do not have to be understood in the Remonstrant sense or in contradiction of the "servum arbitrium" of man, but in such a manner that *in* Christ election truly *takes place* and is *executed.* The real definitive election does not take place *outside of Christ* and may not be abstracted from the incarnate Word. Election, rather, *confronts* us *in* Jesus Christ who Himself is the electing God, the subject of election. "That Christ is the electing God, that is what the Remonstrants failed to say."[34] It is unfortunate that the synod, in setting forth its positive teaching, had an eye only for the (indeed existing!) error but failed to see that the error did not necessarily have to eliminate the idea of Christ as the *foundation* of election. Only a few saw the possibility that stood open here as, for instance, Martini, when he pointed to Christ as the "causa meritoria" of election. The prevailing conception, however, was that the words "elect in Christ" (Eph. 1:4), referred to the *ordo salutis* as God had from all eternity conceived of it and not to election as such in Christ.[35] The decree governing the redemptive order was conceived of as standing independently (i.e., by reason of God's sovereignty) *behind* Christ, while at the same time Christ was pointed to *noetically* and *pastorally* as the way of salvation.

In doing so, however, orthodoxy dug its own grave. The noetic and pastoral superstructure lacked the ontic foundation. This ontic foundation could have become apparent only if *Christ Himself* — the incarnate Word — had been seen as the divine subject of election, in whom it would then have been possible to live and die in peace.

Barth does not see the doctrine of election as presenting us with an *abstract* electing *God* or with *abstract* elect men, but it presents us "concretely with the confession of Jesus Christ as the electing God and as the elect man."[36] Only in this way is it possible to speak truly, responsibly, and comfortingly, both in pastoral practice and theologically. This concentration of election in Jesus Christ stands in the full and exclusive light of God's

34. *Ibid.,* p. 73.
35. *Ibid.,* p. 74.
36. *Ibid.,* p. 81.

revelation and for this reason there is no room for a hidden eternal decree whereby it could be weakened or nullified. On this *revelation* of the mystery of all ages it is possible to build for time and for eternity. Christ is indeed the mirror of election.

*       *       *

This brings us to the question of what this, also in Barth's opinion, incisive correction of the Reformation doctrine of election concretely means. When we enter upon this question we shall discover that it brings us not only to the heart of Barth's doctrine of election but also to the heart of his entire dogmatic vision. The problem is not merely one of an isolated locus in dogmatics, but we come face to face with the whole content of theology, with "the sum and substance of the gospel," with the divine election, the "election of Jesus Christ,"[37] in whom the *fulness* of redemption lies enclosed. This is the wonderful miracle, that Jesus Christ is *at the same time* the electing God and the elect man.[38] When we speak of election we must think of one who is both electing and elect. Jesus Christ is first and foremost the electing God Himself. In Him we stand before none other than God Himself, before the "primal and ultimately determinative decision of God."[39] The fact that He is Himself also the elect one does not exclude His being the electing God.[40] He elects in the communion of the Father and the Son. He is both the primal subject and the primal object of election. He participates in God's election. Because He, as object of election, executes the will of God, "He will, as man, confirm and in a certain sense repeat, the election of God in His electing."[41] If Christ were not Himself the electing God we would have to search outside of Christ for the "primal and ultimately determinative decision of God" as the *real* election, and the only recourse would be a *decretum absolutum*.[42]

---

37. *Ibid.,* p. 101.
38. *Ibid.,* p 110.
39. *Ibid.,* p. 113.
40. "Therefore he is not only the elect, but also the electing One. His election must first of all be understood as an active election, KD II/2, p. 112. Cf. p. 115: "also the Son is active subject in God's eternal predestination of Him to be the Son of Man."
41. KD II/2, p. 112.
42. *Ibid.,* pp. 113, 115.

It is precisely as *God's* election that the election in Christ becomes manifest. Election does not tell us about a dark secret which is and remains inscrutable for us, but it is "the plainly revealed grace of God."[43] Not the slightest room for speculation remains here, for Christ is *the* revelation of God Himself through which all speculative trespassing of the boundaries is once and for all made impossible.[44] In Jesus Christ election is *historical* reality. It is immediately close to us as the *deus revelatus*.[45] The door which might lead to a final uncertainty is hereby forever locked and barred. The will, the election of God, is *not* a background for other things. It is a mystery — the mystery of reconciliation — but it is not an irrational, dark mystery, for Jesus Christ is the electing God. "There is no divine depth in which we shall meet other than Him alone."[46] Christ is not only the manifestation of election, He is Himself the electing God and for this reason He is the *foundation* of our election.[47]

*   *   *

If in the history of the doctrine of election this had been seen, the course of that history, Barth feels, would have been a quite different one.[48] But since, with few exceptions,[49] this insight did not obtain, it was unavoidable that the pastoral pointing to Christ as the mirror of election should be less than fully effective. This could not well be otherwise "if it be not true that Jesus Christ is Himself the electing God."[50] On this basis the shadow of the *deus absconditus* had necessarily to remain suspended over the whole of our life. If Christ be only the elect *means* in the hands of the electing God, then we cannot but "remain restless with re-

---

43. *Ibid.*, p. 113.
44. *Ibid.*
45. For the thesis that Christ Himself is the electing God Barth points to the passages in the Gospel of St. John which speak of Christ's choosing of His disciples, 13:18; 15:16, 19. He wishes to understand these passages "concretely, not figuratively," *ibid.*, p. 113.
46. *Ibid.*, p. 123.
47. *Ibid.*, p. 124.
48. *Ibid.*, p. 118.
49. Cf. Barth's references in this connection to Augustine, KD II/2, p. 115, Athanasius, p. 116, Polanus, p. 119ff, and Cocceius, pp. 122, 123. Concerning the good "beginning" in the Confessio Scoticana cf. *Gotteserkenntnis und Gottesdienst*, p. 102.
50. KD II/2, p. 118.

spect to our own election."[51] But if He be really the electing God, doubt is banished and the foundation has been laid for an impregnable certainty. "As we pass through our concrete historical existence we shall hold to Him with an unshakable certainty. We shall do this because we know that in the eternal background of all history, and in the beginning with God, no other decree was established, no other word was spoken or validated, than that decision which was executed by Him."[52]

\*     \*     \*

We have noted that Jesus Christ is Himself the electing God. We must next observe that He is also the elect one, the man who was from eternity chosen by God.[53] This does not mean that we have been elected *through* Him and *with* Him, but that we have been elected *in* Him,[54] *in* His own divine being-elect through "God's primal decision."[55] His election is not simply exemplary and typical, it is not exhausted in the pastoral-noetic sense of being "the mirror of election." There is also an election of others *in* Him. Here we see the electing love of God. As elect man, Christ is "in His own humanity Himself the God who elects them all."[56] *His* election is a *comprehensive* being-elect because as the elect-man he is the "beginning of all the ways and works of God."[57]

At this point the question arises wherein the election of the man Jesus Christ becomes evident. In the New Testament it appears that the "designation and commission" of Christ, namely, His election, means that He is appointed to *suffer*.[58] The grace of God which is revealed in His election assumes *this* form.[59] The Word

---

51. Here Barth takes sharp issue with Calvin: "That Calvin in particular not only did not answer this question, but obviously did not even see it — that is the decisive objection that must be made against his doctrine of predestination," KD II/2, p. 119. According to Barth, Calvin's electing God is a "Deus nudus absconditus," p. 118, with the result that, notwithstanding his tremendous emphasis on the confession of election "he in the last analysis failed to see ('vorbeiblicken') the grace of God that had appeared in Jesus Christ," p. 118. The "power of the proclamation of the free grace of God" requires a concrete content, namely, Jesus Christ and not "a general and therefore empty divine arbitrariness," p. 120.
52. KD II/2, p. 124.
53. *Ibid.*, p. 125.
54. *Ibid.*
55. *Ibid.*
56. *Ibid.*
57. *Ibid.*, p. 129.
58. *Ibid.*
59. *Ibid.*, p. 131.

became *flesh*. What is the meaning of the election of the man Jesus Christ? "A wrath is kindled, a judgment is pronounced, a punishment is inflicted, a rejection takes place. From eternity it has been decided that it should be so."[60] A *shadow* is necessarily cast over the election of the man Jesus from Nazareth. Man stands under the wrath and the judgment of God. He is subject to rejection, he is guilty of death. But God has, in and with the election of the man Jesus Christ, loved this mankind from eternity. Therefore God commissions Him, in whom He elected mankind, to bear the rejection. He designates the one obedient man to bear what all men had merited.[61] Therein God reveals His grace, and therefore the Lamb that was slain, the crucified Jesus, is the *image of the invisible God*.

Barth's doctrine of election, therefore, also discusses reprobation. The opinion, held by some, that Barth in no sense believes in a double predestination rests on misunderstanding. In 1936 Barth spoke of a "human arbitrariness" in the Lutheran *Formula Concordiae*, in that they are unwilling "to acknowledge more than a comforting significance in the doctrine of election."[62] Over against this emphasis he posits that the doctrine of predestination is a doctrine of *double* predestination.[63] "There is no election apart from non-election, passing-over, rejection."[64] This does *not* mean, however, that Barth now retracts his earlier criticism of the "equality" between election and reprobation. He points instead to God's rejection of Him who is also the elect man, Jesus Christ. "Is Jesus Christ, then, only the bearer of the divine Yes to men? Is He this without being at the same time the bearer of the divine No?"[65]

It is necessary to speak of a double predestination, but this can be done only in terms of Golgotha.[66] This elect man is also the rejected man, the rejected Son of Man, who endures the wrath of God to the end. This elect man must suffer and die. "By

---

60. *Ibid.*
61. *Ibid.*, p. 132.
62. *Gottes Gnadenwahl*, p. 19.
63. *Ibid.*, p. 18.
64. *Ibid.*
65. *Ibid.*, p. 19.
66. Cf. especially KD II/2, p. 191 where Barth speaks about the "relationship of balance." With an eye to Jesus Christ Barth can therefore write, "In obedience and in gratitude we can only rejoice in the *double* divine predestination."

Himself becoming this man, God made Himself responsible and liable for the men who had become His enemies and in so doing made the whole train of suffering which followed in the wake of their sin, namely, their rejection and their death, His own concern." *"That* is what God took upon Himself in His total self-surrender. So radical is His grace."[67]   In Christ God loves man. "His wrath, His judgment, His punishment, now fall upon Him. He is smitten, and in Him His own Son, and in His own Son God Himself."[68] *He* is struck by the judgment and not they whom He, in Christ, has elected.

*       *       *

Therefore Jesus Christ is in the most absolute sense of the word the decision of God, the decision, namely, to become man. What decree *can possibly exist outside of this decision?*[69]   God's election in Christ is the beginning of all His works.  The electing God is not an abstract highest being with all kinds of qualities by reason of which He elects in an absolute decree of which Christ then later becomes the "executor decreti."   Christ Himself is the *decretum concretum,*[70] *the* mode of God's operation.[71]  For this reason, the eternal will of God in Christ is not unknown to us, but is *made known* in the history of God with man.[72]  This is the effulgent light of the overcoming love of God.  This is the mystery, not of an abstract sovereignty, but of the "victorious affirmation and love of God for men."[73]  *"This history is the unique Triumph of Grace and as such the Triumph of the Sovereignty of God."*[74]

In the doctrine of election everything depends on the relationship between *predestination* and *Christology.*[75]  This relationship

---

67. *Ibid.,* p. 133.
68. *Ibid.*
69. *Ibid.,* p. 102.
70. *Ibid.,* p. 108.
71. *Ibid.,* p. 210: "Predestination is not merely a mode of His saving work, but *the* mode of the divine saving work; it is not merely a mode of His work in salvation, but the mode of all His work.
72. *Ibid.,* p. 157. Cf. p. 211: "In that history God's will is wholly clear," and p. 212: "in this history therefore nothing is simply dark or unclear."  This history is not darkness but light, it is not a game of riddles, for the mystery has been revealed and it has a name, namely, Jesus Christ, p. 159.
73. *Ibid.,* p. 214.
74. *Ibid.*
75. *Ibid.,* pp. 161, 211. Note relationship to soteriology also: pp. 183, 205.

we must see correctly.  When we do, we shall no longer find the traditional doctrine of predestination acceptable with its conception of a hidden decree of God which could not but cast men into uncertainty when they regarded their own relationship to God.[76]

Barth is aware of the fact that the correction which he effects in the traditional doctrine of election plunges him into a certain loneliness in the discussion of the very heart of the doctrine. The correction is indeed an incisive one.  He speaks himself of "the need for the total revision of the dogma."[77]  It is for Barth, as he views the matter from the standpoint of the gospel, an historical puzzle[78] that theology has not looked earlier in the direction which he has suggested.  The old conception did not make it possible to enter upon true comfort.  The existence of a mystery was acknowledged, a mystery to which one had humbly to submit himself, but it was not the *true* mystery.  The believer was enjoined to be *silent*,[79] whereas the *revealed* mystery and the knowledge that was given concerning it should have constrained men to *thankful speaking*.  It was not seen that the epistemological ground of election (the mirror of election in its pastoral significance) was also its "Realgrund."[80]

It may be asked whether on Barth's basis election and the knowledge of election are viewed *too simplistically*.  Does he perhaps become guilty of rationalizing the mystery of election?[81] These questions Barth answers negatively.  In his conception, knowledge of election is now possible, but rationalization is excluded.  The light of this knowledge, he would emphasize, is not a natural light which takes its rise in the heart of man, but it is a light which arises from the revelation of the mystery itself, the most unthinkable of all thoughts.[82]  The knowledge of election does not fathom the mystery, nor does it annul or suspend the mystery.  It makes it known *as* the mystery of God's knowledge and grace.  It stands over against the uncertainty of an absolute and hidden decree in which the true mystery is perverted into a

76. *Ibid.*, p. 167.
77. *Ibid.*, p. 373.
78. *Ibid.*, p. 159.
79. *Ibid.*
80. *Ibid.*, p. 366.
81. *Ibid.*, p. 172.
82. *Ibid.*, p. 173.

mystery exclusively of God's sovereignty that stands apart from the grace and mercy of God.[83]  Through Jesus Christ — the election of God — we come to the saving knowledge of faith. The fire which is kindled by the decree (of abstract sovereignty) can only be the fire of *religion,* not the fire of true faith.[84]  True faith rests in the *revelation* of the mystery, it is not silent but it speaks of the salvation that has now been revealed. This fire of faith is kindled in the *decretum concretum* of history and the mystery is no longer made questionable by the existence of an ultimate hidden decision.  In Jesus Christ we can believe in an ultimate certainty because *God will not forsake this work of His hands.*  He Himself, as the one who elects us in Christ, confronts us.  He confronts us in the mystery of His love, and this mystery is not surrounded on every side by question marks that are occasioned by ever-recurring uncertainty.

\*    \*    \*

In extensive discussions Barth indicates why it is necessary, in connection with Jesus Christ, to speak of a *double* predestination. This question is related to the fact that Christ is both the electing God and the elected man.[85]

God has chosen to have communion with man and He has chosen man for communion with Himself.[86]  This latter choice confers a purely unmerited gift.  The former, however — that which God chose for Himself — cannot be a gift.  This choice can only mean "that God, as God, jeopardizes Himself, His deity, His power and His dominion."[87]  For man election is gain, "unheard of exaltation," but *for God* it means "compromise" when He decides to enter upon *this* covenant with man.  When man can only *gain,* God can only *lose.*  Such is, then, the content of

---

83. Barth's intention appears clearly when he writes: "the doctrine of predestination is not to be separated from Christology and soteriology. Faith in the judging and redeeming God is not a direct relationship to the divine majesty and is therefore not to be confused with enthusiasm for God and His honor," KD II/2, p. 210. The sovereignty of God is not a sovereignty of "whim, accident, an arbitrariness," p. 212. It is not exercised outside of Christ but is revealed *in* Him.  For this reason it is not possible to speak of the sovereignty of God as such.
84. *Ibid.,* p. 174.
85. *Ibid.,* p. 110.
86. *Ibid.,* p. 179.
87. *Ibid.*

the *double* predestination which *for man* means salvation but *for God* danger.

Double predestination means election *and* rejection, life *and* death. There is no question here of a distribution of election and reprobation over such and such people, but it is a question of double predestination in and concerning *Christ*. In the election in Christ "God has given to man the former: election, salvation and life; for Himself, however, He has chosen the second: rejection, damnation and death."[88] The danger and the threat confront the Son of God and in Him God Himself. Barth even speaks here of "the deepest compromising of God."[89] God makes Himself — in the rejection — the object of His own wrathful judgment, of damnation, death and hell. God chose our (merited) rejection *for Himself*. The Son of God has taken our rejection upon Himself and therefore (heart of the gospel!) the rejection *is no longer* man's portion.[90]

Predestination is never a mankind-condemning No of God. It does indeed involve rejection, but it is the rejection of *Christ*. Mankind, *we,* deserved this reprobation and therefore there is, so far as man is concerned, not the slightest reason to think optimistically about either election or rejection. It is God's own heart that is touched by our need. Our rejection is borne in His and thereby it is borne away. This is God's mercy, that the sinner in Christ lies enclosed in His own heart and that He has taken the rejection upon Himself. The content of Golgotha is therefore identical with the great *exchange* negotiated at Golgotha, an exchange which cannot be undone through all eternity for it is God's *eternal decision*.[91] Because of this exchange there is nothing to condemn anymore in those who are in Christ. Faith is nothing more than believing in the rejection of the Son of God and — this is the same thing — in the non-rejection of our own life. The rejection in which Christ participates is, in the deepest sense of the word, the rejection of God Himself. Predestination is not a mystery in which our rejection *still* is a possibility, but it is the mystery of the radical substitution which finds its unity in the election of man and the rejection of Christ. Therefore *this*

88. *Ibid.,* p. 177.
89. *Ibid.,* p. 179.
90. *Ibid.,* p. 182.
91. *Ibid.*

election, this *double* predestination, belongs to the kerugma. This is not a doctrine to be reflected upon only in the study-room of theologians and to remain silent about on the pulpit, but it is the light which must radiate from the pulpit in the proclamation of true salvation. This election is *eu-aggelion*. It comes to us as God's certain and irrevocable Word, as the deepest mystery of eternity.[92] *In* the self-surrender of Jesus Christ it is revealed that "the rejection does not concern us because God has made it His own concern."[93] *Belief in our rejection is the perverse belief in what God has not decreed.*

*       *       *

We are aware that the foregoing summary does not even remotely give a complete picture of Barth's extensive treatment of the doctrine of election. One thing, however, should be plain in the discussion which we have presented. It must be evident that in setting forth his conception of election Barth is centrally concerned about the *light* and the *certainty* and the *triumph* of grace. The darkness and the rejection have a distinct place in his treatment of election, but as darkness and rejection whose removal was negotiated for us at Golgotha, that is to say, they are treated as borne by Jesus Christ. To put it differently, the rejection of man has a place in Barth's doctrine of predestination only in the sense that it is carried, put away and destroyed, by Christ. In this sense, *double* predestination lies at the heart of Barth's doctrine. For him election does not mean the irresistibility and the triumph of an almighty "sovereignty." It means the triumph of *grace,* the triumph of self-abnegation, the triumph which is not a triumph of gaining but a triumph of losing, the triumph of the love of God.

*       *       *

In further clarifying the central motifs of Barth's conception of election, it is of importance to give some attention to election and rejection in their relation to the Church and to Israel. Barth emphasizes that there is a parallel between the double predestina-

---

92. *Ibid.,* p. 183.
93. *Ibid.,* p. 184.

tion of Christ and the double aspect of the people of God, namely, Israel and the Church. As the crucified Messiah, Christ, in His rejection, is the "authentic witness" to God's judgment, and as the risen Lord He is, in His election, the "authentic witness" to God's mercy. Similarly, there is a *reflection* of this rejection and election in grace-resisting Israel and in the Church in which His mercy is revealed. This does not mean that election and reprobation are distributed over groups of people, for *both* election and reprobation stand under "the arch of the one covenant."

We must note, in the first place, that Barth discusses the Church in this connection in the chapter dealing with "the destiny of the elect." He speaks here of the elect being destined for salvation.[94] This salvation, however, is not an immanent but a transeunt salvation.[95] It is therefore a salvation which leads to gratitude and in this gratitude to a "representation and portrayal of the glory of God and of its work."[96] In short: the destiny of the Church lies in its *witness-being*. The line of the triumph of grace receives an extension here — from election to the witness concerning God's grace.

Even more deserving of attention is Barth's conception of the function of *Israel*. Her situation contrasts sharply with that of the Church because she resists and rejects grace. Israel, in spite of her rejection of grace, plays a role in God's election because she is the "mirror of judgment."[97] In Israel we see *what man is on whom God has had mercy*. This is Israel's place and function in the witness to God's goodness. The obedient and the disobedient are together "encompassed in the divine election of grace" as *witnesses* to Christ. Also Israel! As part of the totality comprising the people of God, Israel has a *peculiar service* to render. It must serve the praise of God's mercy "in ruin, in death, in the putting away of the old man who rejects his own election and in this rejection rejects God."[98] Israel, that is, the Church in her *Israelitic* expression,[99] reveals how God has mercy on the *unworthy,* and this mercy makes manifest "the enigma of His self-surrender."[100]

---

94. *Ibid.*, p. 455.
95. *Ibid.*, p. 456.
96. *Ibid.*, p. 477.
97. *Ibid.*, p. 294.
98. *Ibid.*, p. 286.
99. *Ibid.*, p. 287.
100. *Ibid.*

It is therefore necessary for the Church "that Israel continue to live on in the midst of her."[1] God's mercy becomes visible only in contrast to the pitiful situation of man in which the Church also participates. To this the whole of Israel's existence witnesses in its *resistance* to grace. Even after Christ has made all things new she continues to resist and to assert herself in her rejection of grace.[2] In doing so she judges herself, but even so she cannot cease to be the people of the risen Christ. What has been decided in Him has also been decided for disobedient Israel.[3] It is Israel's service to embody and exemplify destruction and death.[4] Israel is a witness in the sense that she personifies "a semi-dignified, semi-horrible relic, a wondrously preserved antiquity."[5] Israel disturbs the Church but nevertheless serves her by giving this witness through the fact of her existence. The synagogue does not testify that Christ is risen, but she must say: He is not *here!* Israel sighs as the creature sighs and in so doing becomes a symbol of the suffering of the cosmos.[6] Israel's powerlessness is thus revealed. She can condemn herself but she cannot undo the fact that "also for her a Savior lives."[7]

This explains why Barth sees the service of those who are rejected as lying in *"making visible who are the addressees of the gospel."*[8] They do not disappear from election's field of view but they

---

1. *Ibid.*
2. "She deliberately makes herself guilty of an effort to split the body of Christ."
3. KD II/2, p. 289.
4. *Ibid.*, p. 289. In this connection we wish to point out the dominant place which *illustrative* exegesis of certain parts of the Old Testament has in Barth's exposition. As a very striking example we mention his treatment of Saul and David, pp. 404-434, and the history of the man of God in I Kings 13, pp. 443-453. Barth speaks of the demonstration "of the selective electing of God," p. 434. Saul, the king whom God rejected, is "both prefiguration and copy of Jesus Christ," pp. 431. He bears also the earmarks of election: he is properly and in all earnestness one of the prophets. He stands under the wrath and rejection of God and yet bears something of the glory of God, in all of this reflecting the rejection and the election of Jesus Christ. The history of Israel's kingship illustrates the triumph of grace. David and Solomon may not cause us to forget *Saul*, p. 433. The reflection of God's glory is not absent in Saul, as the shadow of judgment is not wanting in the picture of David. In the light of the fulfillment, that is, in the election and rejection of Christ these things, which could not yet happen to the synagogue, can be seen in Israel's earlier history, p. 429.
5. KD II/2, p. 289.
6. *Ibid.*, p. 290.
7. *Ibid.*, p. 291.
8. *Ibid.*, p. 504.

represent "the world and every single man insofar as they stand in need of the divine election."[9] Here the mankind appears to view for whom God's self-surrender became necessary. Israel herself is not rejected (*Jesus Christ* is the rejected one) and her existence is only a "deceitful representation" of the rejection,[10] but precisely in this way she witnesses to the *nature* of election. In not joining in the praise of the election of Christ and of mankind in Christ, Israel, in her quality as rejected nation, "embodies the fact that this praise is not sung in the void."[11] The rejection of Israel shows what man, *as object of election,* looks like before his election.[12] *Here* we see that election is: sovereign mercy. "Without the rejection this might be overlooked." "The actual existence of rejected men prevents that this should happen."[13] Against the background of godlessness and resistance to grace the nature of election becomes evident. This, then, is Israel's place in history: she is a witness, indirectly and unknowingly, of God's *gracious* election. "Gloria Deo in excelcis" and "gloria Deo ex profundis."[14]

The meaning of the relationship between witness and election is, finally, plainly illustrated in Barth's extensive discussion of *Judas.*[15] Barth has no interest in the New Testament data about Judas from the viewpoint of its biographical value. He sees in Judas, rather, an illustration of the *intent* of reprobation. Barth does not present Judas as a "sample of a general restoration,"[16] nor does he radically exclude his conversion. The Judas-question concerns a wholly different matter, namely, that of grace and the enmity of man which opposes it.[17] We may not attempt to mitigate the guilt of Judas,[18] but we do see that Judas *cannot undo* the decision of election. In his betrayal of Jesus he *co-operates* in the realization of

---

9. *Ibid.*
10. *Ibid.*
11. *Ibid.,* p. 505.
12. *Ibid.*
13. *Ibid.* Cf. also p. 286ff.
14. The relationship between Israel and the Church also comes to expression in what Barth calls "the Church pre-existing in Israel," through which Israel's election is also positively affirmed. This, however, relates only to a *small* and *scattered minority.* "They seem in the end wholly to disappear in the melancholy end of Israel's history," p. 293.
15. KD II/2, p. 598ff.
16. *Ibid.,* p. 528.
17. *Ibid.,* p. 529.
18. *Ibid.,* p. 560.

election. By means of the encounter between Jesus and Judas the superior power of grace becomes manifest,[19] and that precisely in connection with Judas *the reprobate!* Judas was one of Jesus' disciples, participating in the footwashing and the last supper. He was not independently active. "His whole being and action, however bad, and having no less than the authority, weight and power of Satan standing behind them and active through him, can only run their course and develop under the command and control which Jesus exercises over him."[20] Reprobate man plays a *dependent* role and "exists only as a shadow-image."[21] For the doctrine of election this is of "decisive weight."[22] What Judas is as traitor, that is what Israel has always been with respect to the Messiah.[23] All reprobation is, as it were, in a final instance concentrated in Judas as a "compendium." It is, therefore, also the *end*: Judas must die, and with him the nation of Israel. Straight through this rejection, however, shines the light of *election*. The divine "surrender" triumphs over the human "delivering up" of Christ. Reprobation has no independent significance "next to God's election."[24]

Jesus Christ has also died for rejected Israel. The service which the reprobate renders is plain. They are — in spite of themselves — witnesses to the overcoming power of *election* and of the *triumph of grace*.

Therefore it is just the reprobate who must believe, "and as believer be an elect reprobate."[25] In his rejection he is taken up into the great happening. For are not all the elect of the New Testament "reprobates who on the basis of the election of Jesus Christ and because He has surrendered Himself on their behalf, believe in their election?"[26]

\*     \*     \*

It is understandable that in the debate centering around Barth's revision and correction of the Reformation dogma of election, the question should be raised whether Barth's conception of the triumph of election as the triumph of radical grace does not require, as an inevitable corollary, the acceptance of a consistent *univer-*

---

19. *Ibid.*, p. 561.
20. *Ibid.*
21. *Ibid.*
22. *Ibid.*
23. *Ibid.*, p. 562.
24. *Ibid.*
25. *Ibid.*, p. 563
26. *Ibid.*

*salism,* that is to say, the doctrine of the *apokatastasis* (universal restoration). This question has been raised again and again ever since the publication of Barth's views on election. If it be of the essence of the triumph to be revealed over against godlessness and resistance to grace, and if the *real* reprobation consists in the rejection of Christ in contrast to the rejection of others, is it possible to escape drawing the conclusion of the apokatastasis doctrine? If the great decision has been made, if the universal tide has turned, if the great change has taken place through the radical substitution of Christ, then the asking of the apokatastasis question is not illegitimate but is warranted by the simple fact of taking Barth seriously. If the gospel means that the sword of God has smitten once and for all in its striking down of the Son of God, and if in this smiting the *one* rejection has been historically realized and such other reprobation as exists can only attest this fact, is there any possibility open other than to accept the *validity* and the *effectiveness* of the "happening" of this one reprobation? Must it not be *proclaimed* as the most absolute and irrevocable fact that has ever taken place? And, further, must not any other conception of reprobation infringe upon the completeness of the triumph of grace which, as we have seen, is precisely and exclusively a victory over *godlessness* and over *resistance against grace?*[27]

Other questions press themselves forward. In view of the completeness of the triumph, is it still necessary to preach and to call men to believe in the *seriousness* of a human decision? Is *God's* decision not true and effective before and apart from the answer that follows it (belief or unbelief)? Is more needed than the decision that the eternal death and the judgment of God, which man by his guilt has merited, have been so taken away that they cannot meet them as a new possibility or as a new threat either now or in the future?

We are confronted by the indisputable fact that Barth has himself emphatically *rejected* the doctrine of the apokatastasis. This raises the question whether, in presenting Barth's doctrine of election as we have, we have understood him correctly. How is it possible that Barth can reject the, it would seem, logical conclusion of the apokatastasis? This important question makes it necessary to cast a last glance at the central idea in his conception.

---

27. Cf. Barth against synergism, *ibid.,* p. 213.

We may take our point of departure in what Barth writes about the *powerless* attempt to live in terms of reprobation.[28] Man has indeed drawn God's consuming enmity to himself as a deserved judgment, but this merited rejection is that which "in the election of Jesus Christ has been turned against Him, the One, and thereby has been turned away from us all."[29] Thereby God in His grace has made the life of reprobation "an objective impossibility" for us. It is true that the unbeliever attempts to undo this eternal and divine decision, but this is nothing else than an *evil attempt* (the denial of the love of God), and although this attempt resurrects the *shadow* of God's (departed) enmity, still, this attempt is *powerless* because it can never undo the fact that the rejection has been applied exclusively to Jesus Christ.[30]

When unbelief perverts the right that Christ has gained for all, there is heard a "reverberation" of the curse, but of *that* curse "which did not strike them but which, in their place, struck Him."[31] This substitution can be *denied*, but it cannot be *undone*. The guilt of unbelief is a terrible reality, but there is no such thing as an "eternal Jew." "He can eternalize neither himself nor his fate. For to his 'eternity' — and, in and with him, all who are like him — God has in His mercy set limits in the death and resurrection of the Jewish Messiah."[32] Unbelief is a denial of the election in Christ, it is a denial of the definitive "God-for-us" and of the fact that God has taken *our* rejection upon Himself and borne it away. If synergism had a legitimate place in the doctrine of the Church we could place the human decision next to the divine decision. The divine decision, however, has been taken precisely *over against* the human and godless decision and can *therefore* not be undone by any human decision.[33]

---

28. *Ibid.*, p. 381.
29. *Ibid.*
30. *Ibid.*, pp. 381, 382.
31. *Ibid.*, p. 388.
32. *Ibid.*, p. 291.
33. "If predestination is identical with the election of Jesus Christ, then it is not possible that God's freedom in which this decision takes place should be limited and conditioned by the mystery of the existentiality of a corresponding human decision. Were this to be so, the life of the constantly renewed and constantly constituted relationship between God and man would in the final analysis be found to have two sources: the one in God's decision, the other in the corresponding human decision to which the former would have to be related," *ibid.*, p. 213.

It is therefore striking that in this context Barth can, alongside the powerlessness of unbelief, speak of the *deathly danger* of unbelief. In the tension between this "powerlessness" and this "deathly danger" we meet the very heart of the problematics involved in Barth's doctrine of election. Unbelief elicits the "reverberation" of the curse, but it is the reverberation of an already eliminated curse. In terms of this elimination the doctrine of election as God's eternal decision is solely *good news*. The triumph of grace and of the love of God is and remains the mighty theme of the election in Christ.

This lends urgency, however, to the question what the grounds are on which Barth rejects the doctrine of the apokatastasis. When in the course of his Hungarian lectures he was asked, "If God is eternal love, how can we still speak of reprobation?"[34] Barth pointed out that from ourselves we cannot know the love of God because it is not a human love. This answer was given to intercept easy human conclusions drawn from the concept: the love of God. The question could also, however, have been asked less abstractly. He might have been asked whether the *concrete* love of God, the love of God *revealed* in Jesus Christ, could still allow for the rejection of others than Christ. It was on this level that the question was put to Barth in Debreczen: "Does not the universal grace which desires to save all men eliminate reprobation?"[35] Barth's answer is remarkable: "We can be certain that God's lordship is and will be total in all, but what this signifies for us we must leave to God. And therefore we dare not say that in the universal grace damnation is eliminated. The Holy Scriptures speak of election and of rejection."[36]

This answer, obviously, does not provide much clarification. The Scriptures do indeed speak of election *and* of rejection, but according to Barth it was exactly *our* merited rejection which was borne away by Christ. The burden of this revelation is the manifestation of the *deus revelatus* and precisely here, Barth says, there is nothing to leave to God as though there were still a separate mystery outside of the comforting revelation that the rejection had been taken away.

---

34. *Gottes Gnadenwahl*, p. 50.
35. *Ibid.*
36. *Ibid.*

Does Barth's subsequent speaking about "leaving to God" not constitute a curtailment on what God *has done* and on what God *has revealed?* Must the believer not (on Barth's own basis) hold to this for himself and for others? Has not Barth himself said that although there is a difference between the elect and the reprobate, this difference becomes *relative* in Christ?[37]

In view of Barth's emphasis on the factuality of Christ's rejection, it is not possible to close the door to the apokatastasis doctrine by pointing to the fact that the Bible speaks of rejection as well as election and then entrust everything *eschatologically* to the hand of God. Did not the hand of God become visible in His works, and specifically in the one central "modus" of His work in Jesus Christ, in election as the decretum *concretum,* in the triumph of grace?

It is all the more necessary to ask this question because in the discussion centering around the apokatastasis Barth continues to speak about the triumph of grace. There is an overpowering might of grace which continues to rule among men. Does not grace *always* mean the conquest of the deepest darkness and the most stubborn unbelief? Is grace not mightier than sin? "Grace will yet show itself more powerful than anything which the children of this world can in their ignorance and disobedience set over against it."[38] The Church must acknowledge and respect the sovereignty and overcoming power of grace. But, having come so far, Barth suddenly asks the question: "Apokatastasis pantoon?" (the restoration of all?) The answer is in the negative: "No, for grace which would in the end automatically have to reach and embrace everyone and anyone would certainly not be sovereign, would not be divine grace."[39] Barth's conception of grace, as also the immanent analysis of his doctrine of election, compels us to ask what, in terms of

---

37. Cf. especially KD II/2, p. 389: "He is the *rejected* One as He is and in that He is the *elect* One. Seen from the viewpoint of His election there are outside of Him no rejected ones. It is rather so, that for the sake of the election of all the rejected ones He stands alone over against them all. For their sakes He is *the* rejected One (in His reprobation making room for them as the elect of God!) and precisely in this way He is the object of God's gracious election. The antithesis between election and reprobation finds its necessity in Him who is originally both the elect One and the reprobate One. Not only the relativity of this antithesis is grounded in Him, however, but also this: in the whole of their antithetical character they are brethren, in their existence and function they are mutually related to each other, and together constitute an inalienable and indissoluble unity."

38. K. Barth, *Die Botschaft von der freien Gnade Gottes,* 1947, p. 7.
39. *Ibid.,* p. 8.

God's election, the words "automatic" and "would have to" signify. We are not concerned here with a question of human logic but with what Barth himself intended election and rejection to mean.

Considered from the viewpoint of Barth's doctrine of election, it is far from plain what right of existence the rejection of the apokatastasis can have. It is understandable that Barth rejects the idea that man can from himself, or from a humanly construed conception of the love of God, conclude to the election of all. It remains obscure, however, why the apokatastasis is not included *in* the *decretum concretum* of the revelation of Christ.

There is no alternative to concluding that Barth's refusal to accept the apokatastasis cannot be harmonized with the fundamental structure of his doctrine of election. The reason for this refusal must be looked for in another quarter. We must, on the one hand, in no way minimize the *earnestness* with which Barth rejects the apokatastasis idea and, on the other hand, endeavor to understand how he *relates* it to his conception of election.

It would seem that the connection between the two becomes plain from other considerations. We do not mean that there is, after all, a final harmonization. We do suggest that it is possible to discover what it is that creates the tension between these two incompatibles.

*         *         *

In all the phases of Barth's development, in the course of which he time and again rejects the apokatastasis idea, he is manifestly concerned to emphasize that election is an act of God's sovereign grace which must be *proclaimed* to men and be received by them *in faith*. A doctrine of general reconciliation teaching the *effective* universality of salvation for *all* would create the danger that the preaching of election would cease to sustain an adequate relationship to faith. It would then no longer be plain why faith is still necessary or significant. This emphasis of Barth we must further explore.

If election as such were made a purely objective thing the way would be opened to the undermining of human responsibility and of the serious call to believe in the gospel of election. It is unquestionably for *this* reason that Barth, in his rejection of the apokatastasis, has become spokesman for the *open situation* of the gospel

proclamation. It is in this connection that he emphasizes the deathly danger of unbelief. It is remarkable that in the background even
of Barth's joyful doctrine of election *shadows* are to be found.
These shadows fall specifically at that point where he extends the
lines of election and rejection into *eschatology*. Accordingly, he
writes that in the doctrine of election there can be no question of
"elect" or "reprobate," but, he adds, the "being-predestinated"
(which he opposes so sharply as the fatal error of the Reformation
doctrine) can be characterized as a "truth of the eschaton."[40]
"Therefore we cannot say: there are elect and reprobate. We can
and must believe, however, that there will be such. We are on the
way to this reality. That is our human life, that we find ourselves
on this way."[41]

For this reason we may not draw any conclusions in the direction of the apokatastasis, but we must *preach* the triumph of grace
and in so doing set forth "the purpose of the elect."[42] The witness
of the Church is the continuation of God's reconciling activity in
the world. The existence of every elect man constitutes a crossing
of the boundary to the advantage of the Kingdom of God.[43] In
considering the open situation of the proclamation it must be remembered that it is *God* who has made this crossing over eschatologically possible, and who also effects it. "That His salvation
will finally and in the last analysis cover mankind as such (according to the doctrine of the so-called apokatastasis) is a view
which, out of respect for the *sovereignty* of divine grace, we dare
not risk taking."[44] A metaphysics of history is *not* possible. And
as little as we may think in the direction of the apokatastasis, so
little may we think in any *other* direction. "As we avoid the one
view, so we avoid the other. Neither is in its abstraction relevant
to the message of Christ. Both are formal conclusions without substantial content."[45]

---

40. *Gottes Gnadenwahl*, p. 48.
41. *Ibid.*, p. 48. As far as I can see, this thought expressed in 1936 ("there will
be such") finds no clear parallel in Barth's doctrine of election published in 1942.
42. KD II/2, p. 461.
43. *Ibid.*
44. *Ibid.*, p. 462.
45. *Ibid.* We face the fact here that Barth himself drew a direct *conclusion*
which followed from the exclusive rejection of Jesus Christ. It is therefore
understandable that Barth's doctrine of election was regarded as implying the
doctrine of the apokatastasis.

In this manner Barth stands by his thesis that election is the *light* of grace. "We do not know God's gracious election, whether in its aspect as the election of Jesus Christ, or as the election of the Church, or as the election of individuals, other than as a decision of His compassion."[46] The proclamation of election must witness to the shadows of rejection which have fallen over *Christ*. Therefore Barth sets himself sharply against any idea of balance between light and darkness in the preaching of the gospel, and against the conception of those who accept as a matter of course that *grace is not extended to all.* Grace is *free,* and it would not be free if we prohibit it from going out freely to all.

"Has Christ died for our sins alone? Has He not according to I John 1 been sacrificed for the sins of the whole world? Peculiar Christendom, whose most pressing problem seems to consist in this, that God's grace in this direction should be too free, that Hell, instead of being amply populated, might one day perhaps be found to be empty."[47]

The doctrine of election is the doctrine of the *free* grace of God. It emphasizes this freedom and shows us that grace is indeed the grace of *God.* It is therefore not a separate and independent doctrine, but it is the salt in the food of doctrine in its entirety.[48] This freedom of grace, in which the decision of God's-being-for-man has been taken from eternity, is the *triumph* of grace which is taken up in the concrete message of the Church. We — and all men — are called to faith in this triumph. We are called not to resist the *monopleuric* decision of grace but to live gratefully in terms of it. It was the decision of Christ's vicarious work, of the self-surrender of God in measureless condescension in the incarnation of the Word. There are indeed shadows of resistance and unbelief, but

---

46. *Ibid.*

47. *Die Botschaft von der freien Gnade Gottes,* p. 8. In writing to a ministers' conference in 1949 which was to discuss his doctrine of election Barth said: "Will also you find me guilty of the error of holding to the apokatastasis, or will you be one with me in the conviction that it is always more advisable with this danger to preach the life-giving gospel than without this danger to preach the law that kills? Will the acknowledgment — however we may come to it — also strengthen you that the word of God's gracious election is really and truly a word of joy with which, as we face both Christians and non-Christians, we can both begin and end?" O. Weber, W. Kreck, and E. Wolf, "Die Predigt von der Gnadenwahl," *Theol. Existenz heute,* number 28, 1951, p. 7.

48. *Gottes Gnadenwahl,* p. 4.

they are shadows that are cast by the non-acknowledgment of the radicalness and the universality of the divine decision. They are the shadows of resistance against the irresistible, of opposition against what comes to us unconquerably from God's hand, they are the shadows of unbelief in the inviolable fact of history revealed in the *reality* of the rejected Christ.

Therefore Barth continues to speak of the triumph of grace in spite of these shadows and their attendant deathly danger. The shadow does not balance the light, and we are called in the *light* of election. The kerugma itself is shadowless, it is *eu-aggelion,* good news. Unbelief does not have its root in not-being-elect, but it is the denial of *being-elect.* Although the preaching of election causes us to discern a deep abyss, it is "the abyss at whose edge we are kept. We are not able to stare into this abyss, however, as though it also constituted our true place next to our home in heaven where Christ sits at the right hand of God." Therefore God's election is not "a mixture of terror and joy, but only joy, pure joy."[49] It is this message that the Church speaks in her unique witness: "the Kingdom of Heaven opened, Hell barricaded, God justified, Satan refuted, life triumphant, death overcome, faith in this promise the only, unbelief in it, the excluded, possibility."[50]

\* \* \*

It is not accidental that, in the light of these considerations, Barth views *missions* in the light of election. Man must seek refuge at Golgotha because Christ has borne the judgment. That is *the* stimulus to all missionary labor.[51] "The heart of the confession of the New Testament is the consummated judgment of God in the death of Jesus Christ on the cross. No other man stands in this center, none other stands so truly in God's judgment."[52] All other men stand "around this center." There is one remarkable difference among them, however; "the Christian knows, the others do not yet know."[53] The apostles *knew* that the judgment had been executed,

---

49. KD II/2, p. 190ff.
50. *Ibid.,* p. 358.
51. *Ibid.,* p. 738.
52. *Ibid.,* p. 736.
53. *Ibid.,* p. 737.

others did not yet know the true state of affairs, "these fools and deluded ones, with or without the law."[54] They did not surmise that the Judge had appeared on the scene, and that *against* them all — though first and foremost *for* them all — he had rendered the verdict and, once and for all, consummated the sentence which involved their life and their death. This contrast between the *knowing* in the Church and the *not-knowing* in the world is the motive, and the bridging of the chasm between the two is the problem, of the witness of the early Church."[55] Here the compulsion to missionary witness asserts itself: "Woe is me if I preach not the gospel!" (I Cor. 9:16) And this must not be done out of general human love, but because of the urgent content of the message, "the concrete truth concerning Jesus Christ and concerning the life of man." We must preach that death is a sign, but *only* a sign, of God's judgment, for it has *already been executed* in Jesus Christ. We must preach that "mankind, standing around the cross, has, whether as knowing or as unknowing, been placed under that sign in which its death, whether acknowledged or unacknowledged, has been incorporated."[56]

\* \* \*

It should surprise no one that Barth's conception of unbelief as an excluded possibility has led to discussion again and again, even among those who wished, in principle, to establish a relationship between the doctrine of predestination and Christology. Thus, Kreck asks, "whether, in this connection, the thesis that Christ is exclusively the reprobated one is a full statement of the matter. Must not the mystery of this other — from the viewpoint of faith — incomprehensible possibility be allowed to stand?"[57] This question is constantly repeated because the Bible, as we shall later see, places so much emphasis on the call to faith. This question presses all the more because Barth, impelled by his conception of the triumph of grace, uses such strong expressions to show how *impossible* unbelief is, and how *powerless* it is to frustrate *what God has from*

---

54. *Ibid.,* p. 738.
55. *Ibid.*
56. *Ibid.,* p. 739.
57. O. Weber, W. Kreck, and E. Wolf, *op. cit.,* p. 52.

*all eternity decided.*[58]　Kreck asks, "Does this not end in universal restoration, in the apokatastasis, after all, to which Barth does not commit himself?"[59]

＊　　＊　　＊

In coming to the conclusion of this analysis we cannot but be impressed by the unresolved tension between the triumph of decisive election and the rejection of the apokatastasis doctrine. Barth's pointing to the *freedom* of God *could not* remove this tension because such pointing can have meaning only with respect to a haughty human self-determination which takes liberties with the sovereign grace of God.　It cannot have reference to the exercise of God's sovereignty as such.　God's loving self-limitation (the decretum concretum) and the mercy of His eternal decision make a continuing tension between this conception and Barth's rejection of the apokatastasis unavoidable.　It meets us at the point where Barth's No is heard concerning the apokatastasis and his Yes concerning the absoluteness of the eternal decision as the joyful message *par excellence.*　Irrevocable and unassailable is the fact that in cross and resurrection Christ entered history.

Sinful man is *no longer* dangerous in the light of this fact.　"In the death of Jesus, God entered into danger, He exposed Himself freely to it in the death of Jesus in order to cleanse and free sinful man of his sin and to disqualify him as an enemy.　There can be no resistance by man in the face of the disarming which God has effected."　The history of God's faithfulness and of Israel's un-

---

58. In KD II/2, pp. 230-231, Barth writes these remarkable words: "They are not again able to subvert what God in this Jesus Christ has set upright on behalf of men and therefore also on their behalf.　They are not able to give back to the judgment and to the punishment that Jesus bore and bore away, or to the lordship of Satan which He emptied, or to the life of fallen man which He in His saving suffering outlived, the power which according to God's eternal counsel they gained only to lose again.　They cannot give back to these forces the power which God in His eternal counsel denied them and took away from them. They cannot give to the judgment which God willed and executed a purpose that goes contrary to the purpose of God.　They cannot give the lie to God's mercy in this judgment.　With all their contrariness they are unable to bring anything into being against the election of Jesus Christ — or against their own election — that would prove to have any final binding power: nothing that would separate from the love of God in Jesus Christ, nothing that would make of none effect the eternal counsel of God."

59. W. Kreck, *op. cit.,* p. 53. That Kreck, in spite of Barth's warning, nevertheless repeats this question — in addition to expressing much appreciation — underscores the urgency of the discussion surrounding Barth's doctrine of election.

faithfulness cannot be repeated.  "All apparent repetitions of this history are no more than unsubstantial shadows.  That Jesus is Conqueror cannot be undone."[60]

Triumph of election — and unbelief still?  This can only testify to that sin of man for whom Jesus Christ died vicariously.  But *this* joyful message does *not* prejudice the *open* situation of the gospel proclamation.  Barth refuses to permit the concrete significance of the proclamation to disappear behind the fact of the universal divine election.  On the contrary, he wishes to incorporate it *in* this fact.  For unbelief is powerless and is only the recurring witness to that guilt which makes grace necessary.  Therefore man is placed ever anew in the *open situation* of the proclamation concerning the triumph of election, the triumph of the mercy of God.[61]

---

60. KD II/2, p. 555.

61. Cf. Barth's *Die christliche Lehre nach dem Heidelb. Katech.*, 1948, p. 75, in connection with Question 52 of the Catechism. All depends here on the words, "His and my enemies." Barth says that *all men are His* (i. e., Christ's) enemies — also we! — but that we go to meet the Judge who has surrendered Himself for our sakes. "He is the Judge — there can be no question of a reconciliation of all — but the Judge whom we Christians might learn to know." Also here the tension appears. The criticism of the apokatastasis doctrine is definite, but the consistency of the criticism (in the whole of Barth's doctrine of election) is not clear. On p. 76 Barth declares that the seriousness of the judgment may not be weakened, but that we must hold that "Christ has *also* borne *it*." Cf. Barth's *La confession de foi de l'Eglise*, 1943, p. 94. On the basis of all available data we must agree with Brunner when he writes, "It is therefore certainly to be expected that with respect to this matter he (Barth) has not yet spoken his last word," E. Brunner, *Dogmatik*, I, p. 379.

# V

## THE TRIUMPH OF RECONCILIATION

T HE PREVIOUS chapters have already made clear that we must speak not only of a triumph of grace in creation and in election but also, and in intimate connection with them, of the triumph of grace in *reconciliation*. This triumph is not a *new* triumph in distinction from that of creation, it is that triumph which was prefigured in creation. In his K. D. IV/1, 1953, Barth discusses this aspect of the triumph of grace extensively. Although he does not introduce any new themes in this discussion, he does clearly treat the one central theme of his theology from a new aspect. In this part of his dogmatics we see the triumph as the reconciling action of God in the cross and resurrection of Jesus Christ.

\* \* \*

Barth's Christology never involves an antithesis between *Christo*-logical and *Theo*-logical considerations. Through the man Jesus Christ, God Himself is revealed as the divine subject in the work of Christ. This conception brings us to the heart of Barth's doctrine of reconciliation. When we speak of Barth's Christocentric dogmatics, this does not simply mean that Jesus Christ constitutes the "center" of his theology, but it means that the Christocentric emphasis points us directly to God *Himself* who *in Christ* confronts us. For Barth, the truth of the whole of dogmatics rests on this "God Himself." In countless variations we can hear this "God Himself" resounding. In the work of the *man* Jesus Christ we come in contact with a work which cannot be isolated from the *work of God*. Barth has for many years viewed the theological disjunction between Christology and Theology as an abstraction and as a fatal error in theological thinking, and he is unwearied in his opposition to it. As Jesus Christ is Himself the electing God, so His work on earth — in reconciliation — is God's *own* work.

\* \* \*

123

We can best approach the questions which Barth raises in this connection by taking our point of departure in Barth's conception that the work of reconciliation is not the expression of an abstractly understood divine *omnipotence*. God's power revealed in reconciliation is not a "potentia absoluta," the pure might of a majestic and all-powerful God. Such a conception of God's power severs it from the *true* God (Jahwe) and can never produce more than a metaphysics or a natural theology. We can speak of the *true* God only *in terms of Jesus Christ*. Long before Barth published his work on reconciliation he had taught that it is not possible to know the power of God in a single respect outside of Jesus Christ. It is out of the question to speak about the "being" of God apart from the revelation in Jesus Christ. When this is attempted a disjunction is created between the first and the second articles of the Apostles' creed. In this way we can arrive only at an abstract God-concept and we cannot see the true God, the Father of Jesus Christ.

This kind of theology is completely contradicted when Jesus Christ becomes the point of departure for our thinking.[1] Already in 1935, in discussing the first article of the creed, "I believe in God, the Father, the Almighty," Barth pointed out that we may not and cannot interpret this article in terms of our own conceptions of omnipotence and proceed from there to the discovery in the revelation that God is the (this) omnipotent One, who is *also* the Father. Quite the opposite is true: God is revealed to us in Christ as the Father. From this we learn that His power is not an "ability-to-do-anything," but a power which is revealed in His work of reconciliation. In *Christ* it is revealed *who God is*: the Lord of life and death. *This* power has nothing to do with the "omnipotence" of an infinite potentiality or power-possibility, of which no one can form a conception,[2] but it is the *true* power which is revealed in Jesus Christ. Only in this way can the idea of "power" receive content. We can understand the first article of the creed only in the light of the second. The omnipotence of God is "the omnipotence of the decision which has been pro-

---

1. K. Barth, *De Apostolische Geloofsbelijdenis*, 1935, p. 37.
2. *Ibid.*, p. 38.

nounced over us in the fulness of God's judicial right, and must be acknowledged as such by us."[3]

This conception of the true power of God constitutes one of the most essential elements in Barth's theology. It belongs not only to the doctrine of the attributes of God but — in connection with these — it has far-reaching significance for the doctrine of reconciliation. Here if anywhere we must remember that all of God's works can be seen only in the light of His revelation in Jesus Christ. We may not operate with "general," apriori ideas about God, as though we knew something about Him apart from His revelation. We must think about God exclusively in terms of Jesus Christ. It is by way of this emphasis that Barth develops his doctrine of reconciliation. A serious study of it discloses the extent of the consequences of this conception of the power of God for the doctrine of reconciliation.

\*　　\*　　\*

We must note, in the first place, that Barth no longer leaves room for a God-concept whereby it is impossible to conceive of humiliation and self-abnegation on the part of God. Such ideas are *not* applicable to a God who is "infinite potentiality." Every conception of humiliation and self-surrender is excluded by *such* a power, for it would contradict the very idea of the majesty of God.

It is precisely for this reason that every view of God which has been constructed on basis of natural theology, and therefore outside of Jesus Christ, had to lead and has, in fact, constantly led, to a misunderstanding of Scripture. It was not possible to achieve a right understanding of the being and the reality of God because the thinking of natural theology could not free itself from the schematism of what it already knew about God. The one thing needful here is a radical evolution in theological thinking! We must permit ourselves to be corrected and submit to being instructed anew.

We can come to know God only when we cease assuming that we know *beforehand* that, with respect to God, this or that cannot be, is not possible for Him, because it is not to be squared with His infinite potentiality.

When we see God only in Jesus Christ, we come to walk in a new path and wholly new perspectives for the doctrine of recon-

3. *Ibid.*

ciliation appear.    Then it becomes "possible" to see the "God
Himself" in the reconciling work of God in Christ.   It no longer
belongs to the impossibilities of thought to see "God Himself" in
Christ in the most ultimate humiliation, powerlessness and self-
surrender which can — of course! — not be predicated of a God
of infinite potentiality.   Those who think that a self-humiliation
on the part of God is unthinkable and impossible meet the protest of Barth that their exclusion of this possibility flows forth
from erroneous presuppositions about God.   *In and through
Christ* we must learn *who God is and what the really-divine is and
can do.*   In Him we see that God's revelation is precisely *not* concerned about an abstract omnipotence, a potentia absoluta, which
infinitely transcends (as the esse absolutum) any and all humiliation and self-abnegation.   It is God's reconciling activity which
teaches us who the true God, revealed *in* reconciliation, really is.
Not the self-willed logic of natural theology but Jesus Christ
alone must determine our thinking about God.   In *Him* we are
able to discern the true features of this God and discover that He
does not terrify us by His distant and infinite majesty and pure
absoluteness, but that He is near to us in the "powerlessness" of
humiliation and cross.

In order to grasp Barth's intent here, we must rightly under-
sta    this word "powerlessness."   It is not an idea of *inferiority*
that we meet in this conception, whereby we think of human
powerlessness and a worldly antithesis between power and powerlessness.    It is the wonderful divine powerlessness, the powerlessness of the cross, that Barth envisions here.[4]

In this powerlessness the reality of reconciliation lies hidden:
the divine mystery through which the world is saved.    This
"powerlessness" does not stand in contrast with the triumph of
grace but is the channel through which it becomes fully manifest.   The weakness of God is stronger than men, and this weak-

---

4. It is the powerlessness of God, "whose omnipotence goes so far that he is
also able to be weak,    ; to be powerless, as also a man can be weak and powerless," IV/1, p. 142.   It is precisely this that "proves" His *true deity*.   "That is
the nature and being of the true God as He has appeared actively on the scene in
the man Jesus Christ," *ibid.*, p. 142.   God is to be distinguished from the *false* gods
in that "they are not able to do this, that they have not done it, that their alleged
honor, glory, eternity, and omnipotence, does not include but excludes this,"
*ibid.*, p. 142.   They are lords who do not want to be or who cannot be servants
and "whose being is not a genuine being," *ibid.*, p. 42.   Cf. also p. 144.

ness is not a subjective human idea, namely, that it *seems* weak to us, but it is *real* weakness, the essence of God's saving act. In this antithesis to all natural theology, the power of God is identical with *this* powerlessness of the cross. It is the secret of Him who is able to do what is impossible for men to achieve, and in which the triumph of grace is realized. It is the triumph over chaos and the demons which through this powerlessness of the cross are once and for all unmasked as shadow-powers and made ineffective.

*      *      *

From these depths the "God Himself" of Barth's doctrine of reconciliation reverberates. Reconciliation is not the deed of a man, namely, Jesus of Nazareth; it is the deed of *God* in Him. "God Himself wanted to be also the rejected and therefore the perishing man."[5] In the Old Testament the wrath of God is still revealed against *men,* but in the New Testament this antithesis has disappeared. Here God Himself "took the place of those ancient ones and allowed the bitterness of their suffering to become His portion." He "surrendered Himself to this fearful alienation."[6]

In this self-surrender lies the real mystery of Christ's *deity.*[7] What Christ's deity means must not be concluded to from the conception of an infinite divine being, but "must be learned from the Christ event itself."[8] In the incarnation, humiliation and suffering of Christ we see an action of God, "a self-surrender of God to man's contradiction of Him."[9] God Himself places Himself under judgment and bears the curse of death.[10] Reconcilia-

---

5. *Ibid.,* p. 91.
6. *Ibid.*
7. *Ibid.,* p. 193.

8. *Ibid.*
9. *Ibid.,* p. 202

10. Barth presents this thought in a great variety of ways: he speaks of the "self-surrender of God," IV/1, p. 77, of "God's endangering Himself of which John 3:16 speaks," p. 80, of the "humiliation of God," p. 147. By surrendering Christ He put His own existence at stake, p. 76, and gave Himself into the hands of the enemy. Cf. God's "humbling of Himself," pp. 324 and 326. God surrendered *Himself* "in His Son" in order "to suffer the judgment that we men deserved," p. 324. Further: "the fullness of humiliation of God in the crucifixion of Jesus," *Gotteserkenntnis und Gottesdienst,* p. 105, the "self-sacrifice of God," *ibid.,* p. 107, the "boundlessness of the self-sacrifice of God," *ibid.,* p. 107, the "boundlessness of the self-sacrifice," p. 105. In Jesus Christ, "God humbles Himself in order to exalt us. In Him God burdens Himself with the whole of our nature: with the whole of human weakness, shame, unrighteousness and vulgarity," *Die Wirklichkeit des neuen Menschen,* p. 16. He enters "into our damnation and lostness," *ibid.,* p. 16.

tion is indeed the action, substitution, and suffering of the *man* Jesus Christ. It is "an act of God which coincides with the action and suffering of a man, but in such a way that this human action and suffering is to be understood as the action and suffering of God Himself."[11] In Christ the eternal God has given Himself, "and as man has taken this, this human passion," upon Himself.[12]

The question arises whether this confession of the self-humiliation of God, of the "passion of God," does not necessarily involve the presence of an *antithesis,* an inner conflict, in God Himself.[13] It is at this point that the deepest intention of Barth's doctrine of the incarnation becomes evident. He wishes to take this question seriously, and says emphatically that here the praise of God threatens, for the sake of His incarnation, to turn into the grossest *blasphemy.* Against this threatening danger (of God against God) it *must* be maintained that when God surrenders Himself to curse and judgment He *in no sense enters into contradiction with Himself.* His self-surrender does not mean that He, as it were, gives Himself up and loses Himself. "What would His way into alienation help us if by so doing He lost Himself?"[14] In this direction not one step may be taken.[15]

There is only *one* way in which we can understand the mystery of God's being God and of the incarnation of God. There is no paradox or antinomy in God, no schism, "no unfaithfulness to Himself," no shadow of turning. The supposition that incarnation and self-humiliation involve a conflict with the actual being of God rests upon a *human* God-concept according to which self-surrender, humiliation and suffering contradict the "being" of

11. KD IV/1, p. 270.

12. *Ibid.,* p. 271.

13. *Ibid.,* p. 202.

14. *Ibid.*

15. Hence Barth's rejection of the kenosis doctrine of the 19th century: KD II/1, p. 184ff., and IV/1, p. 196ff. This doctrine has, according to Barth, made the biblical teaching that "*God* was in Christ" problematical, IV/1, p. 99. The incarnation does not mean "the self-limitation and the de-deification (Entgöttlichung) of God and of His being." It is precisely *in* the humiliation that Christ is true God, p. 199.

God. Precisely therein lies the great error of this natural thinking about God.

"We must learn who God is and what is divine at that point at which God has revealed Himself, His nature and His being."[16] When God reveals Himself in Christ in this way, i.e., in humiliation and suffering, *we* may not say that this is all really in conflict with Christ's divine nature. We discern exactly in that the *essence* of His deity.

God's self-humiliation and self-abasement correct our ideas about God, and certainly our ideas of what is possible with God and what can and cannot be reconciled with His divine being. There is, therefore, no question of a "contradiction," but much rather of the *deepest revelation* of His being and of His deity.[17] Christ's deity is, consequently, not lost in His humiliation.[18] His self-abasement is not to be limited to His *human* nature. His deity reveals and maintains itself *exactly in* His humiliation. Through it Christ shows what He can do, and through this deed of God's love in Christ we see the very thing which coincides in the most absolute way with His divine nature.[19]

In the incarnation God's omnipotence is not surrendered but, as in the cross, it is manifested. "This is the perfection of His divine omnipotence, that (in distinction from all abstract omnipotence) it can assume the form of weakness and powerlessness, and triumph as omnipotence also and even especially in this form."[20] This is a quotation in which Barth himself has formulated his conception of the triumph of reconciliation most clearly. All that can and must be said about God receives its content from, and must be understood in the light of, this true nature of His deity.[21] In the humiliation His glory is revealed,[22] a glory which

---

16. KD IV/1, p. 203.
17. *Ibid.,* p. 204.
18. *Ibid.,* p. 205.
19. *Ibid.,* p. 204.
20. *Ibid.,* p. 205. Cf. p. 324 where Barth speaks of the *humility* by means of which God wished to make Himself our equal, and of its being "the evidence of His divine majesty."
21. "All that can be predicated of the true God must be filled and interpreted in terms of this first aspect, namely, the act of His self-abasement," IV/1, p. 142.
22. KD IV/1, p. 143. Over against the idea of the laying aside of deity, cf.: that God "even in such humiliation is in the highest sense God, that in this death He was in the truest sense alive, that in the passion of this man as His eternal Son He authenticated and revealed His true deity," p. 271.

is not a worldly glory, but *His* glory. Reconciliation, therefore, does not reveal an "intra-divine paradox" but "the true, majestic nature of God."[23]

When Paul in Philippians 2, in connection with Christ's humbling of Himself, exhorts the Church that this mind should also be in her, he does not speak about something which is really in conflict with God's majesty but he points to the background of ethics which is God's true being. That is to say, God is God in *this* way, in *this* self-abasement. This humility of God — revealed in Christ — is *the* basis of truly Christian ethics.[24]

*          *          *

Barth goes a step further than this, however.[25] Since the self-abasement of the man Jesus Christ was not simply the self-abasement of a *man* but one that was "grounded in the being of God,"[26] we must further say that in this humiliation there was revealed an act of *obedience,* and that all that the man Jesus Christ does is *at the same time* God's own work. "This character of self-renunciation and self-humiliation cannot, as an act of obedience, be foreign to God Himself."[27] We must rather recognize that it belongs to the *inner side* of the mystery of the divine nature that "He is capable of and is free for the rendering of obedience."[28] This does not involve a dialectic of God's divine nature, but a "self-humiliation of God" which is not in conflict with God's nature[29] and which constitutes the presupposition of the real reconciliation. The self-abasement of Jesus has its deep ground in the divine nature of Jesus Christ and therefore *in God Himself.*

Barth is aware that he raises profound questions here. He asks whether we do not, in these questions, touch upon the deepest knowledge of the mystery of God.[30] "We cannot conceal the fact that it is a harsh and even risky matter to speak of an obedience

---

23. KD IV/1, p. 205.
24. *Ibid.,* p. 210.
25. *Ibid.,* p. 211.
26. *Ibid.*
27. *Ibid.*
28. *Ibid.*
29. *Ibid.,* p. 213.
30. *Ibid.*

residing in God Himself."[31]  The reason for this is immediately evident: obedience assumes an "above" and a "below" and seems, therefore, to endanger the unity of the divine being.  Can the one God *command* and also Himself be *obedient*?  Can command and obedience co-exist within the reality of the one true God? Can we perhaps resolve this problem by saying that the question at issue in this obedience is one of a certain economy, a sort of subjection, which does not involve his *essential* being?  Barth rejects this possibility and in so doing rejects anew the doctrine of modalism.[32]  God's own presence in Christ is at stake.  He is *Himself* the subject of reconciliation.  His presence as Reconciler coincides with the existence of the Himself-humiliating Christ.[33] This obedience is the most essential element in His deity.[34]  Jesus Christ is not an appearance-form of the true God, He is the true God Himself.  Therefore we must speak of the obedience of God *without any hesitation*.  "The offense that in God there is an above and a below, a prius and a posterius, may not only not be denied but must be affirmed and understood as belonging to the very essence of God."[35]  It belongs to God's most inner being "that there be in Him also this happening: obedience."[36]

As obeyed, He is the one; as obeying, He is the other.  There is, according to His will, the "lower" of man and cosmos, but this is not the original subordination.  The really original form of this "over against each other" of higher and lower is already present in God.[37]  In this a priori and a posteriori in God no question of inferiority or gradation is involved.[38]  There is not a lack in the one God, but a *peculiar being* which has also this dimension.[39]

---

31. *Ibid.,* p. 211.
32. *Ibid.,* p. 215. In this modalism the being of Christ is seen as "the mode of the appearance, of the revelation, of the operation" of God. The *real* being of God does *not* then belong to Christ. In this manner it was not possible to maintain that God Himself was the subject of reconciliation *in* the self-humiliation of Christ. Cf. J. A. Heyns, *Die Grondstruktuur van die Modalistische Triniteits-beskouwing,* 1953, p. 143 ff.
33. KD IV/1, p. 217.
34. *Ibid.,* p. 218.
35. *Ibid.,* p. 219.
36. *Ibid.*
37. *Ibid.,* p. 220.
38. *Ibid.,* p. 221.
39. *Ibid.*

In confessing Jesus Christ as true God, it is not possible to stop short of the "in every way amazing declaration" of a divine obedience.[40] The One reigning in the highest heavens is at the same time the one obeying in all humility.

The idea of the obedience of *God* affirms anew that the central thrust of Barth's theology is the triumph of *grace*. It is in this self-humiliation of God-Himself in Christ that the triumph is revealed. Here it becomes evident *how* He triumphs. He triumphs not by the majestic, irresistible beating down of all that opposes itself against Him, but by the majestic, irresistible power of His *love* and *grace*. This triumph is not set upon God's own exaltation and glory; it envisions grace for *men*. In abasement and obedience His power becomes manifest. All the questions surrounding the divine reconciliation find their focus and crystallization at this point. It is in *this* way that the Lord of Hosts triumphs. It is another struggle and another triumph than we would expect. It is the struggle and the triumph of the weakness and the powerlessness of the cross. We might say that the sharp accentuation of the "God-Himself" as the true subject of reconciliation makes it possible to speak of a new form of a "theologia crucis," a theology of the cross. The power of God, the *omnipotence* of God, is revealed in the cross.[41] Here God becomes known *in* His deity, in His self-abasement and obedience. Hereby the deepest foundation is laid for an *ethics* of the cross.

\*       \*       \*

This central and basic conception leads Barth to effect an incisive change in the traditional conception of the relationship between the humiliation and exaltation of Jesus Christ. He is fully aware of this and speaks of "far-reaching changes"[42] and of "the greatest offense which, from the viewpoint of the older dogmatics,

---

40. *Ibid.*
41. It is important to note that Barth, precisely in connection with the "God Himself" in reconciliation, raises anew the question of the "natus ex virgine," KD IV/1, pp. 226, 227. The sonship of Christ does not depend on the virgin birth (Barth rejects again the idea of *hieros gamos*). Only in this way is it possible to maintain the "God Himself" in the work of reconciliation. In the work of Jesus Christ the Son of God we must see "God in the mode of being of the Son in relation to God in the mode of being of the Father," p. 228.
42. KD IV/1, p. 145.

will probably be taken at this view."[43]   Barth's conception of Christ's humiliation and exaltation does not involve two successive "states" of Christ but rather two *sides* or *aspects* or *forms* of what takes place in Jesus Christ in His effecting of reconciliation between God and man.[44]   Humiliation and glorification place us before the *double* activity of Christ in His *one* work.   This work can not be distributed "over two different steps or times of His existence," for His whole existence consists precisely in this double form.[45]

Christ was not *first* humiliated and *thereafter* exalted.   He is the *one* Jesus Christ "from whom nothing was taken in His humiliation and to whom nothing was added in His exaltation."   It is evident that in this way Barth *draws the consequences of his view that the being and nature of God are revealed in the humiliation.*   From this he concludes to the conception that the *glory* of God is to be found precisely in the humiliation.[46]   Because Jesus Christ is the self-humiliating God He *is* at the same time the exalted man.   For this reason humiliation and exaltation may not be temporally separated from each other but must be seen together in the one deed of reconciliation.

The modification effected in the doctrine of the two states of Christ has its inevitable consequences for the doctrine of the two natures of Christ.   These two are inseparably related.   In working out this relationship, Barth wishes to abide by the formulation of Chalcedon: *vere Deus, vere homo.*[47]   His concern, however, is not to understand this "vere Deus" abstractly.   *In* the humiliation the *real* deity is made manifest.   It is not true that we can first know God's deity (His omnipotence and majesty) and then later come to an understanding of His humiliation.   On the contrary, it is exactly *here,* in His humiliation, that the *essence* of His deity appears: *vere Deus.*   In this humiliation He is also the *vere* homo who is *exalted.*   In this bi-unity the act of reconciliation consists: the humiliation of God and the exaltation of man.   According to His deity Jesus Christ did not need and

43. *Ibid.,* p. 146.
44. *Ibid.,* p. 145.
45. *Ibid.,* p. 146.
46. *Ibid.,* p. 143.
47. *Ibid.,* p. 146.

could not receive glorification.[48] He was exalted as *man,* as the servant who is the Lord. This is an exaltation which did not take place in the resurrection but which was "only made manifest" by it.[49]

Barth's surmise that especially *this* modification of the traditional doctrine will cause the most offense arises from his realization of what the import of the modification is. His view replaces the idea of *succession* in the humiliation-exaltation relationship by the idea of *contemporaneity.* This means that the doctrine of the two natures and the doctrine of the two states of Christ are, as it were, intertwined into a synthetic relationship between the humiliation of God *and the exaltation of man.*[50] In the concreteness of *this* action of God, which is identical with the action of the man Jesus Christ, reconciliation *takes place.* The triumph of reconciliation is revealed not only in the resurrection but also by way of the cross. The resurrection is the absolute revelation of this triumph which was already a reality *in* the humiliation. When we see the Judge as the "one who was judged in our stead,"[51] the triumph is present *in* suffering. "He conquers in that He suffers."[52] The triumph consists in this great change: the accuser becomes the accused. "In that designation and treatment of the holy God, He becomes as the godless one."[53] This was the *strange* happening which elicited a response even from the cosmos in the signs which it registered on Good Friday. The cross was not the end of the true glory of God, but its *revelation,* for "He saw His glory as God's Sent One triumph in what would happen to Him here, in what He would have to suffer here."[54] Seen from the viewpoint of God's *being,* the triumph lies in this

---

48. *Ibid.,* p. 147.
49. *Ibid.,* p. 148.
50. According to the order in which Barth treats the doctrine of reconciliation he will not discuss until IV/2 the subject, "Jesus Christ, the Servant as Lord," after which will follow "Jesus Christ as Guarantee." In IV/1 Barth finishes the discussion of "Jesus Christ, the Lord as Servant," p. 17ff. The real change which Barth effects in the older dogmatic treatment, via the interweaving of deity and humanity, of humiliation and exaltation, IV/1, p. 148, should therefore become evident especially in IV/2, just as the "God Himself" *in* the humiliation appeared clearly in IV/1.
51. KD IV/1, pp. 231-311.
52. *Ibid.,* p. 262.
53. *Ibid.*
54. *Ibid.,* p. 263.

transition from action to passion.[55] This suffering of God effects the elevation of man, and in this marvelous happening the entire theodicy[56] question pales into insignificance, for man is here reconciled to God.

*   *   *

In order to understand the triumph of grace correctly, it is necessary to note that for Barth this triumph presupposes the reality and actuality of judgment. Grace did not *replace* judgment. We cannot say that anymore than we can say that Christ's substitutionary suffering of the judgment eliminates our suffering of it. That God inflicts His judgment on His Son "does not mean that it does not strike us. It means, rather, that it is executed upon us in its most ultimate seriousness and in its fullest reality. It is in reality and ultimately inflicted upon us because He took our place."[57] Also, that Christ died for us does not mean that we no longer have to die but that we ourselves have died *in and with* Christ.[58]

At this point we meet a new aspect of Barth's doctrine of reconciliation. The substitutionary work of Christ is not a work that takes place outside of us and which is *subsequently applied* to us. We ourselves die in and with Christ. "His dying implied, and to that extent was, our own dying."[59] His death was the death of all, independent of their attitude to this event. The fact that — with Christ — they died, did not find its cause in their belief in the reconciliation. Golgotha was not a *possibility* which is realized and receives its content from faith.[60] The judgment was not cancelled but was executed in full and deepest earnestness. *Man* — all men — are struck by it and through the death of Christ "are made to disappear."[61] "Man could not be helped other than through his annihilation." If the faithfulness and love of God were to achieve their purpose, it would have to be done via the fire of the wrath of God to man in *the* catastrophe that comes over

55. *Ibid.*, pp. 262, 263.
56. *Ibid.*, p. 271.
57. *Ibid.*, p. 324.
58. *Ibid.*
59. *Ibid.*, p. 325.
60. *Ibid.*
61. *Ibid.*, p. 326.

man.[62] "Man who has become an enemy must be totally wiped out of existence and brought to nothing."[63] Therefore the death of Christ and the reconciliation that took place in it can be called the end of the world[64] and of the sinner.[65] This all happens to us in Christ: "Judgment, death, end — have in His person come over us with Him, once and for all."[66]

The triumph of reconciliation, therefore, in no sense means that the judgment has been removed from us. It takes place in its execution upon Christ and, in Him, upon us all. The fact that the pronouncing of this catastrophic judgment over us does not — notwithstanding its radical character — mean the absolute end and the last word reveals the miracle and the mystery of God's grace. Through this mystery, this miracle, a *jenseits,* a beyond, becomes visible on the other side of this catastrophe, this death, this judgment, this end.[67] This "jenseits" is a new act of God which is revealed to us in the resurrection of Jesus Christ from the dead. This is an exclusively divine deed. At the cross men play a role, but *here* God acts without human co-operation or mediation. The resurrection of Christ is a deed which stands in a class with creation.[68] It is a deed of God's *grace.* Jesus Himself is not the subject of the resurrection event — "the New

---

62. *Ibid.,* p. 326. Cf. also p. 100: the Creator "cannot use this man (of sin), cannot further tolerate him. He can only put him away. — And that is what He has done: not simply in the form of a protest whereby He contradicts him, through which the situation between God and man is illumined but not removed, *but through the form of his (man's) extinction,"* (my italics). Barth had expressed this thought earlier in his *Die christliche Lehre nach dem Heidelb. Katech.,* 1948, p. 63: the wrath of God "breaks out, and burns and consumes sinful man."
63. KD IV/1, p. 326.
64. *Ibid.*
65. *Ibid.,* p. 322: "What will he be when he is no longer able to be a sinner, since in Jesus Christ God has cast his being as a sinner behind Him and has made it pure past?"
66. *Ibid.,* p. 327. In no sense, therefore, does Barth mean our *co-operation* in the work of reconciliation. Elsewhere he speaks of Christ's vicarious work in this way, that the New Testament words *anti, huper,* and *peri,* speak of "a place which is really ours and which we should really be occupying. But we are far removed from this our place and in it now stands another," IV/1, p. 253. Cf.: paying "without their co-operation" what they could not pay themselves, p. 253; "consistent exchange," p. 253, "His substitutionary action on our behalf," p. 253. Cf. also p. 278. In this context Barth then expresses the idea that Christ in His work has achieved "the delivering up of sinful man and of sin itself to extinction," IV/1, p. 279.
67. KD IV/1, p. 327.
68. *Ibid.,* p. 331.

Testament does not say it in that way."[69]  He *was raised* from the dead. That He rises and reveals Himself is not the same as His *being raised*.[70]  At least, the being raised as an "experience" that comes over Jesus is *primary*,[71] and His rising and revealing Himself can only follow upon this primary happening. He is exalted through a deed of God and He Himself is "purely object and receiver of the grace of God."[72]

It is in this way that Christ was raised for our *justification*. Justification may not be seen exclusively as an action that is related to the cross, of whose meaning the resurrection is only a sign. The resurrection is, rather, a *new* deed of God, "and therefore not merely the noetic reverse side of justification."[73]  It was possible that the meaning of the cross would be *exhausted* by the cross. In the cross the chaos was allowed — according to the will of God — to triumph over Christ.[74]  Could this not have been the end? Is Jesus' expression of forsakenness by God not a plain indication of "the nearness of this fearful possibility?"[75]  Could the catastrophe of dying *with* Christ not be the end, the revelation of the (effective) repentance of God for having made man?[76]

Barth answers these questions by saying that God could have done it in this way, but that in actuality He *did not* do it in this

---

69. *Ibid.*, pp. 334 and 393. One must "use circumspectly" the idea that "Jesus Christ as the Son of God was, together with the Father, also Himself the subject [cause] of His resurrection. The New Testament does not say it that way." Jesus did have the power to take life again, John 10:18, but Barth here points to John 5:26. Being awakened from the dead and rising from the dead are not "simple interchangeable concepts," p. 334. If this distinction is not made, Barth feels, the difficulty arises that we speak of powerlessness which Christ by His own initiative transcended, a view which in his judgment is a docetic conception of death. Cf. also IV/1, p. 335. It must not be supposed that Barth thinks here only of the resurrection of the *man* Jesus Christ, for he writes: "No, not only as man, but as the Son of God Jesus Christ is here wholly receiver, acceptor." He connects this thought with the earlier discussed "apparently harsh idea" of the *obedience* of God in God Himself. This we see here in the *divine* deed of raising Christ from the dead.

70. KD IV/1, p. 334.

71. *Ibid.*

72. *Ibid.*, p. 335.

73. *Ibid.*, p. 335. Cf. Barth's polemic against Bultmann in various places and — without mentioning Bultmann — IV/1, p. 376 (about "Easter-faith"). That the resurrection is a new deed of God does not mean the insufficiency of Golgotha ("It is finished"). Cf. IV/1, p. 337.

74. *Ibid.*, p. 335.

75. *Ibid.*

76. *Ibid.*, p. 338.

way. He did not vindicate His own right in this way, but *in grace* He raised Christ from the dead and thereby manifested in the highest sense His faithfulness and His love.[77] Therefore the resurrection is the justification of Christ and, in His Person, the justification of "the whole of sinful mankind concerning whose death this event pronounced its decisive word."[78] It is the definite triumph of His unmerited grace.[79]

*     *     *

In the resurrection of Christ as the exclusive act of God's grace, our whole situation and that of the entire world has been changed. In Christ there takes place "a once for all event of the old world of the old man."[80] "The *world, every* man, exists in this change."[81] Jesus Christ *lives* as the crucified One and by virtue of the act of God. He is "pure revelation of God."[82] God's Yes is here spoken in the axiomatic certainty of His judicially binding pronouncement.[83] It is spoken with divine sovereignty, and after it is spoken no problems remain.

The new situation exists independently of the proclamation or non-proclamation of it. It also exists independently of belief or non-belief in it. The Kingdom of God "has its truth in itself, not in that which in pursuance of it happens or does not happen on the earth."[84]

When a king confers a distinction, inability to accept it does not prejudice the integrity of the honor conferred.[85] So it is with respect to the proclamation of grace, although the normal course of things for the New Testament man is that grace is not only

---

77. *Ibid.*, p. 339.
78. *Ibid.*, p. 341.
79. This *grace*-character of Christ's resurrection is essential to Barth's Christology. It is clear that this thought is most closely related to other views of Barth about the punitive suffering of Christ. Barth treats this briefly in KD IV/1, p. 279. Concerning the concept "punishment" Barth writes, with reference to Isaiah 53, "It is therefore not to be wholly rejected." But it may not become a major concept as it did for Anselm, and certainly not in the sense of satisfaction with respect to the wrath of God. "This last idea is wholly foreign to the New Testament." Note the hesitation in the whole of this paragraph, p. 279.
80. KD IV/1, p. 343.
81. *Ibid.*, p. 344.
82. *Ibid.*, p. 394.
83. *Ibid.*
84. *Ibid.*, p. 344.
85. *Ibid.*
89. *Ibid.*, p. 179.

offered to him but that he also accepts it. The *situation* has been changed. It is now an *objective* factuality manifested in the faithfulness of God to Himself and to His will as Creator. The once for all event that took place in the happenings between the Jordan (baptism) and Golgotha has become "an event that took place for all."[86] That which happened is not simply a past event, but "a present, indeed, an event, that fills and determines all the present."[87]

Our concern is not only with Christ who was crucified in the past, but with the Crucified One and the Risen One who now lives. Lessing's problem of the "accidental" historical fact of the crucifixion falls away here because "the moment of this 'accidental fact of history' is the moment of all moments."[88] *The* answer to Lessing's criticism is the intercession of Christ *now.* According to Hebrews, the heavenly representation has no earthly corresponding to it in which the real mystery would then come to manifestation in our time.[89] Christ's once for all history was *God's* history with men. Therefore His act of reconciliation is "our present reconciliation."[90] Here men are turned to God.[91] Not everyone hears it, not everyone believes it, but the change affects all even though it is believed and acknowledged only in and by the Church.[92]

Therefore the Church is in the world to witness to this changed situation which effects all and is reality for all.[93] The catastrophe — the cross — has taken place, and with it the end of the world and the end of the sinner *have come.* We can think now only in terms of the living Lord, in terms of the *jenseits* of sin and death,

---

86. *Ibid.,* p. 345.
87. This does not mean for Barth that the once for all event "happens" again and again. We may not speak of a continuation or a re-presentation or a realization of this event, IV/1, p. 325. "It requires no elaboration, no re-presentation. To place elaborating or realizing events next to this event, or to endeavor to make it a contemporary event, constitutes an offense to its honor and perfection," p. 326. We are far removed here from the representation idea of Casel and others, *and* from the conception of Bultmann.
88. KD IV/1, p. 347.
89. Cf. my *De Sacramenten,* 1954, chapter II.
90. KD IV/1, p. 347.
91. *Ibid.,* p. 349.
92. *Ibid.*
93. "It concerns them all, however; it affects them all, it has been said for them all and to them all; it has also been said loudly and distinctly enough for them all," IV/1, p. 349.

in terms of the grace of God. His resurrection is not, it is true, the ultimate parousia. It is not the second parousia but the first (Easter).[94]

In this radically changed and therefore triumphant situation the Church looks forward to the definite coming of her Lord. This time is, for all its tentativeness, "a time of joy."[95]

The situation is not *half* changed, the thing that has been done is not *partial*.[96] Only, the appearance, the form, in which the new situation is already *now* joyful reality, has not yet been consummated.

*     *     *

Perhaps some will be surprised that, after his extensive exposition of the triumph of grace in the raising of Christ from the dead, Barth now enters upon a discussion of justification by faith.[97] In the nature of the case, the subject does not involve a wholly *new* matter. But we do ask — after the discussion of Christ's being raised from the dead — how the doctrine of justification can be introduced by a section bearing the title, "The Problem of the Doctrine of Justification."[98] The more do we ask this question because the word "unproblematic" still echoes in our ears.[99] It is true that between the discussions on the resurrection of Christ and on justification there is a section on "The Pride and Fall of Man."[100] The reference to the triumph of grace, however, is precisely to *sin*. In fact, is not every problem, one is inclined to ask, resolved finally and for good by the reality of the death of the sinner and the resurrection of Christ? How is it possible that *after* "the judgment of the Father" there can still be a *problem* of the doctrine of justification, even though

---

94. The terms, first and second parousia, are found in IV/1, p. 368.
95. *Ibid.*, p. 361.
96. *Ibid.*, p. 361. The eschatological perspective is not "the minus-sign of a troubled 'not yet'" but the "plus-sign" of the "already," IV/1, p. 361. At this point it is well to be reminded of the criticism of Oscar Cullmann of the so-called consistent eschatology and of the eschatology which centers attention on the idea of waiting for the imminent event ("Naherwartung"). Cf. my *Het Werk van Christus*, 1953, chapter X. With an eye to a number of New Testament passages (e.g. I Cor. 15, Rom. 8, the Gospel of John, passim) Barth writes: "What is really the defect, the limitation, of His present action and revelation? What is still lacking, one is inclined to ask in the reading of such passages," IV/1, p. 361.
97. KD IV/1, pp. 573 - 717.
98. *Ibid.*, p. 573 ff.
99. "Without any problems," *ibid.*, p. 394.
100. *Ibid.*, pp. 395 - 572.

the problem refers not to justification but to the *doctrine* of justification?

Barth's answer to these questions is plain. It is most intimately related to the inserted section about the sin of man. In the light of reconciliation *sin* is exposed. The self-abasement of God fully reveals the *pride* of man.[1] Precisely *here* men are revealed as "those who choose the chaos and have by so doing succumbed to it."[2] The *judgment* became manifest, and when we think of grace we may never forget this. It is this circumstance that creates the *problem* of the doctrine of justification.

The judgment is a real judgment, the wrath is a real wrath, the rejection, and the illumination is a real illumination and grace is real grace.[3] Man exists in the transition from rejection to election. He has God's Yes before him, "but he does not have God's Yes before Him without having God's No behind him."[4] The purpose of the doctrine of justification is to understand God's Yes in a positive sense, "to inquire into it and to understand it." The central question here is, *whether* and *how* man, in his justification, *really* receives a *right* which is *valid* before God; whether *that* man who *as a sinner* stands notoriously guilty before God, the "homo peccator," receives such right.[5]

How can man, when he does not cease to be a sinner, be the "homo justus" before the tribunal of God?

*Simul peccator et justus?* At once sinnner and just? How is God's justifying judgment possible when there is no contradiction in God, no arbitrariness, no disorder, no paradox or darkness?[6] In how far and why is man's justification *not* just a letting bygones be bygones? Why is man's justification *not* in conflict with God's veracity, why is it "not a nominalistic 'as if'?"[7]

This question touches the foundation of the Church, it is concerned with the certainty of faith. The problem is not whether we must take the wholly new situation with less than full seriousness and begin to doubt its full validity. The question must be faced, however, how the possibility of reconciliation is to be con-

---

1. *Ibid.,* p. 574
2. *Ibid.*
3. *Ibid.,* p. 575.
4. *Ibid.,* p. 576.
5. *Ibid.*
6. *Ibid.*
7. *Ibid.,* p. 577.

ceived. Reconciliation is a reality, a divine reality, but how can
we speak of a "genuine justification?"[8]  How are we to understand that there is not only a right of God, but also a right of
man? In which sense is justification more than a hypothesis?

Barth raises this problem with great emphasis. He refers to
"this unusually great difficulty of the doctrine of justification."[9]
The reason for this is his recognition of the decisiveness of the
change which here takes place in man's situation.[10] How is this
possible: peace between God and man "through grace but in a
judicial way?"[11]

In order to understand this we must — first of all — see God's
right over against the guilt of man.[12] In no way may God's right
be prejudiced in our thinking. He knows no change or shadow
that is cast by turning, in Him there is no arbitrariness, no "exlex."[13] Therefore this right of God is in no sense annihilated or
darkened in justification.[14] On the contrary, it is upheld and revealed. This exercise of His right, however, does not exclude the
exercise of His grace. It is rather so, that in the breaking forth
of the wrath of the judgment "grace stands waiting at the end of
the process."[15] "The divine Yes deeply underlies the No." Even
*in* the judgment God does not withdraw His hand from man and
therein it appears that *in* the crisis of judgment "God is merciful
to man also in this form of judgment that overwhelms him and
his unrighteousness."[16]

---

8. *Ibid.*
9. *Ibid.*, p. 580. Cf. "The sweet fruit is indeed found here in an extra-ordinarily
hard and bitter peel," p. 578. The doctrine of justification is the "seat of the
crisis," p. 581. The issue is that of "the problem of the supposition, ,the possibility,
of a truly positive communion of God with men, of peace of man with God," p.
589.
10. KD IV/1, p. 590.
11. KD IV/1, p. 580. It is clear that in all these questions we come substantially
in contact with the background of the debate about the "analytical" and the
"synthetic" doctrine of justification. In its analytic form the doctrine teaches
that God's justifying judgment can be a true judgment only when man has *first*
(through gratia interna) *been made* just. In this way, for instance, Karl Holl
interpreted Luther. In his earlier period Barth expressed himself strongly against
this conception, *Zw. den Zeiten*, 1928, p. 274ff. He is now again concerning himself with this problem.
12. KD IV/1, p. 590.
13. KD IV/1, pp. 590, 591. "Not *exlex*, but Himself lex and in this way the
source, norm, and limit of all *leges*," p. 590.
14. KD IV/1, p. 593, with a treatment of Romans 3.
15. *Ibid.*, p. 599.
16. *Ibid.*

God's wrath has *purpose* and *meaning*,[17] and therefore it is not without limits. The gracious justification is the work of God's righteousness. This does not detract from the seriousness of the judgment, for we can from our side neither count on this grace nor assume that there will be grace in the judgment. We cannot regard grace simply as the reverse side of righteousness.[18] We can receive it only through God's revelation by faith. Judgment means real condemnation, real death, and in this death Christ creates a new right for man. This is not the right of an "as if" but of a *reality*.[19] Because God in Christ identified himself with man,[20] our guilt has really become "of yesterday", it "exists no longer." The thought of the emptying, the annihilation, of the sinner and his sin comes forward anew here. "In Him our sins are gone and we ourselves as sinners are no more."[21] In this way *our new right* comes into being.

In view of this fact, justification has at least as much significance for God Himself as it has for us.[22] God justifies *Himself* in the first place, and that not anthropomorphically but in *reality*. Sin challenged His authority in that the chaos entered His creation. *Is* God really Creator and Lord? This question He answered by taking position against evil and chaos and thus vindicating Himself as Creator. In doing so He at the same time justified man.[23] This truth may be called into question, but it *is and remains* inviolable reality.[24] While it is true that man, notwithstanding the divine vindication, is still a sinner and that we cannot conceive of the absolute justification — not as an as-if but as reality — and that we cannot find it in ourselves, the fact remains that the *separation* between right and left *has taken place*.

In the crisis of the judgment man is seen at *God's left hand* as the worker of unrighteousness, as the sinner who must be abolished. "He can only die and disappear, he has, indeed, already been put to death and been emptied."[25] At the same time, this man also stands at God's *right hand*, he is the object of election in Christ, and has therefore been safeguarded against destruction. There is not a *nominal* condemnation nor is there a *nominal* justification. There is not an apparent, there is a real destruction![26]

---

17. *Ibid.*, p. 600.
18. *Ibid.*, p. 601.
19. *Ibid.*, p. 605.
20 *Ibid.*, p. 617.

21. *Ibid.*, p. 618.
22. *Ibid.*, p. 625.
23. *Ibid.*, p 680.

24. *Ibid.*, p. 681.
25. *Ibid.*, p. 603.
26. *Ibid.*, p. 605.

And there is also a truly new life in Christ! The work that has
been accomplished is not incomplete, nor is it imperfect. It is a
full and complete reality. Our past has been *radically* put away
and at the same time we have been placed in a wholly new situation having a new point of departure.[27] That is the mystery of
the "simul peccator et justus" which has engaged Barth's attention for so long. This two-fold action of God does not constitute
a dualism, it is not a condition consisting of relativized boundaries, but it describes a "whence" and a "whither", a being-on-
the way. There is no paradoxical duality, "no uncertain movement between the most brilliant light and the deepest darkness."[28]
How is it possible to conceive of the just God as the One who has
nothing else to offer man than this "double-existence"?[29] It is a
question of being en route, it is a question of man's *history*. In this
being-on-the-way from the "whence" (unrighteousness, guilt,
dying, destruction) to the "whither" (the *new* man in Christ)
God's action takes place: the justification of the godless. The
reality of this *transition* is the reality of Christ's "*aliena* justitia"
and therefore of *nostra, mea justitia*.[30] In justification the *sinner*
is justified, not the righteous. The *sick* is given medicine, the
*lost* sheep is found.[31]

Only by acknowledging this can we taste the sweetness and the
riches of justification.[32] On the way to our "whither" we know
of this dark "whence." The man who has been found knows,
precisely because he has been found, of this finding of the lost.[33]
Therein lies the "beginning of justification,"[34] "beginning" because of the being lost *and* the being found again.[35] Therefore
justification is not without relation to this past which can be
known and acknowledged only in the way of *confession of guilt*.
"There are, therefore, no men justified by God who must not acknowledge before Him that they are unrighteous, that they are

27. *Ibid.*, p. 669.
28. *Ibid.*, p. 606.
29. *Ibid.*
30. *Ibid.*, p. 613.
31. *Ibid.*, p. 640.
32. *Ibid.*, p. 641.
33. *Ibid.*
34. *Ibid.*, pp. 642, 648.
35. *Ibid.*, p. 641. Cf. the word of the father concerning the prodigal son, Luke
15:32: KD IV/1, p. 607.

proud rebels. They cannot but justify God over against themselves, they cannot but condemn themselves over against God."[36]

In this way man is on the way from his evil past to his *good* future, and his whole life bears the marks of this journey. His guilt will ever constrain him to ascribe glory to *God,* and he will do this precisely *in* his being justified. This man is not *quantitatively* but *totally* justified, and he knows this *as* a sinner in his prayer, Forgive us our debts! Be merciful to me, a *sinner!*[37] The penitential psalms[38] do not posit conditions for justification. They pray for *forgiveness* which they cannot fail to do in the presence of a *gracious* God. Therefore they can also ask for the highest boon obtainable by man: God's gift of fulness of joy (Ps. 51:8). The petitioner proclaims — with all his confession of guilt — the praise of God, and wishes to teach sinners the way.[39] This does not mean an over-evaluation of self, for in justification it is this that has been cut off at the root. The *justified* sinner is the justified *sinner.*[40]

Justification does not weaken the confession of guilt, it elicits it. This is not pessimistic self-accusation which continues to view one's own sin without comfort, but it is correlative to justification which is an act of God's righteousness and therein an act of His grace. There is no question here of doubt or despair in which the symptoms of the old pride come to the fore which may be "the last, perhaps the securest citadel of a tremendous self-denial and self-surrender."[41] All that counts here is the Yes of God, the Yes of His justification. It is only in connection with the hearing of this Yes that confession of guilt can be *serious* and not a *high-minded humility.* Confession of sin and a hopeful pursuing of one's way into the future are indissolubly related to each other.

---

36. *Ibid.,* p. 642. Cf. on Romans 7, KD IV/1, 648ff., especially on the expression, "wretched man that I am!" That is how the justified sinner speaks about his sin, and *this* can be followed by thanksgiving, p. 657. The triumph of grace reveals the depths of guilt. Therefore the necessary reminder of the place from which we come, of the being which, coming from there, is in all its progress still the same human existence: the existence of the sinner who lives only by the grace of God, p. 659.
37. KD IV/1, p. 643.
38. Barth illustrates this transition by means of a discussion of the penitential psalms 32 and 51, *ibid.,* p. 643ff.
39. KD IV/1, p. 647.
40. *Ibid.,* p. 659.
41. *Ibid.,* p. 663.

It is here that God's promise lies, His decision, His "futurum exactum,"[42] in which justification will one day be consummated. Therefore man is not *half* sinner and *half* justified, "but both wholly."[43]

Barth does not wish to understand this "wholly" as a denial of sanctification but as a reality in which the "totus justus" has been pronounced over man in God's judgment and will one day be entirely his. The prayer for forgiveness in the Lord's Prayer is not taken away from us. "Its urgency can never decrease in the Christian life. It should much rather be a test of the genuineness of our justification as life in transition. It should press us to ask whether the significance of this prayer grows with the years or is gradually losing its relevance."[44] Being a child of God becomes reality in the light of the Fatherhood of God in Jesus Christ. This "children's right" is the "sum and substance of the rights of man."[45] Its reality is the Yes of God. It is what God wishes to achieve with man and "what He, in that He justifies the sinner, wishes to achieve with man *triumphantly*."[46] In the adoption God's grace triumphs. It directs man to the fulness and the richness of the future. Not that we have already obtained this or are already perfect, but we press on to make it our own, because Christ *has made us His own* (Phil. 3:12).[47] This is not a "cyclic movement" nor is it a "progressus ad infinitum," but it is a looking forward to the future in which all tentativeness shall have been resolved in the rest, in the achieved goal, where the "totus justus" shall be the uncontradicted and final word of God.

\* \* \*

In concluding his discussion on reconciliation, Barth asks a final question: Is there no doubt respecting *this* reality of justification? Does not the whole matter, in final analysis, become dubious in view of what we know of man, of this justified man?[48] "Is he, does he really exist? Has he ever existed?"[49] Can we be *certain* of this justification, can we know that this reality is more real than

42. *Ibid.*
43. *Ibid.*, p. 664.
44. *Ibid.*, p. 665.
45. *Ibid.*, p. 669.
46. *Ibid.*
47. *Ibid.*, p. 673.
48. *Ibid.*, p. 683.
49. *Ibid.*, p. 680.

any and all other views concerning man? How can we be sure, when it is remembered that we ourselves are concerned and that our "whence" is a past of guilt and sin which are *not* lost to sight in justification but are taken — as *forgiven* sins — in all their seriousness?

These questions can only be answered in the act of *faith*. This faith is not a new work which brings reconciliation into being and makes it real,[50] but it is directed to Jesus Christ alone. Here there is no *striving* after justification, but only an exclusion of striving. In Christ all that is needful for our justification has been accomplished.[51] When Barth so speaks of the negative character of faith, he intends to reject the meritoriousness of faith.[52] It is possible, however, to speak with as much right of the *positiveness* of faith[53] because it is precisely the non-meritorious character of faith, the humble obedience, which "is exactly openness for its object, and in this way it is faith in Jesus Christ."[54] Faith is that most positive factor in which the triumph of grace finds its reflection, its subjective correlate.

\*    \*    \*

This act of faith is possible only through the Holy Spirit. The first part of Barth's doctrine of reconciliation concludes with a discussion of "The Holy Spirit and the Gathering of the Christian Church," and "The Holy Spirit and the Christian Faith."[55] Clearly, this (tentative) conclusion of the discussion cannot stand outside of the triumph of reconciliation. He does not speak here of the human contribution that creates or that complements the reconciliation. The problem is, rather, that of the "subjective realization of reconciliation."[56] The mystery of reconciliation does not take place outside of or apart from man — not even in the "extra nos" of the doctrine of reconciliation of the Reformers. There is an act of man, the act of faith: "participation by man in God's act of reconciliation," the Christian Church, the Christian faith.

50. *Ibid.*, p. 702.
51. *Ibid.*, p. 704.
52. Cf. especially KD IV/1, p. 693.
53. *Ibid.*, contra "apparent humility."
54. *Ibid.*
55. *Ibid.*, pp. 718ff. and 823ff.
56. *Ibid.*, pp. 719, 721.

This does not mean that only *now* — in this "existential" situation! — reconciliation becomes important, for here, too, the issue is the *substance* of the doctrine of reconciliation. In the subjective realization of reconciliation the Holy Spirit makes man "open" for the miracle of reconciliation: credo in Spiritum Sanctum! This does *not* involve distancing ourselves from the objective reality of reconciliation. Therefore the "credo in Spiritum Sanctum," united with the "credo ecclesiam,"[57] is a reality in the world only in terms of the miracle of the Spirit. This reality exists in faith, in faith which cannot be construed or understood in terms of the sinner himself.[58] Faith in Jesus Christ can never arise in the heart of man himself, because sinful man cannot believe, cannot transcend the barrier of his own sinfulness, unless the Son makes him free.[59]

Faith is not possible except through Jesus Christ and the Holy Spirit. Faith can only be *awakened*. But for this very reason faith is not a complementing activity. It is acknowledgment of the reconciliation: "acknowledging, knowing, confessing."[60] This character of faith detracts nothing, however, from its genuinely *human* character. In his doctrine of reconciliation, Barth does not repeat what he said by way of sharp reaction in 1930, namely, that faith is not "an act of human but of originally divine believing."[61] In the reconciliation man is involved in the fulness and reality of his existence. God desires to be *with* man — Immanuel —and this means that the thesis: God is all, man is nothing, *cannot* be a Christian thesis.[62]

There is no pretention, no "claim" made by man in this communion, but the genuinely human act of faith remains. Barth even goes so far as to speak of a "creative" character of faith.[63]

---

57. *Ibid.*, p. 733.
58. *Ibid.*, p. 827.
59. *Ibid.*, pp. 832, 833.
60. *Ibid.*, p. 839.
61. K. Barth, *Philipperbrief*, 1928, p. 98.
62. "Not only a horrible simplification, but complete nonsense," KD IV/1, p. 94.
63. "To that extent, it is not possible to deny the event of faith a creative character," KD IV/1, p. 841. In the nature of the case, all depends here on the words "to that extent." Barth speaks of the creative mystery of the Christian existence, p. 841, but it is plain that he does not understand this as "creative" in the sense that reconciliation takes place (partly) through faith. The whole of IV/1 (as well as other parts of his dogmatics) raises a barrier against this idea.

Having first spoken of its *cognitive* character — as opposed to its creative aspect[64] — he now speaks of faith as having a "creative" character which transcends the cognitive aspect.[65]

It must not be supposed that Barth falls into an unobserved contradiction here. By the cognitive character of faith Barth wishes to indicate the "recognition" function of faith, while by its "creative" character he points to the reality of reconciliation in which the new man is taken up and believes in Him to whom his faith is directed. It is truly man who believes through the power of the Holy Spirit. The Christian faith is not simply an intellectual assent to certain propositions. Faith is *my* faith, as directly involved in the reconciliation wrought by Christ. The creative character of faith comes to rest in the "pro me" of the Christian confession. It does not do so in the individualistic style of "only for me", but in inseparable relationship to the "pro nobis."[66] Only, the "pro me" may not be allowed to be swallowed up or made vague by the "pro nobis." The word "credo" is not an individualistic word,[67] although care must be exercised not to lose the "pro me" on account of this.[68] In the non-abstract "pro me" Jesus Christ is honored who is the Lord of the Church. Here — in the Church — the triumph of reconciliation is reflected in the "credo." "It is not required of me, I am not permitted, I am forbidden, to doubt it."[69]

As opposed to the uncertainty which is contained in Roman Catholic doctrine precisely on the score of the "pro me," we find in Barth the rejection of doubt and uncertainty with respect to the reconciliation which is in Christ. The right not-to-doubt is a bestowed right,[70] but this does not rob it of its character as a right, *our* right. The man with this right, given him through the triumph of the righteousness and grace of God, knows what it means to be a *living* and *ever*-living member of the Church.[71] But the triumph is not exhausted in this realized salvation. The

---

64. *Ibid.*, p. 389: "As this human deed (namely, recognizing, acknowledging, confessing) it does not have a creative but only a cognitive character."
65. *Ibid.*, p. 841.
66. *Ibid.*, p. 843ff.
67. *Ibid.*, p. 844.
68. *Ibid.*, p. 845.
69. *Ibid.*, p. 780.
70. *Ibid.*, p. 864ff.
71. *Ibid.*, p. 867.

Church — in the "pro nobis" and in the "pro me" — knows not only the "history of her soul experience";[72] she also *confesses* before men. As a small light she is "the reflex of the great light."[73] She is a witness to the world in this sense, that she testifies to others who do not know of the salvation that has been achieved for them and of the judgment that has been consummated. They do not know about Christ, and the Church of Christ knows that she herself has not come to faith in her own strength. Therefore she does not witness to herself and to her readiness to believe, but to God who loved the world. The triumph of reconciliation reveals itself in the world in this, that the lost who have been found confess, "God was in Christ, reconciling the world to Himself."[74]

That is the triumph of reconciliation.

---

72. *Ibid.*, p. 868.
73. *Ibid.*, p. 870.
74. *Ibid.*, p. 871.

# VI

## THE ESCHATOLOGICAL TRIUMPH

A FTER having discussed the triumph of creation, the triumph of election, and the triumph of reconciliation as varied aspects of the one triumph of grace, we must, in concluding our analysis of the central motifs in Barth's theology, call attention to his exposition of the eschatological triumph. The conception of overcoming grace which we meet here might also be entitled the triumph of life, or the triumph over death.

Although that part of the *Kirchliche Dogmatik* which will deal specifically with eschatology (the doctrine of redemption) has not yet been published, it is fully possible to include this aspect of Barth's theology in our discussion. From the beginning of Barth's theological development eschatology has played an important role in his thinking. Even in the earliest phase of his thinking he emphasized that eschatology should not merely be a concluding chapter in works on dogmatics, but that it should permeate the whole of our reflection on the gospel.

It is not necessary to trace here the development of Barth's eschatological thought. It is important to note, however, that it was precisely in connection with eschatology that Barth later criticized views expressed in his *Römerbrief*. He felt that his view of eternity had been too much constructed in terms of the idea of a "boundary" of eternity with respect to time. He acknowledged that this conception had prevented him from fully honoring those expressions in Scripture which stress the horizontal line of continuity from present to future in God's redemptive action.[1] His sharp expression that Christianity which was not "absolutely" eschatological had "absolutely" nothing to do with Christianity, was not without warrant in consideration of the emphases of historicism, psychologism and immanentism. He felt, however,

---

1. Cf. my *Wereld Oorlog en Theologie,* 1945.

that he had emphasized too much the idea of the "supra-temporal" and had not given sufficient attention to the actual *end*.[2] God's eternity is the very factor which gives meaning to time and to history. Time is not empty — it has been condemned and brought under judgment! — but, "in terms of its beginning and its end, it is filled and meaningful because of the real and therefore comforting and commanding presence of God."[3] Eternity may not be understood as "a gray monotonous sea."[4] It is directly related to God's *glory* which, according to His eternal counsel, will result in glorification.[5] This glory also manifests itself in the answer to God's action which He has Himself elicited, namely, through the praise of His creature.[6] The creature glorifies God in its gratitude for the salvation given through Jesus Christ.[7] This praise *now* still takes place "in the form of the Church, the proclamation, faith, confession, theology and prayer."[8] But this "temporal form," however real and actual it be, will one day assume its *future* form "which we now await and must await here."[9]

From glory to glorification, from gratitude to praise — this is the movement through which God's eternal glory returns to Himself through the avenues of time. In this praise lies the destiny of the creature, the purpose of the works of God.[10]

It is in this kind of an atmosphere that we find ourselves when we contemplate the eschatological triumph in the theology of Barth.

\* \* \*

The questions which come to the fore in this part of the analysis arise particularly in connection with Barth's anthropology, in which he discusses extensively the eschatological triumph as it comes to expression in the triumph of life over death.[11]

The work of God reveals Jesus Christ as the *Lord* of time. In connection with this theme Barth speaks extensively about

---

2. Cf. especially KD II/1, p. 715ff.
3. KD II/1, p. 719.
4. *Ibid.*, p. 721.
5. *Ibid.*, p. 753.
6. *Ibid.*
7. *Ibid.*, p. 755.
8. *Ibid.*, p. 762.
9. *Ibid.*, p. 763.
10. *Ibid.*, Cf. also KD III/3, p. 556ff.
11. KD III/2, pp. 714 - 780.

our time and then discusses successively the "given time," the "limited time," the "beginning time," and the "ending time." Especially his views about time as ending time claim our attention here. It does not lie in Barth's intention to present a phenomenological analysis of time, of the limitations of human life, and of death, in his discussion of the ending time. All that he wishes to say in this connection he says from the viewpoint of the miracle of Christ's appearance: the "God with us" of *reconciliation*. What consequences does this conception have for the *eschatological* triumph?

\*     \*     \*

In order to gain a right understanding of this "ending time" it is desirable to note first what Barth means by the "beginning time." There was a time in which we were not yet, as also there shall be a time in which we shall not be *any more*. Human life lies between the poles of this two-fold not-being, the "being-not-yet" and the "being-no-longer." We are, it is true, more concerned with our "being-no-longer" than with our earlier "being-not-yet," but there is, for all that, every reason to give attention to this latter form of our being. We are not eternal. We have a *beginning* time. We come out of non-being. That is to say — note the peculiar sequence of thought — "since my very origin I am threatened by nothingness; I stand designated, in a certain sense, as a being which is also able to move toward nothingness."[12]

What lay before us was not *our* time, our "room," for existence. This is the shadow which has been cast over us from the beginning of our being in the world. Man seeks to remove this shadow, and this accounts, according to Barth, for the passionate striving of man to achieve knowledge of the past.[13] This explains the irresistible compulsion to historical study which is the "passionate storming of the gates of time as it has taken form in history," because man, as a searcher into the things of the past, knows of "the abyss of the chaos which lies behind him."[14]

This shadow, however, must also be seen in connection with the *light*. We did not in our beginning time come forth out of

12. *Ibid.*, p. 698.
13. *Ibid.*, pp. 699-701.
14. *Ibid.*, p. 701.

"nothingness, our origin does not lie in the chaos. Our 'beginning' being is from God. *He* is the Creator, not the chaos." Therefore we can receive this limitation of our life as a *good* gift. "We would not be creatures but God Himself if we were eternal."[15]

There is another limitation of our life, however, of which we must be made aware. The knowledge that haunts us at every turn is not so much that our life at one time began, but that the time that has been given to us is a time that will irrevocably *come to an end.* This is the constant concern of man, that he is on his way to being-no-more, that he is on the way to a state of *only-having-been.* This limitation of the life of man casts quite another shadow over his life than that of his earlier being-not-yet. It is *this* limitation of man's ending time which occasions Barth's extensive exposition concerning man's future and which we summarize here as the *eschatological triumph* or as the triumph of grace over death.

At this point Barth asks a decisive question: Is this ending time — "we shall all one day have been"[16] — a *fate*, a *catastrophe*, which comes over us, *or* does this limitation belong to the *good* creation which God made?[17] It is not so much the earlier not-being as the one time no-longer-being which raises the question of how we must understand and come to terms with this coming end! Is this coming end compatible with the idea of a good creation, or is it unthinkable that our good nature could include the idea of life's coming to an end? Is it from a biblical point of view untenable to regard the ending of time in terms of the good creation, or does the Bible present us with a wholly different conception? Does not the Bible say something more about death than that it is a necessary anthropological limitation? Is our "whither" structurally the same as our "whence?" Can death be regarded as belonging to human nature as it came from the hand of God, or is death an alien, destructive power which has penetrated the good creation and is contrary to human nature?[18] Is death not sinister and uncanny? Can we view death in any other way? Is it possible, Barth says, to speak of death

---

15. *Ibid.*
16. *Ibid.*, p. 716.
17. *Ibid.*, p. 722ff.
18. *Ibid.*, p. 723.

other than in this *negative, life-destroying sense?* Is death, although standing under the power of God, anything else than *evil only?*[19]

Must it, then, not be posited that death does *not* belong to the good creation? "Is the end of our existence in time not an unequivocal No spoken to our created existence, which can only be understood to mean that there is in no sense room for it in a doctrine of God's creation?"[20] This question Barth asks with great earnestness. He points out that the limitation of our earlier not-being stands in a different category than our future being-no-longer. Death, empirical death, as we know it and as we know it will one day enter our own life, is not simply a neutral ending of our temporal existence. It is *not* a normal and "natural" return to the not-being whence we came. It is a return to God. We are not on the way to *nothing* or to a neutral and empty being-no-more. We are on the way to the living God and in *this* limitation we come into contact with the sign of God's judgment over our life.[21] We certainly cannot say of this *empirical* death which we know that it belongs to God's creation and therefore to our *good* human nature. On the contrary, it is a *negative* power, an *evil.* It is *not* a formal neutral end to the life of man about which we do not have to concern ourselves as though it were a matter-of-course event in the history of every individual. Death is *that* limitation which is indissolubly related to our *sin* and to our *guilt.* Is *this* death, this *empirical* death, in any sense natural? Is it anything else than curse and misery? When death is called "natural," sin and curse and judgment are denied. It is not permissible to speak of death as a friend or as a kindly release from suffering.[22] The empirical end of man is not the same as the natural end of man. It is, rather, the end of "untruthful existence." "Here we confront quite a different matter than when we ask about the meaning of the beginning of our life."[23] According to Paul, sin has entered the world as an alien power and death entered through sin. It would seem, therefore, that it is quite impossible to speak of death as belonging in any sense to the human nature which came forth *good* from the hand of God.

19. *Ibid.*
20. *Ibid.*, p. 724.
21. *Ibid.*, p. 725.
22. *Ibid.*, p. 727.
23. *Ibid.*, p. 728.

According to Barth, however, there is more to death than this negative meaning. It is striking that he constantly refers to it as the *sign* of God's judgment, not *as the judgment itself*. This is to be explained by the fact that Jesus Christ has on our behalf entered death as the real judgment. With respect to *Him* we must speak not only of death as the *sign* of judgment, but of death as the full, the real judgment in its absolute and deepest sense. After *this* death of Christ, there is for *man* no longer any question of death in the sense of real judgment.

Man's death is no longer the suffering of deserved judgment, "but it is only its sign."[24] The death of Christ sheds a wholly new light over our ending time. Empirical death did constitute a continual threat of all life, but *He* has undergone this threat.[25] Man was deserving of this death and in the Old Testament we see it portrayed in all its seriousness. But light has dawned in the midst of this darkness because the judgment *has been executed*. Jesus Christ has borne it. "No other man stands in this center and therefore no other stands really in the judgment of God."[26] The others — the Christian knowingly, the non-Christian as yet unknowingly — now stand only under the *sign* of the judgment.[27] Through Golgotha man has been spared the suffering of this deserved judgment. The *one* judgment over Christ has become an irrevocable and unalterable fact.

The judgment has been borne, it has been borne *away*, and because of this the character of death has changed. It is not any more, and never again will be, a judgment.

For this reason we cannot comfort ourselves with the "naturalness" of death. When we think of death we should think of "that utterly dangerous and painful nothingness of our reprobacy before God," of the power of God and the might of His law *against* us. This true view of death can change only when we understand that the judgment *has taken place* and that God, who awaits us in our death, is a gracious God who,[28] because of this judgment, is now truly for man. At the horizon of our ending time there stands no longer judgment but the grace of God. Death may be our *bound-*

24. *Ibid.*, p. 730.
25. *Ibid.*, p. 733.
26. *Ibid.*, p. 736.
27. *Ibid.*, p. 737.
28. *Ibid.*, p. 741.

*ary,* but the God of all grace is the boundary of death.[29]  Death is the revelation of the wrath of God, but it is the wrath of His love by which He takes us to Himself in death.  This grace is the triumph, the one and only triumph, over death.[30]  It is not a general doctrine of immortality that can comfort us but only the message of *life* in the midst of death, because death as *judgment* lies *behind* us.  In *Christ* the triumph over death is reality and through Him a higher Power has saved us from the deserved judgment.[31]  Barth speaks expressly of this triumph over death [32] which has become reality in Christ and which was revealed in His resurrection.  *Our death has really become a matter of the past.* "When we regard this one Jesus Christ, no conception is too bold, too high, too inclusive."[33]  In this connection, therefore, Barth speaks of "the triumphant existence and faithfulness of God,"[34] the announcement of which — "the declaration of this victory"[35] — lies in the appearance of God during the forty days between resurrection and ascension.

This consummated reconciliation and redemption, this victory over death, is the *end* of time, the last day, or, rather, the midnight hour which ushers in the last day, last for the individual and last for all men.  Death has been "robbed of its power."[36]  The event that must still come to pass is the *public manifestation* of the "conqueror of Golgotha," [37] and this present continuing time can be no more than a time of *repentance* and *faith.*  For Christ's death, resurrection, and return "are the foundation on which virtually everything stands that can be predicated of man, of his future, of his end and purpose in God.[38]

What does this eschatological triumph mean?  Does Christ's work imply an extension of life on earth?  Will there be "a new beginning, development, and continuation of human life in a time after man's death?"[39]  Is there, perhaps, in Christ *not* an ending time as counter-part to the beginning time?  The answer to *this* question touches the heart of Barth's conception of the ending time.  His answer requires that we return to the question whether death belongs to the good creation as such.

---

29. *Ibid.,* p. 742.
30. *Ibid.,* p. 741.
31. *Ibid.,* p. 746.
32. *Ibid.,* p. 747.
33. *Ibid.*
34. *Ibid.,* p. 756.

35. *Ibid.,* p. 757.
36. *Ibid.*
37. *Ibid.*
38. *Ibid.,* p. 759.
39. *Ibid.*

It is not easy to come to a clear insight with respect to Barth's solution of the problem of the ending time in its relation to eternal life. We must, in the first place, notice that Barth sharply opposes the idea of an extension of human life after death.[40] When Christ through His victory ushers in the last day, and God shall in the end be all in all, there comes into being a "present without an afterward."[41] There is no continuation, no further happening, after the sounding of the last trump. "The hope of the New Testament concerning the beyond of human death is not some sort of changed life which is continued in some sort of unending future. Not this, but the 'eternalizing' of our ending life is the content of the New Testament hope." The hope that we have does not involve an *extension* of our life; its point of reference is our life *as it has been.*[42]    The life that *has been,* life in the *limitations* we have known, is "eternalized," and this action upon the life that has been takes place in such a manner that it does *not* include a *continuation* of our finite existence in the future.

The life that has been, life in all its limitation and finiteness, finds "room" in communion with God.[43]

*This* is the resurrection of the dead.

Barth's conception of the "eternalizing" of our ending life has, so far as I know, no antecendents in the history of Christian doctrine.

\*        \*        \*

The full impact and thrust of this conception we cannot appreciate until we face again[44] the question of the end of man's life and the goodness of created human nature.    When Barth speaks about

---

40. In connection with the problem of the continuation of human life after death cf. also E. Thurneysen's "Christus und seine Zukunfst," *Zwischen den Zeiten* 1931. Over against the doctrine of immortality he rejects the idea of continuity in the sense of an extension of this present life, p. 206. Thurneysen wants to speak of a "new beginning," however, and understands "continuity" as a relativizing of the difference between temporal and eternal life. "Insofar as one wishes nevertheless to speak of continuity, this continuity lies not in the object to which God again gives life, not with man, not in any indestructibleness of his life which at that time becomes manifest, but exclusively and only with the life-giving God Himself," p. 207. It would seem to be clear that this conception of Thurneysen does not yet bring us to Barth's view.
41. KD III/2, p. 759.
42. With reference, among others, to I Cor. 15:53: this perishable nature must put on the imperishable. Cf. also G. C. van Niftrik, *Zie, de Mens,* 1951, p. 494.
43. KD III/2, p. 760.
44. *Ibid.,* p. 761ff.

the "eternalizing" of our temporal life, it appears that all that he had said before about empirical death did not intend to deny that the finiteness and limitation of human life is involved in the *goodness* of human nature.[45]

With an eye to our empirical death, that is, our death as sinful men, it can only be said that the end of life and the abnormality of death *coincide*. Death is our enemy, it is our end, it is "Unnatur."[46] It is precisely at this point, however, that the *cross* pronounces a final decision. The death of Christ was the bearing of an alien burden which did *not* necessarily follow from His being-human.

Christ took death upon Himself *voluntarily*. He did not die because of any anthropological necessity. *In His person*, a human existence was made manifest whose end did not, as such, coincide with His being subject to death as "Un-natur." In Christ — in whom alone we can learn to know man — we see that the *end* of life and *the judgment do not necessarily coincide*. If Jesus is true man, and as true man reveals the essence of being-human, we must conclude that it is not correct to see "human mortality as such as purely negative and evil."[47] If the grace of Christ is to become our portion, it is *necessary* that we have an *end*. It is a human necessity that "we shall one day die and thus become only a having-been."[48]

Christology is decisive for Barth's anthropology as well as for his eschatology. In view of the mortality of Jesus Christ, Barth rejects, because of Christological-soteriological considerations, the identity of *end* and *judgment* as self-evident.[49] We must distinguish between end and curse, dying and punishment, death and the judgment of death.[50] Man's end and man's mortality belong to God's *good* creation. Barth makes this very clear: "It belongs to the nature of man, it is God's creation which determined, and to that extent made it good and right, that the existence of man in time should have an end, that man should be mortal. That we shall one day only have-been answers to a law by which we are not necessarily bound, imprisoned and condemned to destruction. Death is

45. *Ibid.*, p. 764.
46. *Ibid.*, p. 765.
47. *Ibid.*, p. 767.
48. *Ibid.*, p. 768.
49. *Ibid.*, p. 769.
50. *Ibid.*

not in itself the judgment, nor is it in itself the sign of judgment. Factually, however, it is that."[51]

This *factual*, this empirical death, has also a *hidden* aspect in which the boundary as such does not contain a threatening element, and this *hidden* aspect belongs to the *good creation*. Here death as boundary becomes the transition from being to not-being, it is the parallel to man's *beginning* time from not-being to being.

"It is therefore not unnatural but natural for human life to move on to this terminus ad quem. It is natural to ring life out as it was once rung in and therefore it is limited not only at its beginning, but *also with respect to its future*."[52]

Therefore man does not as such have a "beyond," nor does he need one, "for God is his beyond [*Jenseits*]." There is no extension of his earthly temporalness. This thesis, Barth emphasizes, may under no circumstances be understood to mean that death means *finis* [dead is dead] and that there is no reason or room in life for hope and expectation. Also in his quality as having-been man is not *nothing* but "participates in the eternal life of God."[53] It is precisely his life on this side of death, his ending and dying life, that is *glorified*.[54]

This exposition has brought us face to face with the central problem of Barth's eschatology. Continually Barth repeats the polemic against the idea of "continuation," *and* emphasizes man's existence on this side of death. In the totality of this existence, "besides which and after which he has no other," man is grateful to God as his merciful Savior from death.[55]

The earnestness with which Barth holds this view appears from the fact that from this "view of human nature"[56] he draws the conclusion that *this has very great significance for ethics*. The once-for-all and "not to be continued course" of our life receive in this way a peculiar "urgency" which would be *lacking* were we to hope

---

51. *Ibid.*, p. 770.
52. *Ibid.*, Italics by Barth.
53. *Ibid.*
54. *Ibid.*, p. 771.
55. *Ibid.*
56. *Ibid.*

for a being *freed* from the limitation of life and for a "beyond" of this limitation instead of hoping in the eternal God alone.[57]

\* \* \*

Does Barth find the basis for his conception at the end of human life — as non-continuation — in the Bible? To this question he gives an affirmative answer, although he admits that only a "narrow line" is discernible. *Usually* the Bible speaks of our empirical death as the death of *sinful* men. Then death is pictured as an enemy, as judgment or, rather, as *sign* of the judgment. As a rule the Bible regards death from "this second aspect."[58] There is also another aspect of death presented, however, namely in those places where death is seen not simply from its negative side.[59] The Bible does not *always* speak about what Barth calls the *second* death, for there are instances in which the "sinister guest" appears in an aspect which, while not friendly, is, nevertheless, a *natural aspect*.[60] He points to the transition in the lives of Moses and Elijah in which there was not judgment but communion with God in the context of the end of life.[61] The end of human life is not as such a symptom of "disorder" but of *order*, not a "chaotic reign of terror," but a *good* creation of God. And when the Bible says that it is appointed for all men to die, "and after that the judgment" (Heb. 9:27), Barth understands it to be implied here that *dying in itself* does *not* mean judgment, but that it involves a natural happening.[62]

According to God's good creation, therefore, human life has a *boundary*. It is not perpetuated and continued. And yet . . . Barth speaks, in connection with man's end, of a co-existence with the eternal life of God.[63]

The New Testament Christian awaits death without fear, because *he hopes in God* and because "in his end he expects to be

57. *Ibid.*, p. 772.
58. *Ibid.*
59. *Ibid.*
60. *Ibid.*, p. 773.
61. *Ibid.*, p. 776.
62. *Ibid.*, p. 777.
63. *Ibid.*, p. 779.

with Him." Man rejoices in the fact that he will "definitely be
with Him."[64]

*          *          *

In reading Barth on this subject, one asks again and again
whether he has understood him correctly. How is it possible to
square his sharp polemic against the idea of continuation of this
life with this *hope* and this *joy* of the definite "with Him?" What
is meant by the "eternalizing" of our finite life, the emphasis on the
this-side-of-death in ethics, and the urgency of life *here and now*
because man does not have a beyond-death other than God alone?

Answering these questions does not become easier when we take
into account the manner in which Barth treats them also in his
doctrine of providence. In connection with the hidden providence
of God's world government Barth speaks about certain constant
elements which, although they do not prove that God governs the
world, do have the function of serving as signs which point to this
government. As such signs, Barth also mentions, in addition to
the history of Sacred Scripture, the history of the Church, and the
history of the Jews, the limitation of our human life.[65] Especially
these latter have the advantage of presenting an "immediate per-
spicuity."[66] In this limitation a particular period of time is traversed
from beginning to end, it constitutes "a fixed period between birth
and death"[67] as a "fundamental designation" of our existence
Herein lies a sign of God's government. Referring back, in this connection, to his anthropology, he points out that the limited life
*belongs to the good nature of man.* Man's life has a beginning and
it has an end.[68] Herein two acts of God at the beginning and at the
end of all things are reflected, namely, creation and consummation.[69] Human life is a once-for-all matter and this once-for-allness
has profound meaning: "the eternal oneness of God reflects itself
in the small, creaturely once-for-allness of man's once beginning
and once ending life, and who knows whether this life is s
small?"[70] Human life is a history, a drama, in which we are called

---

64. *Ibid.*, p. 780.
65. KD III/3, p. 256ff.
66. *Ibid.*, p. 257.
67. *Ibid.*
68. *Ibid.*, p. 260.
69. *Ibid.*.
70. *Ibid.*, p. 263.

to make decisions which are vastly important. "An unending history would not be history. The lordship under which we live and the once-for-allness which this lordship gives to our life see to it that our history remains a real, that is, a beginning and an ending, history."[71]

In Barth's doctrine of preservation the same problem is again discussed. God wills man and permits him to be that for which He made man.[72] This means that the creature will "within his limits, really and actively be and remain before God."[73] We cannot help asking: continuation, after all? Let us follow Barth in his thought.

The time will come when the whole of created reality shall only have-been.[74] When Jesus Christ shall have been revealed and the history of creation shall have reached its end and achieved its purpose, further continuation will be purposeless. It will be purposeless because the *meaning* of creation will have been fulfilled. "The things that have happened as history pursued its course will then happen in a totality as the comprehension of all individual happenings and become definite: the temporal end of the creature beyond which it will no longer be."[75] And where the creature will *no longer be,* there time as a form of existence will no longer be. But . . . "its preservation by God does not thereby come to an end," even though this be a preservation "within the limits of the creature." *This* preservation does not come to an end with the end of the creature, as little as God first took note of the creature only at the beginning of its history. Already *before* creation — when creaturely reality did not yet exist — God's faithfulness envisioned His creature (in His eternal counsel). In the same way, "His faithfulness remains vouchsafed to the creature also when it has finished its destined course, also then when it will no longer be."[76]

In view of the parallel which Barth draws to the creature in its being-not-yet, it is hardly possible that we can now misunderstand him. It is the drawing of this parallel that makes plain Barth's *protest against the* idea of continuity. Apparently this protest must be taken with complete seriousness. There is not a con-

---

71. *Ibid.,* p. 264.
72. *Ibid.,* p. 99.
73. *Ibid.*
74. *Ibid.*
75. *Ibid.*
76. *Ibid.,* p. 100.

tinuation beyond this life, but there is a *standing* in the attention of God through eternity. "Eternal preservation does not mean that a continuation lies before him."[77] Why should this be necessary now that all has been fulfilled? The eternal preservation of the creature means "positively this — no other possibility remains — that he will eternally be and remain before God."[78] When everything shall have *been,* "then he will, in the totality of his temporal duration be present before God and for God, so he will be *eternally preserved.* He will be seen in his greatness and in his lowliness, he will be judged according to his right and according to his wrong, according to his merit and demerit in God's eyes, but he will also openly participate in the *love* which God has for him."[79]

God permits *nothing* to be lost — no hue in deepest ocean depths, no wingbeat of an insect that lives but a day, nor the earliest time in earth's history, and certainly *nothing* in *our life.* God will not be alone in His eternity, but He will be *together* with His creature, His creature in its limited duration. "Present before God — in *this* way the creature will be and will remain." This is the way in which it will be enfolded in the great rest of God. This is its preservation, a preservation that is not *in addition to* or *after* the preservation in time. This is the *mystery* of the preservation which must be understood in the light of the expression repeated twenty-six times in Psalm 136, "For His mercy endureth forever."[80]

Barth states expressly that it is precisely *his* conception of the future that points to the light which shines incomparably brighter than all other hopes of immortality, and that also of his vision of the future it can be said, "Cannot the jubilation of the resurrection already now be heard above all the sepulchres and urns and faded memories, wherever the Word that proceeds from this light, the Word of our God, sounds forth and is heard?"[81]

---

77. *Ibid.*
78. *Ibid.,* p. 101.
79. *Ibid.*
80. *Ibid.,* especially pp. 102 and 103.
81. KD III/2, p. 744. It is important to take note of Barth's understanding of the "vita aeterna" in his *Credo* of 1935. Already then Barth protested against the view that conceives of eternal life as "a life in one or other supra-temporal state of timelessness or of endless time," *De apostolische Geloofsbelijdenis,* p. 207, (Dutch translation). The point at issue is *our life* which will then have become new "upon an earth, and under a heaven that have been made new, renewed, namely, in their relationship to God the Creator, Reconciler, and Redeemer." It is a question of *revelation,* of the *unveiling* of that which in the glorified life of

We shall later return to the question of Barth's solution of the problem. At this point we wish only to point out that Barth, in his conception of our limited time, does not relinquish the idea of the triumph of grace but considers it to be present also here. Man's coming-to-an-end, the having-been of human life, does not cast a shadow over the triumph, but reveals it from a new aspect. For although there is no continuation, no preservation after and next to the preservation in time, yet there will be a manifestation of the finite, limited life that we shall one day have lived. In this way, *this* life will be glorified with Him as a *justified* and *reconciled* life. This glorification with God is God's triumph, the triumph over death, the triumph of the eschatological future which God has prepared.

---

81. (*Continued from p.* 164)

Christ is already now full reality, although it is still hidden, p. 206. There is not a separate belief in eternal life next to belief in God. There is not a "promise which provides perspectives on what we call a blessed dying"; eternal life is "a creative deed of God through which our fleshly, self-maintaining existence is discontinued and changed into an existence in a heaven and an earth in a time of *peace* with God without any opposition or conflict." In a remarkable comment Barth adds that *if* eternal life is to be union with Christ in this way, then we may also attribute to this life "supra-temporalness, timelessness, or endless time," p. 206. In comparing 1935 (*Credo*) with 1948 (KD III/2) and 1950 (KD III/3) one gains the impression that since 1935 the conclusions which Barth drew from his Christology for anthropology (and eschatology) played an increasingly larger role in his thinking. In 1948 and in 1950 the element of "endless time" *no longer appears*. That God's mercy endures forever (Psalm 136) is directly related to man's "having been." With respect to the resurrection of the flesh, cf. *De apostolische Geloofsbelijdenis*, p. 199, and the *Grundrisz*, 1947, p. 181. In the latter we see Barth en route to III/2 and III/3!

# VII

## THE TRIUMPH OF GRACE IN ITS ANTITHESIS TO ROME

A FTER having noted various aspects of the one triumph of grace, we wish in the present chapter to observe the manner in which this triumph-concept concretely functions in Barth's theology on the score of ecclesiastical and theological *polemics*. It is evident that polemics play a very important role in Barth's dogmatics. It is possible to describe this aspect of his theology from various points of view. It can be seen in its struggle against Rome and modern Protestant theology, against Schleiermacher, Ritschl, Hermann, Brunner, Gogarten, Bultmann, Sartre, Heidegger, Nietzche, Jaspers, and many others.

The significance of the triumph of grace in Barth's polemic against modern Protestant theology presents a concrete area of discussion. The first phase of dialectical theology plainly indicated the main outlines of the rejection of modern Protestantism, and it was clear from the beginning that Barth regarded this dissent as essential to his service as a theologian, a view which he maintains to the present day. Although there were differences between Barth and Brunner in their evaluation of Schleiermacher,[1] there was, nevertheless, a great area of commonness in their rejection of the consciousness- and experiential-theology of the 19th century. When the theology of the Word and of sovereign grace was constructed against this Protestantism, its central criticism was directed against modern Protestantism's misconception of grace.

Barth engaged in this polemic activity also in connection with various questions touching the confession of the Church in which he maintained with vigor the necessity of the Church's rejection

---

1. When E. Brunner wrote his *Die Mystik und das Wort* (the antithesis between the modern conception of religion and the Christian faith as seen in the theology of Schleiermacher), 1924, Barth wrote a review which already pointed to differences in outlook.

of heresy. Barth reminds those who, in the interest of tolerance, appeal to the words "God is love," that in the same fourth chapter of I John in which these words appear the *confession* is seen as the means for discerning the spirits. In principle, tolerance is a closed avenue to the Church.[2] The Church *may not* be tolerant with those who deny that Jesus Christ has come in the flesh, because in this denial the unity, the communion, and the love of the one Church are attacked. Rejection of heresy is part of the calling of the Church: "With her damnamus! the Church safeguards the mystery of grace."[3] It was this that stood central in his polemical concern with modern Protestantism. "In the characteristic affirmations of the 'new Protestantism' we do not recognize the voice of the good Shepherd, but of a strange one."[4] The new Protestantism is a "debate-fellow whose membership in the Christian Church is completely incomprehensible to me."[5] He was willing to call such a Protestant a friend but in no sense "a brother in Christ."[6]

This rejection of modern Protestantism courses through the whole of Barth's dogmatics as an essential part of his polemic. He is convinced that the whole of modern Protestant theology stands or falls with its subjectivistic point of departure and that its anthropology, which forms the background and foundation of its entire structure, stands essentially defenseless against the criticism of Ludwig Feuerbach, because man is more central in that theology than the power and sovereign grace of God.[7]

---

2. Cf. especially Barth's *Das Bekenntnis der Reformation und unser Bekennen*, 1935, p. 10ff, and KD I/2, p. 705: this "No" of the Church is not a disturbing of the life of the Church, it is not a "sin against love," but rather a seeking of lost unity and "the work of love par exellence."

3. *Das Bekenntnis der Reformation und unser Bekennen*, p. 11.

4. *Ibid.*, p. 35.

5. *Ibid.*, p. 34.

6. *Ibid.*, p. 36.

7. Cf. Barth's essay on Ludwig Feuerbach, 1926, "Die Theologie und die Kirche," *Gesammelte Vorträge*, II, p. 212ff. He saw in Feuerbach's system "an insipidity without comparison," p. 236. On the other hand, modern Protestant subjectivistic theology could present him with no effective opposition because it virtually takes its point of departure in man as the measure of all things. Cf. Kurt Leese, *Die Prinzipienfrage der neueren systematischen Theologie im Lichte der Kritik Ludwig Feuerbachs*, 1912, with especial reference to the difficulties of modern Protestant theology in meeting the criticism of Feuerbach, particularly p. 194. Cf. also Barth, "Das Wort in der Theologie von Schleiermacher bis Ritschl," *Gesammelte Vorträge*, II, p. 190, on Feuerbach, p. 207, and on Strausz, p. 208.

It is very difficult, however, adequately to circumscribe Barth's polemic against modern Protestantism because of the undeniable variations within this area. For this reason it will be better to describe his more uniform polemic against *Rome*. Here we can see in an unusually clear manner the polemic significance of the triumph, the omnipotence of grace, in Barth's theology.

We are, moreover, constantly struck by the fact that for Barth this polemic is *essentially* the same as that against modern Protestantism. The triumph of grace does not see in these theologies two *radically* different opponents, but — with all their differences — one opponent. Against the new Protestantism Barth must "with the same definiteness, and ultimately and for the greater part on the same ground, say No in the same way as to Roman Catholicism."[8] This is a thesis which Barth develops in a number of connections in the whole of his dogmatics.[9] For this reason, Barth's struggle against Rome does not reveal simply an "aspect" of his theology, but rather its central and material purpose.

It is of importance to note the essence of Barth's criticism of Rome also for another reason. Roman Catholicism has, in the nature of the case, concerned itself with the question whether there is a connection between Barth's criticism and that of the Reformation, or whether Barth's criticism constitutes such a shifting of ground that there can be no question of identifying the two. Continuing reflection on the Rome-Reformation controversy naturally made this a point of unusual concern for Roman Catholic theologians.[10]

\*          \*          \*

---

8. K. Barth, *Das Bekenntnis der Reformation und unser Bekennen*, p. 35.

9. This does not mean that there is identity. It is true that Barth is of the opinion that the typically new Protestantism is *not* to be explained in terms of the Reformation, but that it can be understood in the light of Roman Catholicism. He adds, however, that the new Protestantism is *also* "a defection to the errors of Arius and Pelagius which were rejected already by the early Church," *ibid.*, p. 33. Cf. further the KD, passim, for valuable surveys of modern Protestant theology, as also his important study, *Die Protestantische Theologie im 19. Jahrhundert*, 1947.

10. Cf. my *Conflict met Rome*, 3rd ed., 1955, p. 202ff. The problem of the Barth-Reformation relationship plays an important role in the expositions of W. H. van de Pol, J. C. Groot, and H. U. von Balthasar, as was earlier the case with E. Przywara. The usual view is that of von Balthasar, who sees in Barth the consistent development of the Reformation and who therefore judges the Reformation in part in terms of the structure of Barth's theology.

Barth's polemic against Rome is most intimately related to his sharp rejection — dominant in his thinking from the very beginning — of *all and every self-justification of man.* His first concern here was not to oppose man's autonomous self-justification, but more specifically the religious justification of the pious man who formally acknowledges that he lives by God's grace alone, but whose life is *de facto* lived in terms of a system of thought which hardly leaves room for grace as sovereign and triumphant. It is in *this* area that Barth discovers the "hubris," the religious pride of the Christian man who, in spite of his profession of living by grace, nevertheless ascribes to man himself, in hidden and refined ways, a *decisive* voice in salvation. It is not Barth's intention to render from the heights a judgment on the human heart. He is concerned about the theological and confessional *framework* within which the Roman Church speaks and testifies. It is in this connection that at a given point — in his discussion of the doctrine of grace — he can suddenly and with sharp criticism say that we *must* assume that she does not actually live in terms of grace because in this way it is *not possible* to do so![11]

This limitation of his criticism to the religious self-justification of the pious man in no wise decreases the seriousness and the necessity of polemics, however, for his concern is with an enemy who threatens not only Roman Catholicism, but also the new Protestantism, traditional orthodoxy, and who, in fact, threatens us all. Over against the experiential theology of the 19th century Barth posited the theology of the triumphant Word of God, the justification of the godless. There can never be any other issue than the conquest of man by grace, the conquest of the old man, the religious man (the religious man in his *own* religion), who must die in order that in the resurrection of Christ he may participate in the victory which grace achieves.

Earlier, however, we heard Barth speak not only of God's right, but also of man's right and of the "self-evident character" of the

---

11. We think here of Barth's discussion of all manner of Roman Catholic distinctions in grace, KD IV/1, pp. 89ff. In connection with this treatment Barth writes, "It is hardly believable that they really live in terms of such a horribly split grace as their dogmatics present. Rather, it is necessary and comforting to believe that they like we — would we did it better — live from the one undivided grace of Jesus Christ," p. 89.

justification of man.[12] The question therefore arises why in *this* conception the triumph of grace is *not* threatened or obscured, and why in *this* connection we do not have to fear the "hubris" and over-evaluation of man.

These central questions inevitably come to confront us when we note the great earnestness with which Barth has from the beginning of his theological labors resisted that form of self-justification which, in his opinion, finds typical expression in the Roman Catholic system of doctrine. There is not in Barth any haughty or improper anti-papalism. He cannot very well be guilty of this, if for no other reason than his pointing again and again to the same danger which threatens *us all*. For this reason, he feels, no one may lightly enter upon the the path of polemic against Rome.

This does not alter the fact, however, that here — in Roman Catholicism — the danger comes to *acute* and *evident* expression. This must always serve as a warning to us. Rome claims to live in terms of the revelation of God and, with this revelation as a background, lives in the pretension that, according to the will of God, she is the one, only, and absolute ecclesia catholica. Even though old and new forms of humanism must also be rejected by the Church,[13] the development of Roman Catholicism enables us to see with unusual clarity the danger of Christian self-justification and the violation of the sovereignty of grace. It is instructurated in the whole system of her doctrine. Precisely for this reason the Roman Catholic conception of justification is so dangerous, for the appearance is created that the grace of God is in no way prejudiced.

---

12. KD IV/1, p. 702.
13. Cf. K. Barth, *Humanismus*, in *Theologische Studiën*, Heft 28, 1950, in which he places the "humanism of God" over against old and new humanism, p. 4, as the essence of the Christian message, and for which the incarnation is decisive, p. 5. This confession stands diametrically opposed to humanism as faith in man. This applies to earlier times, "but when I read Heidegger and Sartre, I ask myself whether the pride of man, despising grace as it does and therefore also bereft of grace, is not fully as unteachable today as it was then," p. 10. The Church must discharge the unpopular task of declaring that "man as he really is, constitutes an unlimited and unholy danger to himself," p. 10. Cf. also Barth's extensive criticism of Sartre's "typically mythological drama of a theogony," KD III/3, p. 394, and of his humanism, p. 391. In it the place of God is taken by *man*, p. 395. With respect to Heidegger cf. p. 394.

This brings us to the real difference between Barth and Rome. In *both* of these theologies there are triumphant elements. Rome has not infrequently chided the Reformation for harboring a certain pessimism because of her conception of the nature of man, and over against this has pointed to the triumphant work of God. How is it possible, and wherein lie the deepest grounds, that Barth's conception of the Christian message as a protest against "all pessimism, tragedy and skepticism,"[14] nevertheless stands diametrically opposed to the triumphant note of Rome's "theologia gloriae?"

\*       \*       \*

Barth has long regarded the Roman Catholic Church and her theology as *the* great opponent of evangelical biblical faith. In the struggle between the two viewpoints, the issue is no less than "the whole" of the Christian faith. Although the existence of Rome must always lead the Protestant Churches to self-examination, in which testing a weakened Protestantism will not be able to vindicate itself,[15] the fact remains that Rome herself has radically misunderstood the meaning of grace, and has come to believe in a *wrong* kind of triumph and to hold to an illegitimate conception of God's salvation. The grace which she confesses is not *truly* the grace of God, it is no longer *free* and *sovereign* grace. "I hold her to be a sinister, strong, and ultimately the only serious, challenger of evangelical theology."[16]

\*       \*       \*

When we follow the consistent line which Barth has pursued in his struggle with Rome from the beginning to the present, we are struck by the very heavy accent which he lays on the Reformation's *sola fide*. Even before 1930 this emphasis played a

---

14. *Humanismus*, p. 11.
15. K. Barth, "Der römische Katholizimus als Frage an die protestantische Kirche," *Zwischen den Zeiten*, 1928. Also in *Gesammelte Vorträge*, II, pp. 329ff. The questions which he asks are: 1. Whether the Protestant Church is really *Church* pp. 336ff., and 2. Whether she is *Protestant* Church, pp. 349ff. Cf. Kurt Frör, *Evangelisches Denken und Katholizismus seit Schleiermacher*, 1932, pp. 185ff.
16. K. Barth, *Theologische Blätter*, 1932, p. 221. Cf. also: "My whole work is concerned with the desperate question of achieving an evangelical theology which can stand worthily over against Roman Catholicism which I hold to be *the* great heresy," p. 222.

decisive role. In a discussion with Roman Catholics in 1927 Barth pointed to an expression in the Catechismus Romanus, "fide solum intelligimus" [by faith alone we understand]. He writes, "We can rest assured that if we were agreed as to the meaning of these three words, there would be no divisions in the Church."[17] It would then be possible to discuss all other questions whether papacy or sacraments, whether dogma or ritual, on basis of this agreement. This is not now the case, however, because the Reformation meant something wholly different by her "sola fide" than Rome means. It understood by this expression the full acknowledgment of the divine favor of grace, which is embraced by faith. In this grace there exists a relationship, but a relationship "without reciprocity,"[18] so that it can never give rise to any pretension from our side. It is precisely the nature of faith and of grace to exclude such pretension.[19] The relationship is not convertible, for we have not chosen Him but He has chosen us. Over against this, Barth finds in Roman Catholicism a *reciprocity* which infringes upon the reality of God's grace.

In faith a new relationship does indeed come into being, an "observing, an acknowledging, an experiencing,"[20] but this action does not bear a competing character, but exists precisely in the acknowledging of grace and therefore *cannot* constitute a limitation of it. That *this* has not been seen by Rome is the "fundamental failing" of Rome and of her theology. Therefore the "sola fide" of the Reformation attacked Roman Catholic heretical thinking at the very root. In the Roman Catholic Church and theology there also comes to expression a triumphant situation, but this manifests itself in terms of *a relationship of balance* between the believing individual and the grace of God. This is plain from the fact that Erich Przywara calmly interprets the "fide solum" of the Catechismus Romanus as the "ecclesia solum"[21] — to which it is, of course, related — and then speaks of the great significance of the "solum which conditions all and constitutes the foundation of all."

---

17. K. Barth, "Der Begriff der Kirche," *Zwischen den Zeiten*, 1927; *Gesammelte Vorträge*, II, p. 293.
18. *Gesammelte Vorträge*, II, p. 295.
19. *Ibid.*, p. 296.
20. *Ibid.*, p. 295.
21 E. Przywara, "Das katholische Kirchenprinzip," *Zwischen den Zeiten*, 1929, p. 284.

Here the difference becomes evident. This identification of the "fide solum" with the "ecclesia solum" discloses the deep divergence between Rome and the Reformation. In this way Roman Catholic theology establishes the balance through which God's hegemony of grace *over the Church* is replaced by a self-apotheosis of the Church.[22] In my book, *Karl Barth*,[23] I spoke of the "evident points of correspondence" between Barth and Calvin in their opposition against Rome. The constant later-recurring interpretation of the "sola fide" [i. e., since 1937] has made ever clearer that, with Calvin, Barth has sharply discerned the essential categories of the Roman Catholic doctrines of the Church and of grace. It may be said that Luther, Calvin, and Barth have all been deeply impressed by the fatal consequences of a specific doctrine of co-operation.

It is striking that nearly thirty years after his conflict with Rome about the "fide solum," the same analysis and the same answer are heard in his work on the doctrine of reconciliation (1953) in which he treats of justification by faith. Here he posits that the issue in the debate about the "sola fide" is that of the distinction between *faith* and *works*. It is erroneous to hold that man now performs the meritorious work of *faith* in the place of what is generally understood as good (meritorious) works. The faith that justifies does not take the place of meritorious work but excludes it, and rests in the grace of God.[24]

Understandably, Barth appeals time and again to all kinds of expressions of Calvin in connection with his discussion about the "emptiness" of faith which involves this, that justifying faith may not be seen as *our* work standing over against the work of God's grace. Neither Barth nor Calvin understand the "emptiness" of faith to mean that it is not a human act. They do mean that faith as a fully *human* act lives from and is directed to the grace of God and can therefore never stand in a *competing* relationship to it. In the "sola fide," faith "is set over against each and every kind of works."[25] Therefore Barth — in agreement with the Belgic Confession, Article 22 — does not consider the

22. K. Barth, *Grundfragen*, 1935, p. 17.
23. G. C. Berkouwer, *Karl Barth*, 2nd ed., 1937, p. 187.
24. KD IV/1, p. 687.
25. *Ibid.*, p. 693.

translation of Romans 2:28 as "through faith alone" to be a slanted translation. Rome has not understood Paul,[26] and all her other conceptions are related to this misunderstanding.

In the light of these considerations, the character of the triumph of grace changes radically. On the background of the significance which the "rediscovery" of Paul had for the Reformation, a certain parallel becomes visible between Rome and Judaism. Rome has not had an eye for "the essential meaning of the distinction that Paul makes between faith and works, she has not seen the wrath involved in this antithesis, or the mutual exclusiveness in terms of which Paul regarded both of them. She has not seen the bearing of this antithesis either for the exposition of the concept of faith or for that of works, and especially not for that of justification itself."[27] Finally, the reaction of the Council of Trent that comes to expression in its decree about justification shows that the Reformation, in its radical accentuation of the "sola fide — sola gratia" over against Rome, had a true insight into the meaning of the Scriptures.[28]

Apparently the Pauline-Reformation distinction did not make any impression upon the council. This is evident from the fact that, although justification was regarded from the viewpoint of the merits of Christ,[29] it was, so regarded, seen as a process in which the free will, weakened by sin, co-operates with grace and in which man is disposed to the reception of grace. Barth rightly emphasizes — as does H. Bavinck[30] — that Trent robs faith of its *central* place and gives it the function of initiating salvation, while justification is seen *analytically* in connection with and on the ground of the infused grace of actual sanctification.[31]

It was therefore natural that Trent rejected the "sola fide" of the Reformation. Apparently it regarded this "sola" as making salvation a one-sided matter! "Paul spoke not only of faith, but also of love and hope, and whoever wishes to think in a Pauline

---

26. *Ibid.*, p. 696.
27. *Ibid.*
28. *Ibid.*, p. 697. Cf. my *Conflict met Rome,* chapter IV.
29. KD IV/1, 698.
30. H. Bavinck, *Gereformeerde Dogmatiek,* I, p. 540.
31. We think of the "analytical" interpretation of Luther's doctrine of justification. Occasioned by this interpretation, Barth writes that if he had to choose between Rome and Luther as Holl interprets him he would choose for Rome, *Zwischen den Zeiten,* 1928, pp. 274ff.

fashion will have to follow him in this. But when he spoke of man's justification he spoke *only* of faith."[32] Therefore Rome, in pronouncing her anathema over the Reformation doctrine of "sola fide" placed herself under the anathema of Galatians 1.[33]

\* \* \*

This sharp dissent from Rome is evident not only in the doctrine of justification by faith, but also in countless other connections in the great controversy. Also in these points, however, we are impressed by the fact that the central issue is the proclamation of the *triumph* and the *omnipotence* of grace in contrast to the Roman Catholic dual emphasis on grace and freedom which, according to Barth, is so typical of Roman Catholic thinking about grace. It is not difficult to illustrate this one theme as it comes to expression on several points.

We meet a very illuminating illustration of Barth's antithesis to Rome in his rejection of her Mariology. Not without justification, he calls the dogma about Mary "nothing more and nothing less than the critical central dogma of the Roman Catholic Church." It is the dogma "in terms of which all her decisive positions must be regarded and with which they either stand or fall."[34] Here we see *the* heresy of Rome through which *all* her other heresies become transparent. Mary has become for Rome "the principle, the primal image, the sum, of the human creature who in his redemption serves co-operatively on the ground of prevenient grace, as she is also the principle, the primal image and the sum of the Church."[35]

Barth does no injustice here to Roman Catholic Mariology. The central function of Mary in redemption is to be the mediatrix of grace. He correctly points out that it is natural for Roman Catholic dogma to emphasize — with Thomas — that Mary is a *creature* and in *that* capacity takes her place in salvation *via* human co-operation. It is true that this co-operation is not autonomous, for it takes place against the background of grace, but against this background the co-operation is *real*. According to Barth, the Ref-

---

32. KD IV/1, p. 699.
33. *Ibid.*, p. 699.
34. KD I/2, p. 157.
35. *Ibid.*

ormation was wholly right in reacting to this only with an angry No, and we are called to continue this protest even more insistently today, now that the evolution of Mariology in the 19th century (1854) and in the 20th century (1950) has made the meaning of this co-operation even clearer than it was in earlier centuries.

To this Mariology, Barth continues, the doctrine of the *Church* also corresponds. Mary is the "mater ecclesiae" and this reflects not merely a romantic sentiment, but the relationship between Mary and the Church in which not only Mary but also the Church functions in the process of salvation.[36] Here, too, a reciprocity is posited between the Church and her Lord in which the intolerable competition again becomes visible, as it does in the relationship between Mary and Christ.[37]

Such reciprocity Barth cannot allow because it violates the being of the Church. All mediation is excluded because the Church lives only in terms of the grace of the one Mediator. "Faith is not some sort of an act of reciprocity, but the act of acknowledging the one Mediator, besides whom there is no other.[38]

\* \* \*

We meet the same point of view in the relationship between Scripture and Church. The purity of this relationship has been violated by Rome in that she has thrust aside the speaking God in His authority over the Church. In the Church there must be the absoluteness of the authority of God and, corresponding to this, the absoluteness of the *subjection* of the Church to her Lord. The protest against Rome may never assume the form of proclaiming one or another freedom-idea.[39] Precisely *in* our protest we must be exclusively concerned to secure the unreserved acknowledgment of Christ's authority. "Roman Catholicism is rebellion against the authority of the Word of God, it is rebellion against the canonical

---

36. With striking correctness Barth writes that there lies a consistency in the proclamations of Pius the IX in 1854 (the immaculate conception of Mary) and in 1870 (concerning the infallibility of the Pope and natural theology), KD I/2, p. 160. Cf. also p. 630.

37. We do not wish to forget here that the encyclical "Ineffabilis Deus" of 1854 accentuates the background of grace in the words "intuitu meritorium Jesu Christi." This accentuation certainly belongs to the whole of Roman Catholic Mariology, but it is far from guaranteeing the freedom and the sovereignty of grace.

38. KD I/2, p. 160.

39. *Ibid.*, p. 747.

Scriptures."[40] The Reformation protested against Rome "not because she knew too much about authority, but *too little.*"[41] There was no longer a true and really higher authority, "one that transcended the authority of the Church herself."[42] The idea of identification between Christ and the Church Barth correctly rejects,[43] because in the deep communion between Christ and His Church we may never forget the "opposition" between the Head and the members.[44]

Rome increasingly allowed tradition to occupy a place next to the Scriptures — tradition as the living Church[45] — with the result that there is no reason to call the decision concerning the infallibility of the Pope a real novum. The necessary confrontation and subordination of the Church to her Lord was lost in the identification, with the consequence that the opposite of true obedience came into being, namely, the self-government of the Church.[46] In this Barth sees the essence of Catholicism, in antithesis to the fact that self-government belongs exclusively to the prerogatives of God.[47] Only when this is first acknowledged will it be possible to speak of the authority — the *real* authority — of the Church "subject to the Word and therefore subject to the Sacred Scriptures."[48]

\* \* \*

In addition to the points that have up to now been mentioned, the controversy with Rome comes to sharp expression in direct connection with the doctrine of free will. Particularly does it come to expression in connection with the manifestation of free will as playing a hidden, and finally as playing a no longer hidden, role. As a typical example we may point to Barth's discussion of the so-

---

40. *Ibid.*
41. *Ibid.*
42. *Ibid.*, p. 640.
43. Cf. my *Conflict met Rome,* chapter I.
44. "The founding of the Church, her mandate and authority, and the personal presence of Christ in the Church do not remove the possibility and the necessity of such an antithesis between His and her authority. Rather in this antithesis and only in it does the unity of Christ with His Church and of His Church with Him *originate* and *exist,*" KD I/2, p. 641.
45. *Ibid.*, p. 628. Eminently noteworthy are the dogma-historical surveys of Roman Catholic theology in the 19th century, pp. 622ff, the Tübingen School, pp. 622ff., and "the inner necessity of the Vatican dogma," p. 633.
46. KD I/2, pp. 639ff.
47. *Ibid.*, p. 639. Concerning the temptation of the "Eritis sicut Deus," cf. p. 644.
48. *Ibid.*, p. 653.

called *scientia media*. The relationship between God and man is here decisively at issue. Again and again the question arose in Roman Catholic theology, in which way it was possible to reserve a place for the creature *within* the framework of God's action without prejudicing that action itself. The problem became particularly acute in connection with the "scientia Dei" because the free will was regarded as also being an object of God's knowing.[49]

In reflecting on the relationship between the knowledge of God and free will, theologians after Trent began to operate with the idea of the "scientia media." This doctrine was taught especially by the Molinists as that knowledge of God whereby He saw and knew beforehand what the creature would decide, and on the basis of this knowledge God then — i. e., via the scientia media — made the decision.

Things future came to stand in the light of the *prescience* of God, the *praescientia* or *praevisio Dei*. The Molinists were not in the first place concerned about the doctrine of this attribute of God as such, but about the connection, the synthesis, between grace and freedom.[50] In opposition to the Dominicans, they formulated the problem in the form of the scientia media and supposed that thereby they had found the point of contact for a balanced solution.[51]

Barth is fully aware that the Molinistic thesis concerning the scientia media has not been able to maintain itself without opposition and that the Thomistic opposition to it obtains to the present day. In spite of this opposition, however, the absence of an official decision makes it clear,[52] in his opinion, that "since the pronouncement of the anathema over the Reformation doctrine, the Jesuitic tendency, at least, cannot be regarded as not having a place in the Roman Catholic system of doctrine."[53]

The extensiveness with which Barth occupies himself with this problem in his doctrine of the divine attributes shows anew how

---

49. KD II/1, p. 640.
50. *Ibid.*, p. 640. Cf. my *Conflict met Rome*, pp. 119ff.
51. *Ibid.*, p. 641. Occasioned by an appeal of the Molinists to Mary, Barth writes, "Of course the maiden of the Roman Catholic tradition had necessarily to put in an appearance here." This remark, although ironically intended, rests materially on Barth's correct interpretation of Mariology (i. e., co-operation).
52. Cf. my *Conflict met Rome*, pp. 121ff.
53. KD II/1, p. 641.

deeply he is concerned with the necessity of tracing heresy to the remotest and most hidden corners of theology. He is here concerned to reject the co-operation and balance motif which for him constitutes a distortion of the nature of true faith and thereby of the sovereignty of grace. This solicitude also appears from the fact that in this very connection he warns Protestantism against thinking too highly of itself. It is precisely *here* that the same danger becomes acute for orthodoxy — and not only for Socinianism and Arminianism — although within the camp of orthodoxy Reformed theology is exposed to it in lesser measure than other theological directions.[54]

*        *        *

Finally, we wish to take note of what may be called the heart of Barth's polemic against Rome, namely, the controversy concerning the currently much discussed *analogia entis,* the analogy of *being* between God and man.

The impression may momentarily be gained that such a controversy is no longer primarily concerned with the doctrine of grace but with philosophical and metaphysical questions. It may be thought that here we are confronted with a problem which entered the discussion incidentally and in which the burden of interest is "ontological" rather than soteriological.

---

54. In connection with Arminianism note Barth's criticism of the ideas of praevisio and praescientia in KD II/2, pp. 72ff. and 363ff. Among the Reformed Barth points to those who discerned the issue, e. g., Voetius who saw the "scientia media" as the "asylum omnium pelagianizantium," II/1, p. 646; further van Mastricht and Turretin, and the Reformed majority who saw clearly here. In his view Gomarus and Walaeus accepted "with certain modifications" the scientia media "in all its forms," p. 647. According to Barth the case is more serious with the Lutherans who stand in the line of Melancthon and Gerhard, pp. 648ff., who laid a connection between the scientia media and the doctrine of grace (in the praevisa fides and the praevisa perseverantia). In his view the Thomists were more evangelical at this point than was this wing of orthodoxy, p. 650. Cf. also Barth's judgment of the Formula Concordiae (on the subject of the praescientia), KD II/2, pp. 75ff. Cf. the judgment of H. Bavinck on the scientia media and the influence which this solution has exercised in theology, *Gereformeerde Dogmatiek,* II, 4th ed., pp. 165-166. Also Bavinck refers to Voetius and Turretin in connection with the rejection of the scientia media. He is of the opinion, however, that Gomarus and Walaeus, in making use of the scientia media, intended something essentially different than the Molinists, and that no objection can be raised against their use of it, p. 167. We cannot now enter upon the difference between Barth and Bavinck on this point. We wish only to point out that, according to Barth, Gomarus did not wish to yield any ground to Jesuitic semi-Pelagianism, but that he wished to reject it even more sharply than had been done, KD II/1, p. 647.

On closer investigation it becomes clear beyond question, however, that for Barth the problem is in principle the same as those discussed above. This becomes apparent when he raises the problem of the analogia entis in connection with the just discussed scientia media. With reference to the Thomistic criticism of Molinism, Barth writes, "an effective denial of Molinism is possible only when thinking in terms of a God-creature-system, when thinking within the framework of the analogia entis, is fundamentally surrendered."[55]

It is clear that Barth's concern in discussing the analogy-of-being doctrine is not with an isolated theory, but with the *central point* of the controversy with Rome. It is not a contradiction when at one time Barth calls Mariology and at another time the doctrine of the analogia entis the real point of defection from the gospel. In his view, both represent, in their deepest thrust, *the same* heresy. As long as twenty years ago Barth summarized his view of the analogia entis as follows: "I regard the analogia entis as an invention of the antichrist, and I consider that because of it one cannot become a Roman Catholic. In saying this, I wish also to say that any other grounds which one may think to have for not becoming a Roman Catholic are, in my opinion, inadequate and are not to be taken seriously."[56] In another connection he speaks of the analogia entis as the "cardinal dogma" of Roman Catholicism.[57]

There is, therefore, every reason to look more closely into the nature of this sharp criticism, even though it will not be possible to discuss the controversy in all its ramifications. Our endeavor at this point is to show that Barth's polemic against the analogia entis intends to maintain that same sovereignty of grace which he defends unweariedly along the whole front of his opposition to Rome. A significant question at this point is whether, as has been suggested

---

55. KD II/1, p. 657.
56. KD I/1, p. vii.
57. KD II/1, p. 275. Cf. also p. 658: ". . . the great deceitful doctrine of the analogia entis as the fundamental structure of Catholic thinking and teaching." In our own time Roman Catholics have on more than one occasion referred to the principle of the analogia entis as the central point of divergence between Rome and the Reformation. Undoubtedly Barth has been stimulated in his analysis by this circumstance. Karl Adam spoke of the analogia entis as "the chief Catholic word," *Gesammelte Aufsätze*, 1936, p. 232, while Peter Wust spoke of the magic wand of the analogy, and Przywara of the crossroads between atheism and Catholicism "in the camp of German Protestantism"!, *Stimmen der Zeit*, 1935, p. 416. Especially E. Przywara has given currency to the term.

in recent discussions, Barth has, in whole or in part, changed his position with respect to his earlier opposition to the analogia entis. The answer to this question will, in the nature of the case, determine our view of Barth's development, especially as that development is revealed in the context of his struggle with Rome.

*    *    *

This discussion is intimately related to the fact that Barth himself speaks emphatically of a certain *analogy* between God and man. He speaks continually, for instance, of an "analogia relationis." Many have concluded that such a relation assumes a *being* and that *therefore* the analogia *relationis* assumes the analogia *entis*. It is very evident, however, that Barth himself places the analogia relationis over against every conception of an analogia entis. Barth wishes to use the concept of the analogia relationis to indicate the *meaning* of the image of God. This may not, however, "be interchanged with one or another kind of analogia entis."[58]

Barth means that in describing the relationship between God and man, we may never speak of an objective state of affairs, but we must speak of a *relationship* which is founded in God and *remains* founded in Him. Barth does not wish to posit a denial of the analogy idea over against the analogia entis.[59] He wishes to speak of the analogy as the analogy of *faith*.[60] There is not in man a point of contact "in the sense of a native or acquired property of man," [61] but *in* faith, *in* the relationship of faith, "God-likeness" *comes into being*. That is to say, the analogy of faith means: "correspondence to the known in knowing, to the object in thinking, to the Word of God in thought and in the spoken human word."[62] It is only in terms of the divine revelation, in terms of the being-known, that there is a "correspondence," an analogy. There is nothing impersonal in this relationship. All depends on the meeting that takes place *in* the revelation to which faith is directed. The way of knowledge is not via conclusions drawn from a fixed

58. KD III/1, p. 219.
59. KD I/1, p. 257.
60. *Ibid.*, p. 257, and also in the *Prolegomena;* and in both places with an appeal to Romans 12:6.
61. KD I/1, p. 257.
62. *Ibid.*, p. 257.

relationship as a state of affairs, but via "confrontation and communion"[63] between God and man.

Although it is relevant to ask why Barth continues to speak of an analogy, it is wholly clear that one cannot, on the basis of Barth's analogy-concept, conclude that he also accepts the analogia entis. This conclusion is unwarranted because, in his view, the analogia entis does not consist in and rest upon the grace relationship, the living encounter between God and man, while the analogia relationis consists precisely in that.[64]

This also reveals, however, why Barth continues to speak of an analogy. There is a connection between the known and the knowing. It is *not* true that there is really no reality that corresponds to our concepts when we speak about God. There is more than simply dissimilarity, more than "something that is exclusively other."[65] "One had better be careful what one asserts when he asserts that." Dissimilarity would mean that *we cannot know God.* "That *we* know Him must mean that *we*, with our views, conceptions, and words, do not designate and give expression to something wholly other than He. It must mean that in and with these means of expression, the only ones available to us, we designate Him, even Him! Without this relationship there could not, on the presupposition of simple dissimilarity, be any possibility of genuineness in our knowledge of God."[66]

Therefore Barth persists in using the word "analogy," be it ever so burdened with associations of natural theology.[67] In this analogy, however, in which the genuineness of our knowledge of God rests in the genuineness of God's *revelation,* something wholly different is envisioned than analogies which we ourselves originate — apart from God's revelation — and use to achieve knowledge of God.[68] This is the heart of Barth's polemic against the analogia entis and therefore there is no possibility that his use of the expression "analogia relationis" should involve any concessions to the analogia entis conception. The "relation" of which Barth speaks refers to a relation which is founded in God's revela-

---

63. *Ibid.*, p. 136.
64. Cf. KD II/1, p. 257.
65. *Ibid.*, p. 253.
66. *Ibid.*, pp. 253-254.
67. *Ibid.*, p. 254.
68. *Ibid.*, pp. 82ff.

tion and which therefore can be and is the basis of true knowledge
of God. He is concerned to reject every conception of the knowledge of God which sustains no relationship to grace and to faith.
Barth's confession is not an incommensurableness between God
and man which would make any predication about God dubious
by virtue of the infinite distance between Him and the creature;
it is rather the revelation of God's grace which alone unlocks the
gates of the genuine knowledge of God.[69]

By means of a criticism of natural theology in which the principle of the analogia entis dominates, Barth thought to be able to
point out clearly the error which threatens here. The issue that
he posits here is the fundamental question about the receptiveness
or non-receptiveness of man to God's revelation. According to
natural theology, man has within himself, specifically in his
reason, the possibility of understanding God's relevation, namely,
the revelation of God in created reality. Because there is an analogy between God's being and man's being, man can by way of
conclusion come to a true knowledge of God. Even though this
natural knowledge of reason is not adequate, it is, for all that,
*true* knowledge. On basis of an objective state of affairs, man
can, *quite apart from grace,* achieve knowledge of God.

Against this conception Barth protests. He posits with the
greatest emphasis that we can achieve knowledge of God *only*

---

69. This point of view does not come to sufficient expression, it seems to me, in
J. C. Groot's discussion, "De analogie in Barth's denken" (in *De Analogie van
het Zijn,* 1942, p. 80). Groot concludes that Barth's analogy conception is in the
final analysis a *denial* of any and all analogy because of the radical distance
through which all correlation with the created word is abrogated, p. 83.
That this does not represent Barth wholly correctly appears also from the fact
that Groot then says that Barth does not continually dare to draw the final consequences of his position, p. 80. In any case it will be necessary to compare with
the idea of distance what Barth writes *against* the idea of the "inequality" of the
creature (KD II/1, p. 257) and against the idea of a two-fold truth and the "as
if" (ibid., p. 258). The divine revelation *in* our creaturely reality is the revelation of the Creator and "not a riotous miracle." Rather, it is a "legal claim"
through which men can come to a true knowledge of God (pp. 258, 259). Barth
does speak here decisively and continually of the *grace* of God's revelation, but
he does not thereby intend to introduce via another way an imputative ("purely
external imputative," Groot, p. 81) "as if", but to point to that gracious revelation of God which leads us by way of creation to the knowledge of God (this
Barth shows very clearly in KD II/1, p. 260). Here Barth polemicizes anew
against the idea of static analogy in natural theology in which the order of
things is reversed and the knowledge of God is derived by means of the analogy
but *apart from the revelation,* KD II/1, p. 260. "We have no reason to say No
once God has in His revelation said Yes. All depends on our saying Yes there
and only there where God has said Yes," p. 261.

through "a reaching out, which has taken place and takes place from the side of God."[70] According to Barth, there is no possibility of the knowability of God or of the knowledge of God apart from this "reaching out." There is no analogy on basis of which, *beginning with ourselves,* we can come to a knowledge of God's being.[71]

Not only do we not know God as Reconciler, as Lord and Savior, but we do not know Him either as Creator. There is no "pre-understanding" (on the basis of an analogy of being) in which room is later given to God's *grace.* In no single respect can we speak of "a prior knowledge about creation which we have of ourselves."[72] It is only God's grace and mercy that make it possible for us to know God also as Creator. Therefore Barth radically rejects the Vatican doctrine of the knowability of God as Creator and Lord by virtue of the natural light of reason.[73] This *partial* knowledge of the true God (outside the *gracious* revelation in Christ) involves a division in the knowledge of God which has as its background a knowledge of God as Creator *in abstracto.* According to Rome man would "also without revelation have knowledge concerning God and in fact has such knowledge."[74] This would be a possibility and an actuality by means of the analogia entis as descriptive of an objective state of affairs, namely, that "God and man are here seen together as standing on a common and therefore neutral basis."[75] There is no question here of an *acting* of God, only of a *being* of God, which is known apart from any action on God's part.[76] This is, in Barth's view, nothing less than an "insult to the Christian idea of God,"[77] because it is imagined that one *can* come to the true God (the "posse" of the Vatican Council) without reference to His grace and mercy.

How is it possible, Barth asks, that natural theology is so vital, since it is so *evident* that the knowing of the true God can take

70. KD II/1, p. 80.
71. *Ibid.,* p. 82.
72. *Ibid.,* p. 83.
73. *Ibid.,* p. 86.
74. *Ibid.,* p. 88.
75. *Ibid.*
76. Occasioned by Söhngen's observation that the knowledge of God's being is subordinate to that of His action, Barth noted that if this were a legitimate interpretation of the analogia entis he would be prepared to drop his criticism of it, KD II/1, pp. 89ff, but that this is not in his judgment the case.
77. KD II/1, p. 93. Cf. also p. 140.

its rise only in His free grace?[78] The only answer he can find to this question is that man resists living *exclusively* in terms of grace. On basis of the analogia entis, natural theology posits an essential readiness, an openness for the knowledge of God as that knowledge is *already* present in natural man *prior to* and *apart from* the encounter with the gracious God.[79] This man of the natural theology is the man who knows God *without* the miracle of grace, he is the *rich* man who can know God *without* standing in need of grace.[80] It is for this reason that natural theology is so vital. Here we see through the "invention of the antichrist"! Natural theology is not a coincidence.[81] In natural theology man *denies* his being completely *closed* to revelation. It is "the one heresy which arises by natural necessity,"[82] and "the vitality of natural theology is the vitality of man as such."[83] For this reason it must be rejected without mercy.

It is therefore plain that in his struggle against the analogia entis, Barth is not concerned about the problem of analogical concepts in general, as these played a role especially in the Middle Ages, but that his concern is with the analogia entis (of God and man) in connection with our knowledge of the true, the gracious God. In distinction from *this* analogy, Barth points to the "experiencing" of God's grace which is founded in God's readiness, and which can never be explained in terms of an already present readiness in man.

This criticism of the analogia entis has through the many years of his development remained constant in Barth and continues to belong to the essence of his theology.

\* \* \*

In the light of the foregoing, we must next face the question how it has come about that some consider Barth now to have accepted *in principle* the doctrine of the analogia entis. If this were indeed true, it would be reasonable to suppose that there would be discernible an incisive modification in his polemic against Rome. The idea that a change has taken place in Barth

---

78. *Ibid.*, p. 139.
79. *Ibid.*, p. 143.
80. *Ibid.*, p. 144.
81. *Ibid.*, p. 149
82. *Ibid.*, p. 159.
83. *Ibid.*, p. 185.

is represented most clearly by the Roman Catholic theologian, Hans Urs von Balthasar, who is of the opinion that Barth has gradually come to a full acceptance of the analogia entis. In support of this thesis he points to Barth's later appreciation for the cosmos as a creature of God.[84] Increasingly he hears Barth speak of an analogy between God and man. Creatureliness has real significance. It is not an appearance, but possesses a relative particularity and independence.[85] There is a being-good of the creature which is dependent upon God, yet is not condemned to not-being. It is *His* good creature, and therewith Barth has, according to von Balthasar, *essentially* accepted the analogia entis and his whole polemic against Rome has — on this point — become meaningless.[86]

It is not possible to enter upon an extensive discussion of von Balthasar's intention to re-open the door to a renewed confrontation between Rome and the Reformation via this analysis of Barth's alleged development in the direction of the analogia entis.[87] We may not ignore it either, however, for the analogia entis touches the fundamental motif of Barth's theology. We are of the opinion that von Balthasar's interpretation that Barth has undergone a "change" is in error at a decisive point and that therein the fundamental fallacy of his masterful and in certain respects irenic book is to be found.

---

84. H. U. von Balthasar, *Karl Barth, Darstellung und Deutung seiner Theologie,* 1951. Concerning this suggestive book cf. M. P. van Dijk, "Een Rooms Katholiek Wrk over Karl Barth, *Gereformeerd Theologisch Tijdschrift,* 1952, Vol. IV, and J. J. Louët Feisser, "Misverstand rondom Karl Barth's leer over de Schepping," *Nederlands Theologisch Tijdschrift,* 1952.

85. With reference to KD III/3, pp. 98, 99.

86. Cf. especially the following sections in von Balthasar's work: "Die Wendung zur Analogie," pp. 93ff., and "Die Vollgestalt der Analogie," pp. 124ff.

87. von Balthasar is aware of "the obvious dogmatic differences" with respect to the Church, the ministry, the sources of revelation, the sacraments, etc., p. 11. He does not wish to obscure these in an unwarranted irenicism. He does eliminate them from his investigation, however, because he wishes to analyze Barth on the score of his view of the *formal structure* of Roman Catholicism (the analogia entis), p. 44. This *key* he wishes to examine, p. 45. With respect to *this* matter he concludes that a schism was not necessary. This does not, it is true, decide the issue at stake in the second complex of questions (the Church, the sacraments, etc.), but it is clear, in von Balthasar's view, that it is not possible to develop and come to a solution of the controversy in terms of the analogia entis. The basis of von Balthasar's opinion is his view of Barth's development in the direction of the analogia entis (cf. the section, "Vollgestalt der Analogie") and of Christocentric theology for which there is also room within the framework of the Roman Catholic Church and her theology. Cf. pp. 335ff., with their references to Schmaus, Mersch, Guardini, and others.

This comes sharply to the fore — though not here alone — in von Balthasar's observations in connection with Barth's criticism of *Quenstedt*. The complicated character of this problem need not prevent us from seeing that *the* central point is raised here anew. Barth discusses Quenstedt in connection with the genuineness of man's knowledge of God.[88] The question that is raised here is, whether and in how far the concepts in terms of which we speak about God are really suitable to indicate the reality of God. When we know God, there is, according to Barth, a *real* analogy between our concepts and God. "The creatures who are the suitable object of our human concepts and words are indeed His creation."[89] There is an analogy, but *that* we know God by way of our concepts is grace, and this grace stands over against the natural self-evidence of knowledge which is from man alone.[90] There is not here an analogy which we discover and from which we can draw conclusions. There is only the grace of God's revelation.[91]

It is in this connection that Barth speaks about Quenstedt. This Lutheran theologian asks whether God and the creature can be subsumed under the same concept. Have God and man a common *being* and are they analogous? In answering this question he rejects both the univocal and the equivocal character of concepts and chooses for that of the *analogia attributionis*. By this he means that the common being is first in the one and thereafter in the other, in the sense that the second is dependent upon the first.[92]

To this Quenstedt adds, that the analogia attributionis is not only *extrinseca,* but also *intrinseca;* i.e., the analogy is in respect of what is *proper* to God and to the creature (by virtue of creation).[93] At this point Barth raises objections. He agrees with the

---

88. KD II/1, pp. 254ff.
89. *Ibid.,* p. 257.
90. *Ibid.,* p. 261.
91. *Ibid.,* p. 263.
92. "Univoca" means that the same word or name is applied in the *same sense* to various entities. "Aequivoca" means that the same word or name is applied in wholly varying senses to various entities. The *analogy* rejects both the univocal and the aequivocal character of concepts, and stands in a certain sense between them. Cf. G. P. Kreling, *De Analogie van het Zijn,* 1942; H. Dooyeweerd, "De leer der analogie in de Thomistische wijsbegeerte en in de wijsbegeerte der Wetsidee," *Philos. Reformata,* 1942, pp. 47ff.; and the extensive study of H. Lyttkens, *The Analogy between God and the World. An Investigation of its Background and Interpretation of its Use by Thomas Aquino,* Uppsala, 1952.
93. KD II/1, p. 269.

attribution, but not with the attributio *intrinseca* which is conceived of as being proper to the creature as such. He does acknowledge that Quenstedt posits dependence in the analogia attributionis, but he does not do this in such a way "that it consists wholly in this relationship."[94] Quenstedt finally falls back on a neutral state of affairs, a relationship, an *existent* relationship, *which is simply there,* and which can dispense with the revelation and *precedes* the revelation. Barth protests against this assumed stable relationship between God and the creature. If this were a correct description of the God-creature relationship, the creature as such would possess revelational qualities and it would no longer be necessary for God mercifully to reveal himself in order to give us knowledge. We meet the same problem here which Barth had earlier discussed, namely, the "world-relatedness" of the revelation, and with which his criticism of Quenstedt fully agrees.[95]

The remarkable thing that calls for attention, however, is that von Balthasar does not take this criticism seriously. He observes, "this [Barth's argument contra Quenstedt] must, in the context of our discussion, be described as a drawing of conclusions which is refuted by the argument itself."[96] This sentence may be called the crux on which the whole of von Balthasar's analysis of Barth turns. Only in this way is it possible for him to maintain that Barth now holds to the "full-fledged acceptance of the analogy [of being]." This reveals, however, the weakness of his effort to remove the stumblingblock of the analogia entis. In all his discus-

---

94. *Ibid.,* p. 269.
95. Cf. my *De Algemene Openbaring,* 1951, p. 251ff. (English translation, *General Revelation,* 1955, p. 297ff.), and *De Persoon van Christus,* 1952, pp. 294ff. (English translation, *The Person of Christ,* 1952, p. 336ff.), in connection with Barth KD I/1, pp. 17ff. On the same question cf. J. J. Louët Feisser, "Misverstand rondom Barth's leer over de Schepping," *op. cit.,* pp. 292ff. Although Louët Feisser's criticism of von Balthasar is, in my opinion, correct, the question may be asked whether in his criticism of Barth he gives a proper rebuttal. He speaks of *"creation and man's being"* as what "in our judgment, they are in the Bible: *in themselves* made after God's image and likeness," p. 298, and further that "the creation participates in God's being," p. 298. Cf. his agreement with Loen that "created reality is in itself revelatory," p. 299, and with his development of the doctrine of creation in the direction of creatio continua. It does not seem to me to be possible to find the solution of the analogy problem in an "analogia existentials," p. 300.
96. H. U. von Balthasar, *op. cit.,* p. 120.

sion, it appears how seriously Barth means his criticism of Quenstedt. The very idea against which he objects is that theology should take its point of departure from an analogy between God and man which resides in the creature and which is stable in character. The factor that makes the creature analogous to God "does not lie in him or in his nature, also not in the sense that God could recognize and accept as an analogy something lying in the nature of the creature as such."[97] But precisely *that* is the nature of the analogia entis, and against that conception Barth continues to direct his criticism. The way to the "full-fledged acceptance of the analogy" on which von Balthasar sees Barth walking remains for Barth a path that leads astray. Barth's criticism of Quenstedt should have prevented von Balthasar from attempting this rapprochement.

Barth does not wish to "draw conclusions." He is concerned about consequences. The seriousness with which he regards his difference with Quenstedt appears from the fact that he introduces into his discussion the question of *grace*. If Quenstedt had no other interest than to discuss justification, Barth argues, it would have sufficed for him to operate only with the analogia attributionis *extrinseca*, i.e., a relationship to the actuality of God's gracious action. When he introduces the "intrinseca" in connection with the question of justification, however, must this not *necessarily* lead to a conception of man's readiness to believe? If Quenstedt can agree with Thomas in the "intrinseca" of analogical knowledge, why can he not also agree with him in his doctrine of *grace?*[98]

Clearly, there is no question here of an approach to the analogia entis which Barth had earlier attacked as *the* Roman Catholic heresy and as an invention of the antichrist.[99] He does speak of an analogy, but this is not an analogy to which we can conclude from some objective state of affairs, but which is founded only in God's *gracious action*.

---

97. KD II/1, p. 270.
98. *Ibid.*, p. 270.
99. It speaks decisively against von Balthasar that already in the time of Barth's sharpest criticism of the analogia entis (KD I/1, 1932, p. 353), he adduces substantially the same objections which in II/1 he raises against Quenstedt. It is true that in I/1 Barth treats of the analogy of the trinity (vestigium trinitatis), but essentially his polemic is the same as that against Quenstedt.

Quenstedt's "intrinseca" means for Barth the entering upon a path which must unavoidably lead to a natural theology. The analogia attributionis intrinseca essentially involves the acceptance of a relationship of being, an analogical co-existence, between God and man. This analogy describes a given and objective state of affairs through which, in principle, the way is opened to a knowledge of God apart from grace.[100] It can only be called a fortunate inconsistency if, in operating with such a conception, we come to conclusions in Christology and in the doctrine of justification in which grace is honored.[1]

Barth continues to reject the analogia entis radically. It constitutes an attack on the divine initiative shown in grace, it infringes upon the power and the triumph of grace in its antithesis to the inability and lost condition of the sinner. The triumph of *free* grace is *the* counter-pole to the analogia entis.

According to the Scriptures, "it is not a being common to God and man which, in the final analysis, constitutes and sustains their communion. It is God's grace which does this."[2] This grace was and is the reality of God's action and constitutes the basis — even when Barth speaks of an "analogy" — for the rejection of the analogia entis.

\* \* \*

The question has been asked, whether Barth has rightly represented the Roman Catholic idea of the analogia entis.[3] Roman Catholic theologians have denied this. They deny that the analogia entis involves the idea of a common participation of God and man in a *third* reality, namely "being."

However important this question of interpretation may be particularly as the analysis bears on Thomism, our first concern is to understand what Barth intends to achieve in his opposition to the analogia entis. His purpose, clearly, is to concentrate on the importance of seeing the "being" in the analogy in its relationship to God's *action.*

The very fact that Barth speaks of an analogia relationis and attributionis, but *not* of an analogia entis, provides strong support

---

100. KD II/1, p. 272.
1. *Ibid.*, p. 273.
2. *Ibid.*, p. 275.
3. Cf. the study of J. J. Louët Feisser, *De Strijd tegen de Analogia Entis in de Theologie van Karl Barth,* 1948, and my *Barthianisme en Katholicisme,* 194

for this thesis. He maintains that the *concept of being* is not a suitable means for pointing the way to knowledge of God, because true knowledge of God is given only in the miracle of God's revelation.[4]

This does not mean that Barth opposes the concept of being as such and undertakes, in so doing, to provide a new and realistic solution to the problem of being.[5] He states emphatically that we may and must concern ourselves with the question of God's being. He does not wish to express this concern in terms of a general conception of being, however, but in terms of the being of *God,* who cannot be known apart from the *act* of His revelation.[6] We cannot, according to Barth, speak of a knowledge of the general being of God, to which later the knowledge of his action can be added. His being is revealed *in* His action. It is precisely God's being, who He really *is,* that is revealed to us "at the point of His dealings with us as Lord and Savior. If we do not meet Him here, we will meet Him nowhere."[7] God *is,* not as an abstract quality of being, but *in* the act of His revelation, *in* His *works.*[8]

He is not the "esse absolutum," but the *living* God, pure in act in the actuality of His *work* and revelation.[9] The question, as Barth characteristically puts it, is that of "God's being in deed,"[10] His *being* "in the modes-of-being of the Father, the Son, and the Holy Spirit."[11] He and His "being" can be found and known only in His *act* and decision: Jesus Christ. "There is not a moment in God's being outside of this act and decision."[12] It is never possible to transcend this conception to get at the *real* being of God as it is *in itself.*

Every pronouncement about the being of God must find its exclusive legitimation in its correspondence to the *act* of His revela-

---

4. It is helpful to compare this criticism of the analogia entis with that of H. Dooyeweerd, "De leer der analogie in de Thomistische Wijsbegeerte en in de wijsbegeerte der Wetsidee," *Philos. Reformata,* 1942, pp. 48-57, particularly with respect to his appreciation for Kreling's observation that the central problem of the knowledge of God lies outside the area of the problem of the analogy of being, p. 54.
5. KD II/1, p. 291.
6. *Ibid.,* p. 292.
7. *Ibid.,* p. 293.
8. *Ibid.*
9. *Ibid.,* p. 295.
10. *Ibid.,* pp. 288ff.
11. *Ibid.,* p. 305
12. *Ibid.*

tion. "God is He who is not only to be found in His act alone, but who can be *found* in His act alone because He is who He *is* only in this *act*."[13] Barth is concerned not only with a noetic problem (the way to the knowledge of God), but first and foremost with an ontic problem, the reality, the dynamic, the actuality, *in* the being of God. In this way alone God *is* and therefore we know Him only here and in this way. Only in this way do we know "God's being as Love."[14]

It is not permissible to object to the conception of being as such.[15] All depends, however, on rightly understanding this being of God and on rejecting an abstract view of it. For this reason von Balthasar was not warranted in concluding that, "in many places in his dogmatics we see him describing the relationship between God and the creature in terms of the classic formulation of the analogia entis."[16] Barth never uses the concept of analogy to refer to the analogia entis which he opposed from the beginning. His references to analogy serve only to exclude the analogia entis from theological consideration *as a description of an objective state of affairs*.

It is of importance to note that von Balthasar also thinks to discern an approach to the analogia entis in Barth in connection with his relationship to Brunner. In the first phase of the conflict between them, Barth opposed Brunner's idea of the "point of contact" because he regarded this as presupposing a "suitability" in man for the reception of God's revelation. He posited that God, in His revelation, *creates* the true point of contact, and that there is in no way a prior habitus in man for such reception. According to von Balthasar, this polemic (against the potentia oboedientialis) became superfluous in proportion to the measure in which Barth began to think more and more in Christocentric terms. In this Christocentric conception, von Balthasar argues, the whole creation is seen *precisely* as "potentiality for the act of revelation,"[17] a *presupposition* of grace. Herein he sees nothing less than the analogia entis: "The fully accepted idea of the

13. *Ibid.*, p. 305.
14. *Ibid.*, pp. 306ff.
15. *Ibid.*, p. 291.
16. H. U. von Balthasar, *op. cit.*, p. 178.
17. *Ibid.*, p. 179. Cf. also p. 390: "The manner in which Karl Barth understands the revelation of God in creation in terms of Christ involves as analogia fidei the analogia entis."

potentia oboedientialis makes more secure the conception of the analogia entis in the very sense in which Barth understands it, namely, as the function of what he designates as the analogia fidei."[18] This latter idea, however, is the crux of the matter. Barth does speak of a destiny of the creature which is "towards Christ," but this is not, in the sense of a potentia oboedientialis, a "natural" presupposition which precedes grace and is then realized in grace. Creation itself is Christologically qualified, and even though man is destined to be God's covenant partner, this does not, according to Barth, involve a human attribute. "We have not been created *as* God's covenant partners, but *with a view to* being such."[19]

It appears, therefore, that also in the Christocentric development of his dogmatics Barth's struggle against the analogia entis has undergone no change. It is therefore a misunderstanding on Brunner's part when he opines that Barth has substantially dropped his objections against the analogia entis. Brunner — like von Balthasar — points to Barth's use of analogy and discovers in it a fortunate shifting of ground. "I am happy that this standpoint, which has occasioned so much discussion, is now no longer an issue."[20] There is every reason to ask, however, whether there is ground for Brunner's optimism, the more so because Barth himself[21] emphatically denies that he has changed his position. In his earlier and in his later writings his concern was not to deny any and every kind of analogy,[22] but rightly to understand the *nature* of the analogy that exists between God and man. The

---

18. *Ibid.*, p. 180.
19. KD III/2, pp. 285-286.
20. E. Brunner, *Dogmatik*, II, p. 52.
21. Brunner has on more than one occasion given expression to an agreement with Barth which did not in fact exist. In 1934 he wrote in *Natur und Gnade*, p. 57, "I am therefore — in fact, already for many years — in agreement with Barth that no legitimate knowledge of God can be obtained by resorting to the principle of the analogy of being, that is, per viam eminentiae, but that it can be gained only in terms of Jesus Christ." This "in agreement with Barth" does not square with the facts. Barth would not write, "no legitimate knowledge," but "no knowledge at all." The difference is everything but subtle.
22. Already in the KD I/1 Barth places the analogia fidei over against the analogia entis, p. 257. Analogia *fidei*, analogia *relationis*, analogia *attributionis extrinseca*, and analogia *operationis* — all these expressions are for Barth antihetical to the idea of analogia entis. Cf. Barth: with the concepts analogia relationis and operationis "we make a *flanking movement* around natural theology and roll up its front from behind," quoted by K. H. Miskotte in *Kerk en Theologie*, 1951, p. 204.

conclusion of Brunner that the analogy *as* analogia fidei "inheres in the God-created *being* as such and does not first come into existence through faith"[23] continues to meet Barth's opposition. He wishes to speak of this "being" only in connection with the gracious *action* of God.

Neither Brunner nor von Balthasar have in their attempts at synthesis done justice to the fundamental intentions of Barth's opposition to the analogia entis. There is no question of a "drawing of conclusions" when he combats Quenstedt. There is, rather, a conscious *maintaining* of his original intention. When we see how positively Barth speaks, for instance, of the *good* creation as such, we are struck the more by his *continued* rejection of the analogia entis.

It can be said of the whole of Barth's development, that his struggle against the analogia entis is for him indissolubly bound up with his struggle against the denial of *sovereign* grace, one can also say, against every form of synergism. This synergism he discerns in the Roman Catholic doctrine of grace, in the doctrine of the Church, in Mariology, and in the analogia entis.

In all of these aspects the issue is the sovereignty of grace, the divine initiative in grace, the triumph of God's grace as *His* exclusive triumph. Because Barth sees synergism as *the* Roman Catholic heresy, and finds it no less in natural theology (on the basis of the analogia entis), the decision respecting the validity of Roman Catholic theology falls for him precisely at this point.

Barth wants to erect a barrier against every effort to achieve a synthesis between grace and freedom, between God and man which would, as creating a "balance," be far removed from the dependence of faith upon the sovereign grace of God. The sharp criticism that is found in his doctrine of reconciliation against Rome's misrepresentation of the difference between faith and works is the continuation of his struggle against the analogia entis.[24]

---

23. E. Brunner, *op. cit.,* p. 51.
24. Whether Barth gives a correct historical interpretation of Rome's position is, in the nature of the case, important. Note the efforts of von Balthasar to show that the deliverance of the Vatican council with respect to the natural knowledge of God can and must be otherwise interpreted than is usually done particularly in the section, "die Natur im Vatikanum," *op. cit.,* pp. 314-335. I my judgment von Balthasar's interpretation of the Vatican council is untenable at this point. A shadow therefore falls over this in itself engrossing discussion

In this one struggle, which comes to expression on various fronts, Barth is consistently concerned to defend the triumph of grace. This triumph can be a triumph of grace only when it is seen as issuing not from man's openness and readiness, but from God Himself. It is the triumph that is indicated in the words of Jeremiah, "O Jehovah, thou hast persuaded me, and I was persuaded; thou art stronger than I, and hast prevailed" (Jer. 20:7).

I am not aware that Barth cites this passage anywhere. But undoubtedly he would see in it the manner in which the triumph of God's grace becomes a reality. He would regard it not as pointing to a competition between the divine persuasion and the human submission to persuasion, but as the joyful acknowledgment of the gracious omnipotence through which God effects His triumph.

---

24. (*Continued from p. 194*).
between the "théologie nouvelle" and Barth. In any case, it will not do to see the work by von Balthasar as, without qualification, *the* Roman Catholic work on Barth *or* on Rome.

# VIII

## AMBIGUOUS TRIUMPHS OF GRACE IN THE HISTORY OF THEOLOGY

I T MAY BE asked whether the dominant note of the triumph of grace in the theology of Karl Barth does not require an immediately favorable decision on the score of the truth and significance of that theology. Is a favorable judgment over a theology which emphasizes the grace of God so centrally and so consistently not a matter of course? When, as we have seen, we find not a theology of crisis and defeat born in a post war mood of desperation, but one of grace and restoration, of the justification of the godless over against the self-justification of man, should this not settle the issue of the validity or non-validity of Barth's conception? Does not its pointing to the triumph of grace and to the joy of the gospel guarantee its biblical character?

*    *    *

Throughout the whole of Barth's dogmatics we hear at every significant point and in every polemic the words of the gospel, the affirmation in terms of which one can live and die.[1] These emphases determine the center of his theology with pronounced and ever increasing clarity. We hear the melody of grace, of fearlessness and of victory, even in the outermost reaches of this dogmatic effort.

Particularly in its polemic against Rome and modern Protestantism, we hear a continual appeal to the evident message of the Scriptures: the decisive and exclusive — and therefore inclusive — gracious action of God over against every form of religious autonomy and synergism. This victory note does not mean the annihilation of man, but rather the gracious *determining of his place* in God's world, the place in which he finds rest and sings his hymn of praise. Does not this hymn of praise correspond to the glory of

---

1. Cf. KD III/4, p. ix.

God?[2] Is further reflection and investigation necessary when in this way the New Testament and the Church in her message of praise are made to speak of the glory of God, of the "superabundance, the overflowing perfection, of the divine being?" Can there be any doubt about the biblical character of a theology which speaks of the creature's overflowing glorification of God, and that not incomprehensibly and in general, but in connection with "His glory revealed in Jesus Christ?"[3]

\* \* \*

It is not at all in conflict with Barth's own conception of theology when we observe that reflection and testing are necessary precisely where the triumph of grace is the issue. That is to say, every theology of grace must be tested on the score of its scriptural legitimacy. Simply to *posit* the theme of the "triumph of grace" does not *in itself* guarantee the purity of a theology. As little as the theme of the "sinfulness" of man excludes the question whether guilt is conceived of in a biblical manner, so little does the motif of the triumph of grace exclude the need of critical testing by the standard of Scripture. Certainly Barth acknowledges the need of such testing when he himself, for instance, subjects the Roman Catholic conception of grace to critical examination and then asks — as he also does with respect to other theologies — whether in the Roman Catholic conception the grace of *God* is truly represented. It is possible to speak with great emphasis about the grace of God and yet obscure the message of God's grace at decisive points because of the total structuration of the theology in which this grace comes to expression. It can be said of Roman Catholic theology — which Barth opposes so strenuously — that it, too, desires to be a theology of grace, although its fundamental structure prejudices the sovereignty of grace.

The whole of the history of dogma demonstrates the moving and dramatic fact that *every* theme must be critically tested in terms of the question: how does it *function* in the whole of the theology concerned? Even the Reformation theme of "sola gratia," corresponding to the essentially identical "sola fide," does not *a priori* guarantee the integrity of a theology built upon that motif.

---

2. KD II/1.
3. *Ibid.*, p. 757. Cf. on the fruitio Dei: *ibid.*, pp. 737, 738.

Also in theology the urgent admonition is in order: Whoso thinketh that he standeth, let him take heed lest he fall. Every motif, even the purest, is threatened by the danger that it will not dominate to the farthest outreaches of the theological structure. When it fails to do this it becomes an abstract principle which, as a "theological" motif, is doomed to fruitlessness.

A clear illustration of the necessity of critical testing is provided by the claim of Rome, especially in her contemporary theological expression, that she *above all* is concerned about the *sovereignty of grace*. When W. H. Van de Pol undertook to approach the difference between Protestantism and Rome from a phenomenological point of view, he came to the conclusion that since the Reformation there exists a serious *misunderstanding* between the two on the score of the "sola fide."[4]

According to Rome, Pelagianism is, next to Arianism, the most dangerous heresy that has threatened the Church. Yet the Reformation accused Rome of having fallen back into this heresy. In order to make an approach to this misunderstanding possible, Van de Pol points out that *also* the Catholic regards salvation to be impossible for fallen man apart from the grace of God. He writes, "The Roman Catholic Church unqualifiedly accepts[5] the 'sola fide' and the 'sola gratia' as Paul understood them in his letters to the Romans and to the Galatians, and as also the Reformed Christian understands and intends them." When we see how here the "sola fide-sola gratia" is taken up and instructurated in Roman Catholic dogma, we can the better understand the necessity of testing, particularly with respect to the theme of grace. For it is precisely where grace, the *superabundance* of grace, is posited that we must be on our guard against every danger that might threaten to overshadow this reality. When reflection of this nature is considered superfluous, it is not possible to escape the danger that we shall speak the same *words* and yet remain alien to each other in spirit.

Another who has undertaken to answer the Reformation reproach against Rome with respect to the relativizing of sovereign grace is G. P. Kreling. In answer to this criticism, he states that

4. W. H. van de Pol, *Het Christelijk Dilemma,* p. 74. Cf. also his "Protestantse misverstanden en hun oorzaken," *Werkgenootschap van Katholieke Theologie,* 1954.

5. W. H. van de Pol, *Het Christelijk Dilemma,* p. 75.

Christianity stands or falls "with the absolute sovereignty of God and the exclusive saving power of Christ, the Redeemer,"[6] and he asserts that the whole of Roman Catholic doctrine rests on this pillar. He grants that the impression may be created — because of the emphasis on human co-operation — that this is not so. According to Kreling, however, the fact is that the Catholic sees the sovereignty of God in so deep and comprehensive a way, that it is not infringed upon or made ineffective by the activity of man.[7] The Roman Catholic "does not suffer from a short-sighted anxiety which sounds alarm when the creature is given a place in the execution of God's decree."[8] This participation of the creature does *not* threaten grace. There is no room for boasting about our achievements.[9] "It is characteristic of the Roman Catholic to know that he is safe in the fold of grace."[10] Kreling considers it amazing to say that one cannot come to true sanctification in Roman Catholicism "since it can take its rise only from the joy that is felt over God's unconditional mercy revealed in Christ's completed work."[11] Although the Roman Catholic Church acknowledges *both* elements: God's decisive grace *and* the work of man, she does not regard this latter as an independent factor, "but as something through which and in which the grace of God reveals itself." According to Kreling, it is precisely *Rome* that can fully confess redemption as being not man's conquest, but God's gift.[12] Kreling would probably appropriate for Rome the well-known theme: sola gratia.[13]

\*      \*      \*

These examples serve to show how necessary it is to test critically every theology which speaks of the sovereignty and the tri-

---

6. G. P. Kreling, *Antwoord op het Herderlijk Schrijven,* 1950, p. 26.
7. *Ibid.,* p. 26.
8. *Ibid.,* p. 27.
9. *Ibid.,* p. 32.
10. *Ibid.*
11. *Ibid.,* p. 33.
12. *Ibid.*
13. Cf. also the view of A. Hulsbosch, *Genade en Kerk,* 1953, pp. 76ff. He takes issue with Miskotte's observation that the words of Paul in their original radical evangelical power no longer function in Roman Catholic exegesis. He writes in this connection: "The whole of the Christian life is born by grace, but within grace the human relationships are maintained," p. 77. Also Hulsbosch declares - in agreement with Kreling - that the redemption of the will as created means also the redemption of the will as free, "which does not detract from God's saving will, but serves to accentuate it," p. 76.

umph of grace. This becomes even more evident when it is considered that we can never speak about grace and its triumph "in abstracto." The reason for this is that the *meaning* of the triumph of grace can only be understood *in relation to that from which it redeems and over which it triumphs.* The message of grace implies this relationship because grace never stands *by itself.* Grace deals with *men* who are redeemed, with a *world* that God loved, with *guilt* which is forgiven, with *death* which is abolished. Therefore an essential part of the understanding of the triumph of grace is an understanding also of these *relations* in which grace stands in triumph.

There is only one true gospel, but this does not prevent Paul from invoking a curse on those who preach another "gospel," even though it be an angel from heaven. Such a gospel is another gospel which is *not* the gospel. In order that the spirits may be discerned, however, it is necessary to reckon with the fact that someone *can* come with the pretension of bringing another gospel in which the good news of Christ is perverted.

In the light of God's Word, it is wholly understandable that the reality of grace should continually be threatened by the unbelieving and rebellious heart of man. This can be done in a variety of ways. The sola-fide — sola-gratia is not an *automatic guarantee* of a true hymn of praise to the grace of God. Obscurations can present themselves even then when we speak of God's grace with the greatest emphasis.

Especially synergism constitutes a threat to the sovereignty of grace. When it makes its appearance, a change takes place which immediately recalls the words of Paul, "And if by grace, then is it no more of works: otherwise grace is no more grace." The shift in accent may at first be hardly noticeable. The emphasis on grace and on its sovereignty continues to be made. In the way of ecclesiastical and theological consistency, however, deviations develop and become more and more evident. Since the doctrine concerning the grace of God touches the very *heart* of the Christian religion, it will always be necessary to test and examine what is said about this center of the faith. Such testing may lead to painful situations, but if we would resist the obscuring of the salvation which God has wrought we may not seek to escape this pain.[14]

The dangers that threaten a right understanding of grace arise in the Church and in theology from the depths of the human heart which has not yet wholly surrendered itself to grace. We must show our love for the neighbor also by exercising watchful regard for each other's theology, and not least when we wish to honor grace as grace. If the triumph of grace is not to become an empty and formal concept, we must be prepared to examine both ourselves and others and ask again and again whether we have rightly seen the *relations* in terms of which the Bible speaks of grace. We must do this in order that none may fall into the error against which Paul warns: "otherwise grace is no more grace."

\*　　\*　　\*

These reflections are underscored when it is considered how frequently in the history of the Church and of theology grace has been treated in a manner which was not to be reconciled with the purity of God's gospel. Dialectical theology has emphasized this from its inception, particularly in connection with its warnings against the so-called "theology of glory."[15] Something wholly different was intended by this theology than what Barth now posits so plainly in his conception of the "triumph of grace." When dialectical theology itself so emphatically rejects every "theology of glory," it is the more necessary to examine the "triumph" which Barth himself sets forth. By putting in the place of the theology of glory the theology of the cross,[16] the dialectical theologians intended not so much to make

---

14. It must be remembered that theological error is not always consistently reflected in the personal life of faith. In speaking about synergism H. Bavinck writes, "One may be Pelagian in doctrine; in the practice of the Christian life, especially in prayer, every Christian is Augustinian. Then he excludes all boasting in self and gives God alone the glory," *Gereformeerde Dogmatiek*, II, 4th ed., p. 339.

15. Although the characterization "theology of the cross" (theologia crucis) in distinction from the "theology of glory" (theologia gloriae) appears in the first phase more frequently than later, this does not indicate an essential change in approach. Cf. a current characterization of the Reformation-Rome controversy by K. G. Steck, "Der evangelische Christ und die römische Kirche," *Theologische Existenz Heute*, Vol. 33, 1952, p. 47. He summarizes the controversy "in the formulation of the young Luther," namely, theologia crucis vs. theologia gloriae. "Today this formulation may be found to be useless and a cheap slogan. It was not that originally and it should not be that now," p. 47.

16. Cf. on this point B. Steffens, *Kreuz und Gewiszheit*, 1929. Earlier he had written *Das Dogma von Kreuz. Beitrag zu einer staurozentrischen Theologie*, 1920.

the cross of Christ the center and content of their theology as to develop a certain method of theological thinking by means of which to approach God's revelation.[17] The criticism of the "theology of glory" appealed particularly to Luther who had strenuously opposed the scholasticism of the Middle Ages as a "theology of glory"[18] because it had refused to follow the narrow way of the *cross*, but had sought to examine *directly* the "being" and the majesty of God. In its endeavor to attain true knowledge of God scholasticism had not held itself solely dependent upon Christ the Crucified[19] apart from whom no one can come to the Father.

Dialectical theology regarded medieval scholasticism[20] as violating the evangelical and Pauline epistemological principle and as ignoring the alarm signal of I Corinthians 1 which speaks of the foolishness and the weakness of God which is wiser and stronger than men. Over against the specter of the "theology of glory," they pleaded for a *broken* theology of the cross. They desired to construct a theology in terms of the cross as the form of revelation, a theology which would set its imprint on *every* pronouncement of theology and which would call men back from finding to seeking, from having to praying, and from triumph to "honorable and complete spiritual poverty."[21]

It was not only Karl Barth who opposed the theology of glory, but also, for instance, Karl Heim. He emphasized the antithesis between glory and cross, between strength and weakness, between riches and

17. Cf. KD I/1, p. 173: "a particular kind of theology."
18. Cf. W. von Loewenich, *Luthers theologia crucis,* 1929, in which he points to Luther's own thesis (theologia crucis) over against the reigning ecclesiastical theology (theologia gloriae) in the year 1518, p. 4. Cf. also in *Zwischen den Zeiten,* 1926, "Die Heidelberger Disputation Dokter Martin Luthers." Übersetzt von Georg Merz, pp. 1-17. Note also the important studies by Erich Vogelsang, *Die Anfänge von Luthers Christologie nach der ersten Psalmenvorlesung,* 1929, chapter I; *Der angefochtene Christus bei Luther,* 1932, with special reference to Luther's use of the term "theologia crucis," p. 20. According to Barth this is not simply a principle of the *young* Luther. Note further, E. Ellwein, "Die Entfaltung der theologia crucis in Luthers Hebräervorlesung," in *Theologische Aufsätze für Karl Barth,* 1936, p. 38; G. C. Berkouwer, "Theologie des Kruises," *Calvinistisch Weekblad,* Vol. I, October 4 - 18.
19. Cf. Barth on the "superbia" in the theologia gloriae as a "speculatio Majestatis," KD I/1, p. 185.
20. Barth is not concerned *exclusively* about Rome. He speaks of a "Catholic *and* a Protestant theologia gloriae," *ibid.,* p. 185.
21. This does not mean the glorification of uncertainty: "there is also a negative theologia gloriae!" *ibid.,* p. 186. On page 276 Barth relates the theologia gloriae to the no longer fully acknowledged fact that the word of God must stand above the Church. Cf. also KD I/1, p. 13: "Dogmatics can exist only as *theologia crucis.*"

poverty. In this contrast he saw the radical difference between Roman Catholicism and Protestantism, and endeavored to indicate in this way that Rome was concerned to think in terms of *glory* and Protestantism in terms of the *cross*.[22]

This emphasis leads us to ask wherein the really objectionable feature of the "glory" was considered to lie. When is it legitimate to speak of a triumph of grace and when is it not?

This is a question which the theological history of the past thirty years puts forward with great prominence. According to Karl Heim, both Roman Catholicism and Protestantism see history epitomized in the drama of the dying and the resurrected Christ. For Rome the center of the drama lies in the resurrection of Christ, by virtue of which the Church already now participates in the *power* and the *glory* of Christ. Protestantism, on the other hand, sees the center of the drama as lying in the consummation at the *end* of time.

This conception clearly provides a point of contact with Barth's earlier eschatological proclamation (which he himself later criticized), with its emphasis on the "not yet" of the kingdom. This must be qualified by the consideration, however, that since the making of this emphasis the definitive character of the resurrection has increasingly come to the fore in Barth's thinking as the decisive triumph which is still to be made manifest. How does Barth conceive of the difference between the triumph of grace in his own theology and the "theology of glory" which he so strongly opposes?

It is not difficult to answer this question. *This* triumph of grace is possible only in terms of the cross and in *contrast to* the "speculatio Majestatis." It is a Christo-centric triumph, it is a "theology from below." He wishes his theology to be fully a "theology of the cross," and even though it is also in connection with this a "theologia resurrectionis"[23] this does not mean that there is another way to the kingdom than the way that leads via the cross. This way is not the high road, but the low road;[24] it is not the way of perception, but of *faith*.

\*     \*     \*

---

22. K. Heim, *Das Wesen des evangelischen Christentums,* a book about which Barth on other counts expressed sharp criticism: "Der röm. Kath. als Frage an die protest. Kirche," *Die Theologie und die Kirche,* II, pp. 344ff.

23. Cf. KD IV/1, p. 622, and further pp. 335, 380, and 587.

24. This "low road" is in the nature of the case not intended as antithetical to revelation, but coincides with it. Concerning Luther's "theologia ab imo" cf. E. Vogelsang, *Der angefochtene Christus bei Luther,* 1932, p. 20.

We wish finally to point out that the need of testing Barth's emphasis on the triumph of grace flows forth from the fact that the history of theological thought has seen more than one triumph-of-grace theology of which it can only be said that in spite of the appearance of honoring the motif of grace, the riches and totality of the gospel were obscured. In saying this we do not mean at all to make the a priori suggestion that the same is true of Barth. This will have to be determined on the basis of Barth's own conception of the triumph of grace. In the examples that we shall adduce from the history of theology, there lies a critical reminder, however, that the triumph of grace in a theology is not guaranteed simply by rejecting synergism. In order to arrive at a mature judgment of such a theology it will be necessary to examine the *nature* of the triumph that is being pleaded. As Barth subjects Rome's glory motif to careful scrutiny, so his own triumph motif cannot be a priorily accepted but must be tested by critical analysis.

*         *         *

The history of doctrine shows that the influence of all manner of theologies of grace has generally been very extensive. The background of the rise of such theologies lies in the utter seriousness with which the Bible speaks of the sovereignty of grace. It need not surprise us that the letters of the apostle Paul to the Romans, Galatians, Corinthians, and Colossians play a significant role in them. The tremendous emphases in these letters on the sola gratia -sola fide exercised an inescapable fascination, as did their radical rejection of all synergism which is found in every age of the life of the Church. The *triumphant* and *definitive* character of salvation found in Paul their chief and unequivocal exponent. Did he not speak of a *disarming* of principalities and powers, of Christ's *conquest,* and did not the depth and the fulness of salvation lie in this conquest?

Without in any way striving for completeness, we wish to point to four striking examples in the history of theology in which the emphasis on the triumph of grace played a decisive role. We think of the "reformer" of the second century, *Marcion,* of *antinomianism,* of *perfectionism,* and of *universalism.* In all of these the triumph motif occupied a central place but, because of the total theological

structure in which it was given this place, justice was not done to
the grace of which the *Bible* speaks.

*       *       *

As first example, we wish to consider Marcion.  His theology
may without fear of contradiction be characterized as grace-theology.
Seeberg speaks not without warrant of Marcion's "attempt at reform," an effort which was plainly directed against legalistic obscuration of the gospel in the second century.  It may be said that Marcion, in his emphatic and exclusive appeal to Paul, wanted to plead
for the "sola fide" and the "sola gratia."  According to Marcion, the
grace of God was sovereign because it did not in any respect depend
on man and on his works, but solely on the *mercy* of the *strange*
God, the Father of Jesus Christ.

This grace-theology received its peculiar emphasis in terms of the
antithesis which Marcion posited between *law* and *gospel*, which
led him to ascribe the law to the Old Testament Creator-god, whom
he regarded as being no longer a valid deity by reason of Paul's opposition to the law.  "Fully taken up by the newness, uniqueness,
and glory of the Pauline proclamation of the grace of God in Christ,
Marcion regarded all other formulations of the gospel, especially
its connection with Old Testament religion, as antithesis and retro-
gression."[25]

A well-known expression of Tertullian characterizes the mainspring of Marcion's theology as the separation between law and gospel.[26]  This separation was made in terms of disqualifying the law,
and was effected with a view to the greater glory of the gospel in
order that *its radical grace character* might receive full expression
and not be threatened by the *law*.  To this grace, faith corresponds.
"Corresponding to this emphasis on grace, he had an appreciation
for the Pauline conception of faith.  Faith is for him trust in the
unmerited grace of God revealed in Christ."[27]  In view of this background, it is understandable that *Luther* has at times been seen as
standing more or less on a line with Marcion.  This parallel is
usually drawn after Marcion and Paul have first been placed in
close juxtaposition.  In this way Harnack speaks of the "Pauline-

25. A. von Harnack, *Lehrbuch der Dogmengeschichte*, 4th ed., Vol. I, 1909, p. 294.
26. "Seperatio legis et evangelii proprium et principale opus est Marcionis,"
Tertullianis, *Adv. Marcion,*
27. A. von Harnack, *op. cit.,* I, p. 218.

Marcionitic view of the distinction between law and gospel," to which Luther again gave a central place.[28] This is a confusing historical judgment as much with respect to Paul as to Luther, but it typifies the problems and connections that can come into being within the area of *grace*-theology. When "grace" is abstracted from the *total structure* of a theology and one has an eye only for the *themes* of "sola fide" or "sola gratia," it is possible to come to an uncritical judgment which places Paul, Marcion and Luther in the same line of descent. It is perfectly plain that Marcion's doctrine of grace cannot for a moment be isolated from his rejection of the Old Testament, of the goodness of creation, and of the law, and therefore from his gnostic antithesis between creation and redemption. Marcion's entire view of grace is wholly determined by his view of that *from which* man is redeemed. His theology is a preaching of the unreserved goodness of God in Jesus Christ. This goodness involves that God need not be feared, although Marcion does not teach the apokatastasis doctrine.[29]

The central problem in Marcion's theology of grace lies in the *relations* in which this grace stands. The accents in Marcion are pronouncedly on the doctrine of *free grace*. He spoke of the love of God which had been revealed in Christ and which was extended freely in Him to the lost world of the Creator-god and of the law. The *free* character of this goodness and grace was directly related to the fact that this world was *not* God's creation, so that the praise of grace concentrated itself in the recognition that this grace given by the *strange* God was unforeseen and was wholly voluntary on His part. Over against the suppression of the agape-motif in the second century, Marcion placed the love of God in the center of his theology.[30] "Marcion can portray the miracle of God's grace in the most eloquent language. It enters the world through Christ as something wholly new and unlooked for."[31] The incomparable newness and wonderfulness of the grace that has appeared lies in the fact that it is a grace that has mercy on *this* world. Nygren correctly observes concerning Marcion's emphatic teaching that the Father of Jesus Christ has nothing to do with creation, that it was

---

28. A von Harnack, *Marcion*, 1924, p. 218.
29. A von Harnack, *ibid.*, p. 138.
30. A. Nygren, *Eros und Agape. Gestaltwandlungen der chr. Liebe*, II, 1937, p. 109.
31. *Ibid.*

propounded by him "in the interest of the agape-idea."[32]  It is the *separation* between the Creator-god and the Father of Jesus Christ that creates the glow in this new and wonderful love.

In the proportion that the *foreignness* of God with respect to the created world is emphasized, the idea of the divine agape becomes *strange, moving* and *paradoxical.*[33]  This divine love is *completely baseless and without motivation.*  It leads to the adoption of men as children of God in the most radical sense of the word.  The separation between creation and redemption opens the way to a *tremendous* accent on *free* grace.  In this conception the law plays no role whatever, and in *that* connection Paul can become *the* great apostle to whom Marcion pays homage.  Paul's opposition to the works of the law and his hymn of praise to sovereign grace are woven by Marcion into the framework of a gnostic melody.  Having done this, he goes on to use many words and expressions in the New Testament to magnify the grace of the hitherto unknown God who has now been revealed *in Christ.*

Since the gospel also speaks decisively of sovereign and unexpected grace (e.g. the mystery that was kept secret for long ages, Rom. 16:25), Marcion supposed that his emphasis lay wholly within the boundaries of the gospel.  The glow and the élan with which Marcion adopted these motifs and proclaimed them make at least understandable the error of relating Luther to Marcion, and which led Harnack to speak of the "Pauline-Marcionitic" line of development.  This is a clear example of the *isolation* of the grace motif from the whole of a given theology.  To do this is a fundamental error which emphasizes the necessity of exercising care in the acceptance of one or another theological motif, even when one is fascinated by the abundance of scriptural expressions.  Moreover, the problem of the *relations* in which grace stands in Marcion's theology becomes plain when it is seen that the grace of the good God achieves redemption from *misery* (the misery of the creation of the Creator-god) rather than from the *guilt* of sin.[34]  Marcion's agape-motif is decisively determined by this emphasis.

---

32. *Ibid.,* p. 110.
33. Nygren points to the word of Tertullian: "Si Christus creatoris est, suum merito amavit, si ab alio deo est, magis adamavit, quando alienum redimit," *Ibid.,* p. 112.
34. *Ibid.,* p. 119.

It is therefore, not an adequate characterization of Marcion's theology to call it a praise of grace. All depends on *how we must conceive of this grace.* Marcion's rejection by the Church as a heretic was most intimately related to her resistance to the *generalizing* of "grace" and to her intuitive understanding that the praise of grace becomes impure when the *components* in terms of which a theology of grace is constructed are not pure. Had the Church not taken a highly critical position with respect to Marcion, there would have been no reason to reject emphatically the gnostic heresy, for gnosticsm, too, spoke with heavy accents of *redemption.*[35]

It was not easy to resist Marcion. It cannot be denied that in his opposition to the legalism of the second century he was profoundly influenced by the biblical emphases on the new, surprising, and unexpected love of God in Christ. He spoke of the agape in a manner that had all but disappeared. But the background of his conception of the agape to it, before long, characteristics which could not be reconciled with the scriptural view of the love of God. In spite of the emphasis on the goodness and the love of God, the whole of the Christian faith was threatened at the foundations: creation, redemption from guilt, eschatology — all were viewed in a manner that was not compatible with the gospel.

This threat to the gospel explains the sharpness of the opposition of Irenaeus and others. The strong influence[36] which Marcion exercised by his use of biblical concepts made it necessary to speak *plainly.* Defenders of the faith realized that precisely at *this* point, at the point where *grace* was emphasized, it was necessary to come to clarity of view. "No other heretic has been the object of such comprehensive efforts at refutation as Marcion."[37] In the nature of the case, the necessity of opposing Marcion involved the danger of eliciting a reaction which would cast shadows over the biblical agape conception. "Every view which endeavored to maintain the unstricted agape motif was regarded as suspect."[38] This is the ever recurring danger in the Church when heresy must be opposed. Then it appears that reaction to heresy has robbed her of the spiritual power to speak the truth fully.

---

35. Cf. especially Hans Jonas, *Gnosis und spätantiker Geist,* 1934.
36. A. Nygren, *op. cit.,* p. 126.
37. *Ibid.*
38. *Ibid.*

Marcion's theology reveals how unscripturally his praise of grace was structured. The grace which he praises is fundamentally a being ransomed from the domination of the world-god. With a view to *this* redemption Marcion sings, "O wonder surpassing wonder, rapture, power and amazement! We can say nothing about the gospel, we cannot think about it, there is nothing to which we can compare it."[39]

\* \* \*

After having seen the need for testing grace-theologies by reference to Marcionism, we can be briefer in illustrating this need in connection with other theologies of grace. We mention, in the first place, *antinomianism*. This keeps us close to Marcion who, as we have seen, placed the love of God *over against* the law.[40] This phenomenon, however, also has a broader reference in the history of the Church. We meet it also without the gnostic-dualistic background of the two gods. We meet it in the formulation that the triumph of grace in Jesus Christ excludes every function of the law. Because of the fulness of the completed work of Christ, any role that is still ascribed to law is regarded as infringing on the accomplished fact of Christ's triumph. Still to have room for law means to turn again to righteousness by the works of the law.

In antinomianism, too, it becomes evident that the theme of the triumph of grace does not in itself guarantee the biblical purity of a theology. It can even be said that it is a peculiar "grace" which antinomianism honors. It is a grace which must be understood in the sense that one can continue in sin in order that grace may abound. The power and the abundance of grace are praised against the background of ever increasing guilt. A peculiar sort of reasoning is applied here of which the idea of the "abundance" of grace forms the central motif. There *is* indeed a connection between the magnitude of our guilt and the abundance of grace, as becomes clear when Paul magnifies the grace that was manifested in him, the foremost of sinners, and when Jesus speaks of the sinful woman whose much love revealed the greatness of the forgiveness that had been extended her.

---

39. Cf. A. von Harnack, *Marcion*, p. 256.
40. Harnack speaks of the "antinomianism of Marcion," *Dogmengeschichte* I, p. 307.

Antinomianism, however, turns these connections into a rational calculation and "concludes" from the increase in sin to the abundance of grace. Opposition against the function of the law in the life of the believer receives its significance from this conclusion. Grace is externalized and loses its effectiveness. The abundance of grace appears, after all, *not* to be present. Therefore Paul writes, "Are we to continue in sin that grace may abound? By no means! How can we who died to sin still live in it?" In the antinomian conception of grace, grace remains a stranger to law and to the ordering of life in terms of the abundance of grace. Life is not redeemed and restored, and it is not possible to understand Paul when he writes, "He who loves his neighbor *has fulfilled the law*." Antinomianism, too, unmistakably shows that it is necessary to scrutinize every theology which has as its central theme the triumph of grace.

\* \* \*

In addition to antinomianism we must also mention *perfectionism*. It, too, be it in a different way, sings of the triumph of grace. Perfectionism does not present a theology in which the humanism of self-justifying man is enthroned, but it constitutes a confession of the *effective* triumph of grace in ordinary life. Perfectionism speaks triumphantly of the power of grace in its all-pervasive effect in the life of the believer in that it speaks of the gift of sanctification as the radical total liberation — already in this life — from all sin and pollution.

Here the confession of the triumph of grace leads to an other conclusion than we discovered in antinomianism, but it is a conclusion which is not less in conflict with the scriptural witness. The reason for this is not that perfectionism overestimates the triumph of grace — how can God's grace ever be "overestimated?" — but the wrong conception of the *manner* in which grace triumphs. The point of departure in the thinking of perfectionism is the perfect work of Christ. From this it concludes, however, to the perfection of the "effects" of this work in the life of the believer. It is striking that in spite of the confession of the *total* liberation from *all* sin, perfectionism again and again manifests tendencies to synergism. In this we must again see a serious warning against the danger of drawing unwarranted conclusions from the triumph of grace.[41]

There is something suggestive not only in antinomianism, but also in perfectionism. This suggestiveness arises from their common emphasis on the triumph of grace. Both illustrate, however, that it is possible to speak responsibly of this triumph only in terms of continual sensitiveness to the entire testimony of Scripture.

\* \* \*

In conclusion, we wish to point to the triumph of grace as it comes to expression in *universalism*. It is not difficult to recognize the idea of triumph in the doctrine of universal restoration. Universalism strongly accentuates the *power*, the *abundance*, the *irresistibleness* of divine grace which does indeed meet opposition on its way but ultimately conquers every resistance. It is, of course, possible to construct a universalistic soteriology by weakening the seriousness of sin and guilt. Usually, however, universalism appeals to the glory of all-conquering grace in the face of the seriousness of sin. We shall later discuss the idea of apokatastasis in connection with Barth's doctrine of election. Here we wish to point out that the irresistibility of grace forms, in one way or another, the central content of absolute universalism. This has been most clearly formulated in Origen's conception that God will achieve the purpose of His creation, and that this purpose includes the subjection of His enemies (cf. I Cor. 15:28), and in this subjection their salvation. This view, according to Jerome's translation of Origen's work, also has implications for the demons, since the punishments of God have a purifying function not only for men but also for the demonic hosts. This purification subserves the perfection of the ultimate triumph of grace. "The power of the Logos finally breaks all opposition and destroys all evil in the soul."[42] In connection with Origen's eschatology Danielou speaks of "this grand theological symphony."[43] However deep Origen's appreciation for human freedom was, still, this freedom was ultimately *subject* to the triumph; resistance lay *within* the framework of an essential divine irresistibility.

---

41. Cf. G. C. Berkouwer, *Geloof en Heiliging*, 1949, chapter III. (English translation, *Faith and Sanctification*, 1952).

42. R. Seeberg, *Lehrbuch der Dogmengeschichte*, 3rd ed., Vol. I, 1922, p. 552.

43. Jean Danielou, *Origène 'Le génie du Christianisme,'* 1948, p. 281. Cf. H. Bavinck, *Gereformeerde Dogmatiek*, IV, p. 687.

It is clear, therefore, that the doctrine of the apokatastasis can find its roots in the desire to elevate God's triumph above every resistance, since the denial of the apokatastasis is regarded as a humiliation for God and a belittling of the triumph of Christ's sacrifice. As F. W. Farrar writes, "How frightful a result, in spite of how infinite a sacrifice!"[44]

\*        \*        \*

The foregoing reflections may suffice to indicate that a speaking about the triumph of grace and of the love of God is always a *complex* speaking. On the one hand, it is deeply under the influence of the testimony of Scripture and, on the other hand, it interprets this testimony in a particular manner. It is not possible to speak simplistically of an abstract "triumph" concept which because of its evident clarity makes further reflection unnecessary. It is not avoidable that *in* setting forth the theme of the triumph of grace, the totality of one's theological conception should play a decisive role. Such exposition involves Christological and pneumatological considerations, the attributes of God, the weight and seriousness of guilt, the responsibility of man, the honor of God and, in this all, the significance of the cross of Christ.

\*        \*        \*

In our analysis of Barth's theology, it became sufficiently plain that its triumphant and joyful character did not arise from a vague and superficially optimistic attitude to life. The triumph to which he gives expression bears, rather, a concrete Name: Jesus Christ as very God and very man. In Him the sovereign and merciful action of God is revealed. Jesus Christ is *the* Conqueror and in *Him* the entirety of the triumph consists and finds its basis.

When we speak of the necessity of testing Barth's conception, therefore, various questions ask for an answer.

The first question that presses itself upon us is, in which *sense* and in which *connections* does he speak of the triumph of grace? What is the meaning of the grace of God that triumphs and from what does it release us? What is the enemy whose defeat constitutes the triumph? Wherein does the triumph consist? What is the nature of the struggle and where is the battle ground on which

---

44. Cited from F. W. Farrar by K. Schilder in: *Wat is de Hel?* 1920, 2nd ed., p. 78.

the decision falls? The answers to these questions involve us in a complex of problems which can be summarized in the problem of the antithesis between sin and grace. All these questions center around this one decisive question: *over which darkness does the light of God's grace triumph?*[45]

The discussion of these questions raises another complex of problems. Correlative to the above mentioned problems is the problem of the relationship of man to the triumph of grace. What is the role of man in this struggle and in this conquest? In which way does he participate in the triumph of grace? Is it, as a "strange" righteousness and as an "objective" reality, external to him? Is this triumph simply a "fact," or is there also a "realization" of this triumph in which its effectiveness as a power and a dynamic in human life becomes evident? And what is the place of *faith* in this triumph?[46]

The third complex of problems which will require our attention is concerned with a specific aspect of the triumph of grace as it finds expression in Barth's theology and which may be circumscribed as the problem of the *divine* character of the triumph. We are constantly struck by the strong emphasis which Barth places upon the "God Himself" and the warnings that are spoken against abstracting Jesus Christ from God the Father. This emphasis involves important questions which are most intimately related to the triumph of grace.[47]

Finally, we wish to call attention to the triumph of grace as an *eschatological* triumph in which the ultimate effect, the realization of the triumph will be discussed. Here we shall particularly consider Barth's earlier discussed conception of eternal life.[48]

The problems which we have here indicated we shall discuss in the succeeding four chapters.

\*     \*     \*

Although the discussion of these four aspects of Barth's theology does not by any means present a complete analysis and evaluation of it, we believe that it does confront us with the central questions

45. Cf. chapter IX.
46. Cf. chapter X.
47. Cf. chapter XI.
48. Cf. chapter XII.

of his dogmatics, and that it will serve to make plain why it is that
Barth's theology is so determinative of European theological thinking today. However we may have to judge of Barth's theology, one
thing is certain: a judgment made in terms of Reformation theology
may detract nothing from the decisive "sola gratia."

# IX

## THE NATURE OF THE TRIUMPH

T HE FIRST question that confronts us in the critical analysis of Barth's theology is, over *what* does grace triumph? We can answer this question by pointing to Barth's continual emphasis on the antithesis between *sin* and *grace*. This raises the question, however, of what we must understand by "sin" and of how grace triumphs reconcilingly over it.

The asking of these questions alone places us before a series of problems all of which bear upon the relationship between God's good creation and the evil which penetrated that creation. In our analysis in Chapter III we learned that we cannot, according to Barth, come to a general knowledge of sin by way of a neutral analysis of human nature. Sin can be known only in terms of the reality and fearfulness of the cross of Christ in which the full seriousness, the corruption and the depth of our guilt are revealed. In the light of the cross, sin is exposed as man's proud refusal to live by grace alone. Sin is never anything else than *this* pride, than this insistence on autonomy and independence, which has taken the place of living in and under the good hand of God, the hand of His grace. Since creation itself is a marvel of God's love and grace, sin is from the beginning the unwillingness to live as "needy" creatures. Sin is never the transgression of abstract law or the violation of a purely *legal* relationship. It is rebellion against grace, the sinister and unfathomable urge to live in alienation from the grace of God.[1]

It is clear that the idea of the grace of creation directly leads Barth to regard the nature of sin in the light of this grace. It is this view that brings Barth to the conception of the incompre-

---

1. Cf. KD III/3, p. 350: ". . . an abstract divine law - whether revealed or natural is not to the point here - if indeed there were such a law, could never be the basis for the true knowledge of sin." There is knowledge of sin only when we understand that "sin is disobedience against the will of God, it is a freeing of oneself from grace and its law."

hensibilty of sin which is so profoundly significant an element in his theology. It is not possible to explain the origin of evil in the world. This impossibility does not, according to Barth, lie in the fact of the limitations of our thinking, but in the fact that sin *itself* is enigmatic, inexplicable, absurd. When it is supposed that sin can be explained, it has thereby been given a "place" in creation, but this is once and for all excluded because creation is *good* and sin can never be explained in terms of it. Moreover, it is impossible to deduce sin from any of the possibilities of created human nature. We have seen that Barth rejects again and again, and with the greatest emphasis, the idea that the "possibility" of sin (the posse peccare) was given with the good creation and that man made use of that possibility in the fall. Man was indeed made *free*, but his freedom was a freedom for *God*, and it did *not* include the possibility of following *two* directions, to evil as well as to good, to the left as well as to the right.[2]

Therefore sin can never be explained in terms of man's *freedom*, since it was precisely his freedom that excluded sin. Sin is without qualification the baffling riddle whose existence cannot and may not be denied and which may, on the other hand, never be otherwise described than as enigma, absurdity and chaos. It has *no* basis whether in creation or in the nature of man.

\* \* \*

It may seem for a moment that Barth refers to the same problem to which Reformed theology referred when it spoke emphatically of the inexplicable character of sin.[3] Particularly did Reformed theology reject the idea of giving sin a place in a causal system through which it received a more or less rational character. It appears, however, that it is not in the first place such antithetical expressions which Barth has in mind when he speaks about the absurdity of sin. When one studies his theology carefully, one soon comes to the discovery that Barth is concerned about something far deeper than the idea that sin is inexplicable

---

2. Cf. K. Barth, *Das Geschenk der Freiheit* in: *Theologische Existenz heute*, Heft 39, 1953, p. 9.

3. In the nature of the case, this problem was extensively discussed in Roman Catholic theology. Cf., among others, R. P. Sertillanges, *Le probleme du mal*, I (*L'histoire*), 1948, and II (*La solution*), 1951, particularly in II, p. 10ff.; "le mal n'a pas de cause premiere" and "le caractère innaturel du mal."

only in terms of our *thinking. It is at this point that, in our judgment, we meet one of the most important problems in Barth's theology.*

\* \* \*

In order to set forth the heart of Barth's conception on this score, it will be well to take our point of departure in Bavinck's emphasis on the inexplicability of sin. He calls the origin of evil "the greatest riddle of life and the heaviest cross that the understanding of man must bear."[4] Sin is a phenomenon which, "in the nature of the case, eludes, on the score of its origin, every explanation."[5] Explanation of it is not only impossible and meaningless, but it is also *dangerous.* "If sin were to be understood and explained, that is, if it were shown that it must necessarily follow from what preceded, its nature would not be adequately described, the boundaries between good and evil would disappear, and evil would in the end be explainable in terms of the good."[6] Sin indeed *is,* it exists, but it can never justify its existence. It is unlawful and irrational.[7] In other theologians, too, we constantly meet this emphasis on the "inexplicability" of sin, in which the chief concern is always to indicate that it is not to be deduced from creation, nor from human nature as such in which there was present a certain disposition, a certain "occasion," to sin.[8] Parallel to this there was always the express rejection of the idea that the origin of sin lies in God and that He could in some way be called the *Author* of sin. There has been a refusal to think about sin and its origin in a deterministic manner. With emphasis Bavinck writes that God is not the "cause" of sin[9] and that it does not have its "origin" in God.[10]

Bavinck does acknowledge that God's counsel and government control sin[11] and that in this way it is *serviceable* to the coming of

---

4. H. Bavinck, *Gereformeerde Dogmatiek,* III, p. 29.
5. *Ibid.,* p. 47.
6. *Ibid.*
7. *Ibid.,* p. 48.
8. Cf. Bavinck's criticism of those who explain sin in terms of man's sensual nature, *ibid.,* p. 30.
9. *Ibid.,* p. 36.
10. *Ibid.,* p. 43. Cf. H. Heppe, *Die Dogmatik der evangelisch reformierte Kirche,* 1861, p. 224, with particular reference to Ursinus, pp. 242ff.; further, *Synopsis pur. Theol.* 1881, pp. 117 and 118, and John Calvin, *The Institutes of the Christian Religion,* I, xiv, 16; I, xviii, 4; and II, iv, 2.
11. H. Bavinck, *op cit.,* p. 36. Cf. J. Calvin, *The Institutes,* II, iv. 2.

the kingdom. This is not, however, to be attributed to *sin*, but to God's omnipotence. He is not a "passive spectator of sin,"[12] but the *living* and *acting* God who, though He is in all things, is Himself spotless and holy and wholly free from unrighteousness. It was, therefore, never attempted to solve the problem of sin as to its origin and reality. It was attempted, rather, to delimit the *boundaries* within which the problem of sin could be discussed. Within *these* boundaries there was not a deterministic but a religious speaking about sin and, in terms of revelation, *man* was referred to as the "causa peccati."[13] Gropingly, theologians have spoken of a divine "permission," in order to retain sin within the area of God's government, while at the same time preventing the idea that the origin of sin should be ascribed to Him. There was a deep awareness, however, that this did not fathom the depth of God's action in relationship to sin.[14]

This theological concern indicates awareness of the danger of becoming lost in the problem of sin and, in becoming lost, of ultimately ascribing the origin of sin and guilt to God while exonerating man. Over against these dangers, Bavinck speaks of one thing that is certain and that stands as a final, *definitive* protection against every attempt to make sin rational and thereby to weaken it:[15] *if* we speak of the "rationality" of sin it may be done *only* in connection with its utterly serious, God's wrath-invoking character, its indisputable reality, its *character* as being "contra voluntatem Dei."

\* \* \*

Against the background of this general Christian conviction with respect to the problem of sin, we are particularly interested not so much in the fact that Barth also speaks of the enigma of sin, but in the specific content that he gives to this enigma.

The observation has been made — and it constitutes a serious accusation — that Barth, in spite of his emphasis on sin as the "mystery of unrighteousness," has not been content to abide by this mystery but that in describing it as absurd and as chaotic he has attempted to give an explanation of it, after all.[16] This criti-

---

12. *Ibid.*, p. 37.
13. Cf. Ursinus in Heppe, op. cit., p. 242, and the *Synopsis,* pp. 117-118.
14. H. Bavinck, *op. cit.,* 36ff.
15. *Ibid.,* p. 35.
16. M. P. van Dijk, *Existentie en Genade,* 1952, pp. 148ff.

cism is occasioned by the fact that Barth has established a *direct connection* between chaos, which in sin receives a concrete form, and God's *election* which, in his theology, always implies God's *rejection*.

The electing Yes of God implies His wrathful No, and *by reason of* this wrathful judgment the chaos, sin, *exists*. Although the chaos is not a creature, still it exists *by virtue of* the divine rejection. It cannot be denied that the chaos appears on the horizon of Barth's theology at the point where he speaks of election. We think here of such expressions as Barth's statement that the chaos has "from the beginning been on the scene,"[17] and that it has its *ground* in God's *not-willing* it,[18] that is, that God did not will it in its quality as chaos which He had rejected already before He spoke the first words that brought creation into being.[19]

At first it might be supposed — in view of God's eternal election that Barth would speak of an eternally enduring chaos as the reverse side of His Yes, that it is eternal, therefore, in its being rejected by God. It appears, however, that this is no sense Barth's meaning. Although the chaos has that significance which "as the unavoidable divine denial and rejection," must be ascribed to it,[20] still, because it is no more than the *reverse side* of God's election, it is only a *passing* reality. "In that God completes His true and positive work, this His negative work becomes *irrelevant,* therefore *superfluous,* and consequently can drop away and *cease to be.*"[21] Barth does not want to become entangled in a logical dialectic, according to which God's eternal love and election requires an *eternal* hating and rejection. Such a "compulsion" does not exist. God's work at His left hand is not necessary and is therefore not equally abiding as the work of His right hand.[22]

God's negative work, the work of His left hand, has its limit at the point at which it has served its purpose.[23] God's wrath does not endure forever, and He is and remains holy also "in the unlimited and no longer threatened triumph of His love, and there-

---

17. KD III/3, p. 406.
18. *Ibid.*, p. 407.
19. *Ibid.*, p. 406.
20. *Ibid.*, p. 417.
21. *Ibid.*
22. *Ibid.*
23. "Having attained this goal, God's *opus alienum* has come to its end," *ibid.*, p. 418.

fore as the God who no longer has to do with *any* enemy, who is concerned only with His creature."[24] This takes place already in the exaltation of Jesus Christ in which God is concerned only with His creature and "has *nothing* to do anymore with the chaos."[25] Where God was wrathful He is wrathful no longer, the enemy *is no more.* "When God has said No, He has said No, and does not have to say it again. Where God has said No, there that to which He has said No, no longer exists."[26]

From this it is plain that Barth does not have in mind a logical dialectic involving an automatic No which is eternally correlative to God's Yes. This does not take away the fact, however, that, albeit with this qualification (the *end* of the chaos), he speaks of sin and chaos exclusively as the *unavoidable* reverse side of election.

It is remarkable that this view of Barth does not first come to expression in his treatment of the doctrine of sin, but that he mentions it explicitly, although in passing, in his doctrine of election. There he speaks of an *eternal self-distinction* in God whereby He distinguishes Himself from that which is *not* God.

In direct connection with this self-distinction, Barth speaks of God's saving work, of His Yes and of His No. In undertaking to show that God's No "constitutes the necessary limitation of the divine Yes," he gives a further clarification of this thought in these words: "as surely as God is *God* and not *not*-God, as surely He Himself lives in the eternal self-distinction from everything which He is not and does not will."[27]

Because God is *such* a God, "therefore He wills and establishes the objects of His love, the witnesses of His glory in the world which He has created, *to be witnesses with a view to this double purpose*: to be witnesses of His Yes and of His willing, and of His No and of His not-willing." God does not "will" evil. He does not "will" sin or the fall but, with a view to the revelation of His glory and His love, He *wills* man *as* sinful man, as man who is *confronted* with that which God has rejected, in the same way in which God Himself is confronted with it in His eternal self-distinction. Man is confronted with what God has rejected as a

24. *Ibid.,* p. 418 and the whole of p. 419.
25. *Ibid.,* p. 418.
26. *Ibid.,* p. 419.
27. KD II/2, p. 152.

power to which *he* [*man*] *is not equal.* For this reason the conquest of sin must for man become history, must become "event." The conquest of evil does *not* for man have "that matter-of-courseness which it has for God."[28]

It will be difficult to deny that we meet here, in a certain sense, an *explanation* of sin. We meet in connection with the eternal self-distinction in God, which occasions the idea of the *witness* to God's glory in its relationship to His self-distinction. "That which is for God Himself the simple and immediate triumph of light over darkness concerning which there is not for a moment or in any respect the slightest question, must in creaturely space, and so for man, assume the form of this history, must in time and in this way become event."[29]

In terms of this relationship sinful and elect man "becomes a demonstration in creaturely time and space of God's eternal self-distinction."[30]

As we shall see later, it is not Barth's intention to relativize the terribleness of sin. It is clear, however, that he wishes in this way to give an insight into the depth of God's counsel. "In the space of creation" the problem of sin becomes an *illustration* of what is *in God* eternal, unproblematical reality, namely, that He is God and *not not-God.* The unacceptableness of this conception (a conception which even leads Barth to speak of a "confrontation" of God with what He does *not will*)[31] lies in the fact that in this manner the connection between sin and the counsel of God is laid *in terms of* the No as "the necessary limitation of the divine Yes."[32] The chaos is made to receive its existence on the basis of God's *rejection,* of His *not-willing.*[33] It exists because it *is* what God does *not* will, to which Barth adds the characteristic words, "because not only God's will but also His not-willing is powerful, and can therefore not be without a corresponding reality."[34]

---

28. *Ibid.,* p. 152.
29. *Ibid.*
30. *Ibid.,* p. 153.
31. In fairness to Barth, it is necessary to point out that he rejects the "felix culpa," KD IV/1, p. 73. We shall return to this point later.
32. Cf. KD III/3, p. 405.
33. *Ibid.,* pp. 406-407.
34. *Ibid.,* p. 406. His rejection has a "real dimension." It is the mighty, wrathful No "through which the chaos receives its peculiar form and existence," *Ibid.,* p. 409.

The objection to this view is not that it is not a logical explanation, but rather that it says *too much*. This "too much" lies in the ideas of confrontation for God and in His eternal self-distinction. This conception gives rise to ideas which lie on a wholly different niveau than those of which the Scriptures speak when they refer to what God *is not*. We meet them not infrequently in the Bible: "Far be it from God that He should do wickedness, and from the Almighty that He should do wrong" (Job 34:10). "Of a truth, God will not do wickedly, and the Almighty will not pervert justice" (Job 34:12). "Thou art not a God who delights in wickedness" (Psa. 5:5); "God is not a man that He should lie" (Num. 23:19), "And also the Glory of Israel will not lie or repent" (1 Sam. 15:29), "It is impossible that God should prove false" (Heb. 6:18), "God is light and in Him is no darkness at all" (I John 1:5).

All these testimonies concerning God are testimonies which, as positive and antithetical expressions, describe God's actions in their holy and glorious character. Occasioned by the wholly unambiguous character of the divine fullness, they are words of praise and adoration which, it would seem, may not be related to a *self-distinction* in God which — here the danger becomes evident — is even called a "confrontation" and from which lines are drawn, lines of necessity, into *time* and *history* where *man* is confronted with evil as an illustration of the divine self-distinction. With the greatest emphasis Barth has rejected the idea of a dualism, of any and every antinomy, conflict, or paradox in God. This does not alter the fact, however, that in the thinking which draws a line from a self-distinction in God to man's confrontation with evil, the problem of the origin of sin soon finds itself coming under the control of speculative ideas. In terms of Barth's conception, it is still possible to speak of the *chaotic*, for man is confronted with it in history.[35] It becomes difficult, however, to accentuate the *enig-*

---

35. It is in agreement with this necessary confrontation that Barth constantly warns against making sin "harmless." In his criticism of Sartre and Heidegger he points out that they have not really recognized the actual chaos and have occupied themselves only with the existentialistic nothingness, *ibid.*, p. 396. They lived in convulsive times and were impressed by the catastrophic times and by the presence and reality of the chaos which was announced by them but they did not *see* it. They did not learn to know it in its *essence* and associated with it as though it were not a dangerous thing. According to Barth, Heidegger has never been a "nihilist," p. 390, and Sartre wishes, in terms of human freedom, to turn to

*matic* character of sin. Connections and relationships appear through which sin as an *inexplicable* phenomenon is relativized. This brings us back to the question of what Barth really means when he speaks of the enigma, the incomprehensibility and the *absurdity* of sin. Upon scrutiny it appears that Barth is not primarily interested in the noetic problem of the incomprehensibility of sin as a sort of crux of our thinking, but that *he is occupied by a wholly different problem.*

When every interpretation which would weaken the reality of sin is rejected,[36] when a man is seen as covered by the *shame* of sin, [37] as *radically* and *totally* evil, [38] as being in enmity to God and thereby unredeemably threatened and on the way to judgment,[39] wherein, then, does the "enigma" of this reality consist?

The answer to this question lies in the fact that the "enigma" of sin can be circumscribed as the *ontological impossibility of sin.*

\* \* \*

In order to understand this strange expression as indicating the enigma of sin, it must be remembered that Barth distinguishes between man's *being* and man's *sin.* Even though man is a sinner and as such sins "against his created being,[40] he remains, even as a sinner, God's creature and his corruption in no wise means the destruction of his being.[41] Man's *nature* remains, even though it be obscured by its radical degeneration.[42] How can Barth come to such a distinction between man's *being* and his *sin* when God's Word speaks of men as radical and total sinners? Only a shameless

---

*deeds.* Is there not a triumphant "nevertheless" in their conception of the chaos, and have they not (Sartre more than Heidegger) left the chaos behind them with the courage born of the freedom of which they consider man capable? Cf. KD III/3, p. 399. They play about sovereignly with the chaos and do not see in it a *fatal* enemy. It becomes for them a "relatively harmless business," *ibid.,* p. 401. "If Heidegger had discerned the chaos for what it really is he would not have described the fear in which, according to him, the chaos manifests itself as being fundamentally no fear, but rest, calmness, and boldness," *ibid.,* p. 401. Cf.: "The sickness unto death with which the chaos confronts man has quite a different appearance." In these and many other places it appears how seriously Barth protests against every "explanation" of sin as necessarily involving a relativizing of it. This would be in conflict with the needed confrontation.

36. KD III/2, p. 35.
37. *Ibid.,* p. 30.
38. *Ibid.,* p. 32.
39. *Ibid.,* p. 37.
40. *Ibid.,* p. 29.
41. *Ibid.,* p. 30.
42. *Ibid.,* p. 33.

over-estimation of self, says Barth, could lead man himself to make this distinction.[43] That this distinction must be made can be understood only in the light of the covenant of grace, namely, "from the knowledge of man as object of the eternal grace of his Creator and Lord."[44] If a man is the object of God's grace, sin cannot be the *only* and the *last* predication that is made of him. Because of *grace* "man's created being cannot, in spite of the shame wherewith he has covered it, be destroyed, it cannot be lost; his falling away cannot alter that which he is for God and has received from God."[45]

It must not be supposed that Barth here has reference to the *formal structure* of man's being in the sense in which Reformed theology spoke of this structure when, in a much used distinction, it referred to the image of God in the *narrow* and in the *broad* sense. This distinction was made to indicate that, according to the Bible, sin did not change man's *being*, that, in spite of sin, man remained *man*.[46] This view stood sharply over against that of Flacius, among others, who taught that because of sin man had become transformed "ad imaginem Satanae."[47]

Barth also speaks of man's "being," but in doing so he refers to something quite different from what Reformed theology had in mind when it used this term. He is not at all concerned about a formal anthropological and ontological humanitas-conception which was not violated or destroyed by sin, but about that "being" of man which can be circumscribed as being *the object of God's grace*. It is in *this* and in *nothing else* that, according to Barth, the *real* humanity, man's true *being*, must be found. "The real man is the sinner who participates in God's grace."[48] The reality of man's being does not simply mean formally that man also as a sinner remains man, but this reality is indissolubly associated with

---

43. *Ibid.*, p. 33.
44. *Ibid.*, p. 34.
45. *Ibid.*, p. 35.
46. Cf. H. Bavinck, *op. cit.*, II, pp. 511 and 515. According to Bavinck this distinction has preserved most purely the connection between creation and redemption, p. 515, although he adds that the distinction has often been conceived of too mechanically and ought therefore to be developed organically, p. 515. Bavinck also says, however, that sin made man lose not only the image of God in the narrower sense, but that it "has also spoiled and ravaged the image of God in the broader sense. It affects man in the whole of his existence."
47. R. Seeberg, *Dogmengeschichte*, IV, p. 494.
48. KD III/2, p. 34.

God's *grace*. This grace is the *first* thing that must be predicated about man, and sin is only the second.[49] It is true that God's judgment over sin strikes man. Judgment, however, is not something that stands by itself, it is always a judgment behind which the grace of God stands.[50] Judgment is always the "form of His mercy."[51] The No of God is *always* spoken for the sake of His Yes, and for *this* reason man remains *man*. "It repeats and affirms that which, according to Genesis 1, happened in creation: the saving separation of light from darkness."[52] Through sin man becomes blind for God, but not God for man.[53] Man breaks the covenant, "but he has not established it and therefore he cannot destroy it."[54] Man can make himself impossible, but only *within* the boundaries of the covenant of *grace*. Man in his sin does not hover about *outside* of these boundaries in a sphere of grace-lessness in which he nevertheless *really* remains man, really retains his *humanitas*. He is and remains "partner in the covenant,"[55] object of grace; he retains "the fundamental character of his being, which is his primary character and which cannot be altered by any secondary factor."[56] It is not a formal structure, an anthropologically determined *humanitas* which is decisive for Barth, but the *being* of man as object of God's *abiding* and *unchanging* grace. It is in *this* way that man remains man. God maintains His faithfulness in spite of our unfaithfulness, His grace in spite of our ingratitude.

Such is God's revelation in Jesus Christ about man as man, "a radiant message of joyful news only." Man may seek to escape this message in his seeking for what he conceives to be his true humanity, but he *cannot* escape it because he actually *is* this man, this object of grace. *"He chooses that which as God's creature he cannot choose."*[57]

Here it becomes plain why, for Barth, sin is a *mystery*. This mystery, this enigma, has nothing to do with the *limits* of our understanding, in the sense of the noetic incomprehensibility of sin. The mystery consists in the fact that sin is something *which in the very nature of the case cannot be*. This is the heart of Barth's doc-

---

49. *Ibid.*, p. 34
50. *Ibid.*, p. 36.
51. *Ibid.*, p. 37.
52. *Ibid.*
53. *Ibid.*, p. 38.
54. *Ibid.*
55. *Ibid.*, p. 35.
56. *Ibid.*, p. 38.
57. *Ibid.*, p. 39 (my italics).

trine of sin, which can be summarized in that strange expression: *the ontological impossibility of sin.*[58]

This ontological impossibility is Christologically grounded. Because Jesus is *the man* in whom God has revealed Himself, every man is a fellow-man of Jesus[59] and therefore being-man *is* being-with-God.[60] For this reason it is possible to speak also of the ontological impossibility of *godlessness.* It is true that people *are* godless, just as they are sinners. But in terms of the man Jesus this is ontologically impossible. Sin and godlessness do indeed constitute a corruption and denial of grace, but they cannot touch the "being" of man because man cannot be lost to the covenant of *grace.* Man wants to be released from this covenant and does all in his power to achieve this,[62] but he *cannot* succeed because of God's grace, which as a canopy of faithfulness and love continues to overshadow him. Man denies what cannot be denied. He rebels, but his rebellion takes place in a kingdom in which grace reigns unassailably.[63]

When sin becomes senseless and chaotic "reality" it has already been intercepted and overtaken by grace.[64] So far as man is concerned, sin seems to be a breaking through and a breaking of the continuity of the covenant, but God's attitude to man "remains, in spite of every alien innovation, in continuity with that in which He created man."[65]

It is not an optimistic and idealistic anthropology that speaks here. Barth wishes to speak about the *being* of man in the light of Christ. Only in this way, he feels, is it possible to hold to an unchanged and unchangeable continuity over against sin.[66] Only in Jesus Christ can the question of who man really is receive a de-

---

58. Very plainly in KD III/2, p. 174: "Here, in this understanding of man's being as resting in God's election, lies the basis and sense of our thesis of the ontological impossibility of sin as descriptive of man." Cf. also the section on "der wirkliche Mensch," *ibid.,* pp. 158-241.

59. *Ibid.,* p. 159.

60. *Ibid.,* pp. 161, 167.

61. *Ibid.,* pp. 162ff. and 166.

62. "This is sin: that man separates himself from the grace of God from which and in which he has his life and being," *ibid.,* p. 39.

63. *Ibid.,* p. 40.

64. KD III/2, p. 44. Cf. also p. 175.

65. *Ibid.,* p. 46.

66. *Ibid.,* p. 50.

cisive answer.[67] We do not come to know the true nature of man with the assistance of words like "responsibility" and "existential" because also such words cannot break through man's autonomous understanding of himself.[68]

It is the gracious election alone that gives us to see man truly. Because of it, sin is ontologically impossible[69] and, in the light of man's true being, chaotic and absurd because the Yes of God preceded this absurd, this impossible thing.

It is striking that Barth, in speaking about the ontological impossibility of sin, continually uses the expression "beforehand." Man was destined beforehand, he was from the beginning appointed, to participate as conqueror in the history of the struggle against the enemy of creaturely being in "the history of victory which Jesus Christ has unfolded."[70]

Sin is ontologically *impossible* because sin means a falling away from grace and it is precisely *God's primordial will* that our unfaithfulness should *not* put to nought His faithfulness. For this reason it is *impossible* to ascribe to the creature "anything that looks like a possibility in the direction of the chaos." Does not man by reason of election live in grace? Has not God come between man and the chaos and "beforehand" *separated* the one from the other?[71] Man who is man in *this* way has neither the right nor the possibility of choosing the wrong direction.[72] It is in the light of these considerations, Barth adds in a remarkable aside, that sin appears in its terrible *absurdity*. When man decides against God, he does this not on the basis of his nature and of a possibility residing

---

67. *Ibid.*, p. 59. "Also our human nature as such we derive wholly and completely from Jesus."

68. This is illustrative of Barth's polemic against Brunner who speaks so emphatically of "actuality." Does Brunner in this usage refer to a disposition or to *the* actuality of God's action? Is there a two-fold possibility in man, a liberum arbitrium?, KD III/2, pp. 143ff. and 153ff., or does Brunner mean the actual man as he stands in grace, in the covenant, and therefore without the possibility of sin as a human possibility? Barth fears the former for in Brunner non-freedom and irrationality are possibilities of man's created nature, III/2, p. 156. Brunner operates with a *neutral* conception of freedom, with a possibility which can express itself in two directions. Therefore Barth asks, *what* election is if, as it appears according to Brunner, it is not yet "in force." The actual man is Jesus' fellowman as he stands in the light of Immanuel about whom we know only in terms of "God's gracious election of the man Jesus," KD III/2, p. 173.

69. *Ibid.*, p. 174.

70. *Ibid.*, especially pp. 174, 175.

71. *Ibid.*, p. 175

72. *Ibid.*

within that nature, but "he reaches in reality for that which has been made impossible for him and *against which he has also been secured.*"[73]

Obviously, Barth has something quite different in mind when he speaks of the "enigma" of sin than when Bavinck speaks of it. The difference between Barth and the general conception of the Church and of theology on the score of the origin of sin lies in this, that for Barth *sin not only has a mysterious, incomprehensible character, but is an ontological impossibility.* This is not a problem of our *knowledge* of sin, but of sin itself. It is a violation of grace, but of *that* grace which because of God's election in Jesus is *inviolable.*

* * *

If man's being, then, is not understood abstractly but as a being in grace, when freedom before God constitutes the being of man[74] and, consequently, man *is* "because God has decided in favor of him,"[75] and if there is *no other* real being of man than *this* being, a new urgency permeates the question of what sin really *is.* Why is sin then not *only* an ontological impossibility? Why is its "reality" not simply an *appearance?* When man's freedom does *not* consist in a choice between two possibilities [76] but between man's own possibility (before God) and his *impossibility,* between being and not-being, when freedom means that man can not-sin and that he cannot sin,[77] why does it not follow that man, when he sins, is no longer man? To this question Barth has only one answer, and that answer is that it is precisely *this* which has been "beforehand" excluded by *God's grace.*

Barth is very positive in affirming that man, real man, is *good.* "In the free exercise of his responsibility before God — the doing of which constitutes his created being — man is factually good and not evil."[78] Barth hastens to add that this is not intended as an optimistic thesis about man.[79] Sin is not an appearance, but reality. God's covenant partner *can* break the covenant and man as he

73. *Ibid.,* p. 176, my italics.
74. *Ibid.,* p. 233.
75. *Ibid.*
76. *Ibid.,* p. 235.
77. *Ibid.,* 235: "potest non peccare" and "non potest peccare."
78. *Ibid.,* p. 235.
79. *Ibid.,* p. 236.

really is "can deny and obscure his true reality."[80]  There *is* an incomprehensible and insane "ability to sin."[81]

From this ability to sin and from this covenant breach, however, Barth turns again to the inalienable character of our true humanity which can be obscured and covered by sin[82] but which is never *lost*.  The power of sin is great, but it is not without limits.[83] It can destroy much, but it can *not* destroy man's being as such which is a being *in grace* and in the Yes of God.

There is a continuity which is unassailable, an "inviolable purpose" of man's creaturely being[84] which *remains* even when it becomes unrecognizable to our eyes.  It is the function of anthropology, in terms of Christology, to demonstrate this continuity. "The practical significance of this question must not be overlooked."[85] Man cannot be man without being a covenant partner of God.[86]

The secret, the mystery of man's humanity lies in this, "that he belongs to God, that God is for him, and specifically that He is for him in the person of the man Jesus."[87]  To this man's being corresponds.[88]

Because Jesus is for us, it follows that man is not man without fellow-man.  Man acts as though he had no God and no neighbor, but this "inhumanity" may not be interpreted as indicating man's true humanity.[89]  We may not regard this "isolation with respect to fellow-man" as belonging to man's being.  This inhumanity does not alter the fact that man remains bound to his Savior, even as the *lost* sheep continues to belong to the flock.[90]  Humanity without fellow-man is impossible.  This humanity may not be seen as a pale and unattainable ideal while the empirical, the "real" man is a wholly different being.  No, it is precisely in this humanity that we are concerned about the *real* man in the "primitive actuality of our situation."  The yearning to be together is most natural,[91] it is the sine qua non of man's humanity,[92] it is not something added, it is an *essential* element of our nature, it belongs to our being-man.

---

80. *Ibid.*, p. 244.
81. *Ibid.*
82. *Ibid.*, p. 246
83. *Ibid.*
84. *Ibid.*
85. *Ibid.*
86. *Ibid.*, p. 247.

87. *Ibid.*, p. 319.
88. *Ibid.*, p. 269.
89. *Ibid.*, p. 271.
90. *Ibid.*, p. 272.
91. *Ibid.*, p. 318.
92. *Ibid.*, p. 328

Man has in his nature no other possibility, no point of contact
for another choice, [93] no possibility for inhumanity.[94] This desire
to be together is not in itself, to be sure, the expression of Christian
love.[95] It constitutes the humanity of human nature in the light
of the human nature of Jesus [96] *This* humanity is inalienable. Although *love* can only be understood in the light of man's walk with
God and of the history which this walk with God creates,[97] we may
not underestimate this humanity. When we ascribe to it its full
value, we do not have to fear that there will not be room left
for grace.[98] Theological anthropology arrives at conclusions at
which others (the heathen Confucius, the atheist Feuerbach, and
the Jew, Buber) have also arrived,[99] but this may not lead us to
surrender our position. The correspondence between heathen and
Christian theses about man, while not complete, cannot be denied.[100] Moreover, the explanation of this circumstance must not
surprise us. It lies in the fact that natural man, too, exists "within
the sphere of divine grace, in the sphere in which Jesus also was
man."[1] It is precisely in the light of grace that we see the connection between Jesus' humanity and humanity in general. There is
"a humanity that is common to the Christian and the non-Christian, and that *not in the formal structure* of being-human, but in
terms of the grace of Jesus Christ. When this is denied, it is overlooked that sinful man "is thoroughly capable of being human in
the sense of having an open heart for his neighbor."[2] For this reason
Barth protests against placing "eros" and "agape" antithetically
over against each other, as is the vogue in recent time, in which
eros must then, of course, typify natural man. This "incitement"
against the "Greek mind" in theology "is not a good thing."[3] The
real man is the man who is *together* with his fellow-man.

Therefore we must say that man *in* his falling away from God,
in his becoming and being sinful, has not been robbed of his
humanity. In his desire for fellowship he reveals his humanity.[4]
Reformed theology has faced the problem of the "goodness" and of
the "corruption" in man by means of the doctrine of common grace

---

93. *Ibid.*, p. 328.
94. *Ibid.*, p. 329.
95. *Ibid.*
96. *Ibid.*, p. 330.
97. *Ibid.*, p. 331.
98. *Ibid.*, p. 333.

99. *Ibid.*
100. *Ibid.*, p. 334.
1. *Ibid.*
2. *Ibid.*, p. 336.
3. *Ibid.*, p. 341.
4. *Ibid.*, p. 348.

through which evil is restrained in man who is *by nature* prone to hate God and his neighbor.[5] The goodness which common grace posits within this framework Barth explains Christologically in terms of man's *being*. Sin, self-isolation and hate with respect to the neighbor are not a revelation of humanity; they constitute rather an attack on man's humanity which is turned back by the unassailable reality of man's true being.

\* \* \*

It is indisputable that Barth's conception of the ontological impossibility of sin (and therewith the "Christological" goodness of human nature) constitutes a decisive background of his view of the triumph of grace. That which other theologians, who also concerned themselves with the "enigma" of sin, posited to reject the idea that man was created evil and that God is the author of sin finds in Barth's doctrine of sin and grace a *positive* place. The shifting which Barth effects in the traditional interpretation of the mystery of sin to that of an ontological impossibility belongs to the most decisive and determinative aspects of his theology.[6]

\* \* \*

It must now be noted that although Barth, on the one hand, speaks anthropologically about the ontological impossibility of sin, he speaks, on the other hand, of man's "ability" to sin, even though this is an "insane" ability. This cannot but give rise to questions, since Barth rejects in countless variations[7] the idea of the "possibility" of sin. How is it possible that he should still speak about

---

5. Cf. Abraham Kuyper, *Gemeene Gratie*, I, p. 11, about the root of the doctrine of common grace, namely, the fatal character of sin, p. 11. Kuyper wishes to detract nothing from this, and at the same time will not close his eyes for "the good and the beautiful outside of the Church, in the world, among unbelievers." He speaks of an "apparent contradiction," because in the light of the restraining effect of common grace there is in reality no question of a contradiction.

6. That this hangs indissolubly together with Barth's conception of freedom is evident not only from our discussion of his polemic against Brunner, but also in many other connections. The ontological impossibility of sin is related to man's *freedom* as freedom before God (which is the only possibility that God gave him). This is not an abstract "non posse peccare," but it is based in *God's* freedom who in Christ has made man free in this way. Without Christ concrete man simply is not. Man *is* in that he lives in *this* freedom, III/2, p. 233.

7. Cf. especially Barth's criticism of Julius Müller's conception of the liberum arbitrium in his *Die christliche Lehre von der Sünde*, 1849, especially the section in II, pp. 152-243, "Die Freiheit als Möglichkeit der Sünde."

the "reality" of sin?  If sin exists *outside* of the "possibility" of human nature then it must for that very reason be described as chaotic, absurd and impossible.  The question arises whether Barth's view of sin as an ontological impossibility does not jeopardize the reality and the serious consequences of the guilt about which the Bible speaks so emphatically in terms of admonition, threat, and judgment.  Scripture certainly does not by means of a phenomenological analysis speak about man's shortcomings, but with a fully concrete accusation it exclaims, Thou, O man!  What are the implications of describing sin as an enigma, a shadow, as absurdity and as chaos?  Since Barth makes plain that we are *not* simply concerned about the psychological inexplicability of man's falling into sin, is it religiously and biblically legitimate to speak as he does about the "enigma" and the "impossibility" of sin?  Do these qualifications have a place within the limits of Scripture?

It is necessary at this point to make a sharp distinction.  Key terms which Barth has introduced into the discussion can be used within the framework of the traditional conception as well as in his conception.  The "mystery" of sin can refer to the incomprehensibility of sin while at the same time holding that God is neither the author of sin nor the "origin" of evil.  The "absurdity" of sin can mean that, in view of the goodness of God's creation and the richness of man's communion with God, there is not a single ground or reason for sin.  Sin can be qualified as *foolishness* and as *absurdity,* as *rebellion* against the goodness and blessings of God's sovereign government, in order that thus, as a confession of guilt, it may be seen in its senselessness, much as the Bible speaks about the *fool* who, in an act of practical atheism, says, There is no God.[8]  Similarly, we can speak of the "chaotic" in the sense of the disorder and disturbance of the riches and beauty of creation which sin always effects.  Such qualifications do not lead us outside of the boundaries of Scripture.

It would seem, however, that we enter upon a wholly different situation when sin is not simply referred to as irrational (how can sin be "rational?") and as disorderly, but the concept "impossibility" is introduced and continually used.  It must indeed be remembered that Barth does not herewith intend to deny the "reality" of sin.  In

---

8. Ps. 14:1 and 53:2: the folly of wishing to evade what cannot be evaded, namely, the reality of God. Cf. A. Weiser, *Die Psalmen,* I, 1950.

spite of this, however, his conception of "impossibility" is unacceptable because the Bible speaks in a wholly different way about the "reality" of sin. When sin and godlessness are designated in terms of a divine accusation of utter seriousness and sin is related to man's responsibility and to death, any and every use of the concept "impossibility" and particularly "ontological impossibility" as a speculative effort to speak where Scripture does not speak is unwarranted. *We do not suggest, therefore, that by "impossibility" Barth means "unreality"; we wish rather to reject the word in the sense in which Barth uses it.*

In order to clarify what we mean here, we point out first of all that Barth's criticism of the traditional view that the "possibility" (to the right *and* to the left) that man has by virture of the gift of true freedom[9] does not solve the problem which he poses but simply shifts it to other ground.

Barth excludes the ability to sin from the good nature with which man was created. Having done this, however, he again asserts this "ability" (as an insane ability) because of the reality of sin in the world. This creates a peculiar tension which we find nowhere in the Bible. Over against this it will have to be acknowledged that when Reformed theology spoke about the "possibility" of sin in man as a good creation it did not thereby present a speculation about "possibilities" in order to give an *explanation* of sin. Rather, it spoke about this "possibility" only in view of the *reality* of sin. In thinking about this reality, Reformed theology was much more concerned to exclude the impossibility than to manifest an independent interest in the "possibility" of sin! Even so, it cannot be denied that on this basis the temptation constantly arose to reflect speculatively on the *rationality* of the "possibility" of sin,[10] and the door was opened wide to all manner of speculation.

The rejection of the "impossibility" of sin — in whatever form it may be posited — is immediately demanded by the reality of guilt and the alienation which it effects. If sin is ontologically impossible, a transition from wrath to grace in the historical sphere is no longer thinkable. It is clear that *this* transition is excluded

---

9. Cf. K. Barth's *Das Geschenk der Freiheit*, 1952, p. 9. Freedom is not simply an *offer*, it is a gift, and therefore not simply a possibility. "It does not place man in the situation of a Hercules standing at the dividing of the ways. Rather it lifts him out of this false situation."

10. Cf. H. Bavinck, *op. cit.*, III, pp. 44ff.

when Barth, consistent with his total view, eludicates what he means by the ontological impossibility of sin by saying that sin is substantially a grasping for that "which has been made impossible for man and against which he has also been secured."[11]

The central thrust of Barth's conception is not an irrational paradox (impossibility *and* reality of sin). The emphasis he wishes to make is rather this: man cannot fall from grace because of the a priori electing love and faithfulness of God, while at the same time sin is a reality. When Barth speaks of chaos, mystery, enigma, shadow and *impossibility,* this last word explains all the others and forms the central category of his doctrine of sin and redemption. This category also stands related to earlier reflections about sin, the devil and the idea of logical inconsistency,[12] but it receives its deepest meaning in the light of triumphant grace.

Barth sees sin as *that* reality which *in* its existence has "beforehand," from the beginning, been overtaken and *therefore* can impossibly effective what it wishes and intends to achieve, namely, the nullifying of grace and the breaking of the covenant relationship with God. The grace which does *not* disappear but which now appears as *unmerited* grace reveals the powerlessness of sin. It is impotent because it is unable to create a really *new* situation but rather finds expression in that area which is the area of God's *grace.* Only in that area can sin happen, but when it does it is precisely within that area that its *impotence* in the face of the triumph of grace becomes manifest.[13]

We see that the triumph of grace is emphatically placed *before* sin and that for this reason sin is anticipated and intercepted and so made ontologically impossible. The triumph of grace is the reverse side of (in a certain sense one can say that it is identical with) the ontological impossibility of sin.

\* \* \*

A decisive question in this discussion is the problem of the reality in history of God's wrath against sin. A few paragraphs earlier

---

11. KD III/2, p. 176.
12. K. Barth, *De apostolische Geloofsbelijdenis,* 1935, p. 52.
13. Cf. KD IV/1, p. 603, about the *impossibility* of the sinner's terminating his own existence in election and as a good creature. Note the reference to the "impossible" flight of Jonah which Barth uses as an illustration when he writes, "Therefore his being saved was not something new, but the execution of the unchangeable, divine counsel against which he had struggled in vain."

we alluded to the transition — in history — from wrath to grace and now we can enter further upon this most important point. It is obvious that this problem must be faced, since the idea of the ontological impossibility of sin raises the question as it were automatically. Does not the triumph of grace in its completely and abidingly a priori character mean that because of grace the wrath of God remains excluded "from the beginning?"

A comparison between Barth and Ritschl on the score of their views of the wrath of God immediately suggests itself at this point. According to Ritschl, God's wrath is really not an actuality but a radical misunderstanding on the part of man from which Jesus as the revelation of God's love came to release us.[14] We must face the fact that Barth has with great emphasis rejected Ritschl's conception of the wrath of God. In Barth's view it is too simplistic a conception and does not do justice to the manner in which the Bible speaks about the divine wrath and the divine judgment. Consequently, he takes issue with Ritschl's "act of exegetical violence"[15] and protests that with the elimination of God's wrath we also "eliminate His grace and His love." On the basis of Scripture it is necessary to speak of the wrath and of the judgment of God. "If God does not meet us jealously, wrathfully, He does not meet us at all, and then man is factually left to himself." It is *precisely* God's wrath, according to Barth, that shows that He is *gracious*.[16] *By way of* wrath and judgment God reconciles man to Himself. It is the *burning* bush in Exodus 3:2 that is *not* consumed. Later, also in connection with his discussion about Ritschl, Barth refers to the separation of light from darkness in Genesis 1:2. The wrath of God does not stand in *antithesis* to forgiveness, but *in* wrath and *in* judgment *reconciliation takes place*.[17] It is grace which "has obviously been the sense of the revelation of God's holiness from the very beginning."

It is plain that Ritschl and Barth may not be identified[18] but, still, there is one clear point of contact between Ritschl's rejection

---

14. Cf. among others A. Ritschl, *Die Christliche Lehre von der Rechtfertigung und Versöhnung*, III, section 42.
15. KD II/1, p. 141.
16. Cf. "That God does not leave him to himself, that God is really gracious to him, is evident from this that He goes to meet man in His holiness," *ibid.*, p. 411.
17. KD II/1, p. 412.
18. Cf. KD VI/1, pp. 421ff.

of the wrath of God and the relationship which Barth posits between the wrath and the *grace* of God. Barth maintains the reality of this wrath, but this reality is the *reverse side,* it is the *working* of grace. Wrath is subordinate to grace in the sense of being the disciplining of grace. For *this* reason wrath is by no means irreconcilable with God's grace and love.[19] It is not necessary for God to reveal Himself "monotonously" as Love. He can speak His No and in so doing "hide Himself as He is in Himself, He can reveal Himself in the strange form of His not-willing and of His wrath." Grace in no sense involves that man remains uncharged with guilt, unjudged and unpunished.[20] Grace without judgment is not grace, and Barth chides Ritschl for not understanding that there is no wrath of God "which is anything else than the gracious burning of His love."[21] Wrath is real, but only as the "modus" of the divine love. As such it really exists *within the area of grace.*[22]

There is judgment and there is wrath. When sin denies grace and attacks that unassailable stronghold, then God meets that attack with holy wrath, but *in* that wrath grace in all its unconquerableness becomes manifest. *This* chaotic and impotent power can offer no resistance against the omnipotent and a priori triumph of grace. When sin has done its worst, it appears — precisely *then* it appears — that grace remained standing as a rock immovable amid the raging sea that dashed its waves in vain against it. Already at the first attack of the chaotic and the absurd reality which sin is its utter defeat is a determined matter.[23] We do not yet see this, but God does. He *has* already achieved the triumph which will now become evident fact in history. We can speak only of the *old* threat which in Jesus Christ has become a matter of the past.[24]

Here the tones of triumph in Barth's thinking resound loudly. The god of this age, he exclaims, "does not concern us. We will not vanquish him, nor do we have to. He has been vanquished."[25]

---

19. *Ibid.,* p. 545.
20. *Ibid.*
21. *Ibid.,* p. 546.
22. Cf. Barth's criticism of Rudolf Otto's conception of "das Heilige," KD II/1, p. 405.
23. KD III/3, p. 343.
24. *Ibid.,* pp. 417, 419. Cf. pp. 421 and 424.
25. K. Barth, *Die Souveränität des Wortes Gottes und die Entscheidung des Glaubens,* 1939, p. 3.

There is no room for anxiety anymore,[26] also not for the Church with respect to the State. One hymn of Paul Gerhardt is stronger than the worst that we can read in the papers about "Russia" and "America."[27]

In our analysis in the first part of this volume we saw that Barth does not regard our actual liberation from the power of the chaos as a matter of the *future*.[28] The liberation has been accomplished and the power of evil is now no more than a dangerous *appearance*.[29] The chaos has *objectively* been eliminated. We do not yet see this, but this is only because of the blindness of our eyes. The chaos has only *apparent* power and therefore it is not dangerous.

The question has more than once been asked whether this kind of triumph is indeed the message of the Scriptures. On the one hand, we constantly meet in the Bible the appeal not to fear, to be of good courage and to believe steadfastly in the victory of Jesus Christ. On the other hand, we see that the believer is continually called to resistance and to struggle. We do not in the Bible gain the impression that the battle is all "an emptied matter" in the sense in which Barth speaks of it. On the contrary, we are warned against a danger that is still very real. When Barth continually speaks of "not-dangerous" and of "apparent power" it is difficult to harmonize this "objective situation" with the New Testament. After Christ's conquest has taken place, the admonitions of which we read are precisely directed against the demonic influence which is apt to close our eyes to the victory. The situation has, as a result of Christ's victory been essentially and triumphantly changed; but, remarkably enough, the New Testament still reckons very realistically with the power of the demons.

The resistance to which we are called is, it is true, not a somber but a joyful matter. The weapons and the full armor of God stand at our disposal. But the *battle* is real now that Christ is no longer on the scene. When in the apocalyptic vision of Revelation the

---

26. K. Barth, *Christliche Gemeinde im Wechsel der Staatsordnungen*, 1948, p. 52.
27. K. Barth, *Die Kirche zwischen Ost und West*, 1949, p. 9. Immediately after this he writes, "Let us *not participate* in this conflict! As Christians we have nothing at all to do with it. It is not a genuine, it is not a necessary, not an interesting conflict. It is a sheer power conflict."
28. KD III/3, p. 420.
29. *Ibid.*, p. 425.

child is suddenly carried away from the woman to the throne of God, the woman must flee away into the desert. The war in heaven against the dragon is won, but the result is that the dragon, who is called the Devil and Satan, is thrown down to the earth and deceives the whole world. The triumphant note dominates in the loud voice that resounds from heaven when the victory song is sung through the blood of the Lamb. But the battle is not yet over. The wrath of Satan reaches its climax precisely at this point when he knows that his "time is short."

The intensified struggle is indissolubly associated with the *victory.* "Then the dragon was angry with the woman, and went off to make war on the rest of her offspring, on those who keep the commandments of God and bear testimony to Jesus." The remarkable thing about Revelation 12 is that the note of *triumph* is directly related to the *new struggle* and to the *new warning*. It is not possible to describe the progress of salvation and victory in the New Testament as a progress from conquest over a *real* enemy to conquest over an *apparent* enemy, or in terms of an antithesis between the powers of evil that have been "emptied" and our blind eyes which do not yet see. On all sides we hear the New Testament speak about the disarming of powers and principalities and of their being overcome, but it is precisely in this new phase of the struggle that we must put on the whole armor of God that we may be able to stand against the wiles of the devil as we contend against principalities and powers, against the world rulers of this present darkness, against the spiritual hosts of wickedness in heavenly places. This struggle bears a very *concrete* character, as appears from Paul's words to the Church of the Thessalonians, "we wanted to come to you — I, Paul, again and again — but Satan hindered us," or from his writing to the Corinthians when all kinds of tensions threatened their fellowship and made necessary his appeal to them mutually to forgive one another as also he had done "for your sake in the presence of Christ, to keep Satan from gaining the advantage over us; for we are not ignorant of his designs." We notice nothing in the New Testament of a silencing of the songs that praise the triumph, but *at the same time* the Church is called to renewed prosecution of the battle, and that on the basis of the decision that has already been made. When there are pseudo-apostles who present themselves as apostles of Christ, Paul does not consider this a thing to marvel at, for Satan himself appears as an angel of light.

When we consider these data, we cannot but ask whether Barth is justified in giving only a "brief look" at the demons in his work on Providence.[30] Undoubtedly he is right when he says that it is possible to have too much respect for this "disorderly business." The manner in which we give this "brief look," however, must be determined by Scripture. Of course we cannot believe in the devil and in the demons in the same way in which we believe in God.[31] Indeed, we can only say that in that sense radical unbelief is the only proper response. This says nothing, however, about the amount of *attention* that we must give to them. It is possible to pray "Deliver us from evil" without having an independent interest in the demons. It is not possible to think rightly about Satan other than in relation to God's revelation. When we take seriously what the Bible has to say about the demons, we may come to the conclusion that Barth's "brief, sharp look"[32] in the last fifteen pages of his doctrine of election is symptomatic of the kind of thinking which we met in his conception of the ontological impossibility of sin. The demonic element becomes vague in its "apparent" reality and in its "being emptied" as chaos. The demons, we discovered in our analysis, have not been created. They exist "only because God, in saying Yes to Himself and to the creature, also necessarily expresses a No."[33] They have been vanquished by the positive Yes of God in His eternal election and in the reconciliation which has historically been achieved by Christ. The sharp issue which Barth took with the bad dream of dogmatics (that the demons are fallen angels)[34] robs the revelation about the demons of its *concrete character*. Biblical demonology is only the "negative reflex of biblical

---

30. *Ibid.*, p. 608.
31. *Ibid.*, p. 611.
32. *Ibid.*, p. 609.
33. *Ibid.*, 613.
34. The argumentation is most remarkable. It is directly related to Barth's criticism of the neutral conception of freedom. In his view, the fall of the angels assumes that "the freedom of these creatures, too, would not be a real freedom if there were not also for them the freedom of the so-called *liberum arbitrium* or at least that in some pre-historical time it meant: the freedom to become fools," KD III/p. 623. The remarkable thing is that with respect to man Barth has the same criticism, but *then* calls sin a reality and speaks of a "fall." Of the angels, however, he writes, "A real, proper angel does not do what is attributed to a part of the angels in this doctrine." He does say in this connection that in terms of this conception of freedom also the human creature cannot be understood wholly correctly, but he does not make plain why man *can* and the angels can *not* fall.

Christology and Soteriology,"[35] for this "kingdom" is the impotent kingdom, the vanquished kingdom, the kingdom of chaos.

Here Barth's "demonology" touches upon his doctrine of creation. The demons stand *outside of creation*. They are not *creatures*. The words of II Peter and Jude are ignored, although they plainly speak of angels that sinned and that did not keep their own position but left their proper dwelling. John 8:44, however, receives full attention, where we read that the devil was a murderer *from the beginning*,[36] who speaks "according to his nature," who is a liar and is the *father* of lies and has nothing to do with the truth.[37]

It is not easy to summarize responsibly what Barth has to say at the conclusion of his treatment of the doctrine of providence. It is clear, however, that the triumph of grace which is prefigured in creation stands over against the powers which *invaded* the creation but which do not themselves belong to created reality. Notwithstanding his criticism of 19th century theology, Barth has in his demonology extended the line of 19th century thinking in this respect that he protests against the "bad dream" of traditional dogmatics. The chaotic stands *outside* of creation and owes its "existence" to the power of God's rejection. At this point we again come into contact with Barth's distinction between the work of God's left hand and the work of His right hand.

The work of God's left hand is His wrath, His wrathful No, while the work of His right hand is His proper work of love. This is a distinction which was originally made by Luther in connection with his discussion of the wrath and the love of God. It is not our purpose at this time to discuss Luther's intention in his use of these terms. It must be pointed out, however, that in Luther's use of them they are related to Isaiah 28:11, "Nay, but by men of strange lips and with an alien tongue the Lord will speak to this people, to whom he has said, 'This is rest; give rest to the weary; and this is repose'; yet they would not hear." The connection between these words and God's right and left hand is not immediately perspicuous, but it must be remembered that the Vulgate translated Isaiah 28:21 as follows, "Alienum est opus eius,

---

35. *Ibid.*, p. 621.
36. *Ibid.*, p. 623.
37. *Ibid.*

ut operetur opus suum." That is to say, God would perform an *alien* work in order to effectuate his *proper* work. Against this background, the alien work is regarded as the work of His wrath in which God's real purpose is the accomplishing of the work of grace in Jesus Christ.

It is clear that Luther as well as Barth distinguishes between the "alien" and the "proper" work of God in connection with God's wrath and God's love. Barth, however, in distinction from Luther, has not, in his use of these terms, referred them to Isaiah 28:11.[38] The reason for this probably is that the distinction between "opus alienum" and "opus proprium," as Barth continually uses it, cannot be based upon Isaiah 28:11 and 21. Isaiah prophesies of the judgment which God will inflict through the Assyrians, men who will speak to Judah in a strange language. Earlier God had spoken, admonishing Judah to trust in Him. But because they had refused to hear Him and had mocked His prophetic word, God will *now* speak in *this* manner, namely, through the Assyrian judgment. We face the fact here that the "strangeness" of the Assyrian language and the "strange" work of God (Isa. 28:21) gave occasion to Luther — via the Vulgate — to introduce the distinction between the alien and the proper work of God, while for Isaiah the "strangeness" served to indicate the nature of the judgment that was to come.

The burden of Isaiah's prophetic judgment was indeed one of wrath and love, but this gives no warrant for saying that the path on which God now leads His people is a path in which He performs a work that is really *alien* to Him. Therefore Barth, in abandoning the connection with Isaiah, used only the terms opus alienum and opus proprium to point to the wrath which is the "alien form" of grace. This relationship between wrath and love also comes to the fore in Luther when he emphasizes that the way of judgment (opus alienum) paves the way for confession of guilt and for the manifestation of God's proper work of love and forgiveness. Barth, however, goes much farther than this. He combines the distinction that we find in Luther with his conception of the chaos which exists at God's left hand and is the expression of rejection, of His "not-willing." This is a thought which we do not meet in Luther

---

38. K. Schilder has correctly pointed this out in his *Heidelbergsche Catechismus,* III, 1950, p. 334.

and indeed cannot meet in him because Luther has a different demonology than Barth.[39] He speaks of them much more concretely and therefore less anonymously. Although Luther does not rationalize the world of the demons, they do not for one moment fall outside the area of creation and are therefore not for one moment withdrawn from the sphere of God's power.

In speaking about the two "works" of God, Luther wishes to illustrate what he himself called the "theology of the cross,"[40] the *strange* way in which God brings His *proper* purpose to manifestation, that is, in the hiddenness of the cross. For Barth, on the other hand, the "opus alienum" involves the whole problem of sin and of the chaos. Here we meet not only God's wrath in its reaction to sin as a phenomenon arising in history, but we meet His wrath as that to which the chaos owes its existence. Therefore *the* expression that captivates Barth is not, as it was for Luther, Isaiah 28:11 (or 21) but Genesis 1:2 (separation of light from darkness)! Luther, at least, leaves room to do justice to the elements of mockery and unbelief between God's first speaking (loving admonition) and His later speaking (through the strange tongue of the Assyrians); for Barth the problem of the opus alienum and opus proprium is removed from this correlative area and becomes one of God's Yes and of His No, of His election and of His rejection. Moreover, where the "bad dream of dogmatics" (the fall of the angels) is rejected, the opus alienum automatically, as it were, receives other characteristics than it had for Luther. For it is now not used, at least not primarily, to designate the problem of the Assyrians in Isaiah, of the theologia crucis and of the "foolishness" and the "weakness" of I Corinthians 1, but its reference is to the non-created chaos which is necessarily rejected by God's eternal No and, with this rejection, receives its own dimension, its own reality.

The results of this difference with Luther are far-reaching. There is no question here of simply effecting a correction in Luther's conception. Rather, Barth arrives at a wholly different kind of "strangeness" than Luther did. Luther emphasized the

---

39. Cf. especially M. Obendiek, *Der Teufel bei Martin Luther*, 1931.

40. In this connection, and also in connection with the exegesis of Isa. 28:11, cf. K. Schilder, *op. cit.*, III, pp. 321ff.; Lennart Pinomaa, *Der Zorn Gottes in der Theologie Luthers. Ein Beitrag zur Frage nach der Einheit des Gottesbildes bei Luther*. Helsinki, 1938; and E. Brunner, *Dogmatik*, I, p. 175ff.

manner of God's dealing with men when He is confronted with unbelief and folly, whereas in Barth's thinking the opus alienum is related to the word God spoke in creating and to the nature of the non-created chaotic and demonic realm which exists at God's left hand by virtue of His opus alienum. Through this action of God there appears at the boundary of creation the shadow of the chaos which was never unreal but which was "on the scene" from the beginning as a rejected reality having its own dimension and character. For this reason Barth goes so far as to speak of the victory of the opus proprium over the opus alienum. With this he does not mean to posit a dualism in God, for the opus alienum is always a rejecting, a wrathful work. This does not alter the fact, however, that the problem of the origin of sin can no longer be isolated from the "strange" shadow of the chaotic and the demonic which God's Yes casts over the creature and *for the purpose of confrontation* with the creature. The struggle against sin does not only have cosmic proportions — it has this in the Bible also — but, in connection with the wrath of God, it has the proportions of a struggle between created and non-created being. For this reason Barth speaks continually of the chaotic. This word refers to more than disorder over against the ordered cosmos and harmony of God's creation. It is also *that* chaotic element which, *as* the rejected reality, is from the beginning "present" and must therefore lead to the "problem" of *creation*.[41]

*   *   *

The foregoing makes evident that Barth does not use the expression "the chaos" simply to indicate the powerlessness of sin in the face of the triumphant Yes of God. The "powerlessness" of the chaos (its being "emptied") does play an important role in his

---

41. K. Schilder, *op. cit.* III, p. 365, writes that according to Barth the chaos already existed because God *did not choose* it. On page 375, however, he writes that in Barth's view the chaos (the work of God's left hand) also belongs to the good creation, a thesis which Barth has continually rejected. The fact that the shadow-side of creation (the work of God's left hand) is taken up in the praise of God is no evidence for Schilder's contention because Barth sets forth extensively that this shadow-side is not the chaos. Perhaps Schilder's interpretation is caused by his reading of Barth's words in III/3, p. 417 that the chaos "has indeed" been created by God. This is a printer's error, however, by which "nicht" (God did *not* create the chaos) became a "wohl" (God has *indeed* created the chaos). Cf. Barth's expression of regret with respect to this error in the Introduction of IV/1. Cf. chapter III, footnote 94.

theology, but over and above this the word involves a "reality" which is "chaotic" in character, and which does not partake of created reality. When one asks himself *what* this chaos with its non-created dimension of being really is, it is necessary to be careful not to identify it with non-being although it does have something to do with "nothing" and "non-being." This appears from the fact that Barth says about the creature that it is by no means "nothing" but rather a creation at "the edge of nothing,"[42] and further when he speaks about our beginning being over which the shadows of non-being fall.[43] Barth refers to non-being in its threatening character, and this comes to more specific expression when he says that creation according to its negative aspect *borders* on the chaos.[44]

At the *edge,* at the *boundary,* of creation the danger threatens to which man is not equal. Although the chaos has not been created, it forms in a certain sense "the horizon of God's creation and of his creature.[45] Therefore Barth speaks of the "ontology of chaos,"[46] and his thinking on the subject is revealed especially in that he interprets *conservatio* (preservation) as *servatio* (salvation), salvation, namely, from the threatening overwhelming power of the chaos.[47] Man can live only in terms of this salvation, in terms of this *merciful* preservation.[48] In this way the chaos, with its own "ontology," receives an integral place in Barth's dogmatic system.

\* \* \*

It is important to take note of the fact that the Bible also makes mention of "non-being" and "nothing." In countless ways it speaks of *not* and *nothing* in the same sense in which we use these words in every-day language. When it does so, it never has reference to a metaphysical problem of "being" or "non-being" but to the reality of the created world, to a denial or a prohibition (thou shalt *not . . . .*) or to an impossibility (without me ye can do *nothing*).

As in our common speech, so also in Scripture these expressions do not represent any theoretical reflections but they are used in a naive and self-evident way. Most assuredly they do not reflect a

---

42. KD III/3, p. 335.
43. *Ibid.,* p. 698ff.
44. *Ibid.,* p. 335.
45. *Ibid.,* p. 406.

46. *Ibid.,* p. 407.
47. *Ibid.,* p. 84.
48. *Ibid.,* p. 87.

threat to creation but rather point positively to the reality of creation and to the will of God. It may safely be said that we in no way meet in them an isolated or independent interest in "nothing" or in "non-being."[49] In this connection we also think of the significance that has been attached in dogmatic thinking to the term "creatio ex nihilo." This expression has at times been interpreted as meaning a creation from an *already* existing "nihilum," and Kuyper has, judging from student notes, protested strongly against this view and called it a magical formula that was well intended but that has done much harm.[50]

Bavinck accepted the term quite readily and understood it as meaning a creative calling forth from non-being to being. He rejects the idea of creation out of an antecedently existing nihilum and considers it to be a trenchant expression of what the Scriptures as a whole teach.[51] He does not understand "creatio ex nihilo" to mean that non-being was the *source* of being, but that what now is, at one time was not and was called into being only through God's omnipotence.[52] In *that* sense the term is fully in harmony with Revelation 4:11 and contradicts every abuse of it which would infringe on God's fully sovereign creative act. The "nihil negativum" directs attention solely to God's creative act, just as Romans 4:17 speaks of God's giving life to the dead and of His calling "into existence the things that do not exist." It is important to note this *positive* function of the scriptural "ex nihilo." The "nothing" as such receives no positive attention or content. It is not associated

---

49. For an example of this abstract interest and reflection we find in M. Heidegger, *Was ist Metaphysik?*, 1929, p. 10: "How must we understand this 'nothing'? Is it an accident that we speak of it as it were automatically? Is it just a way of speaking — and nothing more than that?" He wishes to reflect on this self-evident "nothing" "which slips into our common talk so unobtrusively," p. 13. According to Heidegger, this "nothing" is "revealed" in *fear* and at *this* point we can examine it. "Existence" is: "to be held within the embrace of 'nothing,'" p. 21. Cf. also Heidegger's *Sein und Zeit*, 4th ed., 1935, pp. 184ff. and *Vom Wesen des Grundes*, 3rd ed., 1949, p. 45.

50. A. Kuyper, *Dictaten Dogmatiek, Locus de Creatione*, p. 46. In *E Voto Dordraceno* (Exposition of the Heidelberg Catechism) I, he expresses greater appreciation for the expression, pp. 203, 205.

51. H. Bavinck, *op. cit.*, II, p. 381. Cf. pp. 379-380.

52. *Ibid.*, p. 382: *ex nihilo* regarded as *post nihilum*. Bavinck wishes to retain the expression because "It is peculiarly adapted to cut off all manner of error at the root." For a contrary opinion cf. A. Ehrhardt, "Creatio ex Nihilo," *Studia Theologica*, 1951, pp. 13-43, who judges that the expression, as also that of "creation of heaven and earth" are "largely contradictory."

in the Bible with any metaphysical interest but functions exclusively as a designation of the *omnipotent action of God.*

We meet the same phenomenon of non-independent interest when we observe how the Bible speaks about "nothing." We read that they who rage against Israel shall be ashamed and confounded: "those who strive against you shall be as *nothing* and shall perish" (Isa. 41:12). "The molten images are all a delusion, their works are nothing, they are empty wind" (Isa. 41:29). In the light of the incomparable Jahwe the peoples are as "nothing" before Him, He regards them as nothing and emptiness (Isa. 40:17). To the idols God speaks the threatening word of destruction, "I will destroy the idols and put an end to the images, in Memphis" (Ezek. 30:13).

In all these and in similar expressions the references to "nothing," vanity, and wind plainly point to the *positive* message about Jahwe. We do not meet here any interest in things metaphysical, but we hear God's holy admonition, we see the unmasking whereby that which pretends to be *something* is revealed to be *nothing* and is robbed of all power (I Cor. 1:28). It is He who sits above the circle of the earth, who brings princes to *nought* (Isa. 40:22), and makes the rulers of the earth as *nothing* (Ps. 39:6).

From this usage it is evident that we cannot, so far as Scripture is concerned, speak about an "ontology of chaos." We do not find there a dimension of chaos which according to its nature is related to creation as a *rejected and not-willed* reality. Such a conception can never find a legitimate place on the basis of the revelation concerning creation. It bears, rather, the earmarks of speculative thinking wherein the human choice of one possibility, involving the rejection of other possibilities, is transferred to God and is turned into an independent conception from which all kinds of conclusions are drawn. It is understandable that such an "ontology" makes it extremely difficult to distinguish sharply between what is chaos and what is non-being. Barth uses the terms interchangeably at times,[53] although he declares emphatically that the

---

53. Cf. Barth's striking words about the chaos which God did not will and "to which He gave no being, which exists only as not-being and still as such forms the boundary of that which according to God's will exists, and constitutes its threat," KD III/2, p. 171.

chaos has "reality." As a result the chaos conception loses its concrete and clear character.

H. Van Oyen, who states that he has discussed the problem with Barth, understands Barth's conception to involve a doctrine of sin bearing a pronounced metaphysical-ontological character. "The Platonic distinction between being and non-being as the antithesis between God's lordship and the lordship of chaos brings us to this conclusion. The primordial struggle between light and darkness is reflected in oriental mythical fashion in these ontological categories."[54]

Van Oyen creates the impression that Barth holds to a *primordial* dualism in which light *vanquishes* darkness. The remarkable thing is, however, that for Barth the separation of light from darkness is the *first,* the *original* action of God and that he therefore emphatically rejects any and all dualism. Nevertheless, Barth cannot by means of this rejection be said to escape the impact of Van Oyen's criticism. It is true that Barth views the *duality* of Yes and (the necessary) No in the light of the triumph of grace but, conversely, he sets forth the triumph in terms of this duality. A function, a dimension, a power, belongs to the chaos which exists at the borders of creation [55] and which, although *not created* by God has, nevertheless, been "placed" there. It belongs to the *essence* of the creature to be kept and protected by God's grace against the threat of chaos and non-being. The element of truth in Van Oyen's criticism is that the triumph of grace does not radically exclude the shadow of a dualism between the works of God's *right hand* and those of his *left hand.* The very *components* of the triumph reveal the characteristics of a dualism. Creation and preservation can, in Barth's theology, be understood only in terms of *salvation.* The whole consists in the reality of grace *in Christ.*

There is no room in Barth's thinking for preservation as the sustaining and keeping work of God apart from the idea of *redemption.* For this reason the distinction between pre-fall and post-fall plays no role in his theology. The aspect of *redemption* is dominant from the beginning. To deny this aspect would involve a re-

---

54. H. van Oyen, "De categorie der recognitio en de theologische anthropologie," in *Pro Regno Pro Sanctuario,* 1950, p. 346. Cf. also p. 338.

55. "There is a vast kingdom, a veritable bottomless abyss of chaotic reality," KD III/2, p. 171.

turn to the conception of a creation *independent of* and *preceding* the "needy" creature who must be *kept* against the threat of the chaos.

To surrender his view of the relationship between creation and redemption would mean for Barth that sin comes to stand as an independent incident, as a fragment in history. God's redemptive action can then be described as a reaction to the coming in of sin. Barth does not, to be sure, deny that reconciliation is a "contingent reaction" to sin,[56] that it is God's "reply" to sin and to its consequences.[57] He is not averse to saying that sin is a "coming between,"[58] but this idea is subordinate to the emphasis that God's reaction to sin "stands in one line with the action of God which was from the beginning and throughout its course determined by His will."[59] The most important thing is not God's reaction to sin, but His *faithfulness* which sin, as a "coming between," *is not able to annul.*[60]

It is in *this* light that Barth views sin. It can indeed be characterized as the "sum of things not necessary, not orderly, the sum of all that is contrary to sense and reason."[61] But in the light of God's faithfulness sin is powerless, "the impotent invasion of the chaos,"[62] and subject to "God's victorious No."[63] The first word which God spoke was the word of His grace. Man's sin contradicts this word, but "in this first and eternal word of God sin has already and from eternity been overtaken, branded as lie, and emptied."[64] Although the "enormous coming between"[65] of sin reveals that the triumph of grace is *unilateral, marvelous, free, and sovereign,*[66] that grace is *for the unworthy,* that it is a "nevertheless" and an "in spite of," this is all repealed *in* the impotence of sin to resist grace. The waves of every rebellion break powerlessly upon this rock. Never has theology heard such daring words about the powerlessness of sin and of the chaos as are heard in the theology of Karl Barth. "No praise of the powerful and victorious grace of God as the realization of the covenant in the way of reconciliation can be strong enough."[67] The denial of the seriousness of sin may

---

56. KD IV/1, p. 37.
57. *Ibid.,* p. 48.
58. *Ibid.,* pp. 37, 42.
59. *Ibid.,* p. 37.
60. *Ibid.*
61. *Ibid.,* p. 48.

62. *Ibid.,* p. 49.
63. *Ibid.*
64. *Ibid.,* p. 50.
65. *Ibid.,* p. 72.
66. *Ibid.,* p. 73.
67. *Ibid.*

obscure the praise which is God's due, it cannot abrogate the reality of the victory.

The ontological impossibility of sin is not intended as praise for self-justifying man. It signifies, rather, the "from the beginning" of grace. Although the triumph of grace cannot become ours by a simple and self-evident appropriation, it is for all that real, a priorily real, as the overcoming of all resistance against the grace of God.

\* \* \*

When we note the dominant place which the chaos and the threat which it constitutes for the creature occupy in Barth's doctrine of creation and sin, as also the emphasis which he places upon the rescue of the creature from this threat, a relationship becomes plainly discernible between this primordial "border situation" and the sense of boundary and threat which plays so important a role in modern thought. It is certainly not accidental that Barth, in a sharp polemic against Heidegger, observes that in our catastrophic times we have an unusual opportunity to observe the chaos — something which Heidegger, according to Barth, has precisely *not* done. This threat to the creature on the part of the chaos has not led Barth to set forth a "crisis theology" with pessimistic applications, but this threat is in his theology *radically and legitimately overcome* by the a priori triumph of grace. Barth's theology constitutes a tremendous effort to proclaim the removal of this most serious threat as the *definitive* and *radical* message of joy which is the gospel. The terribleness of the chaos as all that which is "contrary" is for Barth not simply an entity that militates against the love of God. It is not the stumblingblock to a true theodicy; it constitutes rather the *material for confrontation* in which God's original, and the in Christ historically realized, *rejection* of the chaos shines as the light in utter darkness. The emphasis on the chaos and on the chaotic does not relativize the joyful message, but makes possible its being sounded forth in all its clarity and triumph. The message is set forth in all the incontrovertible *factuality* of the "goodness" of Christ's creaturely existence. This reality is the *content* of the gospel, it is the "God with us," and of *this* reality creation formed the impressive prefiguration. In this prefiguration the a priori triumph of grace, the triumph of salvation over the chaos, was delineated and set forth.

* * *

We cannot but ask what, in view of *this* prefiguration, the significance is of history and of the historical triumph which is achieved. It is clear that Barth wishes to answer this question by pointing to the unbreakable *unity* of creation and reconciliation. However much he may distinguish creation from reconciliation as the first work of God's grace, they are constantly — via the prefiguration and the relationship between creation and covenant — woven through each other.

R. Prenter has not unjustly attacked Barth precisely at this point.[68] His criticism is directed against the manner in which creation and redemption cross each other, as a result of which the significance and decisiveness of history are imperiled. The fact that Barth's rejection of a "phase theory" in theology occasions this inter-weaving does not lessen the legitimacy of the criticism. His conception leaves the impression that everything has already been done, all the decisions have been taken, so that one can hardly say that the *historical fall* and the *historical reconciliation* are at issue, but only the *revelation* of redemption in history, the *revelation* of the definitive Yes of God's grace. There is no question of a "stepwise," one after the other, of creation and redemption. The whole of creation fundamentally *rests in redemption*. Creation did not take place through the Logos asarkos (the pre-incarnate Word), but through *Jesus of Nazareth*.

Whatever comes into conflict with this conception Barth rejects as an attempt to give creation independent significance. Here we meet what is undoubtedly one of the deepest motifs of Barth's doctrine of creation. He points continually to the *unity* of God's work from the viewpoint of its a priori omnipotence and irresistibility, and to the eternity-aspect of that work, through which it becomes impossible to separate creation and redemption in terms of historical stages. Barth here touches upon a complex of problems which has also been raised in some Roman Catholic schools of thought and in which particularly the problem of the incarnation

---

68. R. Prenter, "Die Einheit von Schöpfung und Erlösung. Zur Schöpfungslehre Karl Barths," *Theol. Zeitschrift*, 1946, pp. 161ff.

entered the discussion. This has always led, to a certain extent, to "explaining" sin, namely, *in the light of the coming triumph.* It cannot be denied that Barth also thinks in this direction, even though he rejects the "felix culpa"[69] as too simple a solution and in so doing distances himself from R. P. Sertillanges [70] and many others who posit this "felicitas" with emphasis. Notwithstanding this correspondence, Barth differs from the Roman Catholic conception in that he emphasizes even more than it does the unity of creation and redemption. He does so especially by denying the validity of the "step-wise" conception of the before and after of creation and redemption which *continues* to function in Roman Catholic theology. Prefiguration does not simply mean a pointing to, a witness in the formal sense of the word, but it indicates the relationship between reconciliation and creation and eliminates the "stages-theory." It is because of *this* relationship between creation and redemption that R. Prenter, Barth's former disciple, has accused him of "creation docetism."[71] How is it possible that such a criticism can be uttered when Barth so expressly speaks about the creation as a creaturely reality and about the "goodness" of that creation? The answer to this question does not lie in the fact that Prenter accuses Barth of "acosmism," but it arises from the fact that Barth holds to *that* relationship between creation and redemption according to which the world was created *in* Jesus of Nazareth, and exists only in terms of His *saving* grace.

While agreeing with Prenter that Barth attempts to achieve a unified conception of creation and reconciliation, we shall not wish to place over against this view one in which the unity of God's work is broken up into two disparate acts of God, namely, creation and redemption. Belief in the counsel of God is sufficient guarantee against such an error. Therefore the fundamental objection against Barth's view must be otherwise formulated.

---

69. It strikes us, moreover, that Barth objects particularly to the "meruit habere" in the sentence, "O felix culpa, quae tantum et talem *meruit habere* salvatorem !" and to the combination as such of "felix" and "culpa," KD IV/1, p. 73. It is clear that also Roman Catholic theologians are in substantial agreement with Barth on this point because also according to them sin cannot, of course, have any "meritum."

70. R. P. Sertillanges, *Le problème du mal,* II (La solution), p. 60.

71. R. Prenter, *op. cit.,* p. 175.

It has never been the purpose of Christian theology to historicize the works of God.[72]   In holding to the conception of the counsel of God, faith was enabled to retain the inscrutable *unity* of the work of God, as is evident from the frequent appeal that has been made to Acts 15:18 in which the perspective of "from eternity" was considered to be indicated.[73] Moreover, in the debate about infra- and supra-lapsarianism such an historicizing was not the issue, although it cannot be denied that here the question of the order and the unity of God's work was raised.

The real issue raised by Barth's Christological doctrine of creation is not whether his conception may be opposed in terms of the center of the redemptive process, namely, *Jesus* Christ, and therefore by an *historicizing* of the works of God, but rather whether the unity of God's work *may ever be presented in antithesis to what Barth has called the "step-wise" character of God's works and against which he directs his sharp protest.*

The remarkable thing about the Bible is precisely this, that while it speaks clearly about the dimension of "from eternity" and in terms of this dimension speaks of the *unity* and the *omnipotence* of God's works — also with respect to sin — it never devaluates the decisive significance of the historical and the "step-wise" character of creation and redemption but honors them and fully takes them into account. We are aware that the element of "reaction" (against the invasion of evil) in the work of God is never His final word and that it may never be allowed to overshadow the a priori initiative of His works precedent to the entrance of sin.[74]   But this does not mean that God's a priori action may be so viewed that shadows are

---

72. We speak here without making a distinction between Roman Catholic and Reformation theology because this historicizing was rejected not only by Thomistic but also by Scotistic theology. Cf. my *Karl Barth en de Kinderdoop*, 1947, pp. 126ff., and *Het Werk van Christus*, 1953, chapter I.

73. Cf. H. Bavinck, *Gereformeerde Dogmatiek*, II, p. 307. Appeal to this text and to similar passages in the Scriptures show that the attempt to historicize the works of God has always met resistance.

74. Cf. H. Bavinck, *op. cit.*, II, p. 525, in connection with the Adam-Christ parallel in I Cor. 15:45-49 and Rom. 5:12-22. Cf. also III, p. 210, which confesses the unity of the work of God. The decisive factor here is that not a shadow is cast on the historical and "step-wise" aspect of the realization of the covenant of grace. Therefore Bavinck can in this connection speak of the enmity which God set between the seed of the woman and the seed of the serpent, and about the ultimate triumph of the former, III, p. 179. Cf. also Calvin's *Institutes*, II, xii, 7, and my *Karl Barth en de Kinderdoop*, pp. 129ff., and for the entire problem, H. N. Ridderbos, *Paulus en Jezus*, 1952, section 19.

cast over the reality and the *decisive* significance of the fall and of God's reaction to it *in history*.

When it is attempted to construct a *synthesis* of these two elements which will be perspicuous to our understanding, it is inevitable that we shall fail to do justice to one or to the other and that we shall fall into the abyss of either eternalizing God's works or historicizing them. To attempt a synthesis on this score means exposure to the danger of an untenable monism or of an equally untenable *dualism*. Barth's sharp criticism of the "step-wise" relationship between creation and redemption undoubtedly exposes him to the danger of falling into a *monistic* conception of the works of God.

Barth does indeed acknowledge the "reaction" of God against sin, but his emphasis on the a priori power of God's "initiative" threatens to swallow up this acknowledgment. Barth speaks of the fearful reality of sin, but *at the same time* he holds to the ontological impossibility of sin because a *transition* from wrath to grace *in history* has already been excluded and has been changed into a conception in which wrath is no more than "the form of grace." The initiative of grace wholly absorbs the full *historical* significance of evil because this initiative was itself the reaction which, according to God's eternal grace, would be *illustratively* revealed in history and in man's confrontation with the power of the chaos. Hence the words *shadow, riddle, absurdity* and *chaos*. Again, it is not the *noetic* problem of the inexplicableness of sin which is the issue here. Evil as the *"mysterium inquitatis"* is not for Barth a real "mystery" with respect to *knowledge*, it is not a reality which transcends in the first place the knowledge of man. It is rather *the* great mystery, the mystery of *grace* which has been revealed as an "ontological impossibility" in terms of the a priori, abiding, and therefore triumphant grace of God.

Once this conception becomes the basis of theological thinking, it is still possible — as is evident in Barth — to speak of the "contradictoriness" of sin. But it is then no longer possible to make the transition from the "impossibility" to the "reality" of sin and its consequences in history without being confronted by insoluble difficulties and antinomies. God's "initiative" a priorily overshadows all that happens by way of human action and divine reaction, so that Barth can write of God that He "relativizes and overlooks man's sin."[75] This "relativizing" is not intended by Barth as a denial or a minimizing of the seriousness of sin. It is clearly intended as a divine "relativizing" *in Christ* and through grace, and therefore does *not* involve making sin "harmless." But, for all that, the aprioristic conquest of sin moves over the face of the whole of history. The history of sin coincides, as it were, with the contemporaneous conquest of it by the unchangeable grace of God.

It is understandable that Althaus should in a certain connection speak of the "epochlessness" of God's action in Barth's theology. His rejection of creation by the Logos *asarkos,* the pre-existent Son, instead of by the Logos *ensarkos,* Jesus of Nazareth, his thinking in terms of the *center* of the whole process *must* consistently lead to the protest against the "step-wise" conception of God's dealings with men. Over against the historicizing of God's work in which the dimension of "from eternity" was obscured by history, by the activity, the initiative and the merits of man, Barth posits the omnipotent and radical initiative of grace. In doing so, however, the historical perspective is threatened with obscuration.

There *must* indeed be a reason for the unsatisfactoriness of the oscillation between the monistic and the dualistic conceptions of redemption. Whereas dualism destroys the unity of God's work (by means of a corresponding prominence accorded to the place of man in history), monism seeks to effect a sort of rationalizing of the works of God and this endangers the decisiveness of history. The drawing power of both dualism and monism is tremendous. The former derives its power ultimately from the religious autonomy of man, the latter wishes to eliminate this autonomy. For this reason monism has always considered itself to stand in the line of the Church's God-glorifying thinking and confessing. The dimension of "from eternity" comes to stand in the center of attention. The protest against the "step-wise" conception reveals, however, that God's eternal initiative of grace obscures His historical reaction to sin.

Barth teaches that that which is self-evident to *God* — because of the divine self-distinction between what God *is* and what He is *not* — must *in history be revealed to us.* Within *this* frame-

---

75. KD III/2, p. 44.

work of thinking the *decisiveness* of history can no longer be fully honored.

\* \* \*

Within the context of these problems, reference has from time to time been made to Barth's "supralapsarianism." Barth has himself at times spoken appreciatively of supralapsarianism. The word appears in an appreciative sense already in his *Römerbrief* in connection with election and reprobation.[76]

Later, Barth raises the problem of supralapsarianism more specifically and it appears that his preferring it to infralapsarianism is related to his criticism of the "step-wise" character of creation and redemption. His preference flows forth from the fact that the supra view separates creation and redemption *less* than the infra view does.[77] The infra conception — by reason of its fear of the dangers of the supra view — has treated of an "ordering of a separate economy of natural providence"[78] preceding predestination to salvation and thereby has arrived at a view of the world and of history which is not *biblical*. It held that "within the framework of a prior and independently existing natural and world history, room was somehow found for the history of Israel, of Jesus Christ, and of the Church."[79] This brings us to the center of Barth's theology. He appreciates the infra emphasis because it saw that the supra view gives occasion to the charge that God is made the author of sin.[80] The virtue of the infra conception was that it clearly revealed evil to be unfathomable *darkness* and that our redemption is a *real* redemption from a *real* power. The infra view could say this better and more plainly than the supra position could. Although both views are unacceptable because of their common presupposition of the decretum absolutum, the supra conception has "relatively the greater right."[81] There are indeed dangers in this

---

76. *Römerbrief*, 2nd ed., p. 150. It is clear that this appreciation is intimately related to Barth's particular view of election. The relationships which are involved here come to clearer expression, however, in Barth's later works than in the *Römerbrief*.

77. Cf. *Gottes Gnadenwahl*, 1936, p. 43: "In the infralapsarian doctrine creation and reconciliation are severed." In this "sundering and splitting" of creation and reconciliation Barth sees an early indication of the danger of the rise of a natural theology.

78. KD II/2, p. 145.

79. *Ibid.*, p. 146.

80. *Ibid.*, p. 149.

81. *Ibid.*, p. 150.

position, notably the danger of relativizing sin. But these dangers are not essential to the position. Supra has *not* separated creation and redemption. If one wishes to brand supralapsarianism as "theistic monism," it must at all events be admitted that it was "biblical-Christian monism" which its authors had in mind.[82] "Can one really accuse the supralapsarianism that they reached too far?"[83]

In this relative preference for supralapsarianism Barth's criticism of the "step-wise" conception comes to the fore stronger than ever. His treatment of the supra-infra controversy provides a remarkable illumination of his entire doctrine of creation. When Barth undertakes to criticize the traditional supralapsarian view — in terms of his doctrine of election in which Christ is both the electing God and the elected and the rejected man[84] — we suddenly find ourselves confronted by the very center of his doctrines of creation and redemption. In terms of the earlier discussed idea of the self-distinction which exists in God (with respect to what he *does* and does *not* will) he arrives at his (corrected) supralapsarian conception. *Therefore* he teaches not the predestination of the *homo lapsus,* but of the *homo labilis* in order that man as fallen man may be a *witness* of God's glory over against the (for man) insuperable evil, a *witness* and *evidence* of the divine self-distinction which becomes manifest *in* time and in the sphere of *creation.*[85] From the prefiguration of redemption in creation he moves to the triumph that is self-evident for God but not for man, to redemptive "event" in history as the revelation for this triumph. *Therefore Barth's preference for the supralapsarian view is nothing else than the reverse side of the ontological impossibility of sin.*

\* \* \*

While we do not wish to enter here upon a discussion of the motivations of historical supralapsarianism, we do wish to point out that Barth's revised supralapsarianism blocks the way to ascribing *decisive* significance to history. We do not hereby wish to accuse Barth of being guilty of subscribing to a consistently idealistic conception of history in which history serves only to *illustrate*

---

82. *Ibid.,* pp. 139 and 145.
83. *Ibid.,* p. 145.
84. *Ibid.,* pp. 151ff.
85. *Ibid.* p. 153.

an eternal *idea.* Barth has sharply protested against *this* idealism and has even accused himself of not having escaped this error in the *Römerbrief.* He places heavy emphasis precisely on God's revelation *in time,* on the great mystery of the incarnation, on God Himself entering our reality in the fact of His becoming flesh and in His submitting to judgment.

It is striking, however, that Barth in this connection treats the category of *revelation* as revelation of what is *for God* a self-evident triumph. It is certainly not accidental that in his doctrine of reconciliation he does not wish to call Christ's punitive suffering a "main concept," and that he considers the idea of "satisfaction" to be foreign to the New Testament.[86] This is undoubtedly most intimately related to what Barth intends when he speaks of God's wrath as a "form of grace," by reason of which the *transition* in history from wrath to grace is obscured. At this point Barth would interject: Yes, but in the *light* of grace! He can point to this light, however, only by moving into the background the "transition" on which the Bible places so tremendous an emphasis.

That Scripture emphasizes the transition is incontrovertible. We think here of the *change* of which Paul speaks in the midst of his praise of God's initiative in effecting our salvation: that God made us alive, when we were dead through trespasses and sins in which we *once* walked (Eph. 2:1, 2), that we all *once* lived in the passions of the flesh (Eph. 2:3), that we *were* by nature children of wrath (Eph. 2:3), that we *were at that time* separated from Christ and without God in the world (Eph. 2:12), but *now* in Christ Jesus we who *once were* far off have been brought near in the blood of Christ (Eph. 2:13), that God, who is rich in mercy, out of the great love with which he loved us, even when *we were dead* through our trespasses, made us alive together with Christ (Eph. 2:4, 5).

It is the *change* which fascinates Paul when in Romans 9 he speaks of the transition from "not my people" to "my people," from "not beloved" to "my beloved," and in other places from being a slave to becoming a son (Gal. 4:7), from not knowing God to

---

86. KD IV/1, p. 279. Cf. the summary observation: "In Christian theology the idea of punishment entered into the answer of our question from Isa. 53:5. In the New Testament it does *not* appear in this context." Cf. the observation of A. F. N. Lekkerkerker, "Is the word of Isaiah perhaps less central?", "Eerste reacties of KD IV/1" in *Kerk en Theologie,* 1953, p. 234.

knowing God (Gal. 4:8, 9), from the "once walking" in earthly
things, because of which the wrath of God comes, to the "now" in
which they must all be put away since we have put off the old nature and put on the new nature (Col. 3:5-10).

When in the interest of *any* form of supralapsarianism *this* transition becomes obscured, then God's initiative in salvation can still
be praised and a transparency be given to the solution of the problem of "subject" and "object" in the doctrine of reconciliation,[87] but
the history of this doctrine shows that this is a transparency and a
synthesis which fails to do justice to the harmony of the multi-
colored witness of the Scriptures.[88]

At this point we must allude to Barth's frequent protest against
the so-called "double bookkeeping" (the thinking in phases: first in
terms of creation and then in terms of redemption) concerning
which he states that the sun of the Enlightenment revealed that
in the Reformation — and in subsequent theology particularly —
creation and redemption were *torn asunder*. In diametrical opposition to this severance he sets forth his triumphant Christocentric
doctrine of creation as the message of the *already* overtaken, the
*already* conquered enemy, sin, by means of God's primordial confrontation of it which was *prefigured* in creation and *manifested*
in time.

We discern here a remarkable consistency in Barth's thinking:
a Christological doctrine of creation, a biblical Christian monism, a
corrected supralapsarianism, wrath as the "form of grace." And
through this all the "needy" nature of man who can be protected
against the threat of the chaos only by the *mercy* of God. A "step-
wise" succession of creation, fall, and redemption would, in Barth's
view, work destructively upon this conception. Just as law which
would be something more than the *form* of the gospel would receive an *independent* character, so a conception of creation and a
"status integritatis" which would involve the "possibility" of sin,
of disturbance in the established order, and of covenant breaking
would give to man an autonomous status in which he would no
longer live solely and exclusively by grace. Barth's Jesucentric
thinking is the decisive factor in his theology. All thinking about
creation must be permeated with *this* light, the light of *reconcilia-*

---

87. Cf. my *Het Werk van Christus*, 1953, final chapter.
88. KD II/2, pp. 663ff.

*tion.* Therefore we can speak here of a *dialectic* between creation and redemption. Not as though Barth wants to devaluate creation and law in a gnostic sense, for that is already excluded by the thesis of God's love which Barth continually points to in terms of the *good* creation. But it is precisely this goodness which is the *goodness* of the relationship between man's "needy" nature and saving grace. Not only in the noetic but also in the *ontic* sense creation is founded in Jesus Christ, *in reconciliation.*

Barth wants to eliminate every idea of a "double bookkeeping." The expression suggests an untenable relationship between creation and redemption. It receives its suggestive power from the fact that reconciliation has frequently been devalued in the interest of creation. It is not possible, however, that the *distinction* between creation and redemption, as that distinction has been understood in theology, should in itself involve the idea of a double bookkeeping. What the sun of the Enlightenment revealed was *not* the disjunction of creation and redemption, but the gradual denial of *guilt* and *reconciliation.* In this way a double bookkeeping could come into being which paved the way to the "single" bookkeeping of human reason.

The criticism of the Enlightenment has *nothing* to do with the full acknowledgment of the "step-wise" conception in Reformation theology which desired to speak about reconciliation *only* in correlation with *breach that took place in history.* But this does not lead to a disturbance in the unity of God's work. If we wish to respect the Scriptures we shall have to be aware of the fact that it is necessary to recognize *all* the boundaries which its witness indicates. The unity of God's work does not involve the elimination of the historical perspective and does no prejudice to the *historical* relationship between *guilt* and *reconciliation.* The Christological interpretation of the goodness of creation which Barth sets forth in terms of Genesis 1:31 and in which his doctrine of creation may be summarized constitutes a clear illustration of the unresolved problems of his conception. For a goodness which does *not yet* stand in need of *reconciling* grace there is no room in his theology.

Were there to be room for such a view, law would threaten the gospel and creation would threaten reconciliation. Only the reverse order can, in his judgment, do justice to God's work. The relationship between guilt and reconciliation is a *primordial relationship*. Not that this relationship itself belongs to creation but it appears against its background as the struggle — the reconciled struggle — of man to transcend his "needy" nature.

The sharp antithesis does not constitute a profound dualism, for the confrontation takes place in the full light of the triumph and of the *end* of the chaos. The not-willing of God which is the basis of the rejection of the chaos is a *powerful,* a *triumphant* not-willing. For this reason Barth has probably not been deeply impressed by the criticism which suspects him of being guilty of holding to a primal conflict between light and darkness. The whole struggle takes place in the light of the *separation* between light and darkness, of the self-evident fact of God's victory. Therefore Barth can picture sin in all its fearful character, for all its fearfulness falls within the circle of the light of *grace,* and because of the cross appears as *forgiven* sin. For this reason, too, Barth can constantly appeal to all the triumphant grace expressions in the Bible. They function as pointers to the triumph which is the reflection (in time) of God's eternal self-distinction. The drama of the triumph of grace unfolds *within* the systematized relationship that exists between God's Yes and God's No. All the light-beams of Scripture converge here and are focussed on *this* darkness. They are necessary, more than necessary, in view of the non-created *demonic* threat that confronts man. The demons, though not created, "function" as the enemy which is the chaos. The triumph transcends them, however, and that not only in the future, but also in the past. The eschatological triumph will be no more than the revelation of this fact. Only *one* mandate remains for man to fulfill: to see through the *appearance* of things and *not* to fear.

\*   \*   \*

We are indeed far removed here from a "crisis theology" which strengthens and stimulates the despair and hopelessness of the contemporary mood. Barth contradicts this mood radically on the basis of the triumph which he proclaims. This triumph is not contradicted by any empirical reality. It is *eternal* in God and is *revealed* in history.

Man lives in fear and in anxiety because of the uncertainty of the future. But God's triumph, God's *law*, exclude them.[89] Law and gospel may not be separated here.[90]

There remains but *one* imperative: the *manifestation* of *God's* self-distinction *in time.* Man must live by *grace.*

The joyful message of the New Testament resounds here in the cumulative witness of many expressions of scripture[91] which signalize the divine triumph. They are for Barth the counter-part of the *appearance* which is all that is left of the power of the chaos. The triumph is so unassailable that it has become *pure* fact.

For this reason Barth's conception of the nature of the triumph raises the problem of the place of man in this triumph. In which way is he related to it, and is his decision — the decision of faith — still of any significance in the triumph of grace?

These questions place us before the important problem of the *universality of the triumph.*

---

89. *Ibid.,* p. 666.
90. Cf. KD II/2, pp. 663-664 where Barth brings together the many scriptural prohibitions to fear.

# X

## THE UNIVERSALITY OF THE TRIUMPH

The question of the universality of the triumph of grace confronts us squarely with Barth's doctrine of election. The importance of this doctrine in Barth's dogmatic thinking appears not only from the extensive treatment which he accords it, but also in the emphasis with which he, for the sake of the purity of the message, consciously distances himself from the Reformation doctrine of election.

In our analysis of the triumph of election it became evident that for Barth the issue in election is God's gracious decision in Jesus Christ. Man does not, as a co-operating partner, add his own share in the achieving of salvation to this decision. He can only *accept* and *acknowledge* this decision of God in faith. Barth desires above all to give expression to Calvin's emphasis when, in connection with Paul's words in Ephesians 1:4, "even as He chose us in Him," he writes that the name of Christ excludes all merit (*Nomen Christi excludit omne meritum*).

Election is gracious and therefore sovereign election. Barth is of the opinion, however, that the traditional doctrine of election does not sufficiently emphasize this and that consequently the comfort of eternal election cannot gloriously overpower the hearts of men. He judges that this is possible only when it is understood that Jesus Christ is the electing God Himself and that he is at the same time rejected and elected man. It is this conception that determines decisively the place of man in election. In the course of this discussion we met that peculiar tension which characterizes Barth's doctrine of election up to the present moment, namely, the tension between God's universal election and the human *answer*, particularly when this answer is the answer of unbelief which he describes as "fatally dangerous" unbelief.

At the one pole we hear of the eternal decision of God, His Yes to man in Jesus Christ in the rejection and election of the man,

Jesus of Nazareth, in whom the triumph of election becomes visible as a sovereign, divine choice. This decision has been taken. It cannot be undone. Sin takes nothing away from this decision, does not touch its validity, because the decision has been taken precisely over against and in face of the resistance of man as the triumphant decision of God's grace.

At the other pole we discover that man must respond to this decision, that he must react to it, and in connection with this we meet the conception of the ontologically impossible "reality" of *unbelief*. Can this unbelief nullify God's decision? Barth answers this question in the negative. Even though he continues to reject the idea of universal reconciliation (apokatastasis), still he speaks of the powerlessness of unbelief.

In the final analyis it is *impossible* for unbelief to separate us from space. Because of the peace of God which flows forth from the presence of Immanuel, any and every rebellion in the kingdom of Christ is finally overcome and suppressed. Typical of the tensions[1] which have entered the discussion on this point is the criticism which Brunner has made of Barth. He agrees with Barth's emphasis on the knowledge of our election through the revelation of Jesus Christ, but he rejects all kinds of conclusions which Barth has drawn from this conception. Particularly does he take issue with the idea that Jesus Christ is the only man who is rejected. This would, in his opinion, mean that "we cannot speak at all about a being lost, there is then no possibility of damnation, and therefore no divine final judgment."[2] Although Barth does not wish to stand "in the hardly illustrious ancestral line of apokatastasis teachers," still, it is clear that he goes not less far but *still farther* than such men as Arminius: Christ has removed the judgment for all.[3] Brunner emphasizes that this is not *his* but *Barth's own* conclusion. He points out that, according to Barth, man cannot "cancel" God's

---

1. When Barth first wrote about election (in the *Römerbrief*) his accentuation of God's sovereignty was sharply opposed, among others, by A. Messer. He saw in it a sign of the time "which in the collapse of old external authority cannot bring itself to a halt and therefore calls in a slavish spirit for the 'strong man' and for 'dictatorship.'" "A. Gemmer and A. Messer, *Sören Kierkegaard und Karl Barth*, 1925, p. 289. We mention this as casting an interesting light on the first years of the debate.
2. E. Brunner, *Dogmatik*, I, p. 376.
3. E. Brunner, *ibid.*, I, p. 377.

decision,[4] and that the judgment which has *once* struck Jesus Christ can strike no one again.[5]

Brunner considers this to be in diametrical opposition to the New Testament which teaches that there is no condemnation for *those who are in Christ,* and which in *this* connection always speaks of the *decision* of faith. Brunner feels that Barth underestimates the significance of this subjective decision of faith by means of a patent objectivism. This leads him to the conclusion that "the consequence is obvious that the real decision takes place in the objective, not in the subjective sphere."[6] Over against this Brunner posits the "conditionalis divinus" which always lies enclosed in the idea of election.[7] The real issue is "the election of all who believe in Him."[8] Grace is for all "in so far as they believe."[9] "Whoever excludes himself *is excluded.*" There is an identity between being-elect and believing and in terms of this identity Brunner opposes Barth's doctrine of election as a "fundamental alteration of the Christian message of salvation."[10]

It can hardly be denied that Brunner, in positing the idea of the "conditionalis divinus" *in* election, virtually returns to the Arminian conception of the relationship between election and faith. Although Brunner does not conceive of election as resting upon foreseen faith, the "objective" and the "subjective" decisions stand dualistically alongside each other and it is understandable that Barth was not convinced by *this* view of "objectivity" and "subjectivity" in the problem. Brunner holds to an equality of decision which is the very thing that Barth has in the whole of his dogmatics been concerned to oppose.

This does in no wise mean, however, that Brunner's criticism can be called a wild blow. He has sharply discerned the central point in Barth's doctrine of election. He drives home his point by using the illustration of men who are threatened with shipwreck at sea. "In reality, however, they are not at all on a sea where they can founder, but in shallow water in which they cannot drown. They

---

4. KD II/2, p. 348.

5. E. Brunner, *op. cit.,* p. 377.

6. *Ibid.,* p. 379.

7. *Ibid.,* p. 345.

8. *Ibid.,* Cf. my *Geloof en Rechtvaardiging,* 1949 (English translation: *Faith and Justification*), chapter VII.

9. E. Brunner, *op. cit.,* p. 345.

10. *Ibid.,* p. 377.

just do not know it."[11]   It cannot be said that in this illustration
Brunner gives an unfair picture of Barth's doctrine of election. The
already taken and no longer nullifiable decision *is* indeed the fundamental thesis of Barth's view of election. The "not yet knowing"
plays a decisive role in Barth's thinking. The covenant embraces
all.[12]   Only, there is yet a difference among men with respect to the
*knowledge* of this saving fact.[13]

Barth's meaning can also be indicated by the illustration of liberation from an occupying enemy. The armies of liberation have
already entered the occupied city and the capitulation *has* taken
place, but the wonderful news has not yet penetrated into all the
streets and suburbs of the city. Not everyone "knows" that the
liberating event has taken place. This detracts nothing, however,
from the fact of the objective liberation. The *subjective* knowledge
of it does not yet correspond to the *objective* situation.[14]   This objective state of affairs is for Barth the "Christ for all." In this way
there runs through the whole of Barth's dogmatics a strong *univer-
alistic* strain which comes to expression in a variety of connections.

The exclusiveness of the covenant between Jahwe and Israel is
at the same time inclusive: "the covenant which was at the beginning and will be at the end: God's covenant with *all* men."[15]
Hence his criticism — because of the universal strains of his covenant idea — of Calvin's "joyless doctrine" that Christ died only
for the elect.[16]   Election is God's decision concerning all and for
all as the decision of the *gracious* God who is *for* man. In the actuality of this happening "all men are again placed under the consequence and outworking of this confrontation and revelation."[17]

---

11. *Ibid.,* p. 379.
12. "It embraces *very really* the world and the Church, the non-Christian
and the Christian. Its acknowledgment, however, and therefore also its proclamation is the concern of the Christian Church and hers alone," KD IV/1, p.
111. The Church preaches what it *knows* (in distinction from those who do not
know) and therein lies the "exemplary and fundamentally prefigurative existence
of Christianty and of the Christian," KD IV/1, p. 164. Cf. also p. 349, and for
the idea of universality pp. 27, 28, 32-33, 35, 61, 135, and KD III/4 (about
"These who are near and those who are afar off") pp. 349-366.
13. Cf. KD IV/1, p. 344.
14. *Ibid.,* p. 61.
15. *Ibid.,* pp. 27-28, 35. About the exclusiveness and the inclusiveness of the
covenant cf. p. 61.
16. *Ibid.,* p. 61.
17. *Ibid.,* p. 135.

It is therefore not surprising that Barth's theology has again and again raised the question of the apokatastasis. Barth's express rejection of the doctrine of the apokatastasis must be fully taken into account, but it is precisely when we do so that the tensions within his teaching become the more visible. For Barth, unbelief is, in view of the omnipotence of the divine decision, an *impossible* matter. This comes to remarkable expression when Barth speaks somewhere of the "necessity of faith." The whole problem of the "possibility" of faith disappears.[18] It is not so, that man can *choose* between two possibilities, namely, *belief* and *unbelief.* In the object of faith the "necessity" of faith is included.[19] In Jesus Christ — the object of faith — the possibility of unbelief is "rejected, done away with, emptied."[20]

Therefore the inevitability of faith exists "objectively, really, ontologically for all men."[21] Jesus Christ is *not* presented to us as an alternative, he is not an *offer,* for every other alternative has been wiped away. In God's decision "the root of man's unbelief, the man of sin, has been destroyed," so that unbelief has become "an objective, real, ontological impossibility; faith, however, has became an objective, real, ontological inevitability for *all,* for *every* man."[22]

At this point we cannot but think of the connection between the ontological impossibility of sin *and* its reality. The "synthesis" of these two combinations lies for Barth in the triumph of the decision that has already been taken. As sin is ontologically impossible because it cannot achieve what it aims to achieve — man's separation from the grace of God — so unbelief is an *impossible* reality because it cannot touch what in God's decision has become *irrevocable* truth, namely, that God's grace is for man, for *all men.* This line of thought is plain. Even though the expression "ontological impossibility" is an obscure one, it is clear that the actuality of God's decision and the irrevocability of the election of all leads Barth to his view of the *factuality* of salvation. God's decision is a radical decision and affects man truly in the whole of his existence. When man goes contrary to this fact, he is not choosing a "possibility"

18. *Ibid.,* p. 834.
19. *Ibid.,* p. 835.
20. *Ibid.*
21. *Ibid.*
22. *Ibid.*

which is an alternative to faith; his choice is an *impossible* choice which is reminiscent of the chaos. How can man's decision still be "decisive" when it is preceded by God's *a priori* decision? Does faith not know that it lives only because of God's decision and that it can only *accept* this decision? How, then, can unbelief be *the* decision? Who can withstand *His* verdict?

\* \* \*

These considerations leave no alternative to concluding that no serious *kerugmatic* significance can be ascribed to what Barth calls the "fatal danger" of unbelief. In the same moment in which it would become kerugmatically meaningful, unbelief *as a human decision* would again become a competitor of *God's* decision. All of Barth's objections against human co-operation and synergism, against every construction of balance between grace and freedom, would again return.

We can see the problem sharply in connection with the doubts to which H. Berkhof has given expression with respect to the preaching of middle-orthodoxy\* in the Netherlands and which stand related to certain tendencies in Barth's theology.[23] Berkhof is concerned about the nature of the Church's proclamation. He points out that middle-orthodoxy preaches the judgment, but "as the judgment from which we have been rescued."[24] He considers this a salutary correction of earlier emphases, but at the same time considers that the proclamation is in this way threatened with emaciation. Preaching is reduced to "the announcement of an eternal salvation which is in Christ, as it were, self-evidently present and no longer confronts us with a decision."[25] Berkhof acknowledges that the proclamation announces God's Yes as having been sounded forth over our life, but precisely *for this reason* the call now comes to *us* to say yes or no.[26] "God's decision does not make mine un-

---

\* "Middenorthodoxie" or middle-orthodoxy designates the predominant theological viewpoint in the Reformed Church of the Netherlands. It has been strongly influenced by Barth's theology and steers a middle course between the liberalism which earlier characterized much of this communion, on the one hand, and the older orthodoxy, on the other. In distinction from liberalism, however, and in common with orthodoxy, it is evangelical in word and spirit. Translator.

23. H. Berkhof, *Crisis der Middenorthodoxie*, 1953.
24. H. Berkhof, *ibid.*, p. 27.
25. *Ibid.*, p. 38.
26. *Ibid.*, p. 39.

necessary but, on the contrary, lends it eternal significance. The judgment does not lie only behind us but at the same time ahead of us, ahead of us, namely, when we do not believe that in Christ it lies behind us."[27]

It is difficult to see how Barth could answer Berkhof's objections. He would certainly object to the idea that God's decision involves our being called "to say yes or no."[28] He would ask whether in this way God's decisive and all-powerful grace is still fully honored. Particularly would he ask this question when it is insisted that our decision — to the right or to the left — is of "eternal significance." Does not God's decision *include, embrace ours?* Does not grace triumph precisely *in the face of* our *wrong* decision which does not want to have anything to do with grace?

Although Berkhof does not make extensively plain just why God's decision makes ours of eternal value, it is plain that he wishes to point to the evidence of the *scriptural witness* on this score. He points to the many expressions which urgently call to faith and warn against unbelief.[29]

This brings us to the extremely important question of how the Bible speaks about belief and unbelief. Can we in the light of Scripture escape the dilemma: *either* co-operation, synergism, synthesis between God's deed and ours, *or* the ontological impossibility of unbelief? This is *the* decisive question on the score of the problem of universalism.

*    *    *

The problem of belief and unbelief is so profound, that it is not possible to discuss it truly and responsibly apart from a complete subjection to the witness of Scripture. All our reflection on this subject must have as its point of departure the fact that, according to the Word of God, God's salvation is a *sovereign* salvation, that in the most absolute sense of the word it is not from *us* but from *Him,* that it stems from His divine good pleasure alone. *At the same time,* we see with great clarity that in terms of the proclamation of this salvation the human answer, the human reaction, is not without significance. The Bible constantly calls to faith and warns in the most serious terms against unbelief.

---

27. *Ibid.,* p. 40.
28. *Ibid.,* p. 39.
29. With especial reference to John 3:36 and to Hebrews 2:3 *ibid.,* p. 40.

When Jesus Christ was risen from the dead he exclaimed to Thomas, "Be not unbelieving, but believing" (John 20:27). This is the admonition that resounds through the whole of the New Testament. We can hear it clearly in Hebrews when in persecution and distress the Church is warned against unbelief and against failing to obtain the grace of God (Heb. 12:15), against *refusing* Him who is speaking (12:25), against following the example of *disobedience* (4:11), against the *falling away* of those who have been enlightened (6:4-6) and, in sharp language and with the threat of punishment, against the sin of him who has spurned "the Son of God, and profaned the blood of the covenant by which he was sanctified and outraged the Spirit of grace" (10:29).

The biblical antithesis between belief and unbelief makes clear that faith is never a human achievement or merit. The call to faith does not *ex*clude but *in*cludes that the eye of faith is directed to Jesus, the author and perfecter of our faith (12:2). Precisely *this* is the peculiar character of faith, of the wholly unique structure of the activity of faith, that it involves a truly human deed and that this deed is not swallowed up by the overpowering might of grace, but that *precisely as a human deed* it is wholly *full of* and is entirely *directed to* the gospel of grace.[30]

Barth has in many ways illuminated this relationship of faith to its content, particularly over against Pelagianism, semi-Pelagianism, Arminianism, and against the conceptions of "prescientia" and the "scientia media." Especially has he set forth with extraordinary clarity the confusion that obtains with respect to the *function* of faith in the labyrinths of heretical thinking. This necessary and worthy polemic against faith as a human component in salvation — a component bearing a meritorious character — has not, however, led Barth to do justice to the unmistakable earnestness with which Scripture so clearly speaks of the *seriousness* and *danger* of unbelief. In the existential seriousness of God's sovereign decision, the seriousness of the *human* decision was virtually already swallowed up, brushed away by the overpowering, reconciling and existential confrontation between God and man. Barth calls unbelief "fatally dangerous," but this now and then repeated expression is flanked

---

30. Cf. Hebrews 12:4: "In your struggle against sin you have not yet resisted to the point of shedding your blood,"

by extensive reflections on the ontological impossibility of unbelief. This unbelief *has been* put away — the unbelief of the old man — *by* the decisive grace of God, which is *so* decisive that the *inevitability* of faith *lies involved* in it.

It would seem to be plain that the Bible speaks in a different manner about the "dynamic" of unbelief. Not only do the Scriptures warn against unbelief, as we have seen, but often emphasis is laid on significant *relations* which receive a place in the admonition. In a striking manner this comes to expression in Hebrews 4:2: "For good news came to us just as to them; but the message which they heard did not benefit them, *because it did not meet with faith in the hearers.*" This is a remarkable and important passage because in it the *relationship* between *faith* and *proclamation* is indicated. It is plain that the writer does not refer here to a meritorious function of faith. Here we do not meet a pre-Pelagian Pelagius. Nor do these words confront us with a synergist. We do find here the components involved in the tremendous dynamic of the "encounter" between the proclamation and its hearers. At this point Barth's existential understanding of the decision breaks down. These words just *do not leave room* for the view that the human decision has already been taken, is given and is involved *in* the encounter with the revelation. We see rather the components that are involved in the full light of concrete reality. We hear about the proclaimed word which was heard but which was *not profitable,* because it was not accompanied by faith. The word did indeed sovereignly reach the hearers, in accordance with the divine mandate to preach the gospel. But there was no *profit*, no *benefit.* In unbelief, in the dark recesses of the unbelieving human heart, *it broke off.* This fact is taken with full apostolic *seriousness.* The New Testament speaks of belief and unbelief as a choice, a serious, if you will, a *decisive* choice. Whatever the judgment as to the dogmatic place of belief and unbelief, *we will in any case have to take as our point of departure the seriousness with which the New Testament takes the human response to the proclamation.*

In addition to the passage in Hebrews, we wish also to note Paul's words (II Thess. 2:13) in which expression is given to a wholly different reaction to the proclamation. Paul there thanks God continually because "when you received the word of God which you heard from us, you accepted it not as the word of men but as what

it really is, the word of God, which is at work in you believers."
Here the word was *united* with faith and in *this* way was effective.
This relationship we cannot fathom by means of an "existential"
confrontation according to which man's subjective decision already
lies enclosed *in* the confrontation (the ontological impossibility of
unbelief!). We must leave room here for the full message of the
Scriptures and for the concrete components of the dynamic involved in the meeting between the proclaimed word and man's
reaction to it.

The thought expressed in Hebrews 4:2 is remarkable enough to
warrant a further observation. Although the text has given occasion to textual critical discussion,[31] it is plain that the central question in the verse concerns the right relationship between *faith*
and *proclamation*. "The necessity of faith as an act of the hearer
comes to the fore here. The word must not only be heard, it must
also be received in faith."[32] In speaking of the "necessity" of faith
in this sense, something quite different is obviously had in mind
than when Barth speaks of "the necessity of faith" which lies enclosed *in* the existential meeting between the proclamation and the
hearer. Hebrews 4:2 speaks of the "necessity" as a *calling*, as an
*urgent admonition,* so that the proclamation may be profitable and
effective in the way of salvation.

\* \* \*

The clarity with which these components come to the fore har-
monizes fully with the manner in which the Old and the New
Testaments as a whole urge the necessity of faith and warn against
unbelief.[33]

---

31. This refers to the variant readings: *sunkekerasménos* and *sunkekerasménous*.
F. W. Grosheide, *Kommentaar op Hebreen*, 1927, p. 129, and O. Michel, *Der Brief
an die Hebräer*, 1949, p. 10, prefer the first reading. Both authorities point out
that if the second were right it would mean that faith was mixed with the hearers
rather than with the message.

32. O. Michel, *ibid.*, p. 111. H. van Oyen, *Christus de Hoge Priester*, 1939,
speaks of "a word of peculiar pregnancy" in which "the necessity of organic
unity between the word of God and the faith of the Church" is pointed out.

33. Cf. my *Geloof en Rechtvaardiging* (English translation, *Faith and Justification*) chapter VII. In the discussion centering around Barth's theology reference
has more than once been made to John 3:36: "He who believes in the Son has
eternal life; he who does not obey the Son shall not see life, but the wrath of God
rests upon him." Especially A. Lekkerkerker has reminded us of the passage,
most recently in the course of his review of KD IV/1, in which he sought "in
vain" for a reference to it in Barth's exegesis, *op cit.*, pp. 232 and 233.

Undoubtedly, biblical expressions such as we discussed above have led Barth again and again to speak of the decisiveness of belief and unbelief, of unbelief as fatally dangerous, and of the "decision of faith."[34] The clear words of Scripture constitute an unmistakable factor in the tension that is plainly present with respect to the universality of the triumph as Barth understands it. Only, he is not able to give them their full value in the polemic against the synergism which he so much fears.

It is striking that the Bible in using such expressions as "except ye believe" and "whosoever believes" nowhere for so much as one moment creates the impression that they prejudice in any way the *sovereignty* of God's saving work. Apparently *another* relationship is possible between faith and grace than that of synergism in which faith receives a meritorious and co-operative function. In the history of theology we see time and again that synergism (not only with respect to works but also with respect to faith) appears to be *the* favorite means for minimizing the sovereign grace of God. Barth has for thirty years unremittingly warned against making the divine decision dependent upon the human decision. But however much it be necessary to guard against the dangers of synergism which cannot but lead to a proud understanding of the antithesis between Church and world, and however necessary it be to emphasize the *instrumental* character of faith, it is never warranted to ignore or neglect the plainly indicated relations between proclamation and faith of which the Scriptures speak.[35]

When Paul speaks of justification without the works of the law, he is *at the same time* aware of these relations. He gives expression to this with an "if.": "if you confess with your lips that Jesus Christ is Lord and [if you] believe in your heart that God raised him from the dead, you will be saved,"[36] and "No one who believes in him will be put to shame" (Rom. 10:9, 11). Thetically and

---

34. K. Barth, *Die Souveränität des Wortes Gottes und die Entscheidung des Glaubens*, 1939, especially pp. 19ff.

35. Cf. our exposition of Barth's struggle against synergism in chapter VII. In his own characteristic manner Barth summarizes his opposition to synergism in KD II/2, p. 213. Here Barth, from the viewpoint of election, rejects any and all synergism. What happens from the side of man can never bear the character "of an independent mystery which is as such in competition with or stands in some sort of alternating relationship to the mystery of God's prior decision." It is in this connection that Barth calls the history of election "a unique triumph of the grace and therefore of the sovereignty of God."

36. Cf. Acts 16: "Believe (pisteuson) in the Lord Jesus, and you will be saved."

antithetically he preserves fully the seriousness and the reality of this responsibility, as also the meaningfulness of the kerugma. It just cannot be denied that the Bible speaks simply and, so to speak, naively of the relationship between faith and salvation. In this simplicity and naiveté it speaks of the faith *that saves*,[37] and of being justified *by faith*. In the same passage in which Paul reminds his readers that Jesus Christ died for them he speaks of their putting on the *armor* of faith.

In all this emphasis on faith as a human activity, we are struck by the fact that it never leads to a synergistic idea, to the conception of faith as a *creative* component of salvation or as a *merit* which takes the place of good works.[38] Therefore the Pauline antithesis with respect to Judaism is filled from beginning to end with the opposition that exists between justifying faith and the works of the law.

Now it is precisely in terms of *this* conception of *justifying* and *saving* that Scripture lays full emphasis on the call to faith and on the warning against unbelief. In Barth this antithesis plays a powerful role as appears anew in his doctrine of reconciliation. In his theology this antithesis appears in a form, however, that makes the *threat* of unbelief problematical because of the divine decision that has *already* been made. Barth is correct in underscoring that what man does in response to God's message does not involve the existence of a second, a competing mystery in addition to the mystery of reconciliation. Against the background of the sovereignty of grace, however, the Bible leaves room for human decision. This human decision, the decision of faith, to which the message calls, never bears a competing character through which God's salvation is deprived of its sovereign character. Here we see the *depth* and the *mystery* of the correlation between the two. The mystery of the relationship between faith and salvation lies precisely in this, that *this* faith which does *not compete* is *necessary* and *saves*, and that therefore we are called to the acceptance of this faith.

---

37. Matt. 9:22, Mark 5:34, Mark 10:52, Acts 2:21, James 2:14, and especially Heb. 10:39. Cf. also 1 Peter 1:9: the outcome of faith is the salvation of the soul.
38. In the nature of the case, it is not possible to appeal to James 2:22 here because James is concerned here about a "cooperation" of faith *with works*, an aspect which has nothing at all to do with synergism.

There is a great danger that our thinking will rationalize the necessity of faith in its relationship to the completed work of Christ. On the one hand, the necessity of faith and the warning against unbelief can lead to the rational conclusion that faith is a component, even the *decisive component* of salvation. On the other hand, reaction to synergism can relativize the human decision and thereby prejudice the seriousness and the simplicity with which Scripture speaks about the necessity of faith.

In his polemic against the first danger, Barth moves in the line of the Reformation. He has hammered away at the thought that faith is *not* a substitute for the works of the law, that it is not a *new mode* of these works, but that it derives its significance exclusively from its relationship to its *content*. On the score of the second danger, however, it must be affirmed that the problems Barth raises with respect to the "ontological impossibility" of unbelief are wholly foreign to Reformation theology. The Reformation did not permit itself to use a "principle" (that of the sola gratia) as a point of departure for all manner of deductions, but it was guided by the message of the Scriptures which came to her with kerugmatic power that called urgently to faith and warned against unbelief.

The full acknowledgment of these relationships occasioned, in the nature of the case, the possibility that the human decision would, in spite of all, again become *the* central factor in salvation and that faith would become a work of the law. How great this danger was appeared time and again in the post-Reformation period. We think here particularly of the manner in which the Remonstrants fundamentally altered the structure of faith and virtually saw in foreseen faith the basis of election, a conception against which the synod of Dordt was to express its emphatic protest.[39]

The existence of this danger constitutes no warrant for taking liberties with the plainness with which Scripture speaks of calling and warning. We must remain conscious of the fact that the relationship between the message of salvation and the human response to it may never be resolved in terms of a rational synthesis. The relationship may never become humanly transparent. The re-

---

39. Canons of Dordt, Chapter I, Rejection of Errors.

markable thing is, however, that it *is* "transparent" for faith as a human decision that salvation is sovereign, that faith lives because of this, and discovers *in this acknowledgment* its true structure. In terms of *this* transparency the Reformation guarded mightily against both objectivism and subjectivism, against a simple universalism and against synergism. In this way it kept an open vision for the work of the Holy Spirit who is the source of true faith, of *that* faith which is not a second mystery alongside the mystery of reconciliation, but which, filled with this mystery, is constrained to praise the sovereign grace of God and therefore *saves*.

\* \* \*

The present discussion directly confronts us with an immediate consequence of the triumph of grace in the theology of Barth, namely, his conception of *missions*. We have heard him speak of the antithesis (the *relative* antithesis) between *knowing* and *not-knowing* as typifying the difference between the Church and the world, between believers and unbelievers. Barth's view of the triumph of grace is concentrated in this conception. It is difficult to recognize in this view the full significance of the biblical idea of *proclamation*. The Bible speaks in many ways of the proclamation of the gospel to all creatures and about the joyful message of salvation, but this message of joy cannot be satisfactorily described in connection with the categories of *knowing* and *not-knowing*.

When Paul asks, "How are they to believe in him of whom they have never heard? And how are they to hear without a preacher?" (Romans 10:14) and then speaks of the beauty of the feet of those who preach good news, the connections which he establishes between faith and preaching do not coincide with Barth's views about knowing and not-knowing. Barth has reference to the knowing and not-knowing of those about whom an a priori and *identical* decision has already been taken. The *difference* lies exclusively in having or not-having knowledge of the factual happening of God's decision. In this conception, which continually recurs in the writings of Barth, the proclamation can hardly be otherwise understood than as a giving of "information" about a given *state of affairs,* about an already taken decision which is "made known" in the proclamation. We do not wish to deny that Barth gives a place to the *hortatory* aspect of the proclamation by means of another em-

phasis, namely, through the "open situation" of the proclamation.
But this does not alter the fact that his conception of the already
taken decision leaves room for the proclamation only in the sense
of an *informative* declaration concerning the accomplished fact of
God's decisive grace for all.

This brings us into another sphere of discourse, however, than
that in which we find ourselves when the Bible speaks about the
"kerugma" concerning salvation. Undoubtedly we have full right
to speak of a "making-known." This is an expression which we also
find in Scripture. But this "making-known" bears a wholly different
character than that of an informative declaration concerning a
given state of affairs. This is evident from the manner in which
Paul speaks of the "made known" of the mystery which was kept
secret for long ages (Rom. 16:25). According to the command
of the eternal God it is made known "to bring about obedience to
the faith." When Paul writes that God chose to "make known"
how great among the gentiles are the riches of this mystery (Col.
1:27) he adds, "Him we proclaim, warning every man in all wisdom, that we may present every man mature in Christ." God's
declaration is indissolubly united with and directed to *this* proclamation.[40]

Beyond a doubt, the kerugma is a making-known. We cannot do
justice to the concept by turning it into a general admonition. The
kerugma involves preaching, the making known of the great *deeds*
of God, the *proclamation* of the day of the Messiah which has
dawned. The kerugma has not improperly been designated as the
"sounding forth of an event," as the proclamation of what God
has *now* done in Jesus Christ.[41] It is historically qualified in the
fullest sense of the word. It means *preachers, heralds, ambassadors*
of the salvation which has appeared.[42] There is indeed an objective
factuality involved in the kerugma, but this factuality is concerned
with God's reconciling action. Therefore the kerugma comes to us
in the form of a message which is full of *exhortatio*n to faith.

---

40. Cf. G. Kittel, *Theologisches Wörterbuch des Neuen Testaments,* IV, p. 1015:
*katangéllein* in connection with *nouthetéo* as "task and function of the pastor,"
expressed in correction, admonition. Note also its relationship to *didáskein,* Col.
1:28.
41. G. Kittel, *Ibid.,* III, p. 702. Cf. H. N. Ridderbos, *De Komst van het Koninkrijk,* 1950, and *De Apostolische Kerk,* 1954.
42. Cf. II Cor. 5:20 and I John 1:1.

This lifts us above the level where the difference between knowing and not-knowing obtains for, although the "making known" of the proclamation leads from not-knowing to knowing, this transition takes place in the way of exhortation and faith. The coming of the kingdom does not make the human response superfluous but rather urges its necessity with utter seriousness. We see this clearly already in the preaching of John the Baptist. He proclaimed that the kingdom of heaven had come near (Matt. 3:1.) He was the herald of this kingdom which through Jesus Christ broke in upon the world, and called men to repentance precisely *then* when God's redemptive activity began. When Christ made manifest the fulfillment of prophecy (Matt. 4:14ff.) he began at the same time his proclamation of the kingdom: "Repent, *for* the kingdom of heaven is at hand" (Matt. 4:17). The preaching of his disciples is the kerugma of this kingdom that has come near, and the signs that accompany its coming can be understood only in the light of the mystery of its fulfillment (Matt. 10:7, 8). But it is this kerugma that demands decision wherever it is brought: "As you enter the house, salute it. And if the house is worthy, let your peace come upon it; but if it is not worthy, let your peace return to you" (Matt. 10:12, 13).[43] The gospel must be proclaimed from the housetops (Matt. 10:27), which proclamation is since Christ's being received again into heaven a proclamation that is directed to all nations. *In* this universality the loftiness of the kerugma comes to the fore in its demand to be acknowledged and believed: "make disciples of *all nations*" (Matt. 28:19).

The kerugma as a "making-known" is not an empty word which is imparted but which has no effect. It puts the hearer on a *way* in which he can *walk* in the peace of reconciliation, in the peace of sovereign grace. It is the way of proclamation, of instruction and teaching[44] in the driving power of the gospel which *because of* the accomplished work of Christ calls to acceptance and faith. These connections are strikingly brought out in the Gospel of Luke when Christ opens the Scriptures for his disciples, "Thus it is

---

43. Cf. Matt. 10:12-13, and vss. 14-15 in connection with not-hearing, and the entire section 17-23 on the tensions which obedience may bring into being.
44. Teaching (didáskein) and proclamation (euangelízein) are related in Acts 5:42 and in 15:35. In 4:2 (cf. 20:20) teaching is related to anangéllein, and in 28:31 to kerússein.

written, that the Christ should suffer and on the third day rise
from the dead, and that repentance and forgiveness of sins should
be preached in his name to all nations, beginning from Jerusalem"
(24:46, 47). This does not mean a change in the *content* of the
kerugma (from the salvation which God has prepared *to* repentance), but it does indicate the deep *connection* that exists between
the salvation which has appeared, on the one hand, and repentance and faith, on the other.

The kerugma, therefore, is a proclamation, but it is a proclamation in which the loftiness of God's redemptive action calls men
to acknowledge this salvation as *God's gift*. This explains why the
Scriptures emphasize with such great simplicity the decisiveness
of God's action and, on basis of this, the need of the believing acceptance of it. Therefore, too, Paul can write "be ye reconciled to
God" immediately after speaking about the message of the ambassadors concerning God who was in Christ reconciling the world to
himself (II Cor. 5:18-20). It is quite clear that the burden of
these passages is neither one of human co-operation nor one concerning the unimportance of the human decision.[45] There is a
*third* way that is here indicated. It is the way of faith which gives
God the glory in the acknowledgment that salvation is *exclusively*
His gift.

In this connection the seriousness of unbelief also becomes fully
evident. Now that the fulfillment in Christ has come, the rejection
of Christ is set forth in all its terribleness. We can even speak of
the "enigma" of unbelief here on the background of the urgent admonition and the door that has been opened. The enigmatic character of unbelief does not for Mark arise from the sinfulness of
man, nor from its "ontological impossibility," but from the *marvel-
ing* of Jesus about the unbelief He finds in Nazareth where He
could do no mighty work (Mark 6:5, 6). Jesus cannot understand,
He cannot comprehend *this* unbelief, this unbelief after *He* has
taught (Mark 6:2). He cannot fathom the astonishment about
His power and His wisdom which fills the hearts of His hearers
(Mark 6:2) but which is *not* followed by faith.[46]

---

45. Cf. my *Het Werk van Christus*, 1953.
46. Cf. the amazement of Jesus at the faith of the centurion of Capernaum
(Luke 7:9, Matt. 8:10), as contrasted with the unbelief of Israel.

The men of Nineveh will arise at the judgment "with this generation" for they repented when Jonah preached to them and "behold, something greater than Jonah is here" (Matt. 12:41). As Jonah became a sign to the men of Nineveh, "so will the Son of man be to this generation" (Luke 11:30). The preaching that Christ is a sign, a sign that shall be *spoken against,* that He is set for the fall and the rising of many (Luke 2:34) — precisely *in* the time of redemptive fulfillment — shuts off forever the way to relativize the human decision because of the grace of God. When *these* plain words are feared, and the danger of "synergism" is seen lurking in them, it is easy to proceed with the process of relativizing and to do so with an appeal to the triumph of grace and the "necessity" of faith. But then injustice is done to the *message* of salvation which does not call men to co-operate, but to *acknowledge* and *believe.* In Barth's theology the triumph of grace makes vague the seriousness of the human decision, just as the kerugma is threatened with becoming a mere announcement without any vital exhortation.

\* \* \*

In the kind of kerugma to which Barth holds — qualified though it be by the ideas of fatally dangerous unbelief and the open situation of the proclamation — reflection on the grace of God is straight-jacketed by a wholly *objective* conception of the triumph of grace. In criticism of this view it must be said that Barth's emphasis *on the relationships* in which faith stands could have led him more than is now the case to a full acknowledgment of the character of the kerugma as *hortatory* proclamation. The history of both the Church and of theology shows how easily such an acknowledgment can lead in wrong directions in which the sovereign character of salvation is obscured by the co-operative character of faith. These errors *can* be avoided, however, because the *nature* of faith is itself the center to which the problem of the *hortatory* kerugma is constantly oriented.[47] The proclamation will

---

47. We meet the same problem in Lekkerkerker's criticism of Barth when he writes that he "misses" something in Barth's treatment of II Cor. 5:19: "And yet, there is *something* which Barth does not say whereby the impression is made that his exegesis brings him to the outer boundary of 'general reconciliation.' " This "something" is the answer to the question, what it is that gives urgency to the "be ye reconciled to God." This preaching is for Paul a beseeching, an asking, a begging, *op. cit.,* p. 232. Cf. also Acts 2:21 and 2:40.

then no longer be viewed exclusively in terms of "knowing" and "not-knowing" but it will be seen in the light of the kerugma of the kingdom which can be seen and accepted only *in the way of faith.*

The fundamental reason for Barth's conception of "knowing" and "not-knowing" and of the ontological impossibility of sin undoubtedly lies in his view of the decision of *election* that has been made in Christ. It would require a separate study to express a judgment on Barth's entire doctrine of election with all its exegetical and historical-dogmatological expositions. Although space does not permit our doing so, we wish to call attention to some decisive aspects of his view of election. In setting forth the doctrine of election, Barth is concerned about the *comfort* of God's electing act. He is decidedly of the opinion that in the traditional doctrine of election the foundation for this comfort is lacking. Barth wants to throw the doors wide open to a definitely being-comforted. He wishes to emphasize the *omnipotence* of grace and in this way erect a barrier against the shadows that have constantly, also in the churches of the Reformation, been cast over the certainty of salvation.[48]

The heart of the debate about the triumph of election can be summarized in the following question: Has Barth with his doctrine of universal election, the election of all, opened the way whereby he can justly criticize the Reformation doctrine of election? This question may be further specified by reference to Barth's view of the Reformation conception of Christ as the "mirror of election." He acknowledges that in this conception the genuinely scriptural message of election is active. In his judgment, however, this conception does no more than manifest a laudable pastoral concern. It fails to show wherein the pastoral admonition to look to Jesus Christ and to Him alone finds its sure foundation. This explains, in his opinion, why this pastoral effort was not effective. Behind the "mirror of election" there was always visible the threat to all certainty of salvation which arose from the *hidden* will of God. The idea of the "mirror" as the way to the attaining of the certainty of election was in itself a right and good idea. It

---

48. Cf. A. C. De Jong, *The Well Meant Gospel Offer. The Views of Hoeksema and Schilder,* 1954.

could not function comfortingly, however, because there was a *hidden* aspect in the whole of God's works which robbed the pastoral help of its truly confidence-giving character.

The importance of the questions raised by this difference of view between Barth and the Reformation is obvious. This discussion about election touches immediately the problems of *preaching* and of the *certainty* of salvation. We are confronted by the question whether the preaching of the gospel is indeed a *reliable* preaching on which we can depend in life and in death. It is Barth's intention to show anew, and in relation to the theological situation of his day, what the connections are between election and the unassailable certainty of salvation.

* * *

When we do not labor under the illusion that we have reached a "solution" on the score of the problem of election in the Bible, we can learn much from wrong solutions that have been put forward. It has frequently been an unintended function of heresy in the Church that it indirectly called the Church to reflect on the rightness of the path she was following and called her back from misleading ways. One of these has undoubtedly been the way in which election was theoretically and practically equated with a casual and deterministic conception. A comparison between such a deterministic system with Mohammedanism then lay at hand, with the most serious consequences for a right understanding of the true message of the Scriptures.

Who has never encountered "conclusions" drawn from the doctrine of election which cast their chilly shadow over the Church and over the souls of the faithful? There was then no ultimately discernible difference between election and a deterministic causation, and the only distinction that remained between Mohammedan determinism and divine election was that at the top of the deterministic system stood *Allah* and at the top of the causation of election stood *God*.

Such "systems" can produce conclusions in which every human decision, whether for good or for evil, is swallowed up in the iron order of the causal structure. As a result everything becomes devitalized — prayer, faith, conversion — because it all comes to stand within the framework of *this* deterministic causation. There can be no certainty of salvation, nor a really significant way to redemption. Salvation disappeared behind the clouds of a lofty causality. There have been those who in theory and practice have followed this road to the end, and they have become an abiding warning against falling into a way of thinking that is alien to Scripture, that neither sees a historical process any more nor hears a kerugma. Here if anywhere it is true that to be fore-warned is to be fore-armed.

Deterministic causality shuts all the doors of Scripture and deprives us of any and all perspective with respect to the certainty of salvation. In this kerugma-less system the features of a deterministic *hidden* God become enigmatic and terror-inspiring. For this reason alone everyone who understands and trembles at the consequences of this conception will rejoice over the fact that the Reformation, in confessing God's election, did not relinquish but emphasized the connection between election and the proclamation and the pastoral care of souls.

This does not, of course, answer the question whether the pastorate, so considered, has a *basis* (Barth's question), nor does it say that the designated "mirror of election" is a *clear* mirror. We must take note of the fact, however, that the Reformation apparently did not see a "blind spot" here and that it joyfully saw a way indicated to the certainty of salvation. Strong and powerful has the work of *this* pastorate been. With the greatest emphasis it warned against every other way and confessed that only the way of the mirror, the mirror of election, brought rest and peace to the heart.

It is possible to indicate clearly the penetrating earnestness of this pastoral concern. Only when we have been impressed by the seriousness of this concern will we be able to judge the validity of Barth's criticism, namely, that this was not the *deepest,* the *ultimate* comfort that could have been extended.

*    *    *

It is not necessary for our purpose to cite many examples bearing on this point from the Reformed doctrine of election. Suffice it to say, that the anti-speculative emphasis is everywhere observable. We see this especially in Calvin. We think of a well-known expression of his in which theology and pastorate border closely on each other: "If we seek God's fatherly gentleness and His heart which is favorably disposed toward us, we must in the first place direct our eyes to Christ in whom alone the heart of the Father rests."

God has elected and loved us *in Christ* and "if we are elect in Him we shall find the certainty of our election not in ourselves and not even in God the Father if we represent Him to our minds apart from the Son. Christ is therefore the mirror in whom we ought to observe our election, and this we may do without fear of being deceived."[49]

Again and again Calvin warns against curiosity and against transgressing the boundaries of revelation. When he writes (Barth points to this passage in a critical discussion of the traditional doctrine of election), "God's predestination is, after all, in truth a labyrinth" we must, in order to do him justice, note especially the *antithetical* connection in which Calvin writes. It is *recklessness* which plunges men "as into a deep sea when they speak about predestination, because they do not recognize any limits." Only within this limitation does the confession of God's election have value and does it receive significance for the certainty of salvation.[50]

Calvin radically rejects everything which might in a synergistic, Pelagian or semi-Pelagian way point to a foreknowledge of God so that in His electing He would be dependent upon the human decision. "Nothing can tempt him to go farther [than what is revealed in Scripture.] These awe-inspiring mysteries are not for him theoretical doctrines in which man in his littleness can satisfy his desire for speculation in order that he may be able to operate with an order of decrees as Beza already began to do."[51]

It is striking that all Calvin scholars have emphatically pointed to the *anti-speculative* element in Calvin's doctrine of election. He constantly has in mind the connection between election and our

---

49. J. Calvin, *Institutes,* III, xxiv, 5.
50. Cf. A. D. R. Polman, *Onze Nederlandse Geloofsbelijdenis,* II, p. 190ff. who writes that Calvin "also points out the tremendous value of election for the personal certainty of salvation," p. 190, and that Calvin "would have nothing to do with this operating with and speculating about the decrees of God" so that he never "made use of the apriori deductive methods of the later supralapsarians."
51. A. D. R. Polman, *ibid.,* p. 208.

certainty of salvation. Sharply he polemicizes against Gregory: "Gregory speaks badly and corruptingly when he teaches that we are conscious only of our calling but that we are uncertain about our election, and thereby gives to all an occasion for fear and trembling."[52] It is, according to Calvin, rather so that "predestination, when one thinks about it correctly, does not weaken faith but strengthens it wonderfully."[53] The sovereignty of God's grace is not in conflict with the possibility of certainty. For faith it is precisely the foundation of certainty. Nowhere else do we have a support on which we can depend firmly.[54] When Calvin speaks about election, he is at the same time concerned to reveal his conviction *in* the exposition of the doctrine that "our salvation flows from the fountain of God unmerited mercy."[55] Therefore H. Otten, in his treatment of Calvin's view of predestination, can insert a section entitled, "The Significance of Predestination for Christian Piety," and suppport his thesis with many citations from Calvin.[56]

For Calvin election is indissolubly united with the rejection of all work-righteousness. For this reason election is inseparably linked with the confession of the certainty of salvation.[57] This certainty would, in Calvin's judgment, come to hang completely in the air if he were not able at the same time to confess that Christ is the clear light of predestination.[58] It belongs to Satan's most dangerous temptations to lead people who are disturbed by doubts about their election to seek certainty "extra viam."[59] At this point we stand at the very center of Calvin's doctrine of election. He knows the questions that can arise, notably the question about the revelation of one's election: "What revelation do you have of your election?",[60] a question that can have power to the point of despair. Calvin answers this by pointing to the wrong conception of predestination which is reflected precisely by the torturing experience. The doc-

---

52. J. Calvin, *Institutes,* III, xxiv, 9.
53. *Ibid.,* III, xxiv, 9.
54. *Ibid.,* III, xxi, 1.
55. *Ibid.*
56. H. Otten, *Calvins theologische Anschauung von der Prädestination,* 1938, pp. 34ff.
57. H. Otten, *ibid.,* p. 35.
58. J. Calvin, *Institutes,* II, xvii. 1, (with appeal to Augustine) : "clarissimum lumen praedestinationis et gratiae ipse est salvator homo Christus Jesus."
59. *Ibid.,* III, xxiv, 4.
60. *Ibid.,* III, iv, 4.

trine of predestination does indeed have its dangers, but only when they are *sought*, namely, when election is inquired into apart from the word of God.[61]

In the warning against the "extra viam," against the "sine verbo," Calvin lays down the connection between election and proclamation, between election and pastoral care.

It is remarkable that Calvin nowhere appears to be aware that the pastoral care which he advocated really lacks foundation. The contrary is true, because for him the *reliability* of the word of God — this is his point of departure — can *never* be threatened and, therefore *is not* threatened by election. God's sovereign freedom and the profundity of election do not mean for Calvin that there is no "revelatio," no *way* to the knowledge of salvation and of God's election. Therefore he is particularly fond of the idea that Christ is the mirror of election, and this not as a deduction from the loftiness of a "hidden" election, but as the *way,* the *open way* to the certainty of salvation. At this point we stand squarely before the difference between Barth and Calvin. It touches centrally the truth and practicability of Calvin's reference to the *light,* the *mirror* of predestination.

We are aware that this exposition gives far from a complete characterization of Calvin's doctrine of election. One of his central points of departure, however, stands clearly before us. The "mirror of election" is not an incidental matter for him, but it reflects the legitimate relationship between election and pastoral concern, between election and the certainty of salvation. The foundation for this lies, according to Calvin, in the revelation.

This does not mean that Calvin, on the basis of this conception, has in all respects drawn the proper conclusions and formed them into a harmonious "system." He has continually occupied himself with the Scriptures, and in so doing has struggled with Eph. 1:4, Rom. 9 to 11, and with other passages. But the remarkable thing is that *in* this struggling — here the question arises especially as to the validity of Calvin's exegesis of Rom. 9 to 11 — the view of Christ as the mirror of election asserts itself decisively.

This is the point that we are concerned to stress in discussing the criticism of Barth, who is of the opinion that the pastorate of

61. *Ibid.,* III, xxiv, 4.

the "mirror of election" in the Reformed doctrine of election lacks a foundation. In this discussion everything centers about the triumph of reconciliation and about the universality of that triumph.

*  *  *

As we saw earlier, election in the traditional doctrine of election is, according to Barth, really *unknowable* and as a "mystery" is not part of the revelation. In the traditional view, he charges, there is always one question which unavoidably threatens the certainty of salvation, namely, *who* God really is and what His actual, hidden will may be. In contrast to this he posits the knownness or the knowableness of election in its revelation in Jesus Christ. In his judgment there can be no harmony between election and pastoral counsel except in terms of this knowledge.

It is striking that Calvin emphatically rejects such a criticism. He denies that the certainty of salvation is threatened by election and does not know of a "real" God in distinction from and alongside of Jesus Christ. This comes out plainly in the remarkable expression of Calvin that in order to secure certainty of our salvation we must not only seek it in ourselves, but also not in *God the Father*, "if we represent Him to ourselves apart from the Son."[62] Directing our eyes to the Son, however, can be done "without deception."[63]

This "without deception" is Calvin's bulwark against Barth's criticism. It rests upon *the reliability of the revelation* in Christ in which God has come to us.

It can be said, therefore, that Calvin would not have been taken aback by a criticism such as Barth gives expression to, for he does not speak here of the hidden God but of the revealed God. For this reason the suggestion that election constitutes a threat to the certainty of salvation would not have impressed him as valid.

What, then, is the deepest reason for the difference between Calvin and Barth? Our earlier analysis will already have suggested the answer to this question. According to Barth, the Lutheran and the Reformed doctrines of election have weakened the connection

---

62. "Ac ne in Deo quidem Patre, si nudum illum absque Filio imaginamur," *ibid.*, III, xxiv, 5.
63. "Sine fraude licet," *ibid.*, III, xxiv, 5.

between *Christ* and *election.* In that doctrine Christ is seen only as the *executor* of election, not as its *foundation.* Therefore there is a *vacuum* behind election which the pastoral office is not able to fill.

In a certain sense, the debate centers around the exegesis of Eph. 1:4. Barth judges that there can be certainty only when this verse is understood to mean that Christ is not only the *executor* but also the *foundation* of election, because the decision of election is taken in Him and thereby all men have been elected *in Him.* Only then is *certainty* possible, only then can there be a *knowing* unmarred by threat. In the revelation of Christ the *fact* of the election of *all men* has been revealed. This *universal* election stands revealed as *God's* decisive election. All uncertainty is removed by this universally decisive act of God. That which Barth sees as a "blind spot," a sinister "vacuum," in the traditional view, he fills with this decisive act of God which forms the content of the kerugma. In this manner Barth thinks to correct the Reformation doctrine of election on the score of the certainty of salvation and thus do full justice to Eph. 1:4.

This certainty can now point to its foundation: Christ as the rejected and the elected One. The kerugma has this unassailable decisiveness as its concrete content, and as God's definite decision precedes all human decisions. It does not assume the human decision, but in faithfulness it triumphs over that decision which is a rebellion against grace. In this way Christ is not merely the mirror of election, He is the *manifestation* of our election in Him.

\* \* \*

The remarkable element in this conception is that in endeavoring to eliminate the "vacuum" in this way, it returns unavoidably at another point, namely, in the ontological impossibility of sin and unbelief and in the rejection of the apokatastasis. Judging Barth in terms of his own position it can be said that the uncertainty which he discovers in the Reformation conception of election returns in his own system in the problem of subjectivity, namely, the problem of *unbelief.* The a priori divine decision of which Barth speaks really leaves no room for the return of this problem. In theologies that conclude from the nature of God, from His election and love, to a general reconciliation, the problem of subjectivity falls away in sharp reaction to any and every form of synergism. Barth, however, does not follow this path and therefore must deal with the problem of man's response. Even though the vacuum which, in spite of all, appears to exist in his own theology is limited by the conception of the ontological impossibility of unbelief, Barth does *not* draw this line of the ontological impossibility through to the point of teaching the doctrine of the apokatastasis. Were he to do so, the *existential* decision of God would make any existential decision of man unimportant. This Barth wishes to avoid, hence his opposition to the idea of apokatastasis. The tension in Barth's doctrine of election arises from the relationship between *universal election* and *human decision*.

When Barth thought that he had discovered the foundation for pastoral care and thereby had opened the way to the certainty of salvation, the shadows of the vacuum again appeared. It might be expected that this would have suggested to Barth the possibility of reflecting anew on the decision of belief or unbelief in the light of the simplicity with which Scripture speaks of this matter.

Barth clearly feels that by doing so his entire conception would be threatened with ambiguity. He would then have to surrender the idea of the ontological impossibility of sin and . . . the divine decision would become dependent upon the human. Therefore Barth refuses to follow this path because he sees the shadows of synergism falling over every step of it.

This refusal would lead us to expect greater carefulness on Barth's part in evaluating the Reformation doctrine of election. Is there really room in Barth's understanding of the triumph of grace for criticism and correction of the Reformed conception of election?

He would not have exceeded the bounds of carefulness if he had emphatically warned against thinking in terms of an *abstract* God-concept and had urged instead to think of election as having taken place *in Christ*. Nor, in view of the manner in which many have obscured election, would it have been improper for him to ask whether our thinking *really* reckoned with Christ as the mirror of election, and whether in our thinking about election we have not also entertained the idea of a threatening background as an *independent* dogmatic datum *alongside of* or *behind* the revelation in Christ. In view of the confusion that has been apparent in discussions on the doctrine of election, these would have been meaningful dogmatic and pastoral questions. Conclusions drawn now and again from the doctrine of election are disconcerting enough to make continual warning against them eminently proper.

In Barth's criticism, however, we do not meet such *warnings,* but a new *solution.*

It is the solution, suggested by Eph. 1:4, that it is no longer necessary to doubt because the election of *all* is a *fact.* There is no point, therefore, in trying to know what the will of God *really* is because salvation is *objectively* secure in our election in Christ. All of Barth's conclusions compelled him to posit this accomplished fact which must be preached by the *knowing* Church to the *not-yet-knowing* world. Everything which threatened the validity of this definitive and sovereign decision Barth rejected. He not only attacked Reformed theology because, in his judgment, it showed the features of the "deus absconditus" looming up behind the "deus revelatus," but also *Lutheran* theology which in the Formula Concordiae became a doctrine of the general redemptive will of God but gave no full assurance of being efficacious. The attempt was made here to take away the blind spot and to retain fully the comfort of election.[64] But it was not possible to do so.[65] For what is a divine redemptive will which does not achieve its purpose? *Has* God then really chosen, and *is* there a Yes, a Yes which has irrevocably been spoken?[66]

Lutheran theology solves the problem as little[67] as Reformed theology does because it does not see election as being radically Christological.[68] The "empty spot" can be removed only by way of acknowledging the *fact* of the election of all, by believing the decision that *has been made.* This preserves the eu-aggelion and the unbeclouded view of the triumph of grace. The Church must pro-

---

64. KD II/2, p. 77.
65. Barth even writes: "There are in fact grounds that make it understandable that, placed before a choice, Reformed theologians would regard the doctrine of the absolute decree as the relatively better guarantee for the Reformed, the Christian interest in this entire matter," KD II/2, p. 77.
66. *Ibid.,* p. 79.
67. As soon as praescientia is given a place in the doctrine of election "the idea of a free divine choice is cancelled out," *ibid.,* p. 79.
68. *Ibid.,* p. 81.

claim this message as the mystery of election which the others do
not yet know, but which has *objective validity* also for them.

* * *

Probably no one will wish to venture a prophecy as to the direction in which Barth will further develop his thought. It is quite
possible, however, to state in a nutshell his central thesis. This is
that the triumph of election means, centrally and determinatively,
the a priori divine decision of the election of *all* in the election of
Christ.

This a priorism as the content of the proclamation of the
Church involves as a direct consequence for Barth the ontological
impossibility of sin. For is not this unbelief opposition to that
which overcomes the bitterest opposition, namely, God's gracious
election?

At this point Barth stands at a cross-roads in his thinking. He
can move to the right or to the left, not in terms of the demands
of a logical system, but in terms of centrally religious considerations. The one way that is open is that of the apokatastasis in
which the reality of the divine decision which has been taken
is without qualification declared to be identical with the universality of  reconciliation.

The other way is that of *renewed* reflection on the seriousness of
the human decision which, according to the overwhelming testimony of Scripture, is associated with the kerugma that goes out
to the world.

Up to now, Barth has rejected the first possibility. To accept the
apokatastasis would, in his view, make the existential seriousness
of God's decision turn election into a self-evident matter and
prejudice man's subjection to election as *grace*.

Barth has not entered the second way, either. He has indeed
impressively shown the relationship of faith to salvation but, on
the score of unbelief, his conception makes him oppose sharply the
idea that it is a "possibility."

So long as Barth declines to accept either alternative, however,
he must remain standing at the crossroads. This standstill characterizes the present situation in his theology on the score of the
universality of the triumph.

The universality of the triumph of grace in the election of Jesus Christ makes clear what the deepest motif in Barth's thinking is. For him everything in Scripture points to the definitive and irrevocable decision. Everywhere Barth discovers "pointers" to the twofold predestination: rejection and election. In this conception the relationship between Israel and the Church occupies a central position. They are not seen in the light of the history of redemption in its onward moving character, but in the light of the *service* which they render, in the light of their *witness-value*. Israel is *negatively*, the Church is *positively*, a witness of redemption. There is one body, and this body comes to expression in its Israelitic and in its Christian form. Both reveal God's mercy: Israel as addressee of the gospel, the Church as the witness to redemption.

Of real rejection we can speak only in connection with Jesus Christ. His rejection, which is at the same time His election, is the shining center of redemption.

The history of Israel is in itself a terrible history, but *as such* it is taken up into the witness to God's *mercy*. The overpowering might of the triumph becomes unmistakably plain here. Although Barth is concerned to reveal the seriousness of rejection, it continues to stand in the light of election. Historical Israel functions in the total witness to the point of rejecting Christ to show *how free* election is and *how merciful*.

This emphasis is decisive in Barth's outlook. The whole of the history of Israel is seen in this light.

The broadly universal point of view characteristic of Scripture, which has traditionally been regarded as bearing an historical-redemptive character, is crystallized in Barth's theology into a *witnessing function*. By way of this transformation the universality of the triumph is made to stand out sharply. Israel and the Church stand together under the one arch of God's election and mercy.[69]

* * *

69. Th. C. Vriezen has objected to the relationship Israel-Church as Barth presents it: "also the Church has frequently done violence to God's election," *Die Erwählung Israels nach dem Alten Testament,* 1953, p. 111. A little farther on he writes about "the Christian world": "In the rejection and rooting out of Israel by the Christian peoples on the ground that it had rejected Jesus, the Christian world made itself equal with the divine judge." It seems to me that this describes anti-Semitism too simplistically. Vriezen's criticism of Barth, however, touches an essential point: Israel is not the only addressee of the gospel; also the Church knows what it is to be and to remain object of *free* grace.

We are now in position to understand why Barth has attacked especially Calvin and the traditional doctrine of election. Both have failed to teach *universal* election.[70] It is worthy of note, however, that the Reformed opposed the "pro omnibus" of the Remonstrants *not* by way of limitation of the power of Christ's sacrifice, but because the Remonstrants made of the "pro omnibus" an *objective state of affairs* which also in their conception was *not* effectuated.

Within the wide circle of universal reconciliation the Remonstrants had the narrower circle of the *effectiveness* of this reconciliation. Barth also has serious objections against this construction. He saw the vacuum appear in that the spear-head of free human decision penetrated into the universality of Christ's work.

Over against this emphasis he sought a way of his own in which he would be able to escape both the Remonstrant form of the "pro omnibus" and the criticism of the Reformed of this view. The vacuum, the shadow of the human decision falling over the divine decision, had to disappear. It is clear that this shadow disappears in the radical doctrine of universal reconciliation. It is interesting to note that Barth actually believes he has eliminated the shadow and that he can speak of the "original, unilateral, wonderful triumph of God"[71] in the existence of the man Jesus Christ, a triumph of election and of the love of God. It "very really embraces the world and the Church, the non-Christians and the Christians."[72] Unthreatened triumph!

But again the shadow becomes visible when it appears that the universality of the triumph is not developed into the actual reconciliation of all.

"To reflect today with unseemly seriousness about the possibility of the eternal damnation of this one and that one, and tomorrow with an equally unseemly cheerfulness about the ultimate reconciliation of one and all is *one* thing; *another* (and that is the charge that has been given to the Christian Church) is to regard oneself obliged to witness with Christian word and deed to Jesus

---

70. Cf., among other references, KD IV/1, p. 61.
71. *Ibid.*, p. 94.
72. *Ibid.*, p. 111.

Christ as Lord not only but as the Redeemer of the world and, as such, its future."[73]

Here the proclamation, *the witness of the Church,* takes the place of *the empty spot, the traditional doctrine of election.*

This witness cannot, however, fulfill the function which Barth intends it to serve because its *content* is the message of universal election.

The Church has indeed been placed in the world as a witness to God's grace and she has certainly not understood the meaning of election when she does not accept and discharge this calling. But the "open situation" of the proclamation cannot solve the problem posed by Barth's doctrine of election. It is the triumph of election, in the significance which it has in Barth's system, which makes precisely this open situation problematic. *God's* decision, which is the content of the proclamation, leaves room for only one transition: from *not-knowing* to *knowing,* and even the not-knowing has already been overtaken by the knowing, the Yes of God.

Barth's universalism, therefore, makes a problem of the triumph. In 1935 K. H. Miskotte, in discussing Barth's eschatological views, was reminded of a Swiss theologian of an earlier day, namely, Samuel Huber (1547-1624). He supposes "that Barth would be inclined, if not to adopt Huber's views, at least to take them seriously as a way in which in those days it was attempted to relate in a system what Barth relates dialectically."[74] It is understandable that Miskotte should think of Huber in this connection because this theologian concerned himself with the *universal* significance of the work of Christ and therefore with the "pro omnibus" which is involved in it.

Even Huber, however, did not teach the reconciliation of all men. He therefore had to face the question, *how* to square his universalistic conception with the reality of the human decision. It was man's guilt, the guilt of unbelief, which made it possible for him to despise and forfeit the salvation which Christ had provided.[75] He arrived at a view of election which is strongly reminis-

---

73. *Ibid.,* p. 129.
74. K. Miskotte, *De Apostolische Geloofsbelijdenis,* p. 369.
75. O. Ritschl, *Dogmengeschichte des Protestantismus,* IV, p. 137.

cent of the possibility-realization tension which we meet later in the Remonstrants and in many others. "Therefore one either believes or one has been freed in vain and falls again from grace."[76] It is helpful, after the appearance of Barth's work on election in 1942, to recall the parallel which Miskotte drew. It is clear that both Huber and Barth struggled with similar problems. But it is also plain, as Miskotte observes, that Barth would not be prepared to take over Huber's views without qualification.

This is plain from this fact alone, that Huber introduces without hesitation the freedom of human decision with respect to the *already accomplished* salvation, and relates the divine prescience concerning belief and unbelief to it. Barth has emphatically rejected *this* means of solving his problem as a violation of the sovereignty of grace. Huber's view of belief and unbelief as a human decision unavoidably creates a problem which cannot be resolved. In Barth this problem takes the form of the ontological impossibility of unbelief. Nevertheless, the parallel between the two remains striking.[77]

In 1927 O. Ritschl characterized Huber's point of view in a manner that reminds us strongly of Barth: "Through their unbelief they fall back into the condition which Christ through His death had removed."[78] This difficulty remains unresolved in Huber's system. Huber — as does Barth — accepts *this* form of the problem which seems to free us from the "uncertainty" of the traditional doctrine. But in reality the problem has only been shifted to other ground, and is certainly not to be solved in terms of the proclamation of the Church. We meet here the problem of a universalism or, more precisely, a *relative* universalism which rejects the apokatastasis. But it is *in this rejection* that the problem comes to the fore, both in Huber and in Barth. It is the problem posed by the *triumph* of election.

---

76. *Ibid.*, p. 137.
77. Cf. H. E. Weber, *Reformation, Orthodoxie und Rationalismus*, I/2, 1940, p. 98, on "Samuel Huber, the warning voice" and the "disturber from Switzerland," who came to his universalistic views by appealing to Question 27 of the Heidelberg Catechism and to Eph. 1:10, and who was concerned especially about the consequences of the traditional doctrine. For this appeal of Huber cf. O. Ritschl, *op. cit.*, p. 140.
78. O. Ritschl, *op. cit.*, p. 140.

Barth's opposition to all synergism has brought him to the verge of the apokatastasis. At this edge boundaries are fixed in order to accentuate the existential seriousness of the human decision. This problem arises from the thesis of the factual election of all. The light, therefore, does not remain unobscured. Clouds begin to surround it. When Barth's vision has been pursued to the end, it is no longer possible to appeal to God's freedom in election. Barth considered it his duty to point out the danger of arbitrariness, of the "deus absconditus," in the Reformed doctrine of election. But for this very reason he cannot counter the apokatastasis doctrine by pointing to God's freedom. For, according to Barth, it was precisely *this* freedom which was not arbitrary, but the freedom whereby He bound Himself in love, namely, in the concreteness of *the* decision: the election of Jesus Christ.

\* \* \*

We must therefore turn once again to the consideration of Christ as the mirror of election. In the light of the gospel, the way to the certainty of salvation is inviolable. The unacceptableness of Barth's criticism of the inadequacy of the pastoral care allowed by the Reformed doctrine of predestination is the reverse side of the vacuum which appears in Barth's own doctrine of election. We see the shadows fall over the "knowledge" of election. The criticism that the mirror functions only noetically and has no ontic foundation appears to arise from a universalism which itself creates the problem of the tension between the real, universal election of all and the reality of unbelief which, in the final analysis, the ontological impossibility of unbelief is not able to exclude.

In view of these tensions, we are the more deeply impressed by the decisive significance of the manner in which Augustine and Calvin point to Christ as the mirror of election.

Only by way of an extensive treatment of the doctrine of election would it be possible to do full justice to the relations which the Reformation saw between election and the certainty of salvation.[79]

---

79. In the nature of the case, it is not possible to enter upon this question here. We hope to treat it in the following volume of the *Dogmatic Studies* dealing with the doctrine of election — "Deo volente."

We trust it has been made plain, however, that Calvin regarded the *revelation* of election as lying only in Christ as the mirror of election. The "knowledge" of election for which Barth pleads in contrast to the uncertainty of the "deus absconditus" cannot for a moment be found apart from the way in which our election really becomes known to us, namely, the way of faith.

This is the a priori of the gospel in terms of which the mirror of election will have to serve its function to the outermost reaches of the doctrine of election. It is the a priori which is grounded in the reliable revelation itself as the surmounting of both an inflexible objectivity and a narrow subjectivity. It is not a synthesis of objectivism and subjectivism, but the rejection of both. Barth's solution of the universalism of the triumph of election unavoidably brought him into difficulty with the meaningfulness of the horatatory kerugma and of the human decision in the area of history. The "open situation" in his doctrine of election became an alien body, however great the emphasis he placed upon it. The kerugma concerning the mirror of election, however, gives real meaning to the open situation. When we so view the matter, we can understand something of what Christ meant when in answer to the question whether there were few that would be saved He gave a reply which was constantly evasive but which in reality met the question head on: "Strive to enter in. . . ." (Luke 13: 23-24).

# XI

## THE DIVINE TRIUMPH

IN BARTH'S exposition of the triumph of reconciliation he continues his discussion of the one triumph of grace. This does not mean, however, that he simply repeats here what he had said before. In opening this new perspective he presents us with a further development of his thought.

This development comes to expression particularly in the manner in which Barth emphasizes more strongly and consistently the reconciling action of God Himself *in* the person of Jesus Christ. As in the doctrine of election we heard of Jesus Christ who *Himself* is the electing God, so now in the doctrine of reconciliation we meet Jesus Christ as the reconciling God, as God *Himself*, who *in* Christ reconciles the world to Himself. We do not meet this central idea for the first time in his most recent dogmatic study (IV/1). In earlier works he had in a variety of ways emphasized "God Himself" as the divine subject in the act of reconciliation.

This brings us to one of the deepest questions with which systematic theology can concern itself, and especially in our time it stands in the center of interest.[1] It is the question of the relationship between God Himself and history, namely, in the reconciliation, the suffering, and death of Jesus Christ. Barth has now with marked consistency developed his earlier thinking and speaks without hesitation about the suffering of God, of His *obedience,* and of His *self-surrender.*

Various kinds of associations have been laid between the "God Himself" and the suffering of Christ, and I have referred to these conceptions as fundamentally constituting a "violation of the mystery of the trinity."[2] This criticism referred particularly to those

---

1. For several examples of this cf. my *De Persoon van Christus,* 1952, pp. 310-311 (English translation, *The Person of Christ,* pp. 352ff), and *Het Werk van Christus,* 1953, pp. 308-310.
2. G. C. Berkouwer, *Het Werk van Christus,* p. 308.

views which did not shrink from speaking of a "conflict" in God. Barth, however, wants nothing to do with such a conception and calls it blasphemy. In our further discussion we shall have to reckon seriously with this. But this does not alter the fact that Barth gives strong prominence to the "passion of God" and to the "obedience of God." He does not hesitate for a moment to speak in this way because he believes this to be fully in harmony with the confession of the deity of Christ. Although Barth does not, as far as I know, use the term or discuss the concept as an historical phenomenon, he raises here the problem of *theopaschitism* or the suffering of God. The question as to whether it is permitted to speak of the suffering of God has, particularly in our century, been answered in the affirmative by many. What is involved here for many theologians, and especially for Barth, is not a striking way of speaking, such as we meet, for instance, in Ignatius and in other writers in the ancient Church, but a conception which Barth consciously develops in various directions and which for him appears to be of essential importance.

That Barth began without hesitation to think in these terms does not mean that he is not aware of the problems which are involved. As we saw earlier, he refers to the problem of *obedience* in God Himself as a *hard matter*.[3] The question whether commanding *and* obeying can both be *in God* does not restrain him from speaking in this way, however, and that not merely as a way of speaking, but as something very essential, as a necessary description of God's *being*, even though it may be offensive to our thinking.[4]

All considerations which make it incompatible with God's "honor" and with His "being" to speak of God's self-humiliation, self-surrender, humility, suffering, and obedience arise, according to Barth, from an a priori God-concept which is set as a norm for our thinking about God. We do not then in a radically Christocentric fashion take our point of departure from the reality of the revelation in Jesus Christ who is not only true man, but also truly *God*. In a God-concept of natural theology which *we* construe, it is indeed not possible to make such predications about God — the esse absolutum cannot suffer and be obedient — but this has noth-

---

3. KD IV/2, p. 211.
4. KD IV/1, p. 219.

ing to do with *Christian* theology. We come to a wholly different view, according to Barth, when we learn to think about God *in terms of Christ.* Then the confession of Christ's true deity silences all these objections of reason which would determine *what is or what is not possible* for God. When these objections are silenced, we no longer see God as a high and unemotional being, but we see the humble, self-surrendering God. He is the true God *in* the suffering and obedience of Christ.

Barth wishes to teach us to alter radically our thinking about God in order that our conception of Him may not lead us beyond the boundaries of *revelation.* In doing so, Barth draws a remarkable Christological conclusion for our *knowledge of God.* The triumph of grace manifests itself in the revelation of *this* suffering and of *this* obedience of God. It is a revelation of God not in the heights but in the depths, not of riches but of poverty, and in this manifestation the nature, the being of God stands revealed before our marvelling eyes.[5]

\* \* \*

It is necessary to understand clearly that we do not have here a simple repetition of the old theopaschitic conception. It is rather theopaschitism in a new form. Both conceptions end in the suffering of God, but their backgrounds are different. The earlier theopaschitism concluded to God's suffering *from* the unity of Christ's person. The confession of the "vere Deus" meant for the theopaschitists that God suffered. By denying this it was thought that the unity of the person of Christ was violated and that it would not be possible to avoid the Nestorian error of separating His two natures. The suffering of Christ would then be limited to His *human* nature. Many theopaschitic expressions are obviously sharp reactions to Nestorianism. We meet them especially in the monophysitic camp which was strongly opposed to Chalcedon, and particularly against the well-known letter of Leo which

---

5. In short: we must not, according to Barth, have a general conception of "deity" and then think of Christ in terms of this conception and then say that he partakes of *this* deity; rather, we must take Christ as our point of departure in order to know what deity is and who God is. Only in this way can we abolish natural theology.

distinguished emphatically between what Christ did according to His *divine* and according to His *human* nature[6]

At the same time, we notice that Nestorianism protested sharply against every form of theopaschitism, a protest which ran parallel to the criticism of the "theotokos" in its reference to Mary. This has on more than one occasion led to the branding of opposition against theopaschitic formulations as a Nestorian *separation* of the two natures. This may, from the viewpoint of the history of dogma, be a tempting conclusion, but it is not a conclusion which holds, for criticism of theopaschitism can be coupled with a rejection of Nestorianism. The question then arises whether there cannot be *other* considerations that led to the rejection of theopaschitism.

Frequently opposition to theopaschitism has been attributed to a conception of God which viewed him as inflexible and unaffective. It cannot be denied that this conception has often played a role in the opposition to theopaschitism. The idea of the "apathy" of God has frequently led to such a view. W. Elert is not warranted, however, in saying that "the Platonic idea of the apathy of God constitutes to the present day the basis for the God-concept of the whole of orthodoxy." Especially must this view be rejected when we note that it is projected against the background of "the immovable, affectionless features of the God of Plato."[7]

There is not a single ground for affirming that all opposition to theopaschitism arose from *this* conception. On every side we can find misgivings and an intuitive turning away from theopaschitism, and not least when it was desired fully to confess the deity of Christ and the unity of His person. It is peculiar, moreover, that also among the proponents of theopaschitism we frequently discern all manner of hesitation. Only seldom is the theopaschitic line of thought followed consistently to the end. Apologists for the view have, for instance, in speaking of the suffering of God, qualified this suffering as the suffering of the Logos *according to the flesh*. Even more noticeable did this hesitation become in set-

---

6. Concerning monophysitism and theopaschitism cf. among other works Joseph Lebon's "La Christologie du Monophysisme Syrien" in *Das Konzil von Chalcedon. Geschichte und Gegenwart*, I, 1951, pp. 569ff. For the monophysitic conclusion from "theotokos" to theopaschitism cf. p. 570.

7. Cf. W. Elert, "Die theopaschitische Formel," *Theologische Literatur Zeitung*, 1950, p. 196.

ting forth the meaning of the fourth word of the crucified Christ,
"My God, my God, why hast thou forsaken me?" Consistent theopaschitic thinking would lead us to expect that in one way or another its central idea would be developed here. But we observe
a drawing back rather than a moving forward, as Elert indicates
with reference to Cyril who "recoiled from drawing the final conclusion"[8] when he exegeted the word of the cross to mean that
Christ really did not pray here for Himself, a remarkable and
problematical exegesis in connection with the very climax of the
passio Christi. This passage has frequently been a crucial one in
theopaschitic formulations. The unity of the person and especially
the one divine-human nature formed the basis for theopaschitic
thinking, but often the ultimate conclusion of an *absolute* relationship between the divine nature and suffering, forsakenness,
and death was avoided.[9] It is not necessary to pursue these dogma-
historical aspects further. We wish only to point out that the
problem arose in the area of Christology and particularly in connection with the unity of Christ's person.[10]

When Barth speaks of the suffering of God he does so much less
ambiguously and with less involved interpretations than the above
mentioned theopaschitic viewpoints do. His frequent reference to
the suffering of God is free from any and all hesitation. This is
not due to a greater consistency on his part, but to a difference in
motif. The "God Himself" in the passion of Christ does not stand
in need of modification or weakening in the direction of the suffering of the Logos "according to the flesh" but is posited unre-
servedly as an *essentially* divine humiliation. This places us still
more squarely before the question of what the deepest objections
to theopaschitism are, a question which becomes the more urgent
now that it stands before us in a form in which we are, according
to Barth, not concerned about an emphatic manner of expression
but about an *essential* aspect, about *that* aspect of the Son of God

8. W. Elert, *ibid.,* p. 201.

9. Cf. J. Lebon, *op. cit.,* p. 570.

10. We think here of the so-called theopaschitic struggle in connection with the
formula of the Scythian monks: Unum ex sancta Trinitate passum esse carne, an
expression used already by Severus in unmasking the cryptic Nestorians, J. Lebon,
*ibid.,* p. 571. Note especially the addition of the word "carne" which clearly points
again to the central problem involved in theopaschitism.

which comes to expression in His incarnation, His cross, and His death.

* * *

Although we must acknowledge that a variety of motives has played a role in the opposition to theopaschitism, it may not be forgotten that the intuitive resistance to it found its mainspring in the witness of Scripture. This is really the only basis for a *legitimate* opposition. The point of departure *may not be* an aprioristic, naturalistic God-concept, in terms of which we undertake to determine what God Himself can or cannot do. Such a natural (and generally exclusively *transcendent*) God-concept has frequently led to the denial of the incarnation because this was considered to be in conflict with the loftiness, the dignity, and the transcendence of God. The proclamation of the "impossibility" of the incarnation by docetism and gnosticism has been one of the temptations of the ancient Church which her confession of the great mystery made it necessary for her to resist. The Church realized that the denial of the incarnation was nothing less than the denial of what in God's mercy had become reality, and she bowed in faith before the mystery which eye had not seen, nor ear had heard, and which had not entered into the heart of man. It is possible for human thought to deny in its pride that which is undeniable. The human heart is deceitful, also in the labyrinthine ways of theology. It *is* possible in terms of a rigid or loftily transcendent God-concept to arrive at a conclusion concerning what God can *not* do, a conclusion, however, which is contradicted by the revelation: "He who did not spare his own Son but gave him up for all, will he not also give us all things with him?" (Rom. 8:32).

If we will not permit ourselves to think about the suffering of Christ apart from revelation, however, there is no point at which we shall wish to respect the *boundaries* of Scripture so scrupulously as in considering the unfathomable mystery of the incarnation and the cross. In our opinion it is here that consistent theopaschitism has speculatively transgressed the boundaries. We are not concerned to render a uniform judgment about certain terms, as little as that was the interest of the councils of the ancient Church in connection with the term "theotokos." Our concern is to set forth clearly the *thesis* with which we are confronted in modern theopaschitism. Undoubtedly we shall have to remember that not every rebuttal to theopaschitism has a legitimate basis.[11] There is such a thing as an opposition which clearly prejudices the mystery of the unity of the person and which abstracts Christ as man from this unity. Only when we take account of these dangers can we reflect responsibly on the problem of theopaschitism in its older and particularly in its more recent form.

When neither an abstract God-concept nor Nestorianism can provide a legitimate basis for the rejection of theopaschitism, the question arises whether this is possible in terms of Scripture. We believe that this question must be answered affirmatively.

* * *

It is rather striking that in the debate about theopaschitism one side speaks with a certain self-evidence about the suffering of God while the other side denies this emphatically. It is not a debate that simply involves a few texts. Its center has been the person of Jesus Christ. It cannot be denied that theopaschitism in its consistent form has always in one way or another come into conflict with the witness of Scripture concerning Jesus Christ. Particularly does this happen when by way of the "God Himself" (or, in the older form, the divine nature) the subjection of the Son of God to the Father is relativized or obscured.

In theopaschitism the suffering in its quality as suffering of "God Himself" is placed in a perspective other than that in which we meet it in Scripture. Even when there is no question of denying the incarnation, the suffering is a suffering that takes place "within God Himself" and all that Scripture says about the suffering of Christ is understood in this light. It is wholly understandable that theopaschitism should flourish most in monophysitic soil. In monophysitism the human nature of Christ was pressed into the background by the supremacy of the divine nature and its accent on the "God Himself." Whatever took place in the incarnation and on the cross is then placed in this framework, and within *such* a framework there are indeed many possibilities: the dialogue, which virtually becomes a monologue, the tension, the con-

---

11. It must be remembered that not only the Nestorians but also the Arians took sharp issue with theopaschitism. Cf. W. Elert, *op. cit.*, p. 196.

flict. As Nestorianism abstracted the human nature from the unity
of the person, so in Barth's view the "God Himself" becomes the
decisive point of orientation and this sets up a tension which the
scriptural witness does not allow.

When Barth speaks of the suffering of God and even of an
"obedience of God," and this not as a bold manner of speaking but
as an *essential* element in the being of God over against the God-
concept of natural theology, he exceeds the boundaries of the
*revelation* which we have in Christ. The opposition to theopaschitism does not arise from the desire to separate the two natures
of Christ but from the realization of the uniqueness and unfathomableness of the union of the person to which there is no analogy. To conclude from this to a tension and an obedience in God
Himself, to an "above" and a "below" in Him, can only be characterized as speculation. However logical and obvious the theopaschitic conclusion may appear to be (is not Christ "vere homo
et *vere Deus?*"), it is an unacceptable conclusion. It wishes to introduce another dimension of thought into the reflection of the
Church than that with which we are confronted in the biblical
revelation concerning the subjection of Jesus Christ to the Father
as the Mediator between God and man. Most certainly we shall
never be able to comprehend the mystery of the person of Christ,
and neither the divine nature nor the human nature may ever be
abstracted from this unity. But it is precisely because of this incomprehensible mystery that we must clearly recognize the limitations that are here placed upon our thinking.

The whole witness of Scripture with respect to the suffering of
Christ *prevents* us from concluding in an apparently logical directness from the "vere Deus" to the "suffering of God." The above
noted fact that the fourth word of the cross has given theopaschitism occasion for peculiar exegeses (exegeses suggesting retreat!)
is like a beacon at sea. It may be attempted to avoid the "conflict"
in "God Himself" — as Barth endeavors with great exertion to do.
It is not possible, however, for this essential theopaschitism to stop
short at humility, humiliation, and obedience. If the fundamental thesis is to be taken seriously, a place will also have to be found
for curse, death, the wrath of God, and forsakenness by God. We
consider the theopaschitic "conclusion" to be unacceptable, not
because of Nestorianism, nor because of a natural God-concept

derived apart from revelation which thinks to know what God can and cannot do, but because of the life and death of Jesus Christ in his relationship to the Father. Its untenableness becomes manifest when it is confronted with the revelation concerning the *Mediator* Jesus Christ.

\* \* \*

In concluding from the "vere Deus" to the "God Himself" it is not possible to escape falling into difficulties with respect to the biblical conception of the *mediatorship* of Christ. The subjectivity of God in the whole of Christ's suffering cannot but obscure that mediatorship. How can this be avoided when God *Himself* is the subject of the suffering in substitutionary self-surrender? It hardly requires demonstration that in this view of Christ's suffering it becomes difficult to understand that Christ was under the *curse* of the law, that He endured the *wrath* of God, and that He was *forsaken* by God. These are realities which cannot be squared with the suffering of God in which He Himself is *the* subject of the suffering.

At this point it is important to observe that Scripture constantly refers to the relationship between Jesus Christ and the Father. Here the apparently logical conclusion drawn from the "vere Deus" is exposed as an error. In the New Testament this relationship of Christ to the Father occupies a decisive and all-controlling place. We read of His subjection to the will of the Father,[12] of the *command* which He received,[13] of his having been sent,[14] of the work that is given Him to do. We see Him constantly in *prayer* to the Father,[15] we see Him in all the variation and dramatic movement of His suffering and dying which climaxes in His being *forsaken* of God. Countless are the scripture references in which these ideas come to expression. Christ can do nothing of Himself (John 5:30), He proclaims that the Father is greater than He (14:28), He hears and receives from the Father (15:15), He has been

12. Cf. Heb. 10:7; Psalm 40:7-9, "I delight to do thy will, O my God"; John 4:34, "My meat is to do the will of Him who sent me"; cf. John 4:32; Matt. 26:40, 43; John 5:30, 36; 15:10; 17:4.
13. John 10:18, "this *charge* I have received from my Father."
14. John 4:34; 5:24; 10:36, 20:21. Concerning the *giving* of the only begotten Son cf. 3:16, 5:26; 10:29.
15. John 11:41-42; chapter 17.

sealed (6:27), sanctified (10:36), loved (17:23), and glorified (13:32) by the Father.

This is all very difficult to absorb into a theopaschitic conception which always has the tendency to arrive at a Christological view in which the "God Himself" brings more a monologue than a dialogue into being. The "God Himself" conception obscures the concreteness of the way of suffering in the course of which Christ can say that He is not alone because the *Father* is with Him (16:32) and can later give expression to His agonizing *forsakenness*.

It is possible, of course, to point to all these expressions as proving His purely human character and as denying His deity. In that case the subjection of the man Jesus to God is no problem. But when the Church saw that this subjection was associated with the "vere homo et *vere Deus*," this could not but lay upon her the responsibility of respecting the boundaries of revelation with the greatest scrupulousness. There was need for this care, for on one side Arianism, adoptionism, and Nestorianism threatened, and on the other side tritheism which endeavored by means of a "divisio" of the persons to arrive at simple conclusions. The latter problem occupied the attention of Abraham Kuyper in his discussion of the Constitutio Mediatoris, in the course of which he asked, "If there is indeed from eternity a Constitutio Mediatoris, how can we conceive of this to have taken place without falling into tritheism?"[16] He also speaks of the peril that "the persons in the eternal Being are so placed over against each other that there is danger of succumbing to tritheism."[17] It is clear that in the discussion of these problems both Bavinck and Kuyper wish to reckon with the *boundary* that has been established for our thinking.[18] This boundary lies in the acceptance of the harmony which exists between the deity of Christ and the Constitutio Mediatoris or, as Kuyper puts it, the "vocatio Messianica."[19]

The essential element in this harmony is one of *subordination*, of *subjection*. In the unfathomableness of this mystery it is revealed that He who is true and eternal God confronts us in the in-

---

16. Abraham Kuyper, *op. cit.*, Locus III, section 5.
17. *Ibid.*, Locus III, section 5.
18. H. Bavinck, *op. cit.*, III, p. 194.
19. A. Kuyper, *op. cit.*, Locus III, section 5.

carnation of the Word as the *Servant* of the Lord. The very incomprehensibleness of the mystery, however, forbids us to make it the point of departure for a series of conclusions in which the "God Himself" begins to function in determining the being of God, and that with special reference to His obedience and His suffering. This goes beyond the confession of the deity of Christ and constitutes an attempt to comprehend the incarnation. Once foot is set on this road there is no logical place at which to stop. The process of drawing conclusions must then be pursued to the end. It then becomes necessary to speak of what can and does happen *in* God in the way of curse, suffering, and *death*. In this connection it is eminently noteworthy that Barth frequently speaks about the "passion of God" but not so unqualifiedly of the "death of God."[20] This is a remarkable circumstance (symptomatic of the recoil!) which is hardly understandable in terms of his premises.

It is striking that Barth has combined his strong expressions about the suffering and the obedience of God in His vicarious undergoing of the judgment with a sharp rejection of any suggestion that there is a conflict within God. The seriousness with which he presses this point appears most clearly from the fact that, while he speaks of self-surrender, humility, and the suffering of judgment, he does *not* speak of God's self-limitation. This "God Himself" cannot do, because *in* the humiliation He remains wholly and completely the true God. It is in the way of His humiliation that we come to know who He really is. This self-humiliation reveals the essential, the deepest being of God. There is not in Him a sovereignty *as such,* nor is there in Him a glory *as such,* but His sovereignty and His glory are the sovereignty and the glory and the power revealed in His self-surrender. For this reason there is no question of *antinomy* in God, as also there can be no question of a surrender of His divine attributes as was taught in the kenosis theory of the 19th century. There is no change in God, for it is precisely in the way of humiliation and suffering that He stands revealed as the Unchangeable One.

---

20. Barth speaks of this only *indirectly* in the words, "even in such humiliation He was in the highest sense God; in this death He was in the highest sense alive," KD IV/1, p. 271. Thereafter Barth again speaks exclusively of "the suffering of God."

For the same reason God's obedience does not point to an antimony. This "hard" expression offends us because our natural thinking has not become subject to the revelation. The way between Christ's birth and His cross is not a strange intermezzo within the divinity of God. It is His full revelation. Therefore there is no contradiction, no paradox, no antinomy, no chasm in God betweeen His being as it is in itself and His action as Reconciler. He is *not* "wholly other" when He humiliates Himself in Christ. We may never speak of "God against God." There is a "self-surrender of God to man's contradiction of Him, His subjection of Himself to the judgment into which He has fallen in this contradiction,"[21] and the meaning of the incarnation becomes clear in Christ's forsakenness on the cross. But all these things do not ultimately involve a conflict of God with Himself. To say this would, according to Barth, be blasphemy.[22]

When God follows this path He proves thereby that He (He Himself) *can* do so and "that to do such lies wholly in His nature."[23]

It is understandable that Barth should at this point be reminded of Heinrich Vogel[24] who "almost" creates the impression of a "conflict" in God. In his Christology Vogel spoke of the "self-surrender of God to the contradiction of man against God,"[25] "to the curse of death of the contradiction," and of the "self-surrender of God to the powerlessness of death."[26] But he too adds that God reveals Himself precisely in this way "as that one simple truth in which there is no contradiction," and that God reveals His power in this manner. Herein lies the reason that Barth considers Vogel to have escaped after all from the idea of a "conflict" in God.

We face the fact, however, that for both Barth and Vogel the surrender to the contradiction (Barth) and to the "powerlessness of death" (Vogel) is transcended by the "omnipotence" of God.

By this means they wish to eliminate the idea of conflict within God. But the word "omnipotence" which appears here cannot perform this function. We have seen earlier that the idea of omnipotence, according to Barth, cannot add something "new" to

21. KD IV/1, p. 202.
22. *Ibid.*, p. 202.
23. *Ibid.*, p. 204.
24. *Ibid.*, p. 201.
25. H. Vogel, *Christologie*, I, 1949, p. 193.
26. *Ibid.*, p. 193.

God, for this would mean a return to the concept of omnipotence as we find it in natural theology. It can do no more than circumscribe *this* powerlessness of God revealed in the cross. The problem remains, therefore, and it receives even stronger acccentuation in connection with the *wrath,* the *curse* and the *forsakenness* which, according to the New Testament, fell upon Christ. It will not surprise us that others have without hesitation drawn from the "God Himself" the conclusion of a conflict in God.[27]

Essentially we see here the unavoidable consequences of modern theopaschitism. Barth contradicts them emphatically and doubtless this reveals the power of the scriptural witness which again and again keeps the consequences of human thinking from reaching full maturity. This may not keep us from pointing out, however, that the development of thought in and the tensions created by theopaschitism (Barth, Vogel, Gloege) reveal that a boundary was crossed which should not have been crossed. This boundary is not created by an inflexible God-concept. We must discern the boundary, rather, when a conclusion drawn from the incarnation to "God" as subject of suffering and death obscures the scriptural witness to Jesus Christ.

It will not suffice to say that in powerlessness and in death the *omnipotence* and the *life* of God are *revealed*.[28] We see the omnipotence and the sovereignty of God *in* the suffering and death of Christ but this does not mean that they are not to be distinguished from this suffering and death. It is not true that God's "omnipotence" can be defined Christologically in terms of Christ's suffering as though it were identical with the powerlessness in which God's love manifested itself. Greatly though the depths of the humiliation of Christ reveal God's justice and His love, it is not possible to conclude from the "powerlessness" and the "death" in this humiliation to a *new* insight into God's omnipo-

---

27. This happens, for instance, in a discussion of Vogel's *Christologie* by Gloege in "Gott im Widerspruch," *Theol. Lit. Zeitung,* 1951, pp. 79-90. He asks, "Does not the conception of contradiction [in God] need a final clarification, toward which Vogel has already made a beginning?" p. 89. According to Gloege there is indeed a contradiction within God which reaches its profoundest depth there "where God surrenders Himself to His own divine contradiction with which He overcomes the contradiction of man. God surrenders Himself - incomprehensibly - to His own No against sin. Here the horrible pinnacle is realized of the expression: Deus contra Deum!"
28. IV/1, p. 271.

tence. It is peculiar, moreover, that Barth himself in this connection says again and again that God's omnipotence is revealed in the fact that Jesus Christ is *Lord* over life and death, and then adds to this thought, "God, however, is powerlessness neither in whole nor in part, but is real power."[29] It appears that all depends on the content that is put into the concept "omnipotence." The biblical aspects of the true omnipotence of God, of His power and mighty sovereignty, cannot be suppressed and therefore they come to the fore time and again in the theology of the cross which Barth sets forth.

Barth has correctly observed that God's omnipotence does *not* mean that He can do "anything," that His power is "simply the sum of all conceivable possibilities," and that this by no means implies a *limitation* of His power.[30] Also Bavinck pointed this out when he wrote that Scripture nowhere limits the power of God,[31] but added that the nominalists made of this that God not only can do whatever He wills, but "can also will to do anything."[32] But this would mean a potentia absoluta which would sever God's might from His other attributes. This would be an unwarranted abstraction.[33]

By this rejection of a postestas absoluta as a "pure potentiality without any content"[34] on the part of both Barth and Bavinck, the message of the Scriptures concerning the power of God is protected against an abstract power concept. There is a difference, however, in the manner in which these two theologians arrive at this view. Bavinck concludes directly from the data of Scripture; Barth does so in terms of a specifically Christological conception. His opposition to "blind power"[35] as descriptive of God's might arises from his conception of God's power as revealed in *reconciliation*.[36] This is for him the only legitimate framework within which we can speak of God's omnipotence. Here lie the tensions in Barth's conception of divine "power." It is true that God's

---

29. K. Barth, *Grundrisz*, pp. 53, 56.
30. KD II/1, p. 599.
31. H. Bavinck, *op. cit.*, p. 215.
32. *Ibid.*, p. 216. Cf. James 1:13: apeíratos.
33. *Ibid.*, p. 217.
34. *Ibid.*, p. 216.
35. KD II/1, p. 662.
36. *Ibid.*, p. 663.

power is not limited to its manifestation in reconciliation for he distinguishes between God's omnipotence and His omnipresent activity,[37] but it is in reconciliation as the area in which God's power is revealed "that we must take our point of departure if we would rightly think and speak about God's omnipotence."[38] Here we learn to know the "ultimate depths of the being of God."[39] It is also here that the connection with theopaschitism is to be found. Therefore Barth can speak of God's omnipresent activity and at the same time protest against the speculation of "an omnipotent Being as such."[40] It is *in* the omnipotence of reconciliation that we meet the true God and thus learn to know Him as the Father who is the Almighty, the Creator of heaven and earth.

In all this a remarkable shift is discernible in what may be called the character of the theodicy. In a period of human history when "might" in the  view of many reveals demonic features,[41] Barth desires to point to *this* dimension of the power of God.

When Barth hears about the "omnipotence" of the state, he asks whether the fall of Christendom does not lie in the fact that it capitulated not only to the powers of this world in the respect which it has shown for the glory of that power, but especially to the idea of an "absolute power" in God. Has Christianity perhaps lost its ability to recruit followers because of this "natural" God-concept? Was it still possible for men to harmonize *this* power with the love of God?

Modern theopaschitism wants to open new perspectives here. It proposes a *Christological* interpretation of the *power* of God and

---

37. *Ibid.*, p. 662.
38. *Ibid.*, p. 663.
39. *Ibid.*
40. *Ibid.*, p. 662.
41. Cf. K. Barth, *Grundrisz*, p. 54, about the "intoxicating thought" of might *as such* and the related reference to Hitler who also called God "the Almighty." "*Der* Almachtige, that is the chaos, evil, it is the devil," p. 54. This "omnipotence" of being able to do "anything" is the *tohu wabohu* which God left behind Him. Might as such is nothing more than the revolution of nihilism. As over against this, the power of God is "the power of His free love in Jesus Christ." We must observe His *work*, His action, "as the sum total of all that which is called God's ability, His freedom and His possibility."

thereby a central and radical correction of the natural power concept. It proposes a *theodicy of the cross.*[42]

\* \* \*

This theodicy of the cross as the deepest background of the theology of the cross concerns itself with the *true* God who is now no longer obscured by the tension created by the incompatibility between His power and His love. The opposition to the "potestas absoluta" of natural theology has led to the construction of a Christological power concept (cross, death, and curse) in which the suffering of God reveals that His being is *without antinomy.*

It is not possible, however, consistently to retain the cross as the epistemological principle for the understanding of God's "power." The Bible relates the power of God also to the divine act of raising Christ from the dead. And it speaks of the sovereignty and the power of God in connection with the *will* and the *command* of God for the Son, of the *sending* of the Son and of the *work* that has been given Him to do, and of the Servant of the Lord, the Man of sorrows in whose life the *good pleasure* of God to bruise Him and put Him to grief was executed.

These biblical aspects became vague and obscure when from the "vere Deus" the unqualified conclusion is drawn that God is *the* subject of suffering. The transgression of the boundaries of the unique mystery become apparent here. It manifests itself in confusion and leads to the asking of the question that has been put at the fringe of the Church: How can *God* be forsaken of *God?*

When we decline to take this step beyond the indicated boundaries it is possible, of course, to stand exposed to the danger of abstracting the human nature of Christ from the unity of His person. It is possible to fall into the abyss of Arianism, adoptionism, Nestorianism, and even tritheism. But these not imaginary dangers may not tempt us to take the forbidden step. In the theodicy of the cross — often remarkably restrained in its drawing of ul timate conclusions — lies the *extreme* consequence of the Christological God-concept, noetically and ontically, in that it unmistak-

---

42. How seriously we must take this thought in Barth appears from the fact that the "humiliation" of God, His "self-surrender," and all that is related to it is a matter "beside which the theodicy question becomes perfectly pale," KD IV/1, p. 271. Cf. *Grundrisz*, pp. 126, 139, 140.

ably tends to describe the tensions of the power concept with *one* qualification where the Bible constantly speaks with *two*. And when it does so there is no question of a "potestas absoluta et inordinata."

In the crisis of contemporary power concepts there is every reason not to forget that the comfort which God gives us on our way into the future is filled with promises of his *omnipotent* protection. As little as we are warranted in constructing a "natural" God-concept in terms of human conceptions of power, so little are we warranted in allowing the problem of human usurpations of power to cast a shadow over the confession of the omnipotence of God.

The same apostle who speaks about the weakness of God (and about the foolishness of God)[43] speaks also about the riches of His grace which He lavished upon us (Eph. 1:8).

Not a vague and incomprehensible potestas absoluta, but the scriptural conception of God the Father, the Almighty, Creator of heaven and earth gives us to understand why Isaiah, in the midst of the comfort which he extends, can write, "Have you not known? Have you not heard? The Lord is the everlasting God, the Creator of the ends of the earth. He does not faint or grow weary, his understanding is unsearchable" (Isa. 40:28).

\* \* \*

It is striking to note in the present connection that the Bible, without in any way prejudicing the power of God, can speak in a very strong manner about what God *cannot do*. We read that God cannot *deny Himself* (II Tim. 2:13).

We meet this thought in a context that speaks of God's *faithfulness*. What God cannot do is not in Scripture deduced from a humanly constructed naturalistic God-concept, but from His true

---

43. We think here of the appeal to 1 Cor. 1 by the theology of the cross: the foolishness of God is wiser than men and the weakness of God is stronger than men (in connection with the *weakness* of preaching). Paul is concerned not only about an antithesis between weakness and might, but also about the antithesis between folly and wisdom. We may therefore not isolate "weakness" from "foolishness." God has made the *wisdom* of the world foolishness (I Cor. 1:20) and has brought salvation through the "foolishness" of preaching. The motif of "powerlessness'" has not infrequently been unwarrantedly *isolated* from 1 Cor. 1. This does not mean, of course, that the tremendous critical and antithetical proclamation against human folly may ever be allowed to lose any of its significance for us.

being as God in His faithfulness to Himself. In the passage concerned, denial is a human possibility ("if we deny Him") which does indeed correspond to a divine denial ("He will also deny us"), but which excludes all arbitrariness for He remains *the same* and "cannot deny Himself."

Undoubtedly Barth wishes to point to this scriptural witness concerning the immutability of God when he rejects the idea of self-limitation in God. This is impossible in God because, according to Barth's view, it is precisely in the *humiliation* that He remains the same. Hence Barth's protest against the idea of *conflict* in God.

Barth refers, as we noted, to the idea of a conflict in God as blasphemy. Within the framework of this sharp criticism of the idea of a conflict within God Himself there appears to be room, however, for commanding and obedience, for judgment and death in reference to God. For this reason his protest against a conflict in God is no guarantee that this new form of theopaschitism does not become speculative. Where Gloege speaks of "Deus contra Deum," Barth speaks of the realities of wrath and judgment. That this affects God Himself but does not involve His self-limitation or a conflict within Himself only confirms Barth in his view that God is *such* a God as He has revealed Himself to be in *His suffering*.

\* \* \*

In our analysis in Chapter V we pointed out that Barth's thesis of the deity of Christ as the noetic principle for determining who God is has far-reaching consequences for his understanding of the humiliation and the exaltation of Christ. Barth is fully aware of the implications of this position.

In terms of this conception it is no longer possible to speak of a process that moves from humiliation to exaltation, but already *in* the humiliation Christ's exaltation and glorification take place!

The reason for this is clear. Barth's fundamental idea in his doctrine of reconciliation is that God's glory is revealed *in* the humiliation, His power *in* weakness, His life *in* death. Barth himself speaks — quite correctly — of a "very decisive innovation"[44] be-

---

44. KD IV/1, p. 145.

cause in the Reformation doctrine of the two states of Christ's life there clearly obtained a *temporal* element. It was not denied that Christ's entire life revealed a glory and a beauty which the eye of faith could discern.[45] But *this* glory of the incarnate Word nowhere in the New Testament leads to an obscuring of the decisive transition from humiliation to exaltation which took place at the resurrection. When this transition is obscured all that we can still speak of on the score of Christ's exaltation is the "unveiling" of the *previously existing* divine glory. Thinking consistently in this line would require that we see already in the time of His humiliation the presence of His unlimited power and life. This would mean losing from sight, however, the full emphasis which the New Testament places on the *temporal* aspect involved in the progression from humiliation to exaltation. It is precisely this emphasis which Barth's intertwining of Christ's natures with His states is not able fully to honor.

Christ's transfiguration on the mount appears as a momentary interruption of the state of humiliation, which is emphasized by Luke when he lays full emphasis on the events subsequent to this happening (Luke 9:28-45). Christ Himself speaks of His having to *enter* into glory through suffering (Luke 24:26). The epistles also strongly stress the temporal stages involved in Jesus' humiliation and exaltation, as is evident from Philippians 2 in its reference to Christ's form as a servant and to the name which He *receives,* and in Peter when he speaks of the witness of the Spirit concerning the suffering of Christ and the glory that would "follow."[46]

Barth speaks of the offense which his teaching will create especially at this point.[47] This offense cannot be dissociated from the fact that it is not possible, in faithfulness to the New Testament, to replace the transition from humiliation to glory with the idea of the *unveiling* of Christ's (already existing) glory. This, however, is Barth's central idea because he sees the glory in the humiliation. Therefore he writes that humiliation and glory fill

---

45. Cf. John 1:14, 1 John 1:1.
46. 1 Peter 1:11, Heb. 1:3ff., 2:9-10.
47. KD IV/1, p. 146.

the *whole* of Christ's existence and may not be distributed over various phases of His life.[48]

It would certainly be unwarranted to identify Barth's teaching on this point with the 19th century criticism of the doctrine of the two states of Christ. An instructive comparison with the criticism of Schleiermacher suggests itself, however, because of his criticism of the traditional doctrine in terms of the *impossibility* of a real humiliation on the part of God who is "absolutely the highest and the eternal and therefore necessarily ever the same." Barth formulates his objection differently. He does not deny the humiliation. On the contrary, it is the *real,* the *essentially divine* element, the *honor,* the *greatness,* the *glory,* the *depth* of God's being. This necessarily allows him to speak only of an *unveiling* of Christ's glory and prevents him from holding to two phases in Christ's life with a real difference in "glory."

The New Testament speaks of more than an unveiling. This is evident from the connection which it lays between humiliation and exaltation in the name above every name which is given to Christ (Phil. 2:10, Acts 2:36). *This* glory *follows* that of His previous state in which distress and suffering filled His life, "Now is my soul troubled. And what shall I say, 'Father, save me from this hour'? No, for this purpose I have come to this hour. Father, glorify *thy name*" (John 12:27).

It is therefore not possible for a theology of the cross, with its conception of the glory of God *in* the humiliation, to oppose the doctrine of the two states of Christ and to put in its place an intertwined conception of natures and states. The humiliation of Christ as the noetic unveiling of the *being* of God (His suffering and His obedience) leads to positions in which it is no longer possible to do full justice to the historically real progression from humiliation to exaltation as a decisive happening in the reconciling work of Christ. The question must be asked whether this "unveiling" does not press into the background the historical significance of curse and death in the reconciliation, and whether justice is done here to what the Church confesses concerning the *meritorious work* of Christ.

\* \* \*

---

48. *Ibid.,* p. 146.

This brings us to Barth's conception of man's death and judgment in their relationship to the triumph of grace.

The emphasis and the frequency with which Barth asserts that the substitutionary work of Christ does *not* mean that we do *not* come under judgment are striking. The judgment *includes our dying,* and, in view of Christ's work, we have no future anymore. This can even be said to set forth the heart of Barth's idea of substitution. The difficulty here is to understand the expression "in our place" which occupies an important place in Barth's thinking. The question is whether the content which Barth gives to this phrase correctly sets forth the richness of reconciliation. One gains the impression time and again that it has a wholly different meaning for him than it has in the confesson of the Church. The Church confesses "not we, but He" as the *essential* element in Christ's vicarious suffering. Sometimes Barth gives the impression that he wishes to express this thought also as, for instance, when he speaks about the *exchange.*[49] But from everything it appears that this exchange does not exclude but *includes* our extinction. God *did not want* this man any longer who had surrendered to the chaos. He gave expression to this not in the form of a protest, but in the "form of the extinction which He effected."[50]

Here we face not an attitude of God, but "the completion of this rejection."[51]

In that judgment over man the forgiveness of sins takes place, because this man who was abolished in the judgment of God, snatched away in the death of Christ, is again "brought on the scene"[52] in the resurrection of Christ. The substitution of Christ lies for Barth not in the "not *we* but *He*" as the confessions of the Reformation teach, but in the resurrection of the *new* man, while the *old* man is struck by the catastrophe and thereby *disappears, no longer has a future.*[53]

In this conception of Christ's substitutionary work (which Barth has not, to the best of my knowledge, related directly to Ro-

---

49. Cf. *Grundrisz,* p. 135; *Die Wirklichkeit des neuen Menschen,* Heft 27 of *Theologische Studien,* 1950.
50. KD IV/1, p. 100.
51. *Ibid.*
52. *Ibid.,* p. 101.
53. *Ibid.,* p. 326. Cf. our analysis in chapter V.

mans 6)[54] the triumph of reconciliation lies expressed. In terms
of this view of the resurrection of the new man Barth polemicizes
sharply against every conception in which the great event is realized *in us,* that is, in later time, as though it had not *objectively*
and *actually* become a reality in Christ's death and resurrection.

Here Barth allies himself with the consistent polemic of the
Reformation against Rome and against every view which regards
the realization of reconciliation as a *second* mystery, a second and
*independent* action which was not included directly in the reconciling work of Christ.

In this connection Barth strongly emphasizes that justification
is not through works but through faith. He sets forth this emphasis with a penetrating analysis of all refined conceptions of
work-righteousness which have both in the Church and in theology
played so powerful a role. Over against this he confesses the decisive miracle of the triumph of reconciliation. "The 'It is finished'
is objectively true in the whole of its significance."[55] Our knowledge of this fact is limited, it is true, but "its reality is not limited."[56]

"The victory has been achieved but is not yet fully known. The
checkmate of the opponent cannot be prevented anymore, but He
plays the game to the end to convince every man that he has been
defeated. The hour has struck but the pendulum is still in mo-
tion."[57] The good news goes out to man: You *have* died! You, old
man, you, still living in the closing hours of this aeon, "you who
have not yet been reached by the tidings of victory, you foolish one
who continues to play the game that is already lost." This is the
promise that sanctifies. We still live in the shadow of sin which
in Christ has been forgiven and taken away.[58] But what can this
man still produce in the way of evil and error that God has not
already taken seriously?[59] Here lies the basis for the "infallible,
the unshakable certainty of the Christian." This is the air in
which he can breathe.[60] Our cause has become the cause of

54. Cf. my *De Sakramenten,* 1954, chapter VI.
55. K. Barth, *Die Wirklichkeit des neuen Menschen,* p. 23.
56. *Ibid.,* p. 23.          59. *Ibid.,* p. 29.
57. *Ibid.*                  60. *Ibid.*
58. *Ibid.,* p. 28.

Christic.[61] Reconciliation is not a partial, faulty human achievement. It is the divine reconciliation, it is reality because of the omnipotence of God who in humiliation, suffering, death, curse, and actual judgment took upon *Himself* the judgment that we deserved.

Of this fact the justified sinner is *witness*. Reconciliation never becomes a forgotten chapter in the book of our life but continues to involve the acknowledgment of our guilt which in the reconciliation has once and for all been borne away. It is in this way — that reconciliation is revealed as *God's* triumph and confessed as *His* victory in the world.

\* \* \*

The divine *"self-surrender"* in powerlessness and death, in shame and judgment, envisions the "report of victory" in the eschatological situation, the departure of the shadows and the victory of light. Its purpose, in short, is *the gospel*. In Barth's doctrine of reconciliation all problems can, in the final analysis, be reduced to the relationship in which the gospel stands to *the law*.

Is it possible to give a place to the law next to the gospel? Is there room for any new happening subsequent to the triumph of reconciliation?[62] Here we come anew upon Berkhof's objections which include the charge that in the preaching of middle-orthodoxy, as influenced by Barth, there is no room any longer for the *law* to function,[63] that it, at all events, has no *accusing* function any more.[64]

This objection must be seen on the background of Barth's view that the law is nothing more than the *form* of the gospel, a conception which has many consequences. It is not accidental that Barth inverts the traditional order of "law and gospel" to "gospel and law."[65]

---

61. *Ibid.*, p. 16.
62. K. Barth, "Evangelium und Gesetz," *Theologische Existenz heute*, No. 32.
63. H. Berkhof, *Crisis der Midden-orthodoxie*, p. 29.
64. *Ibid.*, p. 29.
65. K. Barth, "Evangelium und Gesetz," in: *Theol. Existenz heute*, No. 32. Cf. also KD II/2, pp. 567ff. and III/4, section 52. For criticism on this transposition cf. P. Althaus, *Gebot und Gesetz*, 1952, pp. 24ff.; W. Elert, "Gesetz und Evangelium" in *Zwischen Gnade und Ungnade*, 1948; H. Thielecke, "Zur Frage: Gesetz und Evangelium," in *Theologie der Anfechtung*, 1949; E. Brunner, *Der Mensch im Widerspruch*, pp. 532ff.

The distinction between gospel and law involves, according to Barth, a distinction within the one word of God. It is not possible to have the law without the gospel and vice versa. The question why we must speak with these *two* words Barth answers by pointing to the gospel as the gospel of sovereign *grace.* In Jesus Christ our human nature has been justified and accepted, and grace triumphed over our lost condition. The law is to be distinguished from the good news of this gospel, but not as a *second* entity standing outside of the gospel. Then the law would be "complementary" to the gospel and would be significant independently of it.

This is not possible, however, since the law has meaning only because of the divine exercise of grace. In this the word of God as *law* has its foundation. When we consider God's election of man the question arises, what does God want with this elect man? The answer is that the electing God gives to elect man his "vocation."[66] When grace governs, it also *commands.* For this reason the law can be called the *form* of the gospel. "How could the lordship of Jesus Christ be proclaimed unless that proclamation as such constituted a demand for obedience?"

The gospel *necessarily* assumes the form of *law,* or, as Barth formulates it in his discussion of ethics, "the one word of God is gospel according to its content, and law as concerns its form."[67] The gospel includes the law and, because of grace, automatically assumes the form of law, of command. Where grace rules, the gospel as command points man to his sanctification and to his future. The covenant therefore is not exhausted by election, but this election "itself and as such"[68] desires to be understood as a *command* directed to man. Therefore Barth can, immediately after setting forth his doctrine of election, treat extensively of "God's command." In this order, the order "gospel and law" finds reflection.

\* \* \*

This order is further emphasized in that Barth points out that the sin of which man becomes guilty in his contact with the *law* is

66. KD II/2, p. 567.
67. *Ibid.,* p. 567.
68. *Ibid.*

specifically this, that man believes that he himself can fulfill the law.[69] He does not realize that God's demand (in the law) is a witness to the righteousness which He Himself has realized for us in Christ.[70] He does not see that the law proclaims our justification by God. Now that is precisely "the decisive element in the law, the content of which the law is only the form,"[71] namely, healing and sanctifying grace. Of the divine "thou shalt" we have made the human "you must."[72] In so doing we are no longer able to understand the law as being the form of the gospel, but we understand it as a law which *we* have to fulfill. This is the reason for Barth's inversion of the order: *first* the gospel and *then* the law, *this* law.

The command follows and is included in the election. The "victory report" of election is the foundation on which the law rests as a call to sanctification. For this reason it may, in the life of the Church and in the proclamation, take its point of departure only in election, in the irrevocable fact of the "God *with* us" and the "God *for* us." The command must be seen against this background. It must be seen as directed against our unwillingness to live in terms of grace, of this grace of election.

When Berkhof sees the law in its accusing function absent in much preaching and relates this to Barth's conception of the relationship between gospel and law, Barth might reply that he wishes fully to respect the law in its accusing aspect. This is no answer to Berkhof's criticism, however, because, according to Barth, this accusing function belongs exclusively to the law *as form of* the gospel. This is really the point at issue in Barth's inversion of the traditional order. He himself is conscious of the fact that in this conception he departs from Luther who laid so strong an emphasis on the accusing function of the law, but i⁻ quite a different sense than he does.

For Barth the law can have a function only *within* and *in terms of* the gospel of reconciliation. When Berkhof in this connection speaks of the danger of "cheap grace" he does not, of course, ignore Barth's strong emphasis — because of election — on command

---

69. *Evangelium und Gesetz*, p. 7.
70. *Ibid.*, p. 10-11.
71. *Ibid.*, p. 16.
72. *Ibid.*, p. 18.

and sanctification. He means that the preaching of the power of grace, of its factuality, can lead to viewing grace as cheap not simply because it can be bought without money and without price (Isa. 55:1) but because there really is no "buying" at all when the kerugma of the gospel shrinks to a simple announcement of *accomplished fact.*

It is true that Miskotte, in answer to Berkhof's criticism, has pointed out that Barth also wishes to do justice to the order "law — gospel." Barth has in fact said that also this order has its good right of existence.[73] He immediately adds to this, however, "This may in no case be determinative for the whole of the doctrine which we wish to set forth here."[74] Later he writes that the distinction "law — gospel" is "legitimate and meaningful."[75] Must we see a concession to criticism here, or does this admission *really* mean "*gospel* and law?"

The context clearly indicates the answer. Man, by not hearing the gospel in the law, pursues his own righteousness in denying that Christ is the *end* of the law.[76] That is our real, our fundamental sin.[77] The gospel is the victory over this our real sin, the sin of unbelief. The law which has been abused but which remains in force places us under judgment, but Jesus Christ turns this judgment into our justification.[78] It is in this connection that Barth calls the order "law — gospel" meaningful. "Through the *content* of the gospel, that is, through Himself, He awakens us to the life of faith in Him who justifies us, but we who are awakened to this life are men who through the *form* of the gospel, that is, through the law, were condemned and cast out into hell in all the nakedness and ugliness of our rejected existence."[79]

[That is] a very involved sentence, but one which makes plain that for him the order "law — gospel" does *not* mean a concession to criticism. He maintains that the order "law — gospel" cannot be determinative because it is the law precisely as the law of the *gospel* that judges man's existence. Within the circle of triumphant grace *this* law as form of the gospel has its place. There can be no question of any function of the law prior to the gospel or prior to the

---

73. *Ibid.*, p. 18.
74. *Ibid.*
75. *Ibid.*, p. 3.
76. *Ibid.*

77. *Ibid.*, p. 27.
78. *Ibid.*, p. 26.
79. *Ibid.*, p. 27.

actuality of grace and justification.[80] When the law accuses it does so against the self-justification which, in the reality of election as content of the gospel, stands revealed as meaningless.

\* \* \*

The background of Barth's emphasis on *"gospel* and *law"* is, it would seem, entirely plain when his whole dogmatics is taken into account. He is concerned about the one word of God which can be described as law (form) and gospel (content). This constitutes a peculiar dogmatic synthesis. Miskotte has pointed out that Barth himself warns against every form of systematic "synthesis." But in the connection which he has laid between the law *as form* and the gospel *as content* he has indeed presented such a "synthesis," as the words "form" and "content" plainly indicate.[81]

There is in Barth's view no room for a law prior to and independent of the gospel because such a law must always lead to self-justification. There is not such a thing as a relatively independent law or ordinance which is knowable as a sort of "law of nature" alongside of God's "word of grace."[82] The question of good and evil does not arise from an abstract law. It can be known and answered only "through the cross and the resurrection of Jesus Christ."[83] Ethics is the "ethics of grace" or it is no theological ethics.[84] God established His command *in grace* and in no other manner. Only where grace is "event and revelation"[85] can the law be promulgated. The law as the *form* of the gospel, as the "dress" of the gospel, is *always* "veiled repetition of the reality of grace and of the promise of grace."[86]

---

80. For this reason Barth will probably not accept what Berkhof writes about "the law as a relatively independent entity," *Crisis der Midden-orthodoxie,* p. 29. He will agree with Berkhof's later observation, however, that "The Gospel must be concretely revealed in its unmasking power. When this is done, we occupy ourselves with the law," p. 30. This unmasking occupies a prominent place in Barth as the unmasking of unbelief with respect to the gospel.

81. Miskotte in *De Waagschaal,* Vol. 7, No. 16) points to KD I/1, p. 187 where Barth writes about the establishing of the covenant in Exodus 19 and 20, and Jeremiah 31, "that a systematic synthesis of both is an impossibility." It must be remembered, however, that precisely in this connection Barth speaks about God's wrath and judgment as "only the hard shell, the opus alienum of divine grace," p. 187.

82. Cf. Barth's polemic against Brunner in KD III/4, pp. 20ff.

83. KD II/2, p. 595.

84. *Ibid.,* 598.

85. *Ibid.,* p. 624.

86. *Ibid.,* p. 625.

For Barth, law never precedes gospel, grace, and reconciliation, as though grace first appears when the law has been transgressed. This priority of the law to the gospel which comes to such clear expression in Question 9 of the Heidelberg Catechism, is wholly wanting in Barth's view of the law. In frequent and varied polemics he opposes this "freeing" of the law from grace, because in this way the law can only lead to attempts at self-justification. Law without grace, law as a "law of nature," can have no other result. There is therefore also no room in Barth's conception for the view that man was placed under the law of the good Creator before the fall into sin and unrighteousness. Just as the goodness of God's creation must be seen Christologically, so God's command is the command of His *reconciling* grace. Law is the form of the gospel and therefore it may be said that Paul's opposition to the Judaistic idea of law and self-justification creates for him the decisive antithetical framework in terms of which he views the total relationship between God and man without thereby feeling any need of different "epochs" in the history of redemption.

Althaus has not without warrant spoken of the "epochlessness in his (Barth's) understanding of God's action."[87] This is the reverse side of Barth's Christological thinking noetically *and ontically*. Corresponding to this is the deep connection that is discernible between Barth's "supralapsarianism" and his conception of "*gospel and law.*" His fundamental point of view does not permit the order "law and gospel" to be determinative for it has never been this and never will be. Only in terms of the gospel can we speak of the judgment of the law as the form of grace, a judgment of which Barth can write, "Whatever the course of this judgment may be, whatever man may reveal himself really to be in this judgment, this is certain — God judges him because He wants to treat him as *His*.[88] In the judgment of God's triumph manifests itself, and *His* decision comes to realization in our confrontation with God's command.[89] Because of this fact, because of this triumph over our entire life, we are *objectively* called to faith.[90] We are not bound by an abstract

---

87. P. Althaus, *Gebot und Gesetz*, 1952, p. 25. This statement remains true, even when one considers that the idea of epochs can be used in many and even in wrong ways and that such is perhaps the case in Althaus.
88. KD II/2, p. 822. Cf. p. 855: grace as the "presupposition" of judgment.
89. *Ibid.*, p. 831.
90. *Ibid.*, p. 857.

law to which we must give a positive content. We are bound by the "mandatum concretissimum."[91] There is not an *unknown* but a *known* command of God,[92] the command of *His* decision, of *His* grace. Our righteousness does not consist in a self-willed fulfilling of the law[93] for the law *has been* fulfilled. It is in this light that we must see the accusing function of the law. Its purpose is to bring us to the true fulfillment of the command which God has given, namely, living in terms of His decision and of His grace.

\* \* \*

The triumph of reconciliation is therefore of decisive significance for the place of the law *within* the framework of the gospel. The debate between Berkhof and Barth touches the very foundation of Barth's dogmatics and the character of the proclamation. The question of "cheap grace" has, in the nature of the case, nothing to do with a closing of God's eyes to sin or with a denial of guilt. (This thought is wholly foreign to Berkhof.) Rather, it finds its center in the completeness of the divine triumph. If anywhere, it appears here that all aspects of the triumph of grace in Barth's theology are concerned to set forth the nature of the one divine triumph. As in the universality of the triumph, the "self-evident" character of salvation is at stake.[94] This comes to expression particularly in connection with the dynamics of the proclamation. Salvation is not, from our point of view, self-evident. Rather, it is the unassailable actuality of God's free action that makes man's relationship to salvation "self-evident." This lies included in the divine triumph of reconciliation, in that deep mystery in which God has taken upon Himself what man deserved.

In this ultimate of love-in-action in God's self-humiliation His being is revealed. This He can do, this His omnipotence, His true, real power can do. It is the radical execution, the concentration, of judgment upon Himself — in Christ — to the point of death, the death of the cross. The law can do no more than function as the form of *this* gospel. It is the law which accuses us and unmasks us in our unwillingness to live in the strength of this grace alone.

---

91. *Ibid.*, p. 745.
92. *Ibid.*, p. 747.
93. *Ibid.*, p. 773.
94 H. Berkhof, *op. cit.*, p. 38.

"God is humble and man is still proud!" Augustine exclaimed. One might be inclined to describe Barth's conception of the relationship between gospel and law, and of the proclamation and election, as the consciously theopaschitic systematization of this word of Augustine. It would not be doing either Barth or Augustine justice, however, so to construe Barth and on the basis of this parallel give a place to his view in the dogma-historical and ecclesiastical tradition. To do this would require either that we give a consistently theopaschitic interpretation to Augustine's expression, or that we eliminate from Barth's conception that which is most essential to it: the suffering, the self-surrender, the humility, the obedience of God as *the* revelation of what is possible for God, the revelation of His true power.

* * *

It is understandable that in our century theopaschitism should assert itself with great force. The confusion attending the effort to understand the living God in His dealings with men today makes it an attractive solution to many problems. There are also those who feel that theopaschitism in its *Christological* form is not the answer to the theodicy problems of our time, but that this answer is to be found in the proclamation of the *now* suffering God. This is a point of view with which we have not occupied ourselves in this exposition and which has no place at all in Barth's theology.

Care must be exercised not only in our approach to any "theodicy" but also with respect to the obscurations that can attend a true theodicy. The offense, the skandalon, over which man stumbles does not lie in the power of God as Scripture sets this forth. Our view of the wonderful power of God (is *anything* too hard for the Lord, Gen. 18:14) can only be obscured when we do not see Him in His love and the fulness of all His virtues. When this is wanting in our God-concept the "powerlessness" of man can make for a life of embitterment and gloom. In praising God we praise also His power, and reaction against the "potentia absoluta" may not lead us to ignore all that the Old and the New Testaments tell us about the power-aspects of God in creation and redemption. It is the message of the Church that the comfort of this power in dark and apocalyptic times is revealed via the cross.

When in the new theopaschitism this comfort is seen only in terms of the deepest humiliation and suffering of God we must remember that the incarnation of the Word and that the cross of Jesus Christ summon us to see the great mystery of the *love* of God. It is for the sake of the ineffableness and the greatness of this mystery that we must respect the scriptural limits that surround it.

# XII

## THE TRIUMPH OF THE END

IT REMAINS to give some particular attention to Barth's view of
the triumph of grace in its eschatological aspect. In our analysis
of Barth's eschatology we saw that this subject confronts us with
the important question of the nature of eternal life.[1] In Barth's theology this means centrally the problem of the *limitation* of our human life, which, in his judgment, belongs to the good creation, to
human nature as such. We observed how strongly Barth emphasizes the eschatological triumph over chaos and death over against
the *continuation* of our human life in a non-ending "eternity."
This emphasis (in contrast to the idea of continuity) was described as the "eternalizing" of our finite life.

\* \* \*

That this is not simply a playing with words appears from G. C.
Van Niftrik's summary of Barth's eschatological views. He writes
that, according to Barth, eternal life cannot possibly be understood
as a new beginning, as the continuation and development of human
life in a time after death.[2] When the last trump shall have sounded
there will be a present *without a thereafter.* Nothing will follow
the introduction of this present because there will not be time anymore. "The eschatological expectation does not mean the continuation of human life in an unending future, but the *eternalizing* of
this our *ending* life."[3]

It is clear that all depends here on the meaning of the word "eternalize." What is certainly not meant is the atheistic idea of "dead is
dead." What is meant rather is the understanding of the *limitation*
of human life as part of the *good* creation. The question that we

---

1. Cf. Chapter VI.
2. G. C. Van Niftrik, *Zie de Mens,* 1951, p. 494.
3. *Ibid.,* p. 494.

must ask here is whether in this triumph of the end we see the light of the biblical proclamation concerning the future reflected.

* * *

It is not surprising that the idea of the "eternalizing" of human life as contrasted with its continuation attracted wide attention.[4]

In view of Barth's positive expressions on this score it was hardly to be expected that in some circuitous way he would again return to the idea of continuation. It is therefore important to take note of H. Vogel's criticism of Barth in this connection. Vogel is particularly disturbed about Barth's view of the "having-been" of human life. His concern is obviously caused by the fact that in this conception he sees the confession of the Church with respect to eternal life threatened.[5]

"The thesis of Barth that man after his temporal being and existence has no further being and existence to look forward to, must be challenged." He knows, of course, that Barth emphatically teaches that "God is my beyond." He asks what we must understand by the word "my" in this expression.[6] In his opinion, Barth's idea of man's "having-been" is in conflict with the positive teaching of the Church, namely, the *life everlasting*.

We do read in Paul that this mortal must put on immortality. The identity of the old man with the new man is doubtless a possibility that only God can envision. This does not alter the fact, however, that man looks forward in hope to "a new being in a new existence."[7] Even when Barth calls the "having-been" a *modus* of

---

4. In O. Weber's *Karl Barths Kirchliche Dogmatik*, 1950, covering the work up to III/2, the weight of this problem does not come to expression, although the problem clearly appears in III/2. The second edition, 1952, up to and including III/4, notes it only in passing (pp. 178-179), and gives no indication of the importance which the problem has for Barth. In other discussions of III/2 the "strangeness" of Barth's conception comes to expression. As an example we mention J.B. Soucek's article, "Man in the Light of the Humanity of Jesus," *Scottish Journal of Theology*, March, 1949, p. 81, where he speaks of a "difficult exegesis" and asks: "Is not the Christian hope too much narrowed down, until it becomes a quite unimaginable moment of meeting with God or an elevation of the mere finite, past and not-to-be-continued existence of man into the light of God's grace, God's forgiveness and God's purpose?" Meanwhile, he awaits "further explanation."

5. H. Vogel, "Ecce Homo. Zur Anthropologie Karl Barths" in: *Verkündigung und Forschung*, 1949/50, p. 119ff. Vogel's criticism is the more surprising because he wholly agrees with Barth's fundamental point of view, namely, the relationship between Christology and Anthropology.

6. *Ibid.*, p. 126.

7. *Ibid.*

being, this is not for Vogel an answer to his question. For him eschatology means "both ontically and with respect to the future"[8] a *new* creation, a *new* heaven, and a *new* earth.

When this perspective is wanting there is not, in Vogel's view, a real eschatological triumph over death.

Barth's strong opposition to any and every idea of neutral continuation of human life in the sense of immortality is striking. Van Niftrik speaks in the same vein when he writes that on the basis of Scripture we cannot hold to more than the eternalizing of our *real* and only life (in time!) and the glorification of the "life of man, which, in its time, *was* in Christ."[9] He warns against "pagan dreams of glory in a time after human death."[10] In short, Barth reacts sharply against a "naturalistic" doctrine of immortality, but *in* this reaction he clearly arrives at a new solution: eternalization *over against* continuation.

Obviously this reaction to pagan dreams of glory and immortality does not bring us a step further in the understanding of the problem of the "vita eterna."

Also Calvin warned against the "diabolical furor of immortal fame," but this in no wise brought him to the conclusion that the mortality of man belongs to man's essential nature. Our concern is not with dreams, or with subjective projections on the screen of an endless-time idea, or with a repristination of the conception of immortality as the Enlightenment understood it, but with the reality of eternal life about which the Scriptures speak with so much emphasis. It is hardly possible to disagree with Vogel when on the score of this scriptural teaching he points to its clear character in the writings of Paul, in the Apocalypse, and in the Gospels. The Bible can be understood only on the presupposition of continuity.

---

8. *Ibid.*, p. 127. Note also his criticism in *Vox Theologica*, 1952, "Das Menschenbild im Neuen Testament" pp. 86-87, where he writes that Barth rejects "any form of existence for man beyond this life." In so doing Barth comes into conflict with the N.T. conception of hope "which gives man as the new creature in Christ (2 Cor. 5:17) the promise of a new existence and being in God's time, in eternity, and extends to him participation in the glory of the incarnate Son of God."

9. G. C. Van Niftrik, *op. cit.*, p. 495.

10. *Ibid.*

This continuity lies in the hand of God, it is true, but *in* that hand it will become reality.[11]

This is clearly expressed when the Bible speaks about the "thereafter" in connection with the new reality of eternal life. We think here particularly of the comfort which Paul presents when he writes that the sufferings of this present time are not worthy to be compared with the glory that is to be revealed *to us* (Rom. 8:18). Here the human subject is presupposed in the encouragement and comfort which are offered. Paul certainly is not interested in vague ideals of immortality. His interest is in the reality of salvation *in Christ,* in the *being with Him,* the always being with Him (I Thess. 4:17). This continuity is concerned with the becoming manifest of the sons of God (Rom. 8:19), with the children of God as heirs (8:17), with participation in Christ's glory (8:17, 30), with hope and expectation (8:25).

The Apocalypse also presents the future of eternal life in this light. It speaks of a not-being, of a having-been, a being-past of the first things (21:4), but this having-been does not exclude the reality of a new being. That which *will not be anymore* is death, sorrow, wailing, pain, the sea, night, the temple. These negative formulations point, however, to a *positive* reality which will be. They do so not in terms of a natural and self-evident ontology, but, for all that, very concretely: the descending of the New Jerusalem, the city of God, the tree of life, the new heaven and the new earth, the fountain of the water of life, the servants of God who will worship Him, and in this all "the dwelling of God *is with men.* He will dwell with them, and they shall be his people, and God himself will be with them" (21:5).

How, in this sharp eschatological light, must we conceive of the "eternalizing" of our life as distinct from its continuation? *Here* the having-been of the first things stands in indissoluble connection with renewal and glory. *This* having-been can be seen only against the eschatological background of the *new deeds of God.*

These things must be pointed out because only in this way can we seriously meet Barth's criticism of the idea of continuity. Vogel's

---

11. Barth had earlier himself written about this *abiding* subject, as in *Das Wort Gottes und die Theologie,* 1924, p. 97: "the Bible speaks of the bodily character of the resurrection, the new world. There is a change in the predicates: sown in changeableness, raised in unchangeableness. The subject abides."

criticism of Barth, we believe, rests on a right understanding of him. If Barth's view were no more than a sharply reacting criticism of the "natural" belief in immortality we would have no choice but to follow him. Otherwise we would not have understood the depths of the transition from death to life *in Christ*. When the significance of this transition is lost to view urgent admonition becomes necessary.

Such an interpretation would do injustice, however, to Barth's positive expressions. That is clear from the fact that he directly relates the "eternalizing" of our finite life to *Christology*, and particularly to the mortality of the man Jesus of Nazareth. With respect to his conclusion of the goodness of the mortal, limited, and finite human nature, therefore, no misunderstanding is possible.

If the *strangeness* of the idea of "eternalizing" still makes one hesitate as to whether he has understood Barth correctly (in spite of Vogel's criticism and the clear exposition of Van Niftrik) he cannot escape coming to certainty in view of Barth's decisive pointing to the once-having-been, to the *no-longer-being*, to our being "in God's mind," and not least through his accentuation (in this connection) of the decisive significance of the "here-and-now" for *ethics*.[12]

\* \* \*

The impression is created by Barth as well as by Van Niftrik that this "eternalizing" contains a thought which rests directly on Scripture. Van Niftrik points to I Cor. 15:53, *"this* perishable nature must put on the imperishable, and *this* mortal nature must put on immortality."[13] The word "this" italicized by Van Niftrik, however, *in no wise* implies the idea of "eternalizing" as over against the idea of continuity.

It is clear that Barth's earlier exegesis ("the subject continues") lies more in the line of Paul's words than the conclusion that "this

12. KD III/2, p. 272. Having established these relationships in III/2, Barth returns to the subject in his treatment of Ethics, III/4, section 56, where he treats extensively of the "once for all opportunity." Limitation is not to be regarded as an inferior something, it is not a curse, p. 651. It is of the essence of man to be "limited." Barth points to other parts of his dogmatics in which he speaks of this limitation: III/3, pp. 70-73, III/4, pp. 653, 657, 666, 669, 670, 676, 681, 682.

13. G. C. Van Niftrik, *op. cit.,* p. 494. Cf. Barth's reference to Rev. 10:6.

perishable nature" which "puts on" the imperishable means a continuing of our earthly life *in the mind of God*.

Paul's words are not *antithetical* to continuity (in the action of God!). He speaks of a real triumph over death, the eschatological triumph of the future which lies in God's hands. This cannot mean a pure having-been with respect to the "terminal character" of our life, however, but it means life and victory (I Cor. 15:56-57), and that in connection with our work in the Lord which is not in vain (15:58).

This victory presents us not with an optimistic anthropology, but it is real and can be understood only as the fruit of Christ's triumph. It effects an eternal restoration in the power of His reconciling work. This is the immortality which Christ's triumph reveals, an immortality which coincides with the reality of His fellowship (I Cor. 15:58).

*     *     *

We cannot but ask what the real background is of Barth's contrast between the "eternalizing" of our finite life and its continuation. In our analysis we noted that in Barth's view temporal limitation belongs to man's *good* creation. Although it is not possible for him to deduce the idea of "eternalizing" directly from the Scriptures, he does believe that the Bible presents a basis for the thought that man, according to the good nature with which God created him, has a temporal terminus and is mortal.[14]

What is involved here is the "clear acknowledgment of man's end."[15] It is true that the Bible presents only a "slender line"[16] in support of this thought because it usually speaks of the end of man's life as the end of his *sinful* life, and of death as an enemy. Barth, however, does not stop here, and it is of central importance to note this. He endeavors to show from the Bible that the transition from being to not-being can be *other* than an overwhelming of the last enemy, that it can be a manifestation of God's *goodness* and *protection*.[17] A dying *is* possible which has lost its terror. Apparently, Barth concludes from the fact that death in communion with God has lost its horror to the idea that death does not at all have to be in

14. KD III/2, p. 771.
15. *Ibid.*, p. 772.
16. *Ibid.*
17. *Ibid.*, p. 773.

conflict with the *good* nature with which God created man. There is a *natural* aspect to death.[18] In support of this Barth points to the death of Abraham and Isaac, but especially to the end of Enoch, Moses, and Elijah. Elijah's departure did not manifest the slightest trace of judgment.[19] At the boundary of his life judgment was taken away, "was made invisible, was annulled by the revelation of what the life which was here brought to an end had all along been: chariots of Israel and its horsemen" (II Kings 2:12).[20] The man Eljah *was no more,* but this end did not mean *darkness.* This death must not be regarded as a sign of disorder, but of God's order and plan,[21] not as a bold stroke on the part of chaos, but as God's *good* creation.[22]

This emphasis Barth also finds in the New Testament. Also here we see that death can be "terminus ad quem" without being the last enemy. The *second* death, that is, *unnatural* dying, is no more. Here man is freed to enter upon a *natural* death.[23] The fact that such a liberation exists shows that "death as such belongs, according to the ordinance of the Creator, to the life of His creature and is therefore *necessary* to it."[24] Sin makes a judgment out of death, but this is not all that can be said about death. It is also the boundary, the good and necessary boundary of our life. The revelation of Scripture that in Christ we do not have to fear death because faith in Him means transition from death to life, Barth understands to mean that death has a *natural* aspect, a necessary *boundary* aspect. From this boundary-aspect man's "having-been" as a *good* thing follows as a matter of course.

It is clear that this conception is fundamentally determinative of the triumph of the end.

Natural death, upon which no continuation of life follows, is related to the revelation of the life that "has-been" and in this revelation lies the *meaning* of our finite and ending life. The fundamental structure of Barth's eschatology is not determined by an ontology of human desire, but by *this* revelation, the revelation of the meaning of our *ending* life in the eyes of God.

\* \* \*

---

18. *Ibid.,* p. 773.
19. *Ibid.,* p. 775.
20. *Ibid.,* p. 776.
21. *Ibid.*

22. *Ibid.*
23. *Ibid.,* p. 777; cf. p. 779.
24. *Ibid.,* p. 779.

What, then, is the real background of *this* interpretation of the vita aeterna? Here we must note two aspects in Barth's thinking on this subject. One is the *dogmatic,* the other is the *exegetical,* basis of his conception. The dogmatic foundation lies in Christology while the exegetical lies in a pointing to the possibility of a believing and fearless death and further in the distinction which Scripture makes between the *first* and the *second* death.

* * *

It is important to examine the nature of this twofold basis.

In the first place, we must note the connection between Christology and our human "limited" time. The remarkable fact is that Vogel also bases his anthropology on Christology but arrives at wholly different conclusions than Barth does. On which grounds then are *Barth's* conclusions founded? In answering this question we must recall once more the decisive point in Barth's argument. We noted that Barth, in his discussion on death, had come so far that the conclusion seemed inescapable that the end of life, that death, could only mean *curse* and *threat,* the realization of chaos. At this point, however, he came upon an "extraordinary difficulty"[25] with respect to his understanding of human nature. "Were we to draw this conclusion (curse, threat, chaos), we would necessarily have to subject to revision everything that we have so far said about the limited time of man."[26]

This revision Barth cannot undertake. It is *not possible* that the limitation of life means only *evil* and *curse.* We do know of *empirical* man in the judgment of God, and of his end as judgment, and of death as an enemy.[27] At this point, however, *Christology* cuts across anthropology and eschatology. Because Christ's death was the *voluntary* end of His human life, because it was the *strange* burden *which did not originally belong to His life,* His death was not *anthropologically* necessary. This fact reveals in Him, the true man, a being-human which is not necessarily to be identified with subjection to death as judgment. For this reason — and this is the

---

25. *Ibid.,* p. 763.
26. *Ibid.,* p. 763. Remarkably enough, we meet a similar argument in connection with the fall of the angels (conclusion of III/3). The danger of *dogmatic exegesis* is clearly apparent here. In pursuing the dogmatical argument the possibility of such a revision may never be excluded.
27. K D III/2, p. 765.

decisive turn in the argument — the fact of human death *as such* is not, as it was not in the case of Christ, a judgment. The being-limited of man's life can therefore be regarded as belonging to man's *good* creation.

Barth's basis for his conception of the end of man is indeed a vulnerable one. All is made to depend here on the *voluntary* character of Christ's death. It is a peculiar abstraction that Barth introduces when he writes, "His human life could also have ended in a wholly different manner."[28] Jesus' dying in judgment was caused by the fact of His bearing of guilt for *others*. His dying in this manner did *not* flow from anthropological necessity. Therefore dying and judgment are not necessarily related. We must distinguish dying which belongs to man's *nature* and dying which takes place in judgment. This Christ made plain when He voluntarily entered into the judgment of death.

This would seem to be a piece of abstract reasoning. Christ's death did, it is true, bear a voluntary character, but it must also be said that in His vicarious suffering He was subjected precisely to the judgment of death and it is hardly possible to speak in an abstract way of some other end of His life through natural death.

It is difficult to escape the thought that this abstract discussion about the end of Jesus' life hardly constitutes a conclusion drawn from the relationship of Christology to anthropology. It is not so much Christology as anthropology that is primary here. It is *anthropology* that primarily gives meaning to man's life as having a "limited" time.

In Barth's theology this conception is intimately related to his view of man's beginning and man's ending time, and it is in terms of this view that Barth's reaction to the idea of continuity must be seen. The argument for man's "limited" life cannot find its deepest basis in Christology. In fact, in terms of Barth's own view one might rather conclude to a non-limited time of man's life since Christ is not only the crucified One but also the risen and *living* Lord, the *man* Jesus Christ, who could explain, "I died, and behold I am alive for evermore" (Rev. 1:18).

For this reason alone Barth's thesis as drawn from the mortality of Jesus is untenable. His argument impresses us with the fact that

---

28. *Ibid.,* p. 766.

*the real origin of the idea of man's "limited" life does not lie here,
but rather in his conception of man, that is, in his anthropology.*
Just as man's earlier not-yet-being casts its shadow over his life, so
man continues in life as a marked being, as a being "which is also
able to move toward nothingness."[29] Here conceptions are involved
which are not derived from Christology but which are *anthropological* in nature. *Beginning* and *end* are placed in a parallel relationship to each other; both are determinative of man's existence
which, [30] in its concreteness, is sign and witness of God's government.[31]

It is open to serious question, however, whether beginning and
end may in this way — anthropologically and phenomenologically
— be placed alongside of each other. Did not man's *creation* create a wholly *new* situation in terms of which it is no longer possible
(in the light of revelation) to speak parallelistically of a "natural"
end of man as a *second* indication of man's finite character?

It is remarkable that Barth who emphasized so strongly God's
first creative speaking, which meant for us the "God with us," can
nevertheless parallelize *beginning* and *end,* thus creating a *twofold*
limitation of man, and can regard as natural the "no longer" as well
as the "not yet." To this phenomenology of man's existence Barth
gave an *a posteriori* dogmatic foundation in terms of the mortality
of Jesus. It was the idea of the "limitation" (forward as well as
backward) of man's life which played the determinative role in his
opposition to the idea of continuity and which led him — via
Christology — to posit the doctrine of the "eternalizing" of man's
life.

It cannot be denied that precisely at this point the eschatological
triumph in the theology of Barth is obscured by the phenomenological idea of "limitation." When the parallel between "not yet"
and "no longer" begins to play a role in eschatology it becomes necessary to confront Barth *critically* with the Church's confession of
*eternal* life and with the *scriptural* conception of eschatology. For
it is only through the conception of "limitation" that Barth was
able to arrive at the idea of "having-been" as an interpretation of
the eschatological expressions of the Bible.

\* \* \*

29. *Ibid.,* p. 698.          30. *Ibid.,* p. 257.          31. *Ibid.,* p. 257.

It is clear that the confession of the Church with respect to eternal life cannot be deduced from some speculation about immortality or from man's sense of his importance through which he then *prolongs* his finite existence in the future. Such thoughts are of course possible and often have found expression in one or another form of subjective projection. But they do *not* form the basis of the Church's confession of eternal life. That confession is not a projection or a postulate, but is exclusively the fruit of divine revelation. The earlier "not yet" does not find a true parallel in the "no longer" of the future. Creation and redemption irrevocably break any systematic correlation between them.

In the light of our earthly time it is possible to speak, as also the Bible speaks, of a "being-no-longer" with respect to this *earthly* life.[32] It is not possible, however, to construe a definitive parallel in terms of this idea between our (earlier) "not-yet-being" and our (later) "no-longer-being."

This parallel, in the definitive sense in which Barth posits it, is precisely the thing that Scripture *denies* us. It is not the idea of continuity that Scripture opposes, but the denial of it. This becomes very clear when Jesus speaks against the Sadducees who repudiated the doctrine of the resurrection of the dead (Matt. 22:23). By appealing to the law of levirate marriage they wish to refute Jesus by an argumentum ad absurdum. From earthly associations they draw lines into the new future and suppose that by so doing they have unanswerably indicated the "impasse" involved in the idea of a future life. In connection with the ideas of "eternalizing" and "continuity" with which we are now concerned, the answer of Christ is of decisive significance. "You are wrong, because you know neither the scriptures nor the power of God." Not for a moment was Christ impressed by the "logic" of the Sadducees. Rather, He places His wisdom over against their argumentation.

In the first place, Jesus here rejects every idea of *simple* continuity: "in the resurrection they neither marry nor are given in marriage, but are like angels in heaven." Here it is not continuity into the future that is rejected, but a wrong representation of that continuity. It is not a simplistic conception that unlocks the door of God's secret concerning the future and concerning those who are

---

32. Cf. Psalm 39:5, 14; Prov. 9:3, 5, 6, 9; Job. 7:6ff., and 10:18ff.

counted "worthy" to take part in *that* age and in *that* resurrection of the dead.[33]

Not only is the wrong idea of continuity rejected by Christ, however, but He also indicates their error and their not knowing the *Scriptures* and the *power* of God by pointing to Exodus 3:6 where God says at a time in which Abraham, Isaac, and Jacob are long since dead, "I *am* the God of Abraham, and the God of Isaac, and the God of Jacob. He is not the God of the dead, but of the living" (Matt. 22:32).

The point of this answer lies in the continuity of their human life and from this it appears that it is precisely *this* continuity that includes the resurrection of the dead which had been called into question. There is no question of a dropping away of the "my" in "God is my beyond." Rather His eternal maintaining of it is emphasized. In this way Jesus praises God's power in His "I am" as the foundation for eternal life and for the resurrection.

It is important to take good note of this passage because in another connection Barth also concerns himself with Jesus' conflict with the Sadducees, namely in connection with *marriage*.[34] Barth interprets the statement that God is not a God of the dead but of the living as follows: God is "the God before whom, before whose ages-encompassing eyes, all are living in their time,"[35] to which he adds, "That they, like Abraham, Isaac, and Jacob, have lived before God in their time *and therefore live eternally,* that will be true only then."[36] Here we see again that Barth's idea of the "limited" time influences his exegesis of Scripture and his teaching concerning the future, and that he permits the *reality* of eternal life to be overshadowed by his controlling idea that man will one day

---

33. Luke 20:34. Cf. "for they cannot die anymore," and "(they) are sons of God, being sons of the resurrection," vs. 36.

34. KD III/2, p. 356ff.

35. *Ibid.,* p. 357.

36. *Ibid.,* p. 357 (our italics). Cf. H. Vogel, *Verkündigung und Forschung,* p. 111. Barth returns to the question in III/2, p. 754: "...a rising from the dead and a continued life of the dead after death is definitely not the positive form of the resurrection. This consists rather in this that they who lived in their time are *as such* (italics by Barth) before God who is not a God of the dead but of the living." It would seem to be plain that Barth does not do justice here to the logic of the argument against the Sadducees which was concerned with the interpretation of Exodus 3:6, specifically the *power* of God that comes to expression in it. The fact that Barth considers Jesus' "angry answer to be wholly appropriate" does not remove the objection to his thesis.

"have been" and by his conception of the "eternalizing" of this present life.

From this it appears, not least with a view to the triumph of the end, that a way of thinking which is alien to the whole of Scripture suppresses the eschatological perspectives of the New Testament. This manner of thinking could, in my judgment, arise *neither* from Christology *nor* from the Scriptures, but only from an anthropology which, in terms of the idea of the "limitation" of human life, dominated Barth's thinking *from the beginning*.

To interpret Barth as "harmless" and to admit some degree of continuity in his ultimate solution of the problem is to misunderstand the fundamental structure of his thinking and to do him a gross injustice. Vogel's opposition to the idea of "eternalizing" has indeed not been a meaningless opposition. Much less has it rested on misunderstanding. Undoubtedly the conflict that has broken out on this point will be confirmed when the last part of Barth's dogmatics (the doctrine of redemption) appears.[37]

\* \* \*

In conclusion, we wish to give some attention to those passages in Scripture which speak of *the second death*. In doing so we are not concerning ourselves with an incidental and subordinate exegetical aspect of Barth's argument, but with a matter that is directly related to his solution.

We noted that Barth distinguishes between death as a natural boundary of human life and death as judgment and curse.[38] *Empirically* these two forms of death coincide, it is true, but this does not alter the fact of a *twofold* aspect of death.

Barth finds the second aspect indicated in the Revelation of St. John when it speaks of the "second death." Obviously, it is important for Barth to find a point of contact in Scripture for his teaching that the "end," the limitation of our life (in death) belongs to the *good* creation of man. Such a point of contact Barth finds there where the second death is distinguished from "natural"

---

37. The hesitation which one meets again and again in reading Barth's expositions about the end and man's "having-been" is to be explained, it seems to me, by his accommodation to the words which both Scripture and the Church use in speaking about eternal life. Thus Barth speaks constantly about "co-existence," "eternal life" (cf. KD III/2, p. 357), and "being clothed upon."
38. *Ibid.*, p. 764.

death, from which it may then be concluded that *death as such* does not fall outside the good nature which God created. Particularly does Barth point to Rev. 20:14, "Then Death and Hades were thrown into the lake of fire. This is the second death, the lake of fire."[39] This death does not belong to the "natural aspect"[40] but it belongs on the level of death as *enemy,* as a *threat* of the chaos, the threat to which Scripture usually points when it speaks about death, the death of *sinful* man. It is *then* that Scripture speaks about the destruction of the name of the godless. *That* death is the second death of the Apocalypse. "This death is pure un-nature. It is, so to speak, the death in death."[41]

From this death, in Barth's view, death in its *natural* aspect is to be distinguished.[42] Blessing and life, curse and death, stand close together in the Old Testament, but they do not coincide. A death *is* possible which is a transition from "being into not-being," an "ultimate having-been,"[43] which does *not* involve a being overcome by the last enemy.

In this way the distinction between this "natural" death and the second death receives in Barth's theology the value of scriptural evidence. Man's future "having been" follows therefore not only from the decisive lines of Barth's Christological thought, but also directly from Scripture itself.

\*   \*   \*

It is not difficult to see that for Barth the "natural" and the *second* death coincide *temporally* and *empirically.* This fact alone, however, makes us ask whether this conception rests on exegesis and whether the data about the second death do not point in a wholly different direction. In addition to Rev. 20:14 we also read about the second death in Rev. 20:6, "Blessed and holy is he who shares in the first resurrection. Over such the second death has no power," and in 2:11, "He who conquers shall not be hurt by the second death."

---

39. *Ibid.,* p. 772.
40. *Ibid.,* p. 773.
41. *Ibid.,* p. 772.
42. The concept "second death" "presupposes a 'first' which is not peculiar to the evil, destructive, unnatural character of the 'second'" (KD III/2, p. 777).
43. KD III/2, p. 773.

It can clearly not be concluded from these texts that the second death involves an act of divine judgment which coincides *temporally* with death as the natural end of life. Revelation rather gives to the second death a place *by itself* in the sense that they who believe are not affected by it. W. Michaelis, who agrees with Barth that death as temporal end and death as curse can be distinguished, does not believe that the idea of the "second death" can be serviceable to Barth on this score. "The expression 'second death' means that two different deaths are mentioned here."[44]

It is also significant that Revelation nowhere speaks of the "first" death.[45] The significant word is therefore the word "second" by which the second death is distinguished not so much from the *first* death as it is from *death as such*. For this reason the concept "second death" cannot be regarded as Barth regards it, namely, that the *first* death is the natural aspect of the end of human life. The Scriptures speak of death as the last enemy which *Christ* has overcome and put to nought (I Cor. 15:26). Death is also referred to as the wages of sin (Rom. 6:23). After Christ had voluntarily suffered this death (as wages) and loosed its pangs (Acts 2:24) it received through Him a character other than judgment. The Heidelberg Catechism teaches that death is no longer a payment for sin but only a dying to sin and entering into life eternal.[46] From this change in the character of death, from this change in its *reality* through the power of the living God, *it does not at all follow that death in itself belongs to God's good creation.* It does mean that for all who believe in Him death — in God's hand — means an entrance into a new dimension which is filled with perspectives to its very horizon.

We are concerned about the light that is shed on *this* reality. It is the light that is to be distinguished from all the vague lights of immortality, for it has been kindled by the great Light, the Light of the world. "Truly, truly, I say to you, if any one keeps my word, he will never see death" (John 8:51). "If any one keeps my word, he will never taste death" (vs. 52). "I am the resurrection and the

---

44. W. Michaelis, *Versöhnung des Alls. Die frohe Botschaft von der Gnade Gottes*, 1950, p. 101.
45. *Ibid.*, p. 98.
46. Heid. Catechism, question 42.

life; he who believes in me, though he die, yet shall he live" (11:25).[47]

It is the same light which is cast over death when Paul exclaims, "O death, where is thy victory? O death, where is thy sting?" to which he adds, "The sting of death is sin, and the power of sin is the law" (I Cor. 15:55-56). In the way of faith everything changes, even the appearance, no, the *reality* of death. The cause of this does not lie in the fact that the "natural" character of death (as creational limitation of man's being) is acknowledged, but in the *taking away* of the *sting* of sin.[48] It is this that changes the triumphant character of death into the subjugation of death as our means of entrance into life eternal.

Not a single ground can be adduced in support of the thesis that in empirical death we are to distinguish between death in its natural aspect and death as judgment. Paul's conception of death is summarized in his characterization of it as wages of sin.[49] "The reality of its gruesome lordship rests on the reality of sin."[50] Nothing that Barth adduces in support of the thought that death need not be feared any longer proves that death was originally a *good* limitation of the life of man. On the contrary, everything points to *reconciliation* as the conquest of the *triumph* of death. Only in this way can the biblical message about death be understood, and about the rest that remains for the people of God (Heb. 4:9) be understood. This rest and fearlessness are to be understood *Christologically*. Therefore the light of the believer's future shines brighter than all the lamps of immortality. It will be difficult to say this, however, when we take seriously Barth's view that man will one day "have been," for in this conception shadows fall over the true *communio* and over the *vita aeterna*. In this "having been" the problems surrounding the idea of limitation change the triumph into a victory which is not free from ambiguity.

---

47. John 11:25. Cf. John 5:24: "he who hears my word and believes him who sent me, has eternal life: he does not come into judgment, but has passed from death to life."
48. Cf. L. Schmid in *Theologisches Wörterbuch des Neuen Testaments*, IV (ketron).
49. Cf. *Ibid.*, V, p. 592.
50. *Ibid.*, III, p. 667.

The true triumph of death's being swallowed up in victory (I Cor. 15:54) does not mean the eternalizing of our present ("diesseitige") life, but the *keeping* of our life for the future. Therein the triumph of the end manifests itself. This is not an ego- or anthropocentric conclusion in which we seek for more than the alloted life-span, but it is revelation from God about the "God with us" in the future that He will create and about our being "children" and "heirs" of God and "fellow-heirs" with Christ (Rom. 8:17).

* * *

We return once more to Barth's fundamental conception.[51] In sharp opposition to the idea of the anthropological "immortality" of the soul Barth concludes — albeit in an incidental, fragmentary chain of thought — from Christ's mortality to the limitation of man's existence. Christ has redeemed us from the *second* form of death. Through Him there is life in communion with God, that is to say, "in communion with God, who as the eternal was, is, and will be, every man's *past life* in its limited time also has a place."[52] Barth's conception of eschatology may be summarized as the *unveiling*, "the uncovering, the glorification of man's past life in Christ as he lived it in his time."[53] This is the resurrection of the dead which we expect. This, Barth would say, is "reality" in the fullest and most complete sense of the word. The revelation of this reality will take place "before the eyes of the gracious God, before their own eyes, and before the eyes of all others."[54] In all these formulations an undeniable tension is discernible, for in this reality which is a reality *not only* for God the "having been" and the "no longer" are not surrendered. Barth continues to hold to a

---

51. It is very difficult to gain a complete understanding of Barth's view of death. Although the materials presented above are plain enough, the difficulty remains of properly understanding the various inter-relationships. Particularly is it necessary to come to a clear view of these when Barth, on the one hand, sees the second death as the essence of death but, on the other hand, declares that in the *sign* of death God is against us, "but *only* in this sign!" (III/2, p. 741). "In death God is against us in hand to hand encounter," but the fire of his wrath is the fire of his wrathful love. This view must be seen in connection with *empirical* death (natural death *plus* judgment) but it is difficult to understand what the relationship is between natural end, empirical death and death as the sign of judgment. Cf. especially KD III/2, pp. 740ff.

52. *Ibid.*, p. 760.
53. *Ibid.*
54. *Ibid.*, p. 771.

once-for-all, limited life which does *not* perpetuate its course.[55]
We have no right to hope for "a liberation from the limitation of
our time and therefore for a beyond."[56]

The idea of limitation is taken up *into* the eschatological conception. To take liberties with this thought and to attempt to ac-
commodate it to the traditional confession of the Church with respect to eternal life is to deny the plainness and the decisiveness
with which this "limitation" received and retains its place in
Barth's conception of the triumph of the future. Here the tension becomes visible between the problems surrounding Barth's
idea of the limitation of our life and the *overwhelming* character
of the biblical testimony concerning the relationship between *sin*
and *death* and concerning the promises of this testimony for the
future. This future lies in the hands of God and becomes *our* future through faith.

One can only hope that Barth, in pursuing his way to a fuller
eschatological statement, will yield to the weight of scriptural testimony *which is concentrated precisely in Christ's triumph.* This
view of the "vita aeterna" is not concerned to proclaim a proud
anthropology which puts man forward and his "eternity." Rather
it is concerned about that importance of man which made Barth
at one time say that the expression, "God is *everything*, man is
*nothing*," is not a Christian way of speaking. This importance is
based not on man's pride or innocence, but in that "love for man"
(philanthropia) of God our Savior (Titus 3:4) that would recon-
cile us to the word "anthropocentric" were it not so frequently
contrasted with "theocentric."

If the incontrovertible biblical witness is accepted it will not be
possible for the shadow of the "limitation" in the sense of "having been" to obscure this new and true communion with God.
Tensions immediately appear when the idea of limitation enters
into the structure of this communion. And who will be convinced
when at the edge of the eschatological vision and mystery of Scripture this "having been" is designated as a "mode" of "being?"

* * *

The Apostolicum in its original form did not contain the words
"vita aeterna." This does not indicate hesitation on this subject

---

55. *Ibid.*, p. 771          56. *Ibid.*

in the early Church, for from the beginning she had in defense against gnostic errors of various kinds confessed the "resurrectio carnis." We will not err when we say that the Church in later adding the words "vitam aeternam" was *not at all* conscious of having added a *new* element. The "vita aeterna" had always been understood to be included in the "resurrectio carnis." For this reason the debate in our day about the eschatological triumph touches the faith of the Church in every age. In his early period Barth expressed himself in a reactionary vein in such sharp eschatological judgments that he later found it necessary to effect a pronounced correction. It was a correction which he found it necessary to make because his earlier presuppositions collapsed under the weight of the scriptural witness. We shall have to await the last volume of his *Dogmatik* to see how his eschatological conception will finally formulate his understanding of the "vita aeterna."

Will he maintain his idea of "limitation" or will this yield place to the scriptural witness concerning God's promise for our future?

# XIII

## THE TRIUMPH OF GRACE AND THE KINGDOM OF GOD

No one will deny that the theme of the triumph of grace is immediately related to the central message of the gospel of God. At the same time, it must be recognized that every theme — also that of the triumph of grace — must in its concrete application be subjected to the test of the gospel in all its parts lest it degenerate into a mere *idea*. As it is possible to suppose one is serving God when in fact he is not (John 16:2), so it is incumbent upon everyone who treats of grace and its triumph to guard against every obscuration of the gospel of the overflowing grace of God. The human heart is deceitful and can exercise its influence also in our reflection about grace.

While it is therefore necessary always to regard the elements of which the triumph of grace consists in the light of God's word, this is particularly a moving matter when a theology is concerned which undertakes so consistently as Barth has done to make the triumph of grace significant for every part of that theology. In his works the biblical words of joy and victory constantly resound and we hear his many testimonies and warnings against the violation of God's sovereign grace.

It is a simpler and more rewarding task to oppose a consistently synergistic system of theology than to concern oneself with a theology which posits with the greatest emphasis — in the light of Christ — the triumph of grace. Especially is this true when, as in the theology of Barth, this grace is placed over against every form of synergism and co-operation. When one takes fair note of this he is impressed with the impossibility of exercising criticism in terms of one-sided reaction in which justice would not be done to the scriptural witness to grace to which Barth's *Dogmatik* does not cease to point. Even when it is felt that the elements that constitute Barth's conception of the triumph of grace clearly evidence the influence of certain presuppositions and peculiar tensions, it

347

is not possible to avoid being impressed by the manner in which the gospel of God's grace breaks through, thetically and antithetically, again and again. Often we are struck by the keen analysis of all manner of refined synergism which has so frequentl̵ʸ threatened the sovereign grace of God in the history of the Church. Therefore it is a responsible undertaking to reflect on a theology of *grace*. This responsibility is determined and qualified by the obligation to detract nothing from the full riches of the grace which is proclaimed to us in the gospel.

In the defense against everything that may obscure the salvation to which the Church and theology are called, reaction is in itself a good and necessary thing. It is possible for the Church to stake everything in defending one sector of her front without resorting to one-sidedness. On that one sector a decision may be reached which is determinative for the whole front when that by which the Church stands or falls is at issue. When such a situation presents itself, strong counter-emphases are made which make on a superficial spectator the impression of "one-sidedness." Upon closer inspection, however, it appears that *here* and *now* these emphases were necessary. This is evident from the "reaction" which we meet in the Bible against the misunderstanding of law and cultus, against the perversion of the freedom which believers have in Christ, against the "emptiness" of faith without works.

We enter upon dangerous ground, however, when reactionary emphases are made which do not have the power to safeguard the full truth as God has revealed it. An example of this we find in the reaction of the post-Reformation Lutheran churches against the meritoriousness of good works which led here and there to the conception of the *hurtfulness* of good works for salvation. In this way the danger always threatens that reaction will not find the *correct* answer. The fatal consequence of such one-sided reaction is that appeal to conscience not only loses its power but that new reactions are later awakened in which that is strengthened which it was desired to oppose in the first place. When these dangers are clearly seen, it can be fruitful to concern oneself with the theme of Barth's theology, namely, the triumph of grace.

*      *      *

Concretely, this means that we may never place over against the theme of the triumph of grace a *lesser* accentuation of the full riches of the grace of God. This would immediately bring us into conflict with the scriptural testimony to the *abundance* of grace. It was not accidental that in our analysis we included Barth's sharp polemic against Roman Catholic synergism. Every reaction against Barth's theology will prove to be powerless when concessions are made to this synergism. Especially in the area of the triumph of grace we see a "pendulum movement" appear in the history of theology. On the one hand, we meet much opposition to synergism which involves an accentuation of the grace of God in such a manner that this grace hardly seems to be other than a deterministic causal system. Disturbed by such a causality, others began to plead for human freedom and for the significance of human decisions only to end in synergism again via another way. In this way the moving struggle to crystallize the relationship between *grace* and *freedom* has manifested itself. It is clear, however, that in this struggle one-sided reaction will not be fruitful because it is powerless to safeguard our view of the fullness of the gospel.[1]

Is it *possible* to give *too much* attention to grace? Are there limits? Can there be a *more* or a *less* in our praise of God's grace? It is plain that there can never be a question of *too strongly* accenting the grace of God. Rather the question is, how shall we lay the *proper* emphases and how can we most *purely* praise this grace.

It is never the *full* accent but the *wrong* accent that obscures the gospel of God's grace.

\* \* \*

Seen in this light, we can say that a criticism of Barth's theology is a particularly responsible matter for *Reformed* theology. For Rome the situation could be called somewhat "easier." In terms of Roman Catholic conceptions it is possible and necessary to counter Barth's theology with the objection that it fails to do justice to human freedom of the will and to human co-operation in salvation. On this basis questions can be raised with respect to

---

1. We think here of the antinomian struggle and of the development of Melancthon and the struggle about synergism in which the above is strikingly illustrated.

Barth's emphases on our calling — because of the gospel of *grace* — to be fearless and to count on the certainty of salvation. In doing so one turns against Barth's theology in terms of *a consciously held synergistic standpoint*.

Reformed theology faces a wholly different situation here. It is not able to think synergistically, but stands committed to the confession of the irresistible power of grace. Herein lies, it would seem, the unique responsibility of Reformed theology in the contemporary theological struggle. It is precisely at this point that we can see that a common "anti" emphasis with respect to Barth's theology does not at all necessarily imply a community of spirit. Also here the "anti" appears to consist of many and varied elements. For this reason a formal "anti" will not suffice. There must be an "anti" that is normatively determined by the gospel itself. In terms of this norm the "anti" can never simply mean that Barth emphasizes grace and its triumph *too much*. Such a polemic would only cast a shadow over the gospel.

*   *   *

All this becomes plain when we observe how Scripture speaks about grace and its triumph. Here we can look in all directions, for it speaks in countless variations of the abundance of grace, of the depths of its riches, of the unutterable mystery, all of them testimonies of which we can hear the echo in the hymns of God's people which praise and extol God's grace in humility, gratitude, and ecstacy, in all of which the accents that are uttered do not fall *one-sidedly* but *rightly*.

Does Scripture not have as its only burden the mighty eu-ag-gelion, the glad message of salvation, which resounds already in the Old Testament? "Behold, on the mountains the feet of him who brings good tidings, who proclaims peace! Keep your feasts, O Judah, fulfil your vows" (Nahum 1:15). Does not Isaiah know this same messenger of joy whose feet are beautiful upon the mountains as he publishes *peace* (Isa. 52:7)? And does not Paul incorporate this word in his message of full salvation when he speaks about the same Lord who bestows his riches on all who call upon Him (Rom. 10:12), the Lord who is *preached:* "How *beautiful* are the feet of those who preach good news!" (Rom. 10:15)?

Can theology indeed have any other concern than to reflect on *this* mystery? Can it do other than point to and interpret the message of this grace which radically excludes all human merit and is therefore indissolubly linked with humility and joy, with our being conquered and overcome by *His* grace? On every page we read of the triumphant, the irresistible, the majestic, the lovely power of the grace of God which has appeared bringing salvation for all men (Titus 2:11), and of the mystery which was kept secret for long ages but is now disclosed and made known to all nations, for which reason Paul exclaims, "to the only wise God be glory for evermore through Jesus Christ!" (Rom. 16: 25-27).

Is not this a conquering, triumphant grace? And does this not come to expression particularly in the fact that it is truly stronger than we? Is not the power of this grace in overcoming the *strongest* opposition an example "for those who were to believe in him for eternal life" (I Tim. 1:16)? Indeed, the gospel is a message of *glad* tidings which are to be proclaimed, a mandate not to fear anymore (Luke 2:10ff.), sending forth preachers and heralds of a wonderful, unsurmised, and all-surpassing grace which eye has not seen, nor the ear heard, nor the heart of man conceived (I Cor. 2:9).

This grace does not confer a moderate, relatively valuable gift, a temporal, limited, and uncertain joy. It confers salvation,[2] life which is life indeed (I John 1:1), the not-seeing of death because of the transition from death to life which has already taken place (I John 3:14), the *bread* of life (John 6:22ff.), the *water* which is drawn with joy from the wells of salvation (Isa. 12:3), comfort, eternal comfort, light, joy, and victory in all distress. And all this is preached to us with *authority*[3] which towers triumphantly above all uncertainty and doubt and thereby lays the foundation for an inviolable certainty.

Is not this grace the conqueror of death and is not its triumph depicted for us in the bold challenge in which Paul takes up the

---

2. Matt. 11:6; 16:17; Luke 19:9; Eph. 1:13; I Cor. 15:2; Rom. 1:16.
3. Cf. G. Kittel, *Theologisches Wörterbuch des Neuen Testaments*, II, the word *euangelizomai*, p. 71: The proclamation is not "simply speaking and preaching, but it is proclamation with strength and power."

prophetic words of Hosea, "O death, where is thy victory? O death, where is thy sting?"

This challenge, which finds its basis in the overpowering might of the grace of God, is wholly in harmony with the entire message of the New Testament which proclaims victory and irresistible power. This power, which extends its conquest to the farthermost reaches of the domain of death and of the valley of the shadow, is not a neutral power but is filled with the loveliness of salvation. It accords wholly with the picture of the Shepherd of the sheep who leads His flock beside the quiet waters, restoring the soul, so that evil will not be feared even in the valley of the shadow of death: "for thou art with me, thy rod and thy staff, they comfort me" (Psa. 23). It is the testimony concerning the safety of those who abide in the shadow of the Almighty (Psa. 91:1) which the power of grace provides, *that* safety which illumines present and future so that they are powerless to separate from the love of Christ (Rom. 8:35, 39). In the face of disturbing heresy it is possible to point to the life that is hid with Christ in God (Col. 3:3).

Moreover, emphasis is constantly laid on the *abundance* of grace, as when Paul speaks of the free gift of grace and the enrichment of the life of the believer, and Peter of "unutterable and exalted joy" (I Peter 1:8). Is it not a boon so rich that we will not be "lacking in any spiritual gift" (1 Cor. 1:7)? It is the shining light of the Father of mercies and the God of all comfort (II Cor. 1:3).

All this does not mean the proclamation of an easy victory in which tension and struggle need hardly be presupposed. It is rather *in* the greatness of the victory that the struggle and the extent of our need and the depth of our guilt become manifest. The *afflicted* are comforted when they are tossed about by the storm (Isa. 54:11). We read of God's *no longer being angry* because of His steadfast love, and of His covenant of peace which puts an end to the struggle and which shall not be removed (Isa. 54:9-10). The abundance of grace stands revealed as the light in reigning darkness, as a gift of the love of God, and as the gospel that is proclaimed to the poor (Matt. 11:5). God's love triumphs over loneliness, while our love is only the response to His (I John 4:10, 19).

He was ready to be sought by those who did not ask of Him, and to be found by those who did not seek Him (Isa. 65:1).

Through the tender mercy of our God the day has dawned upon us from on high (Luke 1:78), and the love of God for man has appeared (Titus 3:4). "For a brief moment I forsook you, but with great compassion I will gather you. In overflowing wrath for a moment I hid my face from you, but with everlasting love I will have compassion on you, says the Lord, your Redeemer" (Isa. 54:7,8).[4] In the overpowering abundance of grace guilt is not weakened or denied, but is *forgiven* and as forgiven guilt it is made manifest. They are *prisoners* who are led away by the mighty chariotry of God, twice ten thousand and thousands upon thousands, the conquered, and also the rebellious, that God might dwell among them (Psa. 68:17, 18). Mourning is turned into dancing (Psa. 30:12) and the fear of the Lord is awakened by the forgiveness of guilt (Psa. 130:3, 4).

In this light we can understand why faith always understands and praises the triumph of grace as a *triumph*. Because of the depths of guilt and because of the rebellious who may dwell with the Lord can this triumph never be regarded as a self-evident matter. The acknowledgment of the triumph coincides and is indissolubly related to confession of guilt, to gratitude for and amazement at *this* triumph which God's grace not only made possible but actualized. In both the Old and the New Testaments we see this wonderment as the subjective correlate of the grace of God. There is reason for this reaction. When the exiles complain, "Our bones are dried up, and our hope is lost; we are clean cut off," the prophet replies, "Thus says the Lord God: Behold I will open your graves, and raise you from your graves, O my people" (Ezek. 37:11, 12). In the crisis of apparent hopelessness this amazement is reflected in Micah's question, "Who is a God like thee, pardoning iniquity and passing over transgression for the remnant of his inheritance? He does not retain his anger forever because he delights in steadfast love" (Micah 7:18). In the New Testament we hear the same echo, but now in terms of fulfillment, "*See* what

---

4. Ps. 30:9, "For his anger is but for a moment, and his favor is for a lifetime. Weeping may tarry for the night, but joy comes in the morning."

love the Father has given us, that we should be called children
of God; and so we are" (I John 3:1).

*  *  *

This amazement and the acknowledgment of the triumph of
grace which it includes, the triumph of *forgiveness* of guilt and of
*life* over death, is not an amazement which is limited individual-
istically by subjective feelings. Rather it is directed to the *deeds*
of God, to the *history* of salvation as the execution of the mighty
Counsel of God. God works still (John 5:17) said the Savior, and
He was working already in the placing of enmity between the seed
of the woman and the seed of the serpent, in His struggle with
the earliest rebellion against His will. Unsearchable are His judgments and inscrutable are His ways (Rom. 11:33). But *in* this
unsearchableness Paul's word is true, *"who* can resist his will"
(Rom. 9:19)? His triumph becomes visible in the face of resistance. This the history of Israel shows, particularly its fall, which
history moves on to the redemption of the world. And this God's
action shows at the point of its most intense concentration, namely,
in Jesus Christ. The rebellious action of men becomes evident in
the gathering of Herod and Pilate with the gentiles and the peoples of Israel "against thy holy servant Jesus," but in this con-
spiracy the light of God's overruling action appears: "to do whatever thy hand and thy plan had predestined to take place" (Acts
4:27, 28). It is the light that shone already in the second psalm,
the psalm that speaks of the conspiring and the plotting of the
peoples, of the kings of the earth and of the rulers. But it is also
the psalm of the laughter of God, of His holy mockery, of His
wrath, *and* of His king whom He has set on Zion, His holy hill.
In this laughter the triumph of God stands revealed, for His wrath
is not opposed by an equally powerful opponent. There is not an
eternal dualism between "powers" of light and darkness, between
good and evil. There is only an indisputable omnipotence which
reveals itself in this laughter. It is the triumph which is concentrated and fully crystallized in Jesus Christ. He is the Conqueror
who overcomes the world (John 16:33), who breaks the power
of the devil (I John 3:8), through whom God disarms principalities and powers, makes a public example of them and triumphs

over them (Col. 2:15). There are no powers who can hold their own in the face of His might.

Here the warning that resounded already under the Old Covenant becomes fully real: "Not by might, nor by power, but by my Spirit, says the Lord of hosts" (Zech. 4:6). Only in this way is the triumph to be achieved in the fullness of "soli Deo gloria." In this tremendous struggle *every* misunderstanding must be removed. We are indeed permitted the boldness of speaking of *man's* triumph, and that in the full sense of the word — are we not *more than* conquerors?[5] — but always with the unambiguous understanding that our victory is *through Him* who loved us.[6] The clear lines of the triumph do not become vague. In faith — the human victory! — they become fully visible. There is not a divided triumph but only the triumph of the grace of *God*.

\* \* \*

These and similar scriptural testimonies can be heard continually throughout the whole of Barth's theology. They form such a dominant emphasis that he has on more than one occasion accused Christianity of being too little a pronouncedly *triumphant* religion and of giving too little evidence that it is really free from anxiety and fear. We still harbor too much of a constricting respect for the devil, as though we — post Christum — still have anything at all to do with the fear of the devil, and as though the devil still has anything at all to do with us. He asks whether the Church of Christ really understands that she has heard and must proclaim a good message. Does she believe that there continues to be a competition between Christ and the principalities, between God and the devil? Has she understood the *command* no longer to fear? Does she not constantly in practice call into question the actuality of the triumph?

\* \* \*

It is clear that these considerations place us before questions which must be determinative of our attitude to the whole of the gospel. It is necessary to ask, however, what the central issue is in these questions surrounding the triumph of grace. We have al-

---

5. Cf. I John 2:13, 14; 5:7.
6. Cf. Jude 20: "keep yourselves *in* the love of God."

ready pointed out that especially in the earliest phase of his development Barth was sharply opposed to triumphant expressions of Christianity which, in his judgment, were hardly distinguishable from phariseeism because of the Church's manifest pride and elevation of self. The dubious "we" (ecclesiam habemus!) was the expression of an intolerable antithesis which could not but alienate the world to the message of the gospel. It is therefore plain, according to Barth, that the Church can also live her life in the world in a manner that is not compatible with the triumph of grace.

Where lies the dividing line between a *true* proclamation of the triumph of grace and that of a *false* presentation of it? This question is of great importance because many, influenced by Barth, made a criticism of the Church's sense of "having attained" the central point of its program. This attack assumed the form of criticism on the Church's (and Christianity's) lack of solidarity with the world, of the phariseeism which spoke piously but gave no evidence of really knowing what grace is, of the self-exaltation which was supposed to be everywhere in evidence. Especially was it emphasized that believers were not "different" than unbelievers and that justification was not the gateway to Christian self-development but that justification was the justification of the *godless*, which may never be regarded as a station on life's journey which comes to lie behind us. "Simul peccator et justus." Therefore no antithesis to the world, but solidarity with her.

It can hardly be denied that in the course of this struggle positive Christian conviction was frequently misinterpreted as exaltation of self. The battle against phariseeism, necessary though it be, always runs the danger of degenerating into generalization. We remember how in the decade between 1930 and 1940 this criticism found a sort of easy expression, particularly in connection with the conception of Scripture, the knowledge of God's command, and the answer in which the possession of this knowledge found expression in the area of politics. Especially the censuring of the desire to "possess" the word of God and the command of God played a strong role in this controversy.

In this "possessiveness" a desire came to expression, according to Barth, to control the grace of God. He saw in it a triumphing of man over the lordship of God.

What then are the boundaries of the true triumph? It is in any case certain that these boundaries cannot be drawn in such a way that standing in the grace of God means to stand without any need for struggle in the world. We remember, for instance, Barth's struggle against National Socialism which he carried on to the point of immediately relating the triumph and the lordship of Jesus Christ to concrete political situations. Later, it is true, a significant discussion developed when Barth gave emphatic expression to the idea that there was now (after the second World War) no need to join the anti-communist front.

In connection with this latter view of Barth, Emil Brunner asked why it was necessary to take issue with National Socialism but not now with Communism. It is not necessary to enter upon this debate here,[7] but it has not become clear why Barth recommended a different attitude to Communism than to National Socialism in view of the fact that what is not a temptation today can become one tomorrow. This is precisely what happened in Germany, especially after National Socialism came into power and was able with this "power" — interpreted as "service" — to fascinate even a part of the Church, particularly the so-called "Deutsche Christen."[8]

It is noteworthy that the triumph of grace has had marked influence on Barth's political conceptions. With especial reference to the threat posed by the state and its views, he writes, "Cast all your burdens upon Him! What has the Christian Church to fear when she lives in faith?"[9] Nowhere in the New Testament do we find fear of the state. When the concrete temptation has not yet come the Church must wait to see "whether and in what manner the situation becomes serious and requires a judgment on her

---

7. The heart of Barth's argument lay in his view that National Socialism had become a temptation while this is not the case with respect to Communism. The spirit of the West is already against it. When the Church *confesses,* then she must "in fear and trembling go against and not with the stream." Therefore, "not with America, not with the papacy," *Christliche Gemeinde im Wechsel der Staatsordnungen,* 1948, p. 69.

8. Barth knew this argument but could not accept it. We may not be anxious for tomorrow. Cf. *ibid.,* p. 51.

9. *Ibid.,* p. 52. "The entire West has fear, fear for the East. It is not right to have fear." According to Barth it is only dreaming "to suppose that we shall see the beast from the abyss walking about on the streets in concrete form." Jesus Christ has closed hell for us. "We may no longer suppose that the hellish form can become a reality."

part."[10] Then the Church can again speak and engage in struggle as she did in Barmen after 1933 in her confession of the one Lord.

It appears that also in the political area the *concrete* application of the triumph of grace requires reflection and discussion. With respect both to a false sense of triumph in the Church and to concrete life the triumph of grace is relevant and demands study. In this reflection the backgrounds of and the elements that constitute the triumph of grace must inevitably come to the fore.

\* \* \*

Amid the undeniable dangers that attend any shiftings in emphasis and distortions in setting forth the triumph of grace, the light of the gospel is the beacon that must guide us. The triumph of grace can be bent to serve the self-righteousness of man, and inner uncertainty can manifest itself in a false conception of the triumph. In Scripture we can clearly discern the critical lines which constitute the norm whereby all "glorying" is to be judged.

There is a glorifying which stands in sharp antithesis to true Christian faith. The scriptural warnings against such glorying are many. When there is really room to glory and God's salvation is poured over the nations, the admonition is heard, "do not become proud, but stand in awe" (Rom. 11:20). There is a pride which is rejected, the pride which manifests itself in self-exaltation and is judged.

The radical difference between the true triumph and the false triumph can be depicted most sharply in terms of the biblical criticism of *false* boasting, a criticism which appears in the Old as well as in the New Testament. It is not boasting that is condemned, but *false* boasting. "Let him who boasts, boast of the Lord" (I Cor. 1:31).[11]

Somewhere, Bultmann mentions as the elements of legitimate glorying: *trust, joy,* and *gratitude.*

The antithesis comes to expression clearly especially in Paul when he rejects a false boasting in connection with self-justification through the works of the law. "Then what becomes of our boasting? It is excluded" (Rom. 3:27). Self-justifying boasting

---

10. *Ibid.,* p. 70.
11. Cf. Jer. 9:24: "let him who glories glory in this, that he understands and knows me, that I am the Lord..."

is the direct opposite of the triumph of grace. Real glorying is glorying *in* Christ Jesus, in the cross (Phil. 3:3, Gal. 6:14). Bultmann speaks continually of the *paradox* that "man can glory only when he looks away from himself and magnifies God's doings." There is actually no real paradox here, but only the meaningfulness of a glorying which arises from grace and knows only of *this* grace. For the New Testament the forsaking of this true glorying constitutes a falling away from the truth, a being bewitched (Gal. 3:1), which affects everything — the tone of the glorying, the color of the joy, which begin to lose their depth of meaning and become oriented to man as the object of boasting.

Therefore the "sola fide" and the "sola gratia" are also founded in real glorying, in the true triumph of grace. The Scriptures are full of testimonies to this and the hymns of the Church sing of it. It is all the one theme of faith which is not to be distinguished from the "soli Deo Gloria" but coincides with it.

For this reason a triumphant theology can never be combated by weakening or relativizing the fulness of the triumph. The triumph of grace must be confessed in a truly Christian manner and it must be preached in spite of any and all danger that genuine glorying will be perverted into false glorying. This danger is so great that nowhere, whether in preaching, confession, or theology, may the door be opened to allow false boasting to enter, however covertly.

This danger is acute also in the area of religion and faith. The warning against false boasting is directed not only against autonomus self-glorification but also against religious self-exaltation in which a refined form of self-glorification can appear in religious dress. The pharisee in the parable glorifies in himself and in his many good deeds, but he begins with "I thank thee", to continue with "that I am not like other men, extortioners, unjust, adulterers, or even like this tax collector" (Luke 18:11). This kind of gratitude brings no healing for self-pride, for the pharisee did not return to his home justified (18:14). Therefore the boundary between true and false glorying must be found in the *nature,* the *structure,* the *direction* of the glorying.

The triumph of grace finds itself reflected in true glorying. It is filled with that grace and its power. It speaks of the Lord and testifies to *His* glory. True glorying also has an eye to its own peace and safekeeping, but this is not a concern for self but for the safekeeping which lies enclosed in Christ and in His grace. Therefore Paul can glory in his sufferings (Rom. 5:3) and sing of the constancy of blessing in Christ, of the constancy of communion in the present and in the future. This glorying is not a passing stage in the life of faith. It is not possible that a Christian life should come into being which can exist independently and have decreasing need of grace. In the true Christian life glorying in grace constantly increases and is deepened. The "more and more" of which the Scriptures and the confessions speak does not mean a being distanced from blessing and from grace but a knowing more and more that we can live only in *this* grace. Sanctification is not a movement from glorying in grace to glorying in self. Grace does not lead us into a terra incognita in which we have to find our own way. God's mercies point out the way to us, the way in which we are transformed by the renewal of our mind, that we may prove what is the will of God, what is good and acceptable and perfect (Rom. 12:2).

In this knowing the triumph of grace becomes evident. It is a knowing which is filled with the repeated prayers of Psalm 119 which ask, "let me not wander from thy commandments!" (vs. 10). Praise continually alternates with prayer and always stands in association with it. With great positiveness we hear, "I have kept thy testimonies" (vs. 22).[12] But this positiveness can be understood only in intimate connection with the prayer for the opening of the eyes (vs. 18), with a cleaving to the Lord's testimonies (vs. 31), with the prayer for instruction (vs. 34), for understanding (vs. 34), for a gracious teaching of God's law (vs. 29), and for the granting of His promise (vs. 58). There is neither hesitation nor a forgetting of God's law but we hear, "May my heart be blameless in thy statutes." It is clear that all praise of self is foreign to the poet when all his love and his praise end with the humble words, "I have gone astray like a lost sheep; seek thy servant, for I do not forget thy commandments" (vs. 176).

Psalm 119 is an amazing psalm in which the changing emphases can be understood alone in terms of the only apparently contra-

12. Cf. verses 8, 51, 53, 56, 63, etc.

dictory elements that constitute the whole.  A. Weiser speaks of
the impression of restlessness which the psalm makes.[13]  If there
is restlessness, it is the restlessness of activity, of dependence, of
prayer and praise, which characterize true faith from beginning
to end.  He refers to the "piety of the law" which does not yet reveal the characteristics of "degeneration and inflexibility which are
characteristic of religion by rote" against which Jesus was later to
protest.  Nevertheless, it manifests, in his judgment, "a tendency
in the direction of a development which ends in the self-righteousness of the pharisees and the scribes."[14]  To me this is an incomprehensible judgment, especially so when Weiser justifies this interpretation by pointing out that in his opinion word and law
take the place of God and His wonderful deeds.  The poet "even
prays to the law," a thought that is occasioned by vs. 48, "I revere
thy commandments, which I love" (more literally, "I lift up my
hands to thy commandments").  This is not an hypostatizing of
God's command, however, for precisely in the uplifted hands we
see the life that wishes to live by grace alone and that knows of the
triumph of grace already in the midst of shadows.

This reflection of God's gracious action in believers is naturally
constantly threatened by the danger that glorying in God's grace
will turn into self-righteousness.  It *is* possible to abstract the law
from the Law-giver, as it is possible to abstract Scripture from the
Author of Scripture.  These things can be done apart from faith and
so can come to live in a triumphant mood which has nothing in
common with the triumph of grace save an appearance.  The message of the Scriptures, however, constantly points us to the boundaries that must be observed here.  These boundaries do not lie
— Psalm 119! — in the mere fact of knowing and keeping God's
commandments, but in knowing and keeping them under the blessing of His mercy, through which alone they can be truly kept
and through which our boasting will not be put to shame as a
false boasting.

*  *  *

When we reflect on the triumph of grace and observe how its
power overcomes the darkness of our heart, we can well understand that the *totality* of the triumph should again and again come

---

13. A. Weiser, *Die Psalmen,* II, 1950, p. 492.
14. *Ibid.,* p. 493.

to the fore. In discussing the universality of the triumph in Barth's theology we noted the connections that become apparent here. It has often been supposed that the radical and irresistible nature of overpowering grace required the conclusion of universalism since only in that conclusion the triumph of grace would be truly reflected. In this way radical grace led to the conclusion of total and universal grace.

This "totality" has often in universalistic fashion been called a *necessary* conclusion from the love of God. Universalism as a religious postulate has in this manner played a role at the fringe of the Church, and not infrequently the Church has been charged with permitting shadows to fall over the totality of the triumph.

It is noteworthy that the debate centering about universalism has always borne a strongly exegetical character. Nevertheless, it must be said that this conclusion — one must say, this a priori conclusion — from the grace and the love of God has played a decisive role. This shows itself in a peculiar shifting in the *message* of salvation in the direction of this supposedly *evident* conclusion. In universalistic theologies grace involuntarily becomes a point of departure for the drawing of logical conclusions. The totality of grace is woven into the texture of the "necessity" of grace which the love of God requires.

The error of universalism does not lie in glorying in God's grace, but in integrating grace into a system of conclusions which is in conflict with grace as a sovereign gift.

The gripping element in all universalism is that at the moment when this integration takes place the seriousness of calling, of responsibility, and of the human decision of faith, is eliminated. When Barth, standing at the threshold of the apokatastasis (the impossibility of undoing God's universal decision), returns again to taking tension, decision, calling, invitation, the open situation, seriously, he does so by pointing to the freedom, the *gift* of grace. We have pointed out the problematical aspect of Barth's doctrine of election in that he, at a decisive moment, makes this turn which, in view of his earlier argument, is hardly understandable. For this very reason, however, the shift in direction calls attention to itself. It points to the *gift-character* of grace which cannot be integrated into a system in which necessity — in terms of human conclusions — plays a role. Universalistic theology can still speak with great emphasis of the triumph of grace,[15] but it becomes a general and aprioristic conclusion which is torn loose from the context of faith and from the real grace of God.

This position is justified by saying that it is impossible *not* to draw this conclusion. The universalistic thesis *must* be posited. There is a *must* in God' love: "its will to lordship is inexhaustible and ultimately unendurable: the sinner must yield."[16] It is a question of *omnipotent* love. J. A. T. Robinson says this has nothing to do with speculation for it is a matter of "the very necessity of God's nature." It is not accidental that the words "must" and "necessity" appear in the exposition of the universalistic thesis. They belong there and constitute its foundation. God *cannot* endure another possibility, "for *that* would be the final mockery of His nature — and He will not."

T. F. Torrance, in replying to this thesis, has correctly called attention to this element of "necessity" and pointed out the speculation involved in it which transgresses the boundaries of revelation and kerugma. "Can we ever get behind God's self-manifestation and His action and discuss the relation of omnipotence and love in terms of the necessity of His divine nature?"[17] Universalism stands or falls, however, with this necessity in which the kerugma is objectified to "factuality" and degenerates into mere announcement of accomplished fact. Only by way of this necessity, it is supposed, can one continue to speak about the *triumph* of grace. Salvation is systematized and it is not realized that the triumph of grace atrophies to a conclusion and that the sovereignty of grace can be known *only in the way of humility and faith*. Because universalism by this "necessity" violates the nature of *free* grace, shadows fall over the grace of God in history and over the *meaningfulness* of Christ's sacrifice which is obscured by the "necessity" of God's nature.[18]

---

15. Cf. E. F. Ströter, *Die Allversöhnung in Christus,* 2nd ed., 1920, who constantly speaks of the *triumphant* gospel. Barth refers to a book by Ströter about Romans 11 (KD II/2, p. 294) as "useful to read in spite of its strong errors." Cf. W. Michaelis, *Versöhnung des Alls,* 1950.
16. J. A. T. Robinson, "Universalism — is it heretical?", in *Scottish Journal of Theology,* 1949, p. 155.
17. T. F. Torrance, "Universalism or Election," *ibid.,* p. 311.
18. Not without warrant Torrance asks, "Dare we go behind Calvary to argue our way to a conclusion, which, if we could reach by logic would make the Cross meaningless?" *ibid.,* p. 311.

The totality of the triumph loses its relevance to history and kerugma so that grace is no longer seen in its unconditional grace-character. Barth has sharply discerned the danger of an ultimately kerugma-less universalism but attempts to free himself from this danger *within* the limits of *God's universal election* as His irrevocable Yes in Christ.

This explains why the tensions in Barth's doctrine of election lead him to conclusions which, in terms of his own presuppositions, cannot be seen as other than a "shadow" that is cast over the triumph of grace. It is the shadow of unbelief with respect to one's own election, the *dangerous* shadow of not believing in God's election which has already made the life that is lived in Christ danger-*less* because of *God's* decision. Barth's attempt to remove this shadow by qualifying unbelief as an "ontological impossibility" — in view of the triumph — does not *eliminate* the problem but *accentuates* it.[19]

\* \* \*

The judgment that universalism misrepresents the nature of grace, unscripturally relativizes the decision of faith, and construes grace in terms of an abstract conception of grace (the idea of necessity), does not require a hesitant speaking about grace. Scripture itself speaks of the grace that *reigns* through righteousness to eternal life through Jesus Christ our Lord (Rom. 5:21).[20] *Omnipotence* and *grace* are not mutually exclusive conceptions. When the *power* aspect is considered to be incompatible with the grace aspect a secularized conception of power has obscured the biblical message of grace. Scripture does not know of such an antithesis.[21] The relationship which Scripture conceives to exist between the two is of decisive significance for properly understanding the nature of grace. The word which Paul uses for the *reigning* of

---

19. We meet the same problem in Torrance's article, p. 316, where he endeavors, as does Barth, to untie the two elements: "The amazing message of the Gospel is, that Christ has chosen all men, died for all men" and at the same time: the rejection of the apokatastasis by pointing to the "mysterium iniquitatis," to the "bottomless dimension of sin in the human heart" (p. 317). The point of union between the two elements lies in the open situation of preaching: "Woe unto us, if we preach not the Gospel" (p. 318).

20. Rom. 5:21 (*basileuo*). This *reigning* of grace accentuates its triumph, as is also clear from the relationship obtaining between Christ and the believer, Rev. 5:10; 22:5.

21. In connection with the reigning of grace (Rom. 5:21) cf. the abundance of grace (5:20).

grace is related to the words *king* (basileus) and *kingdom* (basileia), and reveals grace in its relationship to the kingdom of God.[22] This does not mean that we can speak about the kingdom *apart from* and *independently of* grace. It does mean that we cannot speak about "grace" and draw all kinds of conclusions from the concept without keeping the eye fixed on the concept of the kingdom of God. The gospel which proclaims the grace of God confronts us with the gospel of the kingdom of God.[23]

For this reason it will never be possible to speak in a scripturally legitimate manner about the grace of God when the biblical message about the kingdom of God is not fully recognized and honored. This does not involve a tension or conflict between the aspects of love (grace) and power (kingdom) but rather it keeps in view the connection between them and the depth of God's gracious action which is so revealed.[24]

In this way the connection is retained between grace and the greatness and the glory of the kerugma of the kingdom whereby a safeguard is provided against obscuring the concepts of grace and of the triumph of grace. In Scripture the triumph of grace does not stand alone but is related to the totality of God's action in the old and the new covenants. By faith we can understand the triumphant words which announce that God's counsel shall stand and that He shall accomplish all His purpose (Isa. 46:10). We do not now fix our attention on an inflexible sovereignty concept *instead of* on grace. We wish only to underscore that the message of grace may never be abstracted from the relationships in which we meet it in Scripture. We can hear the warning in connection with the sovereign action of God in history. The triumphant word of Isa. 46:10 stands in the context of urgent admonition to the transgressors (vs. 8). In His righteousness God triumphs over their counsels: "Hearken to me, you stubborn of heart, you who are far from deliverance [righteousness, A. V.]: I bring near my

---

22. Cf. A. Nygren, *Der Römerbrief*, 1951, p. 169. "The Greek word that is used here, *basileuein*, directs the attention in an immediate way to the kingdom of God proclaimed by Jesus, the *basileuo theou.*"

23. Matt. 4:17; Mark 1:14, 15, and especially Matt. 4:32: the gospel of the kingdom of God.

24. Cf. H. N. Ridderbos, *De Komst Van Het Koninkrijk*, esp. section 23: the kingdom and the cross.

deliverance, it is not far off, and my salvation will not tarry; I will put salvation in Zion, for Israel my glory" (vss. 12, 13).

We meet connections here which appear everywhere in Scripture. They are connections and relationships that belong to the divine triumph. In the revelation of God's love and righteousness in Jesus Christ, in the execution of His counsel, according to which Christ does not come into the world to condemn but to save, we see a way opened which is full of tension and drama, of calling and responsibility.

God's action does not exclude these emphases but rather includes them in the calling to faith, acknowledgment, and acceptance. God's triumph in Christ stands revealed specifically as the triumph of *His* kingdom. The aspects of love and power do not clash but find their harmony in the kingdom. The Messiahship of Christ is utterly unique. When we try to parallelize it with a political messianic ideal the gospel immediately speaks its corrective word.[25] The wisdom of those who wish to strive for Christ by protecting Him against the dark way of the cross is rejected as a wisdom in which not the things of God but the things of *man* are considered (Matt. 16:23).

The way of the cross as a way of suffering is at the same time the way to *true* power and authority. To the question *who* the Son of man is, Jesus answers with the promise that the powers of death shall not prevail against His Church (Matt. 16:18). It is precisely the way of the cross that will effect the powerlessness of *this* attack.[26] The powers of darkness[27] are serviceable — in the way of the cross — to the conferring of power on Christ. Because of this power John can say that in the apocalyptic struggle the Lamb shall conquer (Rev. 17:14).

This is not a triumph that is set forth in terms of human deductions or that can be construed on the basis of our insight into the "necessity" of God's being. It is the triumph of the kingdom. It is

---

25. Cf. among others John 6:15: Jesus withdrawing himself into the solitude of the mountains when he noticed that "they were about to come and take him by force to make him king." Cf. Matt. 26:51 and Luke 22:35 about the swords, and, on this subject, Ragnar Leivestad, *Christ the Conqueror*, 1954, pp. 27ff.

26. Cf. G. Kittel, *op. cit.*, III, p. 401: the Church is the "congregation of those who are stronger" in connection with Luke 11:22: *ischuteros* as over against *ischuros*.

27. Luke 22:53 (*exousia tou skotous*); Col. 1:13.

not the triumph of the kingdom outside of the gospel, but in indissoluble relationship to it.

In many and varying accents this relationship is made explicit. Paul thanks God "who in Christ always leads us in triumph, and through us spreads the fragrance of the knowledge of Him everywhere."[28] We read of the Rider on a white horse who makes war in righteousness, His robe dipped in blood, the name by which He is called being the Word of God (Rev. 11:11-13). Here resounds the word of the Almighty and of the name: King of kings and Lord of lords (vs. 16). The struggle is not one of an eternal dualism between hostile powers, but it is a truly real struggle and full of cosmic perspectives.

The kingdom of God has these power-aspects which derive their meaningfulness from the nature of this kingdom. The biblical apocalypse is not the mythological formulation of a "simple" grace but a designation of the tremendous aspects, the cosmic and world-historical proportions, of the kingdom of God.[29] The gospel is the proclamation of this kingdom. But it is a proclamation that is *full of exhortation,* and that because of the *eu*-aggelion, the grace of this conquering kingdom.[30]

For this reason alone criticism of universalism may never posit a *partial* triumph and thus belittle God's action. How can the word "partial" be harmonized with the eschatological emphasis of Scripture and with Paul's "from him and through him and to him are all things?" (Rom. 11:36).

There is but *one* answer to universalism, namely the kerugma, according to which God's triumph does not follow as a *second* and *uncertain* something upon His revelation in Christ.[31] It knows

---

28. II Cor. 2:14, *thriambeuo*. ". . .he regards it as grace that he may at all times and everywhere march in such slave chains in God's triumphant procession," G. Kittel, *op. cit.*, III, p. 160.

29. Cf. E. Stauffer, *Christus und die Ceasaren,* 1948, p. 112ff., and *Die Theologei des Neuen Testaments,* 1948, passim. Also, H. Ridderbos, *Paulus en Jezus,* 1952, p. 72ff.

30. This hortatory aspect detracts *nothing* from the aspect of proclamation, as also not from the *factual* aspect of which the apostles are *witnesses.* Cf. R. Schippers, *Getuigen van Jezus Christus in het Nieuwe Testament,* 1938, on the witness of *facts,* p. 198, which demand a decision. Through this factuality the Johannine witness becomes an accusation against unbelief, p. 199. In this way the apostles stand in the world as witnesses of Jesus' glory, p. 200.

31. In connection with the idea of "the failing god" and with the the criticism of Pierre Bayle, cf. the paragraph on "l 'échee initial de Dieu" in R. P. Sertillanges, *Le problème du mal,* II, 1951, p. 58ff.

only of the triumph of grace in connection with the revealed mystery itself.

When we have a proper regard for Jesus Christ as He is revealed to us in Scripture, no conclusions are possible or warranted which are drawn outside of faith. In the way of faith we see the glorious reflection of the triumph of faith. Also to the Church we must speak of this glory in the relationships in which Scripture presents it.

Salvation does not run dead in the alley of a self-sufficient Christianity which knows only that the world lies in the evil One. With an eye to this condition of the world the Church must know that she has been called precisely from this condition into her present state: "But you are a chosen race, a royal priesthood, a holy nation, God's own people, that you may declare the wonderful deeds of him who called you out of darkness into his marvelous light" (I Peter 2:9). Here we hear of election and grace and distinction from the world, but with a total exclusion of any distorted antithesis. All glorying in self is unmasked. Was this call not a calling *out of darkness?* And from this darkness to His *marvelous light?* As an *eternal* remembrance there will be inscribed above the life in glory, "Once you were no people but now you are God's people; once you had not received mercy but now you have received mercy" (vs. 10).

In this transition the marvelous light is reflected to which we are called. Boasting in self forgets the being called *out of* darkness. It ignores the "once not" to fix all attention on the "now" only. Glorying in self does not realize that this relationship is an inseparable one. *Here* we find with the most pronounced clarity the *boundary* between the triumph of grace and a false, misplaced triumph. God searches the heart,[32] and this searching is admonishingly included in the message of the gospel.

\* \* \*

The calling out of darkness into the marvelous light leads to the proclamation of the gospel to the world (I Peter 2:9). The way to the river of the water of life which flows from the throne of God and of the Lamb (Rev. 22:1) passes through history. It

---

32. Jer. 17:10. Cf. Ps. 139 vss. 1 and 23.

is the way to the great multitude which cannot be numbered, from every nation, from all tribes and peoples and tongues, standing before the throne and before the Lamb (Rev. 7:9), in connection with which we hear the hymn of praise, "Amen! Blessing and glory and wisdom and thanksgiving and honor and power and might be to our God for ever and ever! Amen!" (7:12).

This way to our wonderful future (7:16, 17) is a way of calling and invitation, of proclamation and admonition. It is not possible to speak meaningfully about God's grace in Jesus Christ outside of these contexts. Grace can be understood only by faith, and that as an incomprehensible gift and as an eschatological mystery. In the knowledge of guilt and through the gift of the Spirit the Church confesses and proclaims in the world the triumph of grace as the triumph of the kingdom. It is not a relationless triumph but one which we meet everywhere in the New Testament in its bearing on the mystery of godliness: "He was manifested in the flesh, vindicated in the Spirit, seen by angels, preached among the nations, believed on in the world, taken up in glory" (I Tim. 3:16). The triumph is not a purely objective something possessing a glory which stands apart from grace. The triumph stands in the context of the history of redemption and as such in the context of glory which is reflected in faith.

It is striking how strongly the New Testament emphasizes this triumphing of the kingdom. It shows us perspectives to which Christ Himself pointed in the course of His work: "The harvest is plentiful, but the laborers are few; pray therefore the Lord of the harvest to send out laborers into his harvest" (Matt. 9:37, 38).

The *Lord* of the *harvest*: also in this way can the relationships involved in the triumph of grace be summarized.

In all these relationships we see the history of God's salvation and the dynamic of the message: the proclamation of the gospel of the kingdom of God. Reflection on this triumph and on the harvest is legitimate only when it is done in the context of this mercy of Christ and of the preaching of the gospel.[33]

\* \* \*

This context is unable to function, however, when the gospel is overshadowed by an objective message about election which bears

33. Cf. G. Kittel, *op. cit.*, III, p. 133.

no vital relationship to the *proclamation*. Indeed, such a message concerning election *cannot* bear a vital relation to the proclamation even when it is later — because of the power of the scriptural witness — again brought into relation with it.

The *a priori* idea of the election of all cannot later again be given a place in the kerugma. The proclamation concerning the Messianic kingdom has already been reduced to a mere announcement about a given state of affairs which cannot subsequently be re-formed into a real proclamation. Over against this effort to make the proclamation significant we see in Scripture the concrete area of conflict in which the kingdom manifests itself triumphantly. We must allude here to our earlier discussion concerning Barth's conception of the unity of creation and reconciliation. His "supralapsarianism," we saw, casts a haze over the entire historical area because he concludes from the a priori triumph to the ontological impossibility of sin. All that occurs in the area of history in the way of guilt and rebellion has already been taken away by the *a priori* triumph. The transition from "once not" to "now," from wrath to grace, from "far off" to "near," came in its *extraordinary* importance to stand in the background. The New Testament is full of this transition in its historical significance.

The struggle could in this way assume the form of an a priori conquest of the enigmatic chaos which was rejected already at creation by virtue of the divine No. The "mysterium iniquitatis" came in a peculiar way to stand in *this* triumphant light. Even though creation and reconciliation were not identified but distinguished, the real *confrontation* took place between the chaos rejected at creation and the reconciliation which effected this rejection. The prefiguration of the triumph of grace in the revelation of creation is for Barth more than a "significat." When one takes note of the "tertium comparationis" it can be said that creation provides a real "est." The chaotic — in its quality as rejected possibility — is an aspect of creation and receives in this way its own dimensions which can be depicted in all their horribly threatening character. It functions as antithetical material against the background of which the triumph of grace stands revealed. All that is left, in terms of this triumphant fundamental structure of creation, is to pursue the necessary way to the radical "emptying" of the chaos which in Christ has become *manifest*.

The summons to fearlessness is based on the *apparent* reality of the darkness and of the chaos.

Barth's speaking about the triumph of grace centers about this conception and is immediately significant for preaching and pastoral care. He wishes to point to the shining and radiant light as *the* source of comfort, also in catastrophic times. The struggle against the "powers" becomes a struggle against the *as yet blinded eyes.* Because of the triumph the powers appear only as the *fatal creation* of man in his blindness, in his not-yet-seeing what the true and inviolable reality is. It is only because of the blindness of unbelief that the powers are clothed with the appearance of reality.

There is every reason to call attention to this once again in this final chapter.

Barth's theology discusses the "powers" at a decisive point in his exposition and it does so in its quality as a theology of *grace.* Even though Barth consciously limits his attention to "God's adversary" to the smallest degree possible, it is not inconceivable that precisely at this point the validity of his theology of grace will be determined. The *unusual* attention which the New Testament gives to the need of resisting the demons indicates that the triumph of grace can be understood only when it is seen in its concrete context. The New Testament, one could say, does not speak *less* but rather *differently* about the vanquishing of the demons than Barth does. Believers are called not to fear so much as a single threat, but this call comes in the midst of real *conflict.* Nowhere is the disappearance of the enemy and the incipient end of the struggle implied. On the contrary, we read of a struggle whose bitterness is derived from the fact that it takes place "post Christum."

We hear the message of the kingdom which has come in Christ and of the signs of triumph that accompany it. We hear of the decision that has been taken in the cross and the resurrection of Jesus Christ, to whom *all* authority has been given in heaven and on earth. There has been a *dethroning* of the powers, a conquest by Christ of the principalities and powers of which he has made a public example (Col. 2:15). The coming of the kingdom has radically altered the situation in the battle area. A decision *has been taken* with respect to the powers. It is the decision of the fulness of time which has been revealed in the appearance of Jesus Christ "who abolished death and brought life and immortality to light through the gospel" (II Tim. 1:10). He came, He was revealed for *this* purpose, namely to destroy the works of the devil (I John 3:8), to enter the *strong* man's house, to bind him and to plunder his goods (Matt. 12:29).

But this unmasking, this dethroning, do not yet mean, according to the New Testament, the definite end of the struggle. There has indeed come a mighty, decisive, concretely historical turning point in it, but this turning point directs our eyes to the future in which Christ's omnipotent power will be manifested in the *end* of the conflict when Christ will deliver the kingdom to God the Father "after destroying every rule and every authority and power" (I Cor. 15:24). Ultimately there is only one dethronement by the one Christ, but if we wish to do justice to the New Testament we may not fail to recognize these perspectives that characterize history and the end of history. In the last days the conflict bears the *unique* character of a struggle that takes place *after* the issue has been decided and in the *light of* this decision. In the last days the spirit of antichrist will be revealed who does *not* confess Christ. "This is the spirit of antichrist, of which you have heard that it was coming, and now it is in the world already" (I John 4:3). It is precisely *in* the coming of the antichrist and of many antichrists that *"we know that it is the last hour."*[34]

The last hour does not exclude this reality but it stands revealed *as the last hour* precisely *in* the reality of *this* denial. The date of the antichrist is strictly a date in the *history of redemption*. *In* his denial and in his continued tempting he is an utterly dependent figure, the antithetical correlate of the outpouring of the Holy Spirit through which men call upon the name of Christ and learn to say that Jesus is *Lord* (I Cor. 12:3). There is not therefore a sort of dualism of two equal powers which fascinates with its drama. It is rather a *unique* conflict which is indissolubly related to the issue that has been *decided*, with the turning point which *has taken place,* with the great *historical* transition: "the darkness

---

34. I John 2:18. With his warning signal (the antichrists) John "wishes to characterize his time as eschatologically significant." They are "characteristic signs of this peculiar time," R. Schnackenburg, *Die Johannesbriefe,* 1953, p. 125.

is passing away and the true light is already shining" (I John 2:8).

That this reality — "I saw Satan fall like lightning from heaven" (Luke 10:18) — together with the present activity of the antichrist, is now disclosed to us in no sense devaluates the triumph and the comfort of grace. Believers do not pursue their way in the knowledge that the threat is no longer a real one, but they do know that this threat has been overruled in their communion with Christ. And they know of an *ultimate* total annulment of this power which will become manifest in the parousia. Whatever the threat can and does in fact effect, it can never effect separation from the love of Christ (Rom. 8:38ff.).

In this communion the triumph of the love of God comes to full revelation in the lives of believers. It is the divine comfort which does not consist in the absence of threat, but in the radical *boundary* which has been set to its power and effectiveness. The conflict of the last days is a conflict of faith, love, and expectation. It is not the *self-evident victory* that characterizes the last hour, but *this struggle*. It is the struggle of confrontation not with an unqualifiedly strong power, but with *this* power of temptation which takes place *after* the issue has been decided. Paul sends Timothy to Thessalonica that he might know their faith "for fear that somehow the tempter had tempted you and that our labor would be in vain" (I Thess. 3:5). This concern can be understood only in the light of the *reality* of the danger that threatens the Church.

It is not possible to escape being impressed by the reality of the demonic world to which the New Testament points. It speaks of the snare of the devil,[35] of varying forms of temptation,[36] of the need for soberness and watchfulness,[37] of the danger of giving opportunity to the devil.[38]

For these reasons it is not possible to speak about the triumph of grace and of the kingdom of God without taking full note of this emphasis. The eschatological perspectives of victory do not appear apart from grace but in direct connection with it, and this not in a few apocalyptic parts of Scripture, but in daily and joyful

---

35. I Tim. 3:7; II Tim. 2:26.
36. Cf. I Cor. 7:5; Eph. 6:11.
37. I Peter 5:8; James 4:7; Eph. 6:16; Acts 13:10.
38 Eph. 4:27. Cf. 6:10ff.

admonition to the Church. The words, "the God of *peace* will soon crush Satan under your feet. The *grace* of our Lord Jesus Christ be with you" (Rom. 16:20), stand wholly in the context of the admonition of vss. 17-19. They are words of triumph in their bearing upon Satan *and* upon the grace of Jesus Christ. In *this* way they speak about the God of *peace*.[39]

It is well to remember these things when we speak about the triumph of grace, lest we create tensions between the triumph of *grace* and the triumph of the *kingdom*.

All depends here on the reality of the threat which characterizes the last days. Unquestionably, the New Testament reckons with the reality of the threat of the demons continually and in a very concrete manner.[40] There is indeed a blindness of the eyes, but the origin of this blindness lies in the reality of the threatening power. It is not occasioned by self-deception or by a misunderstanding caused by unbelief. Nor is the "reality" of the demons an original creation of man. On the contrary, there is a *meeting* of, a confrontation with, a concrete *adversary*, as Peter calls him (I Peter 5:8), there is a trial which is coming on the whole world (Rev. 3:10), a synagogue and a throne of Satan (2:9, 13), a being cast into prison by him (2:10).

This places the apostolic witness in full accord with the eschatological witness of Christ (Matt. 24:21, 24) in which He indicates the reality of the danger by saying that if those days had not been shortened no human being would be saved.[41] A sharp look at this reality appears, according to the whole of the New Testament, to involve not a threat to joy but reveals rather the context in which the joy is experienced.

In the 19th century the process of "Entmythologisierung" began in which the demons were eliminated from the relationship between God and man. This relationship was spiritualized and deprived of its "mythical" aspects. In later time — in our time —

---

39. Cf. the benediction in Romans 15:33.
40. The concrete variations with which Paul speaks of this reality are striking. Cf. I Thess. 2:18 (Satan hindered us) and the "hindering" in Rom. 1:13; 15:22; Acts 16:6-7 (without demonic aspects). Note also II Cor. 12:7 (the messenger of Satan), I Cor. 5:5 (in connection with discipline), and II Cor. 2:11 (in connection with conditions in the Church). Note further the words of Christ in the Gospels which are striking by reason of their concreteness: Luke 22:31-32; Luke 10:18; John 14:30; 12:31.
41. Matt. 24:22. Cf. Mark 13:20: He *has* shortened those days.

the "suprapersonal" aspects of evil came to the fore again and gradually men began to speak about the "demonization" of life.  It appeared that the demons were the objects of renewed attention, that
the "power" of demonic manifestations of catastrophic suprapersonal character was bringing about a new "acknowledgment."
Denis de Rougemont and C. S. Lewis have impressed many with
all manner of forgotten but very real aspects of the demonic world.

It was a sign of the times when a book appeared — of 666
pages! — entitled "Satan," advertized with the question, "Who is
the Master who, invisible and intangible, hidden behind the cur-
tain of our life, directs wth unparalleled genius the drama of world
evil?"

In a variety of ways attention is here called to the many dark
corridors through which this power moves in history and in the
conscious and subconscious life of man.  It is hardly possible to
think of a sharper contrast than is found between this comprehensive and all-too-interested attention for the "Master-director"
and the mere fifteen pages about "God's adversary" of Barth's
*Dogmatik.*  Even when we clearly discern the dangers of this concentrated attention we will not be able to close our eyes to the
peculiar problem involved in Barth's "demonology" in which his
conception of the triumph of grace as it were *culminates.*  It culminates in the *brevity* of the look that is cast at this wasteland of
the spirit.

The question arises —  an important question in connection
with the triumph of the kingdom — whether Barth, too, is introducing a program of "Entmythologisierung."  He himself has answered this question.  He is willing to avail himself of the word
"Entmythologisierung" but *not* "in the current, somewhat banal
and phenomenological sense."[42]  There can be a "demythologizing"
only in the sense of *theological exorcism,* namely, as "an act of unbelief arising from belief."  The "foundation lie underlying
all lies" must be seen for what it is in terms of *Christian truth.*
The demonic world is not seen as a fallen angelic host but as that
*chaotic* power which exists under God's "No," as that *unreal* reality which is "unreal" because it is not the being of God nor the
being of the creature.[43]

---

42. KD III/3, p. 611.        43. *Ibid.,* p. 613.

Here we stand before the problem of Barth's *brief* demonology to which we referred earlier. We stand before the fact of the *existential* brevity of this part of Barth's *Dogmatik*. The attention to *this* subject can, in his judgment, be brief because it is attention that is given to a *fallen*, a *conquered* power. It could again receive the appearance of a great power only if we were to give much attention to it and treat it as a matter still deserving of respect.

We ask again, however, what this exorcism, this theological *ban* is. Is this "exorcism" supported by appeal to the New Testament? It is remarkable that Barth hardly discusses the New Testament data about the demons.[44] In view of the emphasis which the New Testament lays on the *concentration* of opposition *after* the completion of Christ's earthly work and at the coming of the kingdom, there is every reason why Barth should have discussed this aspect of the New Testament witness. The New Testament itself sees to it that we shall not give the demons *independent* attention. Its attention is an attention given in the context of *relations*. In the apostolic witness the triumph of the kingdom is a triumph that takes place in relation to Christology and soteriology. The struggle that leads to this triumph is not simply a power conflict. It is rather a struggle that is elicited and decided *in terms of reconciliation*. Cross and resurrection determine the nature of the struggle.

The legitimate place which our confrontation with evil, which is the real front in the conflict, finds in the New Testament is indicated by Jesus' weaving the petition for deliverance from evil into the Lord's prayer. This petition reflects the little time that is left to the powers of darkness. The summons not to fear is legitimate only when it is seen in this context. It comes to us in the whole of the dynamic situation of the last days. In that situation the summons has its place, its truly honorable place. When it is robbed of this concreteness, however, the danger of underestimating the dethroned powers immediately arises. Temptation may not be changed into a subjective blinding of the eyes.

There is indeed a "Jenseits" in which the conflict is at an end. But, however strongly the New Testament makes us yearn for

---

44. On this cf. Bent Noack, *Satanas und Soteria. Untersuchungen zur N. T.-lichen Dämonologie*, 1948, and Ragnar Leiverstad, *Christ the Conqueror, Ideas of Conflict and Victory in the New Testament*, 1954.

this "Jenseits," it clearly indicates the contours of the battle area for the period of the last days, the period that may be designated as *post Christum*. We read of the mystery of lawlessness which is already at work (II Thess. 2:7). There is a working of Satan "with all power and with pretended signs and wonders, and with all wicked deception" (II Thess. 2:9,10). This does not, however, involve the giving of *separate* attention to dark apocalyptic events, for all this stands written in a chapter that speaks of *gratitude* and *love*, of *sanctification* and *faith*, and of the *glory* of Christ (vss. 13ff.).

Not least because of these relationships Bultmann's "Entmythologisierung" constitutes a weakening of true Christian alertness against the powers of evil, and Barth's (different) "Entmythologisierung" has the same effect. In Bultmann this is all quite plain. Certain it is that there is nothing to fear from the evil powers as a "myth." Barth, on the other hand, while he does not wish to eliminate the evil powers, does wish to eliminate fear of and respect for them. Not the demons are banned, but the unbelief is which reckoned with their chaos-power. In Barth's demonology we meet the danger of a self-evident fearlessness, of the denial of the activity of the dethroned powers post Christum, concerning which the whole of the New Testament testifies.

It is therefore not accidental that in this final chapter we make the lines of the discussion converge on the "brevity" of Barth's demonology. Particularly at this point we see how dogmatics touches the proclamation, the pastoral office, and prayer. How is it possible that Barth's view of the "unreality" of the demons should *not* influence the total attitude of the Church during the period of the last days?

In dark and crucial times it is, of course, possible to "overestimate" the demons and to turn them into God's equals in strength as they engage Him in a breath-taking conflict. It is possible — as is in fact being done in the 20th century — to speak of the "enigma" and the "demonization" of man's life, and suppose that this is the hour of the powers of darkness.

We must remember, however, that in another period of history these words were spoken: "this is your hour and the power of darkness" (Luke 22:53). It was in the time of the "passio magna," in the time of judgment, that these words were uttered. Since that time we hear the message, "the darkness is passing away and the true light is already shining" (I John 2:8). But although even in the 20th century a *dualistic* world and life view has no right to existence, still it would not be warranted to underestimate the dethroned powers. We must always be able to understand *in concreto* and in the *dynamic of responsibility* Paul's concern about the threat of having labored "in vain" (I Thess. 3:5). The problem of how rightly to evaluate the power of the demonic host can never be solved abstractly and theoretically. It can be resolved only *in Christ,* in faith, love, and prayer. The "sola fide" and the "sola gratia" retain their actuality and concreteness in the last days. They may not be seen out of relation to the tempting evil which is overcome and will be overcome only in communion with the living Lord.

Had Barth allowed his thinking about the demons to be corrected by the witness of the New Testament, his view of the triumph of grace would have been affected. It would have been affected not in the sense of a weakening or of an attenuation of the triumph of grace, but in the sense of larger appreciation for the relationships in which the Scriptures speak of the triumph of grace. In casting his "brief glance" at the demons he did not choose to follow this course but continued to oppose the "bad dream" of dogmatics, namely, the fallen angels.

It is clear that this conception is not an unimportant digression in Barth's dogmatics. Inseparably related to it is the whole problem of the non-creaturely chaos which now in Christ — the revelation of *grace* — belongs radically to the past. We can now live only in terms of this universal and juridically effective Yes to which we are called in Christ. In Him we cannot again enter into the "impossibility" of living in the shadow that belongs *to the past.* Barth's "demonology" is the reverse-side of his view of the triumph of grace because the "realization" of the prefiguration of the triumph of creation constitutes its *exclusive* content.

It would seem that Barth, at least in his "demonology," stands rooted in the 19th century more than appears at first glance to be the case.[45] It is true that deep differences can be pointed out between his conception and that of 19th century thinking. Its rejection of demonology and Barth's "brief look" at it cannot be brought together in the common denominator of an "optimistic" world and life view.[46] Nevertheless, the comparison is instructive. When Brunner in 1924 published his study about Schleiermacher, he typified the contrast between Schleiermacher and the "theology of the Word" as that of "the optimism of development" in antithesis to "the idea of the antichrist."[47] Over against Schleiermacher's "monism"[48] he posited the New Testament witness concerning the *judgment* which was not weakened by the knowledge of the grace of God.[49]

Brunner's criticism of Schleiermacher pointed to the existence of an "eschatological vacuum" in his theology.[50] When after the passing of thirty years we recall this judgment, it appears that Barth's "Entmythologisierung," his exorcism of the demons — in terms of Christ — has something else in mind than the simplistic criticism of the 19th century which had little eye for the destructive power of evil. Barth's emphasis falls precisely on the terror-inspiring chaos which now no longer affects us because it has been overcome. It is not because of any confidence in man but only because of Christ, because of the "sola fide" and the "sola gratia" that the look at the demons can be *brief*. In the midst of the chaos problem stands the *grace* of God. Barth certainly has no desire to

---

45. It may be asked how far this is true also with respect to Barth's *angelology*. Cf. KD III/, pp. 426-608, where Barth's views about the angels come to expression in terms of "function" and "service." Angels are "not to be regarded as independent subjects but as, in a certain sense, consisting in their function which is wholly, which is exemplarily, one of service" (p. 429). In this way they are representatives of the mystery (p. 434). On the subject of orthodox angelology cf. p. 438. Note the concept "to exist in relation," p. 477, and the creation of the angels, p. 526. With respect to *individual* angels of which the Bible speaks, this is not "to be pressed ontologically," p. 532.

46. Note, for instance, the acknowledgment of Schleiermacher, *Der Christliche Glaube*, 6th ed., 1884, I, pp. 198-199, that the devil "appears frequently in the New Testament, but neither Christ nor the apostles teach a new doctrine about him," p. 202. Belief in a continuing kingdom of Satan would weaken joyful courage and would be destructive of Christian love, p. 209. Poetical usage (personification) need not be disadvantageous to piety and therefore the representation of Satan does not have to be removed from the Church's treasury of song.

47. E. Brunner, *Die Mystik und das Wort*, 1924, pp. 288-312.

48. *Ibid.*, p. 219: His philosophy of history is an open and uncompromising confession of Monism.

49. *Ibid.*, p. 308.

50. *Ibid.*, pp. 268-287.

give comfort to a pessimistic view of life which, influenced by a catastrophic period in human history, does not regard joy in Christ to be the answer to the heaviness that fills the hearts of men. Rather he wishes in his dogmatics to sound forth the witness to the *radical* joy that is in Christ, in which confession alone, according to Barth, one can live and die.

This is the gripping thing in every confrontation with Barth's "triumph of grace" and calls for responsible analysis of his theology. For the accents of the triumph — "the word of God is not bound" (II Tim. 2:9) — resound continually and break their way through all presuppositions as we hear the call in these apocalyptic times not to close our eyes for the great *Light*.

The criticism that Barth accentuates grace *too much* is a senseless criticism. It cannot be denied, however, that the fulness of the grace of God in its significance for the proclamation and the worship of the Church will not receive its due place until the witness of the New Testament breaks through Barth's demonology in its inseparable relationship to the connection that Barth posits between *creation* and the *chaos*. For in both the demonology and the creation-chaos relationship that one non-created chaos "reality" is concerned which falls outside of the dimension of created being and which therefore gives rise to the uncertainties that cast their shadow also over the triumph of grace. Only by such a breakthrough can Barth's opposition against synergism and modern Protestant theology become fully effective. For then these uncertainties, this problem, would recede into the background. Then the "a priori" triumph would no longer lead to an obscuration of the *history* of redemption. Then election could be meaningfully confessed without introducing the problem of the dangerous unbelief which is in the end unable to put to naught the grace of God. Then the opposition to natural theology would not lead to a "supralapsarianism" in which there is no real place for a transition from creation to the fall and, in the fallen world, from wrath to grace. Then too, finally, eschatology would no longer because of the triumph of grace be overshadowed by the idea of the "eternalizing" of this present existence.

\* \* \*

When we think about these things we are impressed anew by the significance of *sin* in theological reflection. When the Reformation replaced the scholastic antithesis between *nature* and grace with that between *sin* and grace, it entered directly into the area of total corruption *and* of sovereign grace. In doing so the Reformation spoke plainly and rejected the accusation of "pessimism" with respect to human nature. It was not interested in an independent "pessimistic" approach to man but with the reality of guilt in connection with the reality of grace. Not only in the Reformation, but in the entire history of the Church and of theology it appears that the relationship betweeen sin and grace is of decisive significance. It is this even when it assumes the form of an antithesis between nature and grace. The confession of the triumph of grace is always correlative to the confession of *guilt*. It need therefore not surprise us when we find this relationship also in Barth's thinking. It is the antithesis between chaos and grace that stamps his theology. His entire theology is a theology of grace against the background of this chaos. It is not a crisis-theology that he proposes, but rather an *overcoming* of the crisis through grace.

This conquest is not an incidental historical event, but it takes place in terms of the eternal counsel of God. This explains why Barth's thinking about the triumph of grace followed the path of the radical a priori character of the triumph. This a priori factor proved to be of immediate significance for his understanding of the origin and the reality of sin. They came to stand *in the light* of the a priori consideration through which sin as the chaos, as the judged and rejected evil, was closely related to God's eternal self-distinction, *i. e.* with respect to what God is not. The counsel of God functioned as the principle of explanation whereby sin became even more "understandable" than in the view from time to time expressed by the "felix culpa." It became "understandable" not in any excusing sense, but as the echo of God's eternal Yes. Because sin is *this* echo, the triumph of grace is the center of Barth's theology.

The problem posed by this "necessary" a priori character of the triumph in its relationship to history became *the* problem of Barth's theology. It will never do to criticize Barth's theology by

placing over against it *another* explanation of sin and of its reality. Whenever sin is "explained" shadows fall across the path
of the Church and of theology. The way of speculation always
leads to confusion. The Reformation took position over against
this confusion. It refused to go beyond the limits of revelation
to construct a rational "unity" which would endanger the reality
of guilt and its historical reconciliation. It was therefore willing
to speak of creation and reconciliation but not of "nature" and
grace. In construing the relationship between them it did not
historicize salvation but retained the correlation between guilt and
reconciliation.

The "problem" of the origin of sin was in this way clearly circumscribed. Sin lost every trace of anonymity. It was often indeed referred to as an "enigma," but this qualification had standing only with respect to efforts to deprive sin of its culpable character whereby it was given a natural place in the life of man.
Apart from this consideration any designation of sin as "enigmatic"
is illegitimate. It is also illegitimate to designate the enigma as the
"impossibility" of sin in terms of the a priori triumph. Only when
sin is freed from its "enigmatic" character can it be correlative to
reconciliation. The full concreteness and the dynamic of history
then appears.

In this context we must speak of the triumph of grace, of the
triumph of the kingdom. It is a triumph that places us in the midst
of promise and responsibility, of calling and admonition. Where
the triumph of grace is acknowledged and confessed, there the
eu-aggelion of the kingdom is preached in the world. When the
Spirit of Christ is poured out over all flesh we are carried along
in the *victory procession* of Christ throughout the world. In times
of stress and conflicting powers Christ's course through the world
may not seem to be a victory procession. But it is that nevertheless, and transcends any possibility of human usurpation. It is the
revelation of triumphant authority, of power and might, of *royal*
lordship. It is the lordship of the conquering gospel, of the good
message which calls for response. It is the proclamation of the
kingdom and the exhortation to enter it. It is calling and invitation.

In this triumph of the kingdom all human self-elevation, all
phariseeism, can only be radically condemned as a threat to the

Church of Jesus Christ. The certainty of the Church that she will participate in the triumph against the gates of hell is the certainty of faith which pursues its way in fear and trembling. This certainty knows that he who stands must take heed lest he fall. In this way the victory is realized. The victory is not without threat, but it faces and overcomes the threat. It is the victory about which we cannot speak abstractly, but only in terms of the conquest of our own rebellious heart by *this* irresistible power. *This* knowledge must continually be in the mind of the Church and must constitute the background of her whole life. With this knowledge, and filled with the irresistible power and the marvel of the triumph about which it speaks, she must go forth to encounter the world. She does not go about construing, she does not wander outside the limits of her calling, but she rests, ashamed of her own small faith, in the word of the Lord: "The harvest is plentiful, but the laborers are few; pray therefore the Lord of the harvest to send out laborers into his harvest" (Matt. 9:37, 38).

Jesus spoke this word after he had gone about all the cities and villages, teaching in their synagogues and *preaching* the gospel of the kingdom. He had seen the crowds and was filled with compassion for them because they were harassed and helpless, like sheep without a shepherd, vss. 35, 36.

*This* Lord has spoken His decisive word: ". . . be of good cheer, I have overcome the world," John 16:33.

# THE PROBLEM OF INTERPRETATION

In the discussions surrounding the theology of Karl Barth the matter of interpretation plays a very important role. It would be possible, in connection with Protestant and Roman Catholic literature on the subject, to write a lengthy study on the variations in the interpretation of Barth. This whole issue is intimately related to the danger of *subjectivity* in the interpretation, a danger which is not in the least imaginary in the case of so comprehensive a work as Barth's dogmatics.

In connection with this it presumably is not superfluous in this appendix to give some account of the criticism which I made in various footnotes of the Dutch edition of my book of the interpretation of Professor C. Van Til, who, in his volume *The New Modernism: An Appraisal of the Theology of Barth and Brunner* (2nd Edition, 1947) and in his later study "Has Karl Barth Become Orthodox?" (*Westminster Theological Journal*, 1954), passed a radically critical judgment on the theology of Karl Barth by entering a negative reply to the question of that second book. He set the new modernism over against orthodoxy, and it can be said that this is just the bone of contention in the various interpretations. Since my footnotes on Van Til have been omitted from the English edition of my book, and in view of certain discussions of mine in the American press, I present here a summary of my position. For the question is and will remain an important one in connection with the issue of Barth and the influence of his theology, and is one, therefore, which compels us all to make a serious and a responsible analysis of his work. It is my idea that the criticism of Barth's theology and the objections to it can have importance in the responsible discussion of our time only if they are based upon a legitimate and warranted analysis of his work. If that is not altogether the case, one can summarily reject Barth, but there will be no real opposition in the argument for the simple reason that those who thereupon proceed to read Barth himself will not be able to recognize the relevancy of the criticism presented.

\* \* \*

The struggle going on around the interpretation of Barth is concentrated for the most part upon what we call "the philosophical background" of his thought. In any theology there is threat of the danger that particular philosophical presuppositions will cast their shadow upon the light of God's Word, and it is, accordingly, always a good and necessary thing, by way of warning, to conduct an investigation into whether or not in a given writer this is so. It certainly is not right to hold — and in this I quite agree with Van Til — that the philosophical assumptions underlying a theology are of no importance. Think, for instance, of the tremendous influence of Hegel's philosophy on the Christological development in the theology of the nineteenth century. One cannot easily over-estimate the influence of philosophy in theology. It has often had a serious influence for the bad: for example, when principles that were incompatible with the Word of God affected the interpretation of the gospel.

Van Til, however, on the basis of philosophical assumptions which he thinks he finds in Barth, comes to some very audacious utterances. I am thinking of his statement about Brunner: "a theology of revelation without revelation, a theology of creation without creation, a theology of sin without sin, a theology of Christ without Christ" (*The New Modernism,* p. 267); and, concerning Barth, I am thinking of Van Til's statement: "If we substitute the word 'reality' for Barth's word 'God', we shall not be far amiss in catching his meaning" (*The New Modernism,* p. 231); and of his saying that Barth's theology leads to the view that people may think "that they are not subject to the wrath of God, that their sins need not be washed away through the blood of the Son of God and Son of Man, Jesus of Nazareth, who was born of the virgin Mary, died and rose again with the same body with which he was laid in the tomb. For men to depend upon the Jesus Christ of Barth is to depend upon themselves as inherently righteous" ("Has Karl Barth Become Orthodox?", p. 181).

In regard to such statements it is evident that whoever has read the last part of Barth's *Dogmatik* (IV/1, 1953, IV/2 is about to appear), that part of it, namely, which deals with the atonement and the substitution of the servant of the Lord, must necessarily react with a number of questions. It is altogether understandable, consequently, that others who themselves stood critically disposed in many ways to the theology of Barth could nevertheless not go along with Van Til's analysis and hence with his criticsm of Barth. I am thinking, for example, of the celebrated book of Hans Urs von Balthasar (*Karl Barth: Darstellung und Deutung seiner Theologie*, 1951), in which he calls Van Til's presentation of Barth "völlig grotesk" because of the fact that Van Til deduces Barth's whole theology from the philosophical assumptions which he thinks are underlying it. And I think also of the book of a Reformed theologian in The Netherlands (M. P. Van Dijk, *Existentie en Genade*, 1952) which itself sharply criticizes Barth but the author of which nevertheless rejects the analysis and the method of Van Til's criticism. Such a rejection, consequently, does not in the least imply an acceptance of Barth's theology, but constitutes only a criticism of an unsound analysis which draws conclusions which Barth himself draws least of all, conclusions, in fact, *which he himself has more than once and at great length opposed.* The motives of such criticism are not apparent in Van Til, and it is this that is unsatisfactory in Van Til's analysis and constitutes the reason why those motives are not appropriated by those who also criticize Barth and who are by no means silent about their objections and regard them as important. Van Til has no eye for the fact that often in the history of dogma particular philosophical assumptions played a part in a theology, assumptions, that is, *in which* and *alongside of which* an influence of the Word of God makes itself felt in such a way that it is impossible *to deduce* the theology logically and consequentially from the particular philosophical assumptions. Because Van Til thinks that he can point out certain assumptions in Barth, he thinks he can draw the lines of them *on through,* and so essential statements of Barth are neglected or distorted. Accordingly, he no longer has an eye for particular facets of Barth's theology; so much comes out in Van Til's view of Karl Barth's defense of the doctrine of the virgin birth. Van Til has no appreciation for this defense. Since 1927 Barth has defended the reality of the virgin birth over against Brunner, who, also since 1927, has launched a sharp and inclusive attack upon this doctrine. In his defense, Barth is going counter to a tradition of criticism of approximately a century's standing. But Van Til has no appreciation for it, since he writes as follows of this defense: "Barth's criticism of Brunner's rejection of the virgin birth is therefore far from being undertaken in the interest of a return to orthodoxy. Quite the contrary" ("Has Karl Barth Become Orthodox?" p. 165). As I see it, Professor Dr. Z. U. Zuidema's judgment is sounder when he writes of Barth's defense of the virgin birth: "Thanks also to the career of Barth, the doubt on exegetical and textual critical grounds of the scriptural foundation for this doctrine — and it was such doubt that Brunner and Kohnstamm used as a weapon in attacking the dogma — has had to give way to a renewed acknowledgment of the reliability of the scriptural basis."

But that is not the only point. I think also of the views of the concept of God and of the Trinity in Barth. More than once Barth has simply been accused of modalism. This charge was brought to the fore again, also recently and in connection with the problem of the ontological trinity. Van Til thinks that Barth rejects the ontological trinity. How, indeed, could it be otherwise when according to Van Til the situation is such that "for Barth there is no transcendent or antecedent God at all. But he continues to use the word God as modern theology in general continues to use it"? Whoever wants to criticize Barth in this line has, as I see it, first of all the task of penetrating *deeply* into the elaborate explanations in which Barth *defends* the ontological trinity and *attacks* modalism. It certainly does not suffice to say: He denies all that, and never once to enter upon Barth's expressed defense. This seems to me to be an elementary requirement of scholarship, and when we attack each other in such a way, the attack, as I see it, is fruitless. At any event, one would have to take account of Barth's argumentation, as, for example, was done in the calm and deliberate dissertation of Dr. J. A. Heyns of South Africa on the subject *Die Grondstruktuur van die Modalistische Triniteitsbeskouwing* (Dissertation, Free University, Amsterdam, 1953). Certainly also an investigation ought then to be made of the significance of the criticism which Barth himself has made of particular philosophical influences which had formerly exerted an influence upon him — namely, in his *Römerbrief* — as well as of the significance of the sharp criticism which Barth has directed against modern theology, a criticism of which his attack on Bultmann especially is a very clear example. One can say that Barth denies the resurrection from the dead, but one ought sometime to try to demonstrate this from the criticism which Barth in his *Dogmatik* (III/2) directs against the denial of this resurrection of Christ by Bultmann. My main objection to Van Til's interpretation is not that he criticizes Barth. I criticize Barth also, and in this very book, but Van Til's analysis does not correspond to the deepest intents of Barth's theology. Hence it does not surprise me that Barth says in *amazement* that he *cannot recognize himself at all* in *The New Modernism.*

As I see it, the deepest ground of this unwarranted interpretation consists of this: that only particular parts of Barth's theology come into consideration — a factor which makes for great one-sidedness — and that the *whole* of Barth's theology is not discussed in terms of all his writings. Hence the motivating lines of Barth's development in contrast to the modern theology and his great appreciation of Kohlbrugge do not become at all clear. Nor does it become clear why so sharp an attack upon him is being conducted by most of the prominent liberal theologians. Apparently they recognize that in Barth's theology they are coming into contact with a form of theological thought which they cannot merely subordinate and work into their *own* theological system.

And in general I should like to remember in connection with Barth what Schrotenboer wrote with reference to Brunner: "It cannot be denied that in many places the light of the truth of the Word breaks through and finds expression in his theology" (Paul Schrotenboer, *A New Apologetics: An Analysis and Appraisal of Emil Brunner's Theology*, Dissertation, Free University, 1955). Personally I judge that this happens less in Brunner than it does in Barth. I think of Brunner's sharp attacks upon the virgin birth, of his playing fast and loose with many scriptural data without attempting any thoroughgoing and serious exegesis; but what, together with Schrotenboer, I should like to see applied to Brunner,

I should like to see applied to Barth also. Such is the problem of synthesis which Van Til, as I judge it, has not sufficiently seen. It is a problem which indeed plays a role not only in Barth. It is a general problem in the whole of the history of dogma. It applies — to mention no others — also to Augustine and Thomas. Anyone who undertook to judge of their theology on the basis of particular philosophical influences would simply have to arrive at a negative judgment, both of Augustine (Neo-Platonism) and of Thomas (Aristotle). But it is evident that the relationships are too complicated to permit of this kind of argumentation. This implies no weakening of criticism, but it does imply a clearer view of the situation; and it takes account of the powerful influence of the Word of God, which, as I view it, is the secret of the history of dogma, and which, frequently also in the Reformed theology, into which scholasticism has ever again tried to penetrate, has offered strong resistance along ways which were not in themselves above suspicion but rather were fraught with danger.

\* \* \*

Whoever leads a person out of particular assumptions to an absurd position seems to be a sharp critic. But at bottom such criticism is weak and such as cannot in the long run hold its own against exhaustive analysis. The impression can, of course, easily be created that those who oppose unsound and partial or inexhaustive criticism do this because they are in agreement with Barth's theology. But that is not the situation. At issue in this is the matter of a truly *responsible* analysis, for it is only on the basis of a penetrating and thoroughgoing analysis of a person's intents and bearings that solid criticism can be based.

\* \* \*

I am aware of the fact that anyone who risks an appraisal of Barth's theology is surrounded by dangers. It is by no means a simple matter, and it probably is true that in such a judgment also one's personal insights play a considerable role. But it is precisely when all together we want to proceed from the riches and truth of the Reformed confession, and in that confession from the absolute authority of Holy Scripture, that light should in the long run dawn on our discussions. Personally I think that at bottom the difference in interpretation springs from our view of the relationship obtaining between theology and philosophy in the history of dogma. And in the background of this difference there lies also a difference in our view of *orthodoxy*. More than once Van Til, also again in his last brochure, has in his opposition to Barth drawn a picture of orthodoxy in which I cannot recognize the features of the real *Reformed* orthodoxy. This took on concrete significance in connection with the fact that when in the Dutch edition of this book I had at several points reproduced Van Til's meaning it was said that in these instances I had been reproducing the meaning of Barth. I eagerly take opportunity, therefore, to explain all this once more in greater detail. It is indeed true that Van Til often *paraphrases* Barth. But the difficulty arises from the fact that in this paraphrase an image of "orthodoxy" is being presented which as I see it does not square at all with the reality of orthodoxy. In the paraphrase of Barth's criticism of orthodoxy it is remarked, among other things, that Barth opposes the idea of orthodoxy which holds to God as "God in himself" and as "self-contained God" (a phrase which recurs a good deal in Van Til). After the paraphrase which on just about *all* points does not correspond to Barth's own representation, there follows this sentence: "for this orthodox scheme Barth substitutes his idea . . ." (*The New Modernism,* p. 161). Thus, for example, Van Til represents Barth as saying that the persons of the Godhead are not "three centers of self-consciousness" (p. 162) and he then deduces Barth's modalism from this. So too he says that Barth "clearly rejects the Chalcedon creed with its notion of the second person of the ontological trinity taking to himself in permanent union without confusion an already existent human nature" (p. 162). The criticism of Barth, as is evident from the paraphrase in which we often cannot recognize Barth, rests at bottom on a particular conception of orthodoxy, a conception characterized by the notion of the self-contained God. Very probably the discussion will now have to be continued about that (not about the theology of Barth, but about the doctrine of God, the Christology, and the doctrine of the Trinity). More than once I have thought that the difference was a matter of analysis. But, as I see it, a difference in *theological* problematics is also becoming more and more apparent. More specifically, I now see that when Van Til speaks of the "self-contained" God and the assumption of an already existent human nature, he recognizes the danger of *modalism,* indeed, but not the danger of *tritheism* and *Nestorianism.* It was to the latter danger that Kuyper so earnestly addressed himself. And behind all these questions there arises, I think, in the final analysis the question of the self-contained God in relation to the *Counsel of God.* This becomes clear to me particularly as I read the latest of Van Til's books, namely, *The Defense of the Faith.* It is not my intention at this point to consider the interesting questions which this book raises. But there are points in it which are intimately connected with the matters here under discussion. Such is the case, for instance, when Van Til, to my great amazement, pleads for the equal ultimacy of election and reprobation. In response to the criticism directed against this position, he writes: "Well. I do indeed maintain the equal ultimacy of election and reprobation." And Van Til motivates this position by adding: "since I take my point of departure in God and his plan" (*The Defense of the Faith,* 1955, p. 413ff.). And these observations immediately touch on his view of Barth. For Van Til says that Barth rejects the "equal ultimacy" of election and reprobation. This is to state the problem in an absolutely inadequate way, since it suggests that whoever rejects the "equal ultimacy" of election and reprobation by that token comes to stand in the line of Barth. Nothing could be less true. I am of the opinion that the "equal ultimacy" of election and reprobation is rejected already by the Canons of Dort, and that one can judge soundly of the scriptural doctrine of election only when one in very fact rejects this symmetry. I think of those beautiful words in the Conclusion of the Canons in which it is said that the signatories "detest with their whole soul" also the view that "in the same manner in which the election is the fountain and the cause of faith and good works, reprobation is the cause of unbelief and impiety." This is an utterance in which that symmetry which plays so tremendous a role in theological determinism is emphatically *repudiated.* This has nothing to do with a denial of the Counsel or Plan of God, but most certainly does have something to do with the criticism of an unbiblical distortion of the message of the Divine election, a distortion according to which the Counsel of God is made to serve as the principle accounting for both faith and unbelief. We should be particularly grateful that the Synod of Dort warned us about that so very emphatically.

But think, then, of how unwarranted it is to relate the rejection of "equal ultimacy" to *Kierkegaard* and *the dialectical theology*. This is to act as though the problem of symmetry and its rejection had not already played a conclusive role in Bavinck and Kuyper and in the whole history of the doctrine of election. It is not possible to treat at further length of these matters here, but perhaps I may refer on this point to my latest volume, *De Verkiezing Gods* (Divine Election), 1955, in which I have treated of these considerations at elaborate length. But it seems clear to me that these theological backgrounds also play a role in Van Til's analyses and criticisms.

But is it not merely a difference between philosophy and theology? Very probably not. The difference in interpretation is related to the difficult and responsible struggle which theology must conduct in this dynamic time of ours — dynamic also in the sphere of theology. Since such is our responsibility we must all alike realize that we must all together in the fellowship of the Christian faith serve the cause — the cause also of theology. For theology is not merely a phenomenon of the study. At all times, whether for good or for evil, theology has influenced the preaching of the Church. And it is not without reason, therefore, that we shall at all times have to remain critical of *all* that is merely human work, also in theology. We shall have to remain always critical also, certainly, of every form of theological thought which does less than justice to the faith which God has entrusted to us for our salvation. We are at the present standing in the middle of that struggle. It is difficult, sometimes, to make out just who the warriors are. The fronts change every day. But that makes it all the more necessary to see *clearly* just *where* we ought to conduct the fight, on *which front*, and with *which weapons*. May the consideration, also of the interpretation of Barth's theology, contribute to that clarity of vision. This is the more important when it is clear — as no one will care to deny — that Barth's main concern is to speak of the all-conquering grace of God in Christ Jesus. In my book I have a special chapter (VIII) on the types of theology which purport to be "theology of grace" but nevertheless do not do full justice to the Biblical idea of triumph as set forth in the entire New Testament. It is to that issue, I think, that discussion should be directed. It can, if sharply focussed upon that point, be a fruitful discussion which contributes to the good of the Church of God. This, too, is the joy of all theologians that they know no more than the simple believers know, that they may *serve*, want to *serve*, and can *serve* that Church of God for which Christ died outside the gates of Jerusalem.

# LIST OF WORKS CITED

Adam, Karl, *Gesammelte Aufsätze*. Augsburg: P. Haas, 1936.

Althaus, P., "Theologie und Geschichte. Zur Auseinandersetzung mit der dialektischen Theologie," in *Zeitschrift für systematische Theologie*, Vol. I, 1923.

——, *Gebot und Gesetz*. Gütersloh: C. Bertelsmann Verlag, 1952.

von Balthasar, H. U., *Karl Barth*. Darstellung und Deutung seiner Theologie. Köln: Jakob Hegner Verlag, 1951.

Barth, K., *Christus und Adam nach Römer* 5 (Theologische Studien, Heft 35). Zürich: Zollikon Verlag, 1952.

——, *Credo*. München: C. Kaiser Verlag, 1935.

   (*Credo*. New York: Scribner's, 1936)

——, *Das Bekenntnis der Reformation und unser Bekennen*. München: C. Kaiser Verlag, 1935.

——, *Das Geschenk der Freiheit* (Theologische Existenz heute, Heft 39). München, C. Kaiser Verlag, 1953.

——, *Das Wort Gottes und die Theologie*. München: C. Kaiser Verlag, 1924.

   (*The Word of God and the Word of Man*. Boston: The Pilgrim Press, 1928)

——, "Das Wort in der Theologie von Schleiermacher bis Ritschl," in *Gesammelte Vorträge*, II. München: C. Kaiser Verlag, 1926.

——, *De Apostolische Geloofsbelijdenis*. Nijkerk: G. F. Callenbach N. V., 1935.

——, "Der Begriff der Kirche," in *Zwischen den Zeiten*, 1927.

——, *Der Heilige Geist und das christliche Leben*. München: C. Kaiser Verlag, 1930.

——, *Der Römerbrief*. 2d ed. München: C. Kaiser Verlag, 1932.

   (*The Epistle to the Romans*. London: Oxford University Press, 1933)

——, "Der römische Katholizismus als Frage an die protestantische Kirche," in *Zwischen den Zeiten*, 1928.

——, *Die Botschaft von der freien Gnade Gottes*. Zürich: Zollikon Verlag, 1947.

——, *Die christliche Gemeinde im Wechsel der Staatsordnungen*. Zürich: Zollikon Verlag, 1948.

——, *Die christliche Lehre nach dem Heidelb. Katech.* Zürich: Zollikon Verlag, 1948.

——, "Die dogmatische Prinzipiënlehre von W. Herrmann," in *Zwischen den Zeiten*, 1925.

——, *Die Kirche zwischen Ost und West*. Zürich: Zollikon Verlag, 1949.

——, "Die Lehre von den Sakramenten," in *Zwischen den Zeiten*, 1929.

——, "Die Neuoriëntierung der Prot. Theol. in den letzten dreissig Jahren," in *Kirchenblatt für die ref. Schweiz*, Vol. 7, 1940.

——, "Die Not der evangelische Kirche," in *Zwischen den Zeiten*, 1931.

———, *Die Protestantische Theologie im* 19. *Jahrhundert.* Zürich: Zollikon Verlag, 1947.

———, *Die Souveränität des Wortes Gottes und die Entscheidung des Glaubens.* Zürich: Zollikon Verlag, 1939.

———, "Die Theologie und die Kirche," in *Gesammelte Vorträge*, II. München: C. Kaiser Verlag, 1926.

———, *Die Wirklichkeit des neuen Menschen* (Theologische Studien, Heft 27). Zürich: Zollikon Verlag, 1950.

———, *Dogmatik im Grundrisz.* Zürich: Zollikon Verlag, 1947.
(*Dogmatics in Outline.* New York: Philosophical Library, 1947)

———, *Evangelium und Gesetz* (Theologische Existenz heute, Heft 32) München: C. Kaizer Verlag, 1936.

———, *Fides quaerens intellectum. Anselms Beweis der Existenz Gottes.* München: C. Kaiser Verlag, 1931.

———, *Gottes Gnadenwahl* (Theologische Existenz heute, Heft 47). München: C. Kaiser Verlag, 1936.

———, *Gotteserkenntnis und Gottesdient nach reformatorischer Lehre.* Zürich: Zollikon Verlag, 1938.
(*The Knowledge of God and the Service of God According to the Teaching of the Reformation.* London: Hodder and Stoughton, 1938).

———, *Grundfragen.* Nijkerk: G. F. Callenbach N. V., 1935.

———, *Humanismus.* (Theologische Studien, Heft 28). Zürich: Zollikon Verlag, 1950.

———, *Kirchliche Dogmatik*, Vols. I-IX. Zürich: Zollikon Verlag 1932-1955.
(*The Doctrine of the Word of God*, Vol. I, parts 1 and 2. New York: Scribner's, 1936—).

———, *Komm, Schöpfer-Geist.* (with E. Thurneysen). 2d ed. München: C. Kaiser Verlag, 1924.
(*Come, Holy Spirit.* New York: Round Table Press, 1933).

———, *La confession de foi de l'Eglise.* Neuchatel, 1943.

———, "Ludwig Feuerbach," in *Zwischen den Zeiten*, 1927.

———, "Parergon. Karl Barth über sichselbst," in *Evangelische Theologie*, 1948-1949.

———, *Philipperbrief.* München: C. Kaiser Verlag, 1928.

———, "Polemisches Nachwort," in *Zwischen den Zeiten*, 1927.

———, *Prolegomena.* München: C. Kaiser Verlag, 1927.

———, "Quousque tandem?", in *Zwischen den Zeiten*, 1930.

———, *R. Bultmann. Ein Versuch ihn zu verstehen* (Theologische Studien, Heft 34). Zürich: Zollikon Verlag, 1952.

———, "Rechtfertigung und Heiligung," in *Zwischen den Zeiten*, 1927.

———, "Unerledigte Anfragen an die heutige Theologie" (1920) in "Die Theologie und die Kirche," in *Gesammelte Vorträge*, II. München: C. Kaiser Verlag, 1926.

Bavinck, H., *Gereformeerde Dogmatiek*, I. Kampen: J. H. Kok, 1920.

Berkhof, H., *Crisis der Middenorthodoxie.* Nijkerk. G. F. Callenbach N. V., 1953.

———, "De betekenis van Karl Barth voor theologie, kerk en wereld," in *Wending*, 1947

Berkouwer, G. C., *Barthianisme en Katholicisme*. Kampen: J. H. Kok, 1940.
———, *Conflict met Rome*. 3rd ed. Kampen: J. H. Kok, 1955.
———, *De Algemene Openbaring*. Kampen: J. H. Kok, 1951.
(*General Revelation*. Grand Rapids: Eerdmans, 1955).
———, *De Persoon van Christus*. Kampen: J. H. Kok, 1952.
(*The Person of Christ*. Tr. by J. Vriend. Grand Rapids: Eerdmans, 1952)
———, *De Voorzienigheid Gods*. Kampen: J. H. Kok, 1950.
(*The Providence of God*. Tr. by L. Smedes. Grand Rapids: Eerdmans, 1952)
———, *Geloof en Heiliging*. Kampen: J. H. Kok, 1949)
(*Faith and Sanctification*. Tr. by J. Vriend. Grand Rapids: Eerdmans, 1952)
———, *Geloof en Openbaring in de nieuwere Duitsche theologie*. Utrecht: Kemink, 1932.
———, *Geloof en Rechtvaardiging*. Kampen: J. H. Kok, 1949.
(*Faith and Justification*. Tr. by L. Smedes. Grand Rapids: Eerdmans, 1954)
———, *Het Werk van Christus*. Kampen: J. H. Kok, 1953.
———, *Karl Barth*. 2d ed. Kampen: J. H. Kok, 1937.
———, *Karl Barth en de Kinderdoop*. Kampen: J. H. Kok, 1947.
———, *Kohlbrugge in Onze Tijd*. Kampen: J. H. Kok, 1948.
———, "Theologie des Kruises," in *Calvinistisch Weekblad*, Vol. I, Oct. 4-18.
———, *Wereld Oorlog en Theologie*. Kampen: J. H. Kok, 1945.
Bronkhorst, A. J., *K. Barth*. Den Haag: Boekencentrum, 1953.
Brunner, E., *Das Ewige als Zukunft und Gegenwart*. Zürich: Zwingli Verlag, 1953.
———, *Der Mensch im Widerspruch*. Berlin: Furche Verlag, 1937.
(*Man in Revolt*. Tr. by O. Wyon. Philadelphia: Westminster Press, 1947).
———, *Der Mittler*. Tübingen: Verlag J. C. B. Mohr, 1927.
(*The Mediator*. Tr. by O. Wyon. New York: Macmillan, 1934)
———, "Der neue Barth," in *Zeitschrift für Theologie und Kirche*. Vol. 48.
("The New Barth," in *Scottish Journal of Theology*, June 1951)
———, *Die Grenzen der Humanität*. Tübingen: Verlag J. C. B. Mohr, 1922.
———, *Die Mystik und das Wort*. Tübingen: Verlag J. C. B. Mohr, 1924.
———' *Dogmatik*, I (1946); II (1950). Zürich: Zwingli Verlag.
(*Dogmatics*, Vol. I (*The Christian Doctrine of God*) and II (*The Christian Doctrine of Creation and Redemption*). Tr. by O. Wyon. Philadelphia: Westminster Press, 1950).
———, *Erlebnis, Erkenntnis und Glaube*. Tübingen: Verlag J. C. B. Mohr, 1923.
———, *Natur und Gnade*. 2d ed. Tübingen: Verlag J. C. B. Mohr, 1935.
Brunner, P., *Vom Glauben bei Calvin*. Tübingen: Verlag J. C. B. Mohr, 1925.
Calvin, J., *Institutie*. Delft: W. D. Meinema, 1931.
(*Institutes of the Christian Religion*. Grand Rapids: Eerdmans; reprint, 1949).
Danielou, J., *Origene "Le genie du Christianisme."* Paris: La table Ronde, 1948.

De Jong, A. C., *The Well-Meant Gospel Offer. The Views of Hoeksema and Schilder.* Franeker: T. Wever, 1954.

De Vogel, C. J., *Ecclesia Catholica.* Utrecht: Het Spectrum, 1946.

Dooyeweerd, H., "De leer der analogie in de Thomistische wijsbegeerte en in de wijsbegeerte der Wetsidee," in *Philosophia Reformata,* 1942.

Ehrhardt, A., "Creatio ex Nihilo," in *Studia Theologica,* 1951.

Elert, W., "Die theopaschitische Formel," in *Theologische Literatur Zeitung,* 1950.

————, "Gesetz und Evangelium," in *Zwischen Gnade und Ungnade.* München, 1948.

Ellwein, E., "Die Entfaltung der theologia crucis in Luthers Hebräervorlesung," in *Theologische Aufsätze für Karl Barth.* München: C. Kaiser Verlag, 1936.

Frör, K., *Evangelisches Denken und Katholizismus seit Schleiermacher.* München: C. Kaiser Verlag, 1932.

Gemmer, A., and Messer, A., *Sören Kierkegard und Karl Barth,* 1925.

Gloege, "Gott im Widerspruch," in *Theologische Literatur Zeitung,* 1951.

Gogarten, F., *Gericht oder Skepsis. Eine Streitschrift gegen Karl Barth.* Jena, 1937.

————, "Karl Barths Dogmatik," in *Theologische Rundschau,* 1929.

————, *Von Glauben und Offenbarung.* Jena, 1923.

Grot, J. C., "De analogie in Barths denken," in *De Analogie van het Zijn.* Utrecht: Het Spectrum, 1942.

Grosheide, F. W., *Kommentaar op Hebreen.* Amsterdam: Bottenburg, 1927.

Haitjema, T. L., "Een Amerikaanse aanval of de dialectische theologie," in *Pro Regno pro Sanctuario.* Nijkerk: G. F. Callenbach N. V., 1950.

————, *Karl Barth.* Wageningen: Veenman, 1926.

Hamer, J., *Karl Barth. L'occasionalisme theologique de Karl Barth.* Paris: Desclee, de Brouwer et Cie, 1949.

Von Harnack, A., *Lehrbuch der Dogmengeschichte.* 4th ed., Vol. I. Tübingen: J. C. B. Mohr, 1909/1910.

————, *Marcion,* 1924.

Heidegger, M., *Sein und Zeit.* 4th ed. Halle: Max Niemeyer Verlag, 1935.

————, *Vom Wesen des Grundes.* 3d ed. Frankfort a. M.: V. Kloostermann Verlag, 1949.

————, *Was ist Metaphysik?* Bonn: Cohen, 1929.
  (In *Existence and Being.* Tr. by R. F. C. Hull and A. Crick. Chicago: H. Regnery, 1949)

Heim, K., *Das Wesen des evangelischen Christentums.* Berlin: Furche Verlag.

Hein, A., "Moderner Marcionitismus und practische Theologie," in *Theologische Blätter,* Vol. 1, Berlin: Furche Verlag, 1922.

Heppe, H., *Die Dogmatik der evangelisch reformierte Kirche.* 1861.

Heyns, J. A., *Die Grondstruktuur van die modalistische Triniteitsbeskouwing.* Kampen: J. H. Kok, 1953.

Hulsbosch, A., *Genade en Kerk.* Utrecht: Het Spectrum, 1953.

Jonas, H., *Gnosis und spatantiker Geist.* Göttingen, 1934.

Kittel, G., *Theologisches Wörterbuch des Neuen Testaments.* Stuttgart: W. Kohlhammer Verlag.

Kreling, G. P., *Antwoord op het Herderlijk Schrijven.* Utrecht: Het Spectrum, 1950.

————, *De Analogie van het Zijn.* Utrecht: Het Spectrum, 1942.

Kuyper, A., *De Gemeene Gratie.* Kampen: J. H. Kok, 1902-1904.

————, *Dictaten Dogmatiek,* Locus de Creatione. Kampen: J. H. Kok.

————, *E Voto Dordraceno.* Kampen: J. H. Kok, 1904/1905.

Lebon, J., "La Christologie du Monophysisme Syrien" in *Das Konzil von Chalcedon. Geschichte und Gegenwart,* I. 1951.

Leese, K., *Die Prinzipiënlehre der neueren systematische Theologie im Lichte der Kritik L. Feuerbachs.* Leipzig: J. C. Hinrichs Verlag, 1912.

Leivestad, R., *Christ the Conqueror. Ideas of Conflict and Victory in the New Testament.* New York: Macmillan, 1954.

Lekkerkerker, A., "Eerste reacties of KD IV/1" in *Kerk en Theologie,* 1953.

von Loewenich, W., *Luthers theologia crucis.* München: C. Kaiser Verlag, 1929.

Louet Feisser, J. J., *De Strijd tegen de Analogia Entis in de Theologie van Karl Barth.* Amsterdam: Uitgeverij H. J. Paris, 1948.

————, "Misverstand rondom Karl Barths leer over de Schepping," in *Nederlands Theologisch Tijdschrift,* Vol. 6, 1952.

Lyttkens, H., *The Analogy between God and the World. An Investigation of its Background and Interpretation of its Use by Thomas Aquino.* Upsala, 1952.

Merz, G., "Die Heidelberger Disputation Doktor Martin Luthers," in *Zwischen den Zeiten,* 1926.

Metzger, M., "Gottes Gnadenwahl," in *Verkundigung und Forschung,* 1941-1950.

Michaelis, W., *Die Versöhnung des Alls. Die frohe Botschaft von der Gnade Gottes.* Berlin, 1950.

Michel, O., *Der Brief an die Hebräer.* Göttingen: Vandenhoeck und Ruprecht Verlag, 1949.

Miskotte, K. H., *De Apostolische Geloofsbelijdenis.*

————, "Naar aanleiding van een diagnose II," in *De Waagschaal,* Vol. 7, No. 16.

————, "Schepping en Verbond," in *Kerk en Theologie,* Vol. II.

Müller, J., *Die christliche Lehre von der Sünde.* Breslau, 1849.

Noack, B., *Satanas und Soteria. Untersuchungen zur N. T.-lichen Dämonologie.* 1948.

Nygren, A., *Der Römerbrief.* Göttingen: Vandenhoeck und Ruprecht Verlag, 1951.

————, *Eros und Agape. Gestaltwandlungen der chr. Liebe, II.* 1937.
    (*Agape and Eros.* Tr. by P. S. Watson, New York: Macmillan, 1953).

Obendiek, M., *Der Teufel bei Martin Luther.* Berlin, 1931.

Otten, H., *Calvins theologische Anschauung von der Prädestination.* München: C. Kaiser Verlag, 1938.

Pinomaa, L., *Der Zorn Gottes in der Theologie Luthers. Ein Beitrag zur Frage nach der Einheit des Gottesbildes bei Luther.* In *Annales Academiae Scientiarium Fennicae.* Helsinki, 1938.

Polman, A. D. R., *Onze Nederlandse Geloofsbelijdenis.* Franeker: T. Wever.

Polyander, J., *Synopsis purioris Theologiae.* ed. by H. Bavinck. Leiden: Donner, 1881.

Prenter, R., "Die Einheit von Schöpfung und Erlösung. Zur Schöpfungslehre Karl Barths," in *Theologische Zeitschrift,* Vol. II, 1946.

Przywara, E., "Das katholische Kirchenprinzip," in *Zwischen den Zeiten*, 1929.

Reid, J. K. S., "The Office of Christ in Predestination," in *Scottish Journal of Theology*, Vol. I, nos. 1, 2.

Riddell, J. G., "God's eternal decrees," in *Scottish Journal of Theology*, Vol. II, no. 4.

Ridderbos, H. N., *De Apostolische Kerk*. Kampen: J. H. Kok, 1954.

———, *De Komst van het Koninkrijk*. Kampen: J. H. Kok, 1950.

———, *Paulus en Jezus*. Kampen: J. H. Kok, 1952.

Ritschl, A., *Die christliche Lehre von der Rechtfertigung und Versöhnung*. Bonn: A. Markus, 1908.

Ritschl, O. *Dogmengeschichte des Protestantismus*, III. Göttingen: Vandenhoeck und Ruprecht Verlag, 1926.

Robinson, J. A. T., "Universalism — is it heretical?" in *Scottish Journal of Theology*, 1949.

Schilder, K., *De Heidelbergsche Catechismus*, Vol. III. Goes, 1950.

———, *Wat is de Hel?* 2d ed. Kampen: J. H. Kok, 1920.

Schippers, *Getuigen van Jezus Christus in het Nieuwe Testament*. Franeker: T. Wever, 1938.

Schleiermacher, F., *Der Christliche Glaube*. 6th ed. Berlin, 1884.

Schnackenburg, R., *Die Johannesbriefe*. Freiburg; Verlag Herder, 1953.

Schrotenboer, P., *A New Apologetics: An Analysis and Appraisal of Emil Brunner's Theology*. Dissertation, Free University, Amsterdam, 1955.

Seeberg, R., *Lehrbuch der Dogmengeschichte*. 3d ed. Leipzig, 1922.

Sertillanges, *Le problème du mal*, I (L'histoire) 1948; II (La solution) 1951. Paris: F. Aubier.

Severijn, J., *Vragen van tijd en eeuwigheid. Bezwaren tegen het nieuwmodernisme*. Maassluis, 1947.

Soucek, J. B., "Man in the Light of the Humanity of Jesus," in *Scottish Journal of Theology*, March, 1949.

Stauffer, E., *Christus und die Caesaren*. Hamburg, 1948.
    (*Christ and the Caesars*. Tr. by K. and R. Gregor Smith, Philadelphia: Westminster Press, 1955)

———, *Die Theologie des Neuen Testaments*. 5th ed. Stuttgart: W. Kohlhammer Verlag, 1948.
    (*New Testament Theology*. Tr. by J. Marsh. New York: Macmillan, 1955)

Steck, H. G., *Der evangelische Christus und die römische Kirche* (Theologische Existenz heute, Heft 33). München: C. Kaiser Verlag, 1952.

Steffens, B., *Das Dogma vom Kreuz. Beitrag zu einer staurozentrischen Theologie*. Gütersloh: C. Bertelsmann Verlag, 1920.

———, *Kreuz und Gewiszheit*. Gütersloh: C. Bertelsmann Verlag, 1929.

Ströter, E. F., *Die Allversöhnung in Christus*. 2d ed. Berlin, 1920.

Tertullianis, *Adversus Marcion*. Tübingen: Verlag J. C. B. Mohr.

Thielecke, H., "Zur Frage: Gesetz und Evangelium," in *Theologie der Anfechtung*. Tübingen: Verlag J. C. B. Mohr, 1949.

Thurneysen, E., "Christus und seine Zukunft," in *Zwischen den Zeiten*, 1931.

———, "Zum rel. sozialen Problem," in *Zwischen den Zeiten*, 1927.

Torrance, T. F., "Universalism or Election," in *Scottish Journal of Theology*, 1949.

Tromp, D., *Nieuwe Theologie*. Baarn: Hollandia, 1926.
Van de Pol, W. H., *Het Christelijk Dilemma*. Roermond, 1948.
(*The Christian Dilemma*, 1952)
———, "Protestantse misverstanden en hun oorzaken," in *Werkgenootschap van Katholieke Theologie*, 1954.
Van Dijk, M. P., "Een Rooms Katholiek Werk over Karl Barth," in *Gereformeerd Theologisch Tijdschrift*, Vol. IV, 1952.
———, *Existentie en Genade*. Franeker: T. Wever, 1952.
Van Niftrik, G. C., *Een Beroerder Israëls*. 2d ed. Nijkerk: G. F. Callenbach N. V., 1949.
———, *Zie de Mens*. Nijkerk: G. F. Callenbach N. V., 1951.
Van Oyen, H., *Christus de Hoge Priester*. Nijkerk: G. F. Callenbach N. V., 1939.
———, "De categorie der recognitio en de theologische anthropologie," in *Pro Regno Pro Sanctuario*. Nijkerk: G. F. Callenbach N. V., 1950.
———, "Over wijsgerige affiniteit van Barths theologie," in *Onder Eigen Vaandel*, 1938.
Van Teylingen, E. G., "Over de wijsgerige achtergrond der dialectische theologie," in *Philosophia Reformata*, 1945.
Van Til, C., "Has Karl Barth Become Orthodox?", in *Westminster Theological Journal*, 1954.
———, *The Defense of the Faith*. Philadelphia: Presbyterian and Reformed Publishing House, 1955.
———, *The New Modernism. An Appraisal of the theology of Barth and Brunner*. 2d ed. Philadelphia: Presbyterian and Reformed Publishing Co., 1947.
Vogel, H., *Christologie*, I. Berlin: Lettner Verlag, 1949.
———, "Das Menschenbild im Neuen Testament," in *Vox Theologica*, 1952.
———, "Ecce Homo. Zur Anthropologie Karl Barths," in *Verkundigung und Forschung*, 1949/1950.
Vogelsang, E., *Der Angefochtene Christus bei Luther*. Berlin, 1932.
———, *Die Anfänge von Luthers Christologie nach der ersten Psalmenvorlesung*. Berlin, 1929.
Vriezen, T. C., *Die Erwählung Israels nach dem Alten Testament*. Zürich: Zwingli Verlag, 1953.
Weber, H. E., *Reformation, Orthodoxie und Rationalismus*. Gütersloh: C. Bertelsmann, 1940.
Weber, O., *K. Barths kirchliche Dogmatik. Ein einführender Bericht*. Neukirchen, 1950: I/1 to III/2; 2d ed., 1952: I/1 to III/4.
(*Karl Barth's Church Dogmatics. An Introductory Report*. Tr. by A. Cochrane. Philadelphia: Westminster Press, 1954)
———, Kreck, W., and Wolf, E., "Die Predigt von der Gnadenwahl (Theologische Existenz Heute). München: C. Kaiser Verlag, 1951.
Weiser, A., *Die Psalmen*. Göttingen: Vandenhoeck und Ruprecht Verlag, 1950.
Wust, P., *Stimmen der Zeit*. 1935.
Zuidema, S. U., "Het nieuw modernisme," in *Mededeelingen v. d. Vereeniging voor Calv. Wijsbegeerte*, Dec. 1946.

# A LIST OF ENGLISH TRANSLATIONS OF
# KARL BARTH'S WRITINGS*

*Against the Stream.* Shorter post-war writings; 1946-1952. Ed. by R. G. Smith. New York: Philosophical Library, 1954.

"Barth to Bereczky: A Letter," *Christian Century,* July 30, 1952.

*Christian Life.* London: SCM Press, 1930.

*Church and State.* Tr. by G. R. Howe. London: SCM Press, 1939.

*Come, Holy Spirit* (with E. Thurneysen). Sermons. Tr. by G. W. Richards, E. G. Homrighausen, K. J. Ernst. New York: Round Table Press, 1933.

"Continental vs. Anglo-Saxon Theology," *Christian Century,* Feb. 16, 1949.

*Credo. A presentation of the chief problems of dogmatics with reference to the Apostles' Creed.* Tr. by J. S. Mc Nab. New York: Scribner's, 1936.

*Dogmatics in Outline.* Tr. by G. T. Thomson. New York: Philosophical Library, 1947.

*God in Action.* Theological addresses. Tr. by E. G. Homrighausen, K. J. Ernest. New York: Round Table Press, 1936.

*God's Search for Man.* (with E. Thurneysen). Sermons. Tr. by G. W. Richards, E. G. Homrighausen, K. J. Ernst. New York: Round Table Press, 1935.

"How My Mind Changed, 1938-1948," *Christian Century,* March 9 and 16, 1949.

"How My Mind Has Changed In This Decade," *Christian Century,* Sept. 13 and 20, 1939.

"Letter to American Churches," *Christendom,* Autumm, 1943.

"No Christian Marshall Plan," *Christian Century,* Dec. 8, 1948.

*Prayer According to the Catechisms of the Reformation.* Stenographic notes of a seminar adapted by A. Roulin; tr. by S. F. Terrien. Philadelphia: Westminster Press, 1952.

*The Church and the Churches.* Grand Rapids: Eerdmans, 1936.

*The Church and the Political Problem of Our Day.* New York: Scribner's, 1939.

*The Church and the War.* Tr. by A. H. Froendt. New York: Macmillan: 1944.

"The Church — The Living Congregation of the Living Lord Jesus Christ," in *Man's Disorder and God's Design*: the Amsterdam Assembly Series. New York: Harper & Brothers, n. d.

*The Doctrine of the Word of God,* Vol. I, parts 1 and 2. Tr. by G. T. Thomson and H. Knight. Authorized translation of *Kirchliche Dogmatik.* Further volumes in preparation. New York: Scribner's, 1936 —

*The Epistle to the Romans.* Tr. from the 6th ed. by E. C. Hoskyns. London: Oxford University Press, 1933.

*The Germans and Ourselves.* Tr. by R. G. Smith. London: Nisbet & Co., 1945.

---

\* This list was compiled largely from the Library of Congress Catalog, the Cumulative Book Index, and the Reader's Guide to Periodical Literature. It should not be considered exhaustive. — *The Publisher.*

*The Holy Ghost and the Christian Life*. Tr. by R. B. Hoyle. London: F. Muller, 1938.

*The Knowledge of God and the Service of God According to the Teaching of the Reformation*. Gifford Lectures. Tr. by J. L. M. Haire and I. Henderson. London: Hodder and Stoughton, 1938.

*The Only Way. How Can the Germans Be Cured?* Tr. by M. K. Neufeld. New York: Philosophical Library, 1947.

"The Protestant Churches in Europe," *Foreign Affairs*, July 1943.

*The Resurrection of the Dead*. Tr. by H. J. Stenning. New York: F. H. Revell, 1933.

*The Teaching of the Church Regarding Baptism*. Tr. by E. A. Payne. London: SCM Press, 1948.

*The Word of God and the Word of Man*. Tr. by D. Horton. Boston: The Pilgrim Press, 1928.

*Theological Existence Today!* Tr. by R. B. Hoyle. London: Hodder and Stoughton, 1933.

*This Christian Cause*. New York: Macmillan, 1941.

*Trouble and Promise in the Struggle of the Church in Germany*. Tr. by P. V. M. Benecke. Oxford: The Clarendon Press, 1938.

Aulen, Gustaf, *et. al., Revelation*. New York: Macmillan, 1937. Contains a chapter by Karl Barth.

Weber, O., *Karl Barth's Church Dogmatics*. An Introductory Report. Tr. by A. Cochrane. Philadelphia: Westminster Press, 1954. An outline and digest, largely in Barth's own words, of the existing eight volumes of *Kirchliche Dogmatik*.

# INDEX OF SCRIPTURE

*Note:* *References include footnotes*

GENESIS
1          12, 13, 58, 225
2              12, 13
1:2      58. 61, 70, 76,
                235, 242
1:31       59, 64, 259
3          53, 62, 83
18:14           326

EXODUS
3:2             235
3:6             339
19, 20          323

NUMBERS
23:19           222

I SAMUEL
15:29           222

I KINGS
13              109

II KINGS
2:12            334

JOB
7:6             338
10:18           338
34:10, 12       222

PSALMS
2               354
5:5             222
14:1            232
23           35, 352
30:9            353
30:12           353
32              145
39:5            338
39:6            246
39:14           338
40:7-9          305
51              145
51:8            145
53:2            232
68:17, 18       353
91:1            352
119:10, 18, 22, 29,
        31, 34. 48,
        58, 176     360

130:3, 4            353
136           164, 165

PROVERBS
9:3. 5, 6. 9       338

ISAIAH
11:6                 68
12:3               351
28:11     240, 241, 242
28:21       240. 242
40:1-6, 7-8,  9     39
40:17, 22          246
40:28              313
40:33               34
41:12, 29          246
46:8, 10           365
46:12, 13          366
52:7               350
53:5               257
54:7                61
54:7. 8            353
54:7-10             40
54:9, 10. 11       352
55:1               322
65:1               353

JEREMIAH
9:24               358
20:7               195
31                 323

EZEKIEL
30:13              246
37:11, 12          353

MICAH
7:18               353

NAHAM
1:15               350

ZECHARIAH
4:6                355

MATTHEW
3:1                277
4:14               277
4:17          277, 365
4:32               365
8:10               278

9:22                273
9:35, 36           383
9:37, 38      369, 383
10:7, 8, 12, 13, 14,
        15, 27     277
11:5               352
11:6               351
12:29              372
12:41              279
16:17              351
16:18. 23          366
22:23              338
22:32              339
24:21. 22, 24      374
26:40, 43          305
26:51              366
28:19              277

MARK
1:14, 15.          365
5:34               273
6:2, 5, 6          278
10:52              273
13:20              374

LUKE
1:78               353
2:10               351
2:34               279
7:9                278
9:28, 45           315
10:18         373, 374
11:22              366
11:30              279
13:23, 24          296
15:32              144
18:11, 14          359
19:9               351
20:34              339
22:31, 32          374
22:35              366
22:53         366, 377
24:26              315
24:46. 47          278

JOHN
1:14               315
3:16          127, 305
3:36               268
4:32. 34           305
5:17               354

| 5:24 | 305, 343 |
| 5:26 | 137, 305 |
| 5:30, 36 | 305 |
| 6:15 | 366 |
| 6:22 | 351 |
| 6:27 | 306 |
| 8:44 | 80, 240 |
| 8:51, 52 | 342 |
| 10:18 | 137, 305 |
| 10:29 | 305 |
| 10:36 | 305, 306 |
| 11:25 | 343 |
| 11:41-42 | 305 |
| 12:27 | 316 |
| 12:31 | 374 |
| 13:18 | 100 |
| 13:32 | 306 |
| 14:28 | 305 |
| 14:30 | 374 |
| 15:10, 15 | 305 |
| 15:16, 19 | 100 |
| 16:2 | 347 |
| 16:32 | 306 |
| 16:33 | 354, 383 |
| 17:4 | 305 |
| 17:23 | 306 |
| 20:21 | 305 |
| 20:27 | 269 |

**ACTS**
| 2:21 | 273, 279 |
| 2:24 | 342 |
| 2:36 | 316 |
| 2:40 | 279 |
| 4:2 | 277 |
| 4:27, 28 | 354 |
| 5:42 | 277 |
| 13:10 | 373 |
| 15:18 | 252 |
| 15:35 | 277 |
| 16 | 272 |
| 16:6, 7 | 374 |
| 20:20 | 277 |
| 28:31 | 277 |

**ROMANS**
| the book, | 198, 204 |
| 1 | 26, 34 |
| 1:13 | 374 |
| 1:16 | 351 |
| 2:28 | 174 |
| 3 | 142 |
| 3:27 | 358 |
| 4:17 | 57, 245 |
| 5 | 84, 85 |
| 5:3 | 360 |
| 5:12-22 | 252 |
| 5:13 | 86 |

| 5:14 | 87 |
| 5:20 | 87, 364 |
| 5:21 | 364 |
| 6 | 318 |
| 6:1 | 210 |
| 6:23 | 342 |
| 7 | 145 |
| 8 | 140 |
| 8:17 | 331, 344 |
| 8:18, 19, 25, 30 | 331 |
| 8:32 | 302 |
| 8:35 | 352 |
| 8:38 | 373 |
| 8:39 | 352 |
| 9 | 257 |
| 9:19 | 354 |
| 9:11 | 285 |
| 10:9, 11 | 272 |
| 10:12, 15 | 350 |
| 10:14 | 275 |
| 11:6 | 200, 201 |
| 11:20 | 358 |
| 11:33 | 354 |
| 11:36 | 367 |
| 12:2 | 360 |
| 12:6 | 181 |
| 13:8 | 210 |
| 15:22, 33 | 374 |
| 16:17-19, 20 | 374 |
| 16:25 | 207, 276 |
| 16:25-27 | 351 |
| 22:5 | 364 |

**I CORINTHIANS**
| the book, | 204 |
| 1 | 202, 242, 313 |
| 1:7 | 352 |
| 1:20 | 313 |
| 1:28 | 246 |
| 1:31 | 358 |
| 2:9 | 351 |
| 5:5 | 374 |
| 7:5 | 373 |
| 9:16 | 120 |
| 12:3 | 372 |
| 15 | 140 |
| 15:2 | 351 |
| 15:24 | 372 |
| 15:26 | 342 |
| 15:28 | 211 |
| 15:45 | 85 |
| 15:45-49 | 252 |
| 15:53 | 332 |
| 15:54 | 344 |
| 15:55 | 352 |
| 15:55, 56 | 343 |
| 15:56, 57, 58 | 333 |

**II CORINTHIANS**
| the book, | 204 |
| 1:3 | 352 |
| 2:5 | 41 |
| 2:11 | 238, 374 |
| 2:14 | 367 |
| 5:7 | 76 |
| 5:18-20 | 278 |
| 5:19 | 279 |
| 5:20 | 276 |
| 12:7 | 374 |

**GALATIANS**
| the book, | 198, 204 |
| 1 | 175 |
| 3:1 | 359 |
| 4:7 | 257 |
| 4:8, 9 | 258 |
| 6:14 | 359 |

**EPHESIANS**
| 1:4 | 94, 98, 262, 285, 287, 289 |
| 1:8 | 313 |
| 1:10 | 294 |
| 1:13 | 351 |
| 2:1, 2, 3, 4, 5, 12, 13 | 257 |
| 4:27 | 373 |
| 6:10, 11, 16 | 373 |

**PHILIPPIANS**
| 2 | 130, 315 |
| 2:10 | 316 |
| 3:3 | 359 |
| 3:12 | 146 |

**COLOSSIANS**
| the book, | 204 |
| 1:13 | 366 |
| 1:27, 28 | 276 |
| 2:15 | 355, 371 |
| 3:3 | 352 |
| 3:5-10 | 258 |

**I THESSALONIANS**
| 2:18 | 238, 374 |
| 3:5 | 373, 378 |
| 4:17 | 331 |

**II THESSALONIANS**
| 2:7, 9, 10 | 377 |
| 2:13 | 270 |

**I TIMOTHY**
| 1:16 | 351 |
| 3:16 | 369 |
| 6:16 | 30 |

II TIMOTHY
| | |
|---|---|
| 1:10 | 372 |
| 2:9 | 380 |
| 2:13 | 313 |
| 2:26 | 373 |

TITUS
| | |
|---|---|
| 2:11 | 351 |
| 3:4 | 345, 353 |

HEBREWS
| | |
|---|---|
| the book, | 139 |
| 1:3 | 315 |
| 2:3 | 268 |
| 2:9, 10 | 315 |
| 4:2 | 270, 271 |
| 4:9 | 343 |
| 4:11 | 269 |
| 6:4-6 | 269 |
| 6:18 | 222 |
| 9:27 | 161 |
| 10:7 | 305 |
| 10:29 | 269 |
| 10:39 | 273 |
| 12:2, 4, 15, 25 | 269 |
| 12:29 | 30 |

JAMES
| | |
|---|---|
| the book, | 80 |
| 1:13 | 310 |
| 2:14, 22 | 273 |
| 4:7 | 373 |

I PETER
| | |
|---|---|
| 1:8 | 352 |
| 1:9 | 273 |
| 1:11 | 315 |
| 2:9, 10 | 368 |
| 5:8 | 373, 374 |

II PETER
| | |
|---|---|
| the book, | 240 |
| 2:4 | 79 |

I JOHN
| | |
|---|---|
| 1 | 118 |
| 1:1 | 276, 315, 351 |
| 1:5 | 222 |
| 2:8 | 378 |
| 2:13, 14 | 355 |
| 2:18 | 372 |
| 3:1 | 354 |
| 3:8 | 354, 372 |
| 3:14 | 351 |
| 4 | 167 |

| | |
|---|---|
| 4:3 | 372 |
| 4:10, 19 | 352 |
| 5:7 | 355 |

JUDE
| | |
|---|---|
| the book, | 79, 240 |
| 20 | 355 |

REVELATION
| | |
|---|---|
| the book, | 237, 330, 340, 342 |
| 1:17, 18 | 41 |
| 1:18 | 336 |
| 2:9, 10 | 374 |
| 2:11 | 341 |
| 2:13 | 374 |
| 3:10 | 374 |
| 3:11, 17 | 35 |
| 4:11 | 245 |
| 5:10 | 364 |
| 7:9, 12, 16, 17 | 369 |
| 10:6 | 332 |
| 11:11-13, 16 | 367 |
| 12 | 238 |
| 17:14 | 366 |
| 20:6, 14 | 341 |
| 21:4, 5 | 331 |
| 22:1 | 368 |

# INDEX OF PROPER NAMES

*Note: References include footnotes*

Adam, K., 180
Althaus, P., 12, 23, 24, 26, 254, 319, 324
Anselm, 42, 93, 138
Aquinas, Thomas, 20, 21, 71, 175, 189, 389
Aristotle, 389
Arius, 168
Arminius, 263
Athanasius, 100
Augustine, 20, 21, 71, 100, 295, 326, 389

von Balthasar, H. U., 11, 13, 15, 33, 37, 38, 43, 168, 186, 188, 189, 192, 193, 194, 195, 386
Barth, K., see Index of subjects
Barth, H., 21
Bauer, F.C., 20
Bavinck, H., 174, 179, 201, 211, 217, 218, 224, 228, 233, 245, 252, 306, 310, 392
Bayle, P., 367
Beidermann, A. E., 20
Berkhof, H., 12, 267, 268, 319, 321, 322, 323, 325
Berkouwer, G. C., 11, 12, 15, 16, 24, 38, 48, 60, 67, 139, 140, 168, 173, 174, 177, 178, 188, 190, 202, 211, 252, 258, 264, 271, 278, 297, 318, 392
Beza, T., 283
Blumhardt, J. Chr., 45, 46, 48
Bronkhorst, A. J., 45
Bruhn, W., 24, 26
Brunner, E., 11, 12, 15, 16, 24, 27, 44, 122, 166, 192, 193, 194, 227, 231, 242, 263, 264, 265, 319, 323, 357, 379, 385, 387, 388
Brunner, P., 36
Bultmann, R., 9, 16, 20, 21, 44, 137, 166, 358, 359, 377, 388

Calvin, J., 14, 15, 36, 47, 48, 84, 94, 95, 101, 173, 217, 252, 262, 265, 282, 283, 284, 285, 286, 291, 295, 296, 330
Cocceius, 100
Confucius, 230
Cullmann, O., 140
Cyril, 301

Danielou, J., 211
DeJong, A. C., 280
De Rougemont, D., 375
De Vogel, C.J., 15
Dooyeweerd, H., 187, 191

Ehrhardt, A., 245
Ellwein, E., 202
Elert, W., 300, 301, 303, 319

Farrar, F. W., 212
Feuerbach, L., 167, 230
Frör, K., 171

Gemmer, A., 263
Gerhard, 179
Gerhardt, P., 237
Gogarten, F., 16, 25, 26, 43, 44, 166
Gomarus, F., 179
Gregory, 284
Groot, J. C., 168, 183
Grosheide, F. W., 271

Haitjema, Th. L., 11, 43
Hamer, J., 11
von Harnack, A., 205, 206, 207, 209
Hegel, G.W.F., 20, 48, 385
Heidegger, M., 20, 166, 170, 222, 223, 245, 249
Heim, 202, 203
Hein, A., 11
Heppe, H., 217, 218
Herrmann, W., 18, 166
Heyns, J.A., 131, 387
Hitler, 311
Holl, K., 142, 174
Huber, S., 293, 294
Hulsbosch, A., 199

Ignatius, 298
Irenaeus, 208

Jaspers, K., 166
Jerome, 211
Jonas, H., 208
Jülicher, A., 11

Kant, I., 21, 32
Kierkegaard, S., 392

Kittel, G., 276, 366, 367
Kohlbrugge, F., 46, 47, 48, 50, 388
Kohnstamm, P., 387
Kreck, W., 118, 120, 121
Kreling, G.P., 187, 191, 198, 199
Kuyper, A., 47, 231, 245, 306, 391, 392

Lebon, J., 300, 301
Leese, K., 31, 167
Leibnitz, G.W., 48, 67, 68, 69
Leivestad, R., 366, 376
Lekkerkerker, A., 257, 271, 279
Leo, 299
Lessing, G.E., 139
Lewis, C.S., 375
von Loewenich, W., 202
Louet Feisser, J. J., 186, 188, 190
Luther, M., 14, 15, 92, 173, 174, 201, 202, 203, 205, 206, 207, 240, 241, 242, 321
Lyttkens, H., 187

Marcion, 11, 204-209
Melanchthon, 179
Mersch, 186
Messer, A., 263
Metzger, M., 91
Michaelis, W., 342, 363
Michel, O., 271
Miskotte, K. H., 56, 193, 199, 293, 294, 322, 323
Mozart, 66, 67, 69
Müller, J., 231

Nietzsche, F., 166
Noack, B., 376
Nygren, A., 206, 207, 208, 365

Obendiek, M., 242
Origen, 211
Otten, H., 284
Otto, R., 236
Overbeck, 50

Pelagius, 168
Pinomaa, L., 242
Plato, 21, 31, 32, 247, 300
Polanus, 100
Polman, A., 283
Pope Pius IX, 176
Prenter, R., 56, 250, 251
Przywara, E., 168, 172, 180

Quenstedt, 187, 188, 189, 190, 194

Reid, J.K.S., 89
Riddell, J.G., 89

Ridderbos, H.N., 252, 276, 365, 367
Ritschl, A., 93, 166, 235, 236
Ritschl, O., 293
Robinson, J.A.T., 363

Sartre, J., 166, 170, 222, 223
Schilder, K., 11, 212, 241, 242, 243
Schippers, R., 367
Schleiermacher, F., 9, 38, 69, 70, 166, 316, 379
Schmaus, M., 186
Schnackenburg, R., 372
Schrotenboer, P., 388
Seeberg, R., 205, 211, 224
Sertillanges, R.P., 216, 251, 367
Söhngen, G., 184
Soucek, J.B., 329
Spengler, O., 23
Stauffer, E., 367
Steck, K.G., 201
Steffens, B., 201
Ströter, E. F., 363

Tertullian, 205, 207
Thielecke, H., 319
Thurneysen, E., 16, 25, 39, 44, 45, 46, 48, 50, 158
Torrance, T.F., 363, 364
Tromp, D., 11

Ursinus, 217, 218

Van de Pol, W. H., 168, 198
Van Dijk, M. P., 38, 49, 50, 89, 186, 218, 386
Van Mastricht, 179
Van Niftrik, G. C., 89, 158, 328, 330, 332
Van Oyen, H., 11, 21, 247, 271
Van Teylingen, E.G., 21, 26
Van Til, C., 11, 384-393
Vilmar, A.F.C., 48
Voetius, 179
Vogel, H., 48, 308, 329, 330, 331, 332, 335, 339, 340
Vogelsang, E., 202, 203
Vriezen, Th. C., 291

Weber, H., 294
Weber, O., 13, 118, 329
Weiser, A., 232, 361
Wolf, E., 118
Wust, P., 180

Zuidema, S.U., 11, 21, 387

# INDEX OF SUBJECTS

*Note: References include footnotes*

Abraham, 334, 339.
Adam, 83-88.
Adoptionism, 306, 312.
*Aliena justitia*, 30, 36, 47, 144.
*Analogia attributionis*, 187 - 190, 193.
*Analogia entis*, 179-194
*Analogia fidei*, 181, 192-194.
*Analogia operationis*, 193.
*Analogia relationis*, 181, 182, 187, 189, 190, 193.
Angels, 12, 76-80, 239, 240, 242, 335, 338, 375, 378, 379.
Anthropology, *see* Man, nature of.
Antinomianism, 209-210.
Apokatastasis, 112-117, 121, 122, 206, 211, 212, 263, 266, 287, 288, 290, 294, 295, 362. *See* Universalism.
Apostles' Creed, 18, 124, 345.
Arianism, 198, 306, 312.
Arminianism, 179, 264, 269.

BARTH, K., works cited,

*Christliche Gemeinde im Wechsel der Staatsordnungen*, 75, 237, 357.
*Christus und Adam nach Römer*, 5, 84, 85.
*Credo*, 164.

*Das Bekenntnis der Reformation und unser Bekennen*, 167, 168.
*Das Geschenk der Freiheit*, 216, 233.
*Das Wort Gottes und die Theologie*, 31, 39, 331.
"Das Wort in der Theologie von Schleiermacher bis Ritschl," 167.
*De Apostolische Geloofsbelijdenis*, 54, 63, 124, 125, 164, 165, 234.
"Der Begriff der Kirche," 172.
*Der Heilige Geist und das christliche Leben*, 18.
*Der Römerbrief*, 10, 11, 20, 21, 26, 27, 28, 29, 31, 32, 33, 35, 36, 37, 38, 39, 42, 43, 44, 45, 49, 151, 255, 257, 263, 388.
"Der römische Katholizismus als Frage, an die protestantische Kirche," 48, 171.

*Die Botschaft von der freien Gnade Gottes*, 115, 118.
*Die christliche Lehre nach dem H. K.*, 122, 136.
"Die dogmatische Prinzipiënlehre von W. Herrmann," 18.
*Die Kirche zwischen Ost und West*, 237.
"Die Lehre von den Sakramenten," 13.
"Die Neuoriëntierung der Prot. Theol. in den letzten dreiszig Jahren," 15.
"Die Not der evangelische Kirche," 18.
*Die Protestantische Theologie im 19. Jahrhundert*, 38, 45, 48, 67, 168.
*Die Souveränität des Wortes Gottes und die Entscheidung des Glaubens*, 236, 272.
"Die Theologie und die Kirche," 167.
*Die Wirklichkeit des neuen Menschen*, 127, 317, 318, 319.
*Dogmatik im Grundrisz*, 54, 55, 56, 57, 60, 62, 165, 310, 311, 312, 317.

*Evangelium und Gesetz*, 319, 321, 322.

*Fides quaerens intellectum, Anselms Beweis der Existenz Gottes*, 42.

*Gotteserkenntnis und Gottesdienst nach reformatorischer Lehre*, 15, 93, 94, 96, 100, 127.
*Gottes Gnadenwahl*, 14, 89, 91, 94, 102, 114, 117, 118, 255.
*Grundfragen*, 21, 32, 173.

*Humanismus*, 170, 171.

*Kirchliche Dogmatik*, 12, 14, 15, 16, 17, 21, 26, 32, 36, 37, 38, 42, 44, 46, 49, 52, 54-79, 81-113, 115, 117, 119, 120, 121, 123, 126-165, 167, 169, 170, 173-193, 196, 197, 202, 203, 215, 219, 220, 221, 223, 224, 225, 226, 227, 228, 229, 230, 234,

235, 236, 237, 239, 240, 243, 244, 246, 248, 251, 254, 255, 256, 257, 258, 261, 264, 265, 266, 271, 272, 289, 292, 297, 307, 308, 309, 310, 311, 312, 314, 315, 316, 317, 319, 320, 323, 324, 325, 329, 332, 333, 334, 335, 336, 339, 340, 341, 344, 345, 346, 347, 375, 376, 379, 386, 388.

*Komm, Schöpfer-Geist*, 39, 40, 41.

*La confession de foi de l'Eglise*, 122.

"Ludwig Feuerbach," 47.

"Parergon. Karl Barth über sich-selbst," 12, 42.

*Philipperbrief*, 148.

"Polemisches Nachwort," 24.

*Prolegomena*, 15, 26, 42, 43, 47, 49, 51, 181.

"Quousque tandem?" 18.

*R. Bultmann. Ein Versuch ihn zu verstehen*, 16, 20.

"Rechtfertigung und Heiligung," 47.

"Unerledigte Anfragen an die heutige Theologie," 18, 43.

Belgic Confession, 12, 173.
Bible, the, *see* Scripture.
Boundary-idea, 31, 32, 39, 41, 57, 58, 59, 65, 66, 67, 151, 157, 160, 161, 243, 244, 247, 249, 334.

Chalcedon, 133, 299, 390.
Chaos, 12, 57-82, 88, 127, 137, 141, 143, 219-223, 227, 234, 237, 240-261, 311, 317, 328, 334, 335, 370-381. *See* Creation; Evil; No, God's; Sin.
Christological orientation, 12, 17, 18, 37, 42, 43, 49, 53-56, 60, 64, 65, 67, 69, 72, 73, 74, 75, 76, 80-122, 123-150, 156, 157, 158, 159, 165, 186, 191, 192, 193, 203, 212, 226, 231, 250, 251, 252, 258, 259, 262, 263, 266, 280, 286, 287-296, 297-327, 332, 335, 336, 337, 341, 343, 344.
Church, the, 9, 15, 17, 18, 19, 21, 24, 28, 34, 35, 39, 48, 50, 74, 96, 107, 108, 109, 110, 113, 115, 117, 118, 119, 120, 130, 139, 140, 141, 147, 149, 150, 152, 162, 166, 167, 170, 171, 172, 173, 175, 176, 177,

194, 197, 198, 201, 202, 203, 204, 208, 209, 228, 231, 237, 238, 254, 255, 265, 267, 269, 272, 275, 279, 281, 289, 290, 291, 293, 294, 302, 304, 306, 312, 316, 317, 318, 321, 329, 337, 338, 345, 346, 348, 355, 356, 357, 358, 362, 366, 368, 369, 373, 374, 377, 380, 381, 382, 383, 392, 393.
Covenant, 53-60, 82, 87, 105, 108, 193, 224-229, 248, 250, 258, 265, 320.
Creation, 10, 12, 13, 18, 52-88, 123, 154, 155, 157, 160, 161, 162, 163, 192, 206, 215, 240-261, 328, 333, 334, 337, 338, 342, 370, 380, 382.

*Das Nichtige*, 62, *see* Chaos.
David, 109.
Death, 153-165, 317, 328-346, 352, 354.
Demons, 12, 76-80, 127, 211, 239, 240, 242, 260, 371-380. *see* Satan.
Demythologizing, 9, 16, 77, 374, 375, 377, 379.
*Deus absconditus*, 92-101, 289, 295, 296.
*Deus revelatus*, 11, 92-101, 114, 289.
Devil, the, *see* Satan.
Dordt, Synod of, 47, 97, 98, 274, 391, 392.
Dualism, 80, 81, 144, 222, 243, 247, 253, 254, 260, 354.

Election, 9, 15, 17, 18, 52, 60, 65, 77, 89-122, 141, 143, 219, 220, 227, 228, 239, 242, 255, 256, 262-296, 297, 320, 321, 323, 362, 364, 368, 370, 380, 391, 392, *see* Reconciliation. Universalism.
Elijah, 161, 334.
Enlightenment, the, 77, 258, 259, 330.
Enoch, 334.
*Entmythologisierung*, *see* Demythologizing.
Eschatology, 66, 117, 140, 151-165, 203, 328-346, 371-380.
Eternal life, *see* Immortality.
Eternalization, 158-164, 328-346, 380. *See* Immortality.
Eternity, 151, 152.
Ethics, 14, 130, 132, 160, 162, 323, 332.
Evil, 57, 62, 66, 67, 68, 72, 73, 78, 82, 113, 143, 155, 215, 216, 217, 220, 221, 222, 223, 228, 231, 232, 237, 238, 239, 252, 253, 255, 256,

311, 318, 323, 335, 375, 376, 377, 378, 379, 381. *See* Chaos, Sin.

Faith, 27, 30, 33, 36, 47, 48, 74, 77, 105, 106, 135, 140, 141, 143, 147, 148, 149, 150, 172, 173, 174, 175, 176, 179, 181, 183, 194, 203, 205, 213, 252, 261, 262-280, 284, 290, 318, 324, 334, 343, 348, 353, 355, 363, 365, 368, 369, 383.
Fall, the, 53, 61, 79, 82-84, 216, 220, 247, 250, 253, 324, 380, *see* Man, Nature of.
Formula Concordiae, 102, 179, 289.
Freedom, 61, 63, 79, 148, 175, 176, 177, 178, 194, 211, 216, 222, 227, 228, 231, 233, 239, 267, 294, 295, 348, 349.

Gnosticism, 66, 207, 208, 209, 302, 346.
Gospel, 17, 18, 21, 22, 31, 35, 48, 49, 50, 91, 92, 93, 97, 99, 104, 106, 109, 112, 116, 118, 151, 180, 196, 200-209, 249, 258, 259, 261, 269, 270, 275, 276, 277, 281, 291, 295, 296, 319-326, 347-358, 364-369, 382, 383, 385. *See* Kerugma, Reconciliation, Salvation.
Guilt, 82, 87, 93, 112, 122, 142, 144, 145, 147, 155, 197, 207, 209, 211, 215, 232, 241, 259, 260, 319, 325, 336, 352, 353, 354, 369, 370, 381. *See* Evil; Judgment, God's; Sin.

Heidelberg Catechism; 14, 294, 324, 342.
Herod, 354.
History, 162, 163, 250-261.
*Hohlraum*, 32, 36, 173.
Holy Spirit, 58, 87, 147, 148, 149, 275, 315, 369.
Humanism, 170, 210. *See* Righteousness, man's.

Immortality, 153-165, 328-346. *See* Eternalization.
Incarnation, the, 16, 54, 65, 74, 118, 127, 128, 129, 250, 257, 302, 303, 307, 308, 309, 327.
Infra-lapsarianism, 252, 255.
Israel, 82, 86, 87, 88, 107, 108, 109, 110, 111, 121, 255, 265, 278, 291, 334, 339, 354.

Jacob, 339
Jesus Christ, ascension of, 16, 74, 157.
  death of, 87, 119, 121, 135, 136,

143, 156, 157, 159, 302, 317, 318, 325, 335, 336.
  person of, 16, 94, 127-134, 159, 230, 298-307, 312, 314, 315, 390, 391.
  resurrection of, 16, 121, 123, 136, 137, 138, 140, 157, 169, 203, 315, 317, 318, 323, 371, 376.
  states of, 132, 133, 134, 297-327.
  work of, 17, 84, 85, 86, 95, 99, 100, 101, 123-135, 139, 146, 149, 157, 159, 176, 210, 274, 287, 305, 311, 316, 317, 318, 333, 342, 344, 371, 372, 376, 382.
Jesus Christ, *see also* Christological orientation.
John the Baptist, 277.
Jonah, 234, 279.
Judaism, 174, 273, 324.
Judas, 88, 110, 111.
Judgment, God's, 23-41, 46, 48, 49, 61, 70, 72, 73, 77, 81, 83, 85, 102, 103, 106, 112, 113, 119, 120, 134, 135, 136, 140, 141, 142, 146, 150, 155-164, 219, 225, 235, 236, 263, 264, 267, 268, 317, 319, 322, 323, 324, 325, 334, 335, 336, 340, 342, 343, 344. *See* No, God's; Wrath, God's.
Justification, 30, 47, 85, 137-147, 169, 170, 173, 174, 175, 189, 190, 196, 272, 318, 321, 322, 323, 356.

Kerugma, 9, 107, 119, 273, 276, 277, 278, 279, 280, 282, 287, 290, 296, 322, 363, 364, 365, 367, 370. *See* Gospel.
Kingdom of God, 75, 117, 138, 203, 277, 365-383.
Knowledge of God, 178, 181-195, 299. *See Analogia attributionis; Analogia entis; Analogia fidei; Analogia operationis; Analogia relationis.*

Law, 17, 48, 87, 120, 205, 206, 207, 209, 210, 215, 258, 259, 261, 273, 274, 319-326, 360, 361. *See* Gospel.
*Liberum arbitrium*, 61, 97, 227, 239, *See* Freedom; Man, nature of.
Life, eternal, *see* Eternalization; Immortality.
Life, limitation of man's; *see* Death; Eternalization; Immortality.

Logos, 211, 250, 254, 300, 301.

Lord's Prayer, 146, 376.
Love, God's, 37, 60, 81, 93, 101, 102, 103, 105, 107, 113, 114, 116, 129, 135, 138, 157, 164, 206, 207, 208, 219, 220, 234, 235, 236, 240, 241, 257, 259, 287, 292, 295, 309, 311, 312, 326, 327, 352, 353, 355, 362, 363, 366, 373. *See* Yes, God's.

Man, nature of; 15, 61, 62, 64, 79-86, 141-148, 152-162, 169, 171, 174, 179-195, 215-233, 256-260, 328, 330, 332, 333, 334, 335, 336, 337, 340, 341, 343, 345, 381.
Marcionism, 204-209.
Mariology, 175, 176, 178, 180, 194, 300.
Middle-orthodoxy, 267, 319.
Missions, 119, 275.
Modalism, 131, 390, 391.
Mohammedanism, 281.
Molinism, 178, 179, 180.
Monism, 12, 253, 254, 256, 258, 379.
Monophysitism, 303.
Moses, 86, 87, 161, 334.

Neo-Manicheism, 11.
Neo-Marcionism, 11
Nestorianism, 299, 300, 301, 303, 304, 306, 312, 391.
New-Modernism, 11, 16, 384.
New Testament, 9, 17, 24, 30, 46, 78, 79, 94, 101, 110, 111, 138, 158, 161, 197, 207, 237, 238, 257, 261, 264, 270, 271, 305, 309, 315, 316, 326, 334, 340, 352, 353, 358, 359, 369, 370, 371, 372, 373, 374, 376, 377, 378, 379, 380, 393. *See* Scripture.
No, God's, 23-41, 57, 66, 69, 70, 71, 72, 73, 74, 77, 82, 91, 102, 106, 141, 142, 155, 219, 220, 221, 225, 236, 239, 240, 242, 247, 248, 260, 370, 375. *See* Chaos; Judgment, God's; Wrath, God's.

Occamism, 11
Old Testament, 17, 156, 205, 206, 271, 326, 341, 350, 353, 358. *See* Scripture.
Omnipotence, God's, 11, 92, 124, 125, 126, 129, 132, 192, 193, 250, 308, 309, 310, 311, 312, 313, 325, 326, 363, 364.

*Opus alienum*, 73, 74, 219, 240, 241, 242, 243, 323.
*Opus proprium*, 73, 74, 241, 242, 243.

Pauline writings, 204, 205, 206, 207, 209, 273, 324, 330.
Pelagianism, 36, 93, 198, 269, 270, 283.
Perfectionism, 210-211.
Phariseeism, *see* Righteousness, man's.
Philosophy, *see* Theology and philosophy.
Pilate; 87, 88, 354.
Polemics, 166-195.
Politics, 10, 26, 237, 356, 357, 358.
Pope, infallibility of, 176, 177.
*Potentia absoluta*, 124, 126, 310, 311, 326.
*Potentia inordinata*, 11
*Potentia oboedientialis*, 192, 193.
*Potestas absoluta*, 92, 310, 312, 313.
*Potestas inordinata*, 92.
Power, God's, *see* Omnipotence, God's.
Prescience, God's, 178, 269, 289.
Preservation, *see* Providence.
Protestantism, 15, 166, 167, 171, 179, 198, 202.
Providence, 63, 67-72, 80, 162-165, 240, 244, 247, 333.

Reconciliation, 14, 18, 52, 56, 65, 69, 72, 76, 81, 82, 83, 84, 88, 89, 90, 116, 123-150, 173, 194, 234, 235, 247-260, 273, 275, 277, 286, 297-327, 370, 376, 382. *See* Salvation; Universalism.
Redemption, *see* Reconciliation.
Reformation, see Theology, Reformation.
Religion, *see* Righteousness, man's.
Remonstrants, 47, 97, 98, 274, 292, 294.
Reprobation, 17, 60, 91, 102, 120, 219, 221, 255, 391. *See* Election.
Resurrection, the, 158, 164, 338, 339, 344, 346.
Righteousness, God's, 25, 27, 28, 30, 34, 39, 42, 65, 143, 145, 322. *See* Justification; Yes, God's.
Righteousness, man's, 17, 25-42, 47, 169, 170, 196, 210, 249, 322, 356, 358, 359, 361, 382.

Sadducees, 338, 339.

Salvation, 25, 29, 30, 31, 36, 47, 48, 53, 59, 67, 71, 72, 78, 81, 87, 88, 90-97, 105, 106, 107, 108, 117, 149, 150, 152, 169, 171, 174, 175, 176, 201, 204, 238, 244, 247, 250, 255, 257, 258, 262-296, 325 331, 348, 349, 350, 352, 354, 358, 362, 363, 368, 382. *See* Reconciliation, Universalism.

Sanctification, 47, 146, 174, 199, 210, 320, 321, 322, 360.

Satan, 75, 77, 80, 111, 238, 239, 240, 284, 311, 354, 355, 368, 372, 373, 374, 375, 377, 379.

Saul, 109

Scholasticism, 202, 389.

*Scientia media*, 178, 179, 269.

Scotism, 252.

Scripture, 9, 14, 15, 21, 36, 39, 45, 53, 60, 77, 83, 85, 114, 115, 120, 125, 151, 154, 161, 162, 174, 176, 177, 190, 196, 197, 200, 201, 204, 210, 212, 222, 223, 224, 232, 233, 235, 237, 239, 243, 244, 246, 252, 257, 258, 259, 260, 261, 268, 269, 270, 271, 272, 273, 274, 275, 276, 277, 278, 281, 282, 283, 285, 288, 290, 291, 302, 303, 304, 305, 310, 312, 313, 326, 330, 331, 332, 333, 334, 335, 337, 338, 339, 340, 341, 342, 345, 347, 348, 350, 356, 358, 359, 360, 361, 364, 365, 366, 367, 368, 370, 373, 378, 385, 386, 387, 388, 389.

Semi-Pelagianism, 36, 93, 179, 269, 283.

Sermons, Barth's, 17, 38, 39, 40, 41.

Sin, 17, 62, 63, 69, 70, 73, 79-88, 93, 115, 122, 140, 141, 143, 145, 147, 155, 210, 211, 215-260, 263, 318, 322, 325, 334, 343, 345, 381, 382. *See* Chaos; Evil; Guilt; Judgment, God's; Unbelief.

Sin, ontological impossibility of, 88, 215-260, 266, 278, 280, 287, 288, 290, 370.

Socinianism, 179.

*Sola fide*, 43, 45, 47, 171, 172, 173, 174, 197, 198, 200, 204, 205, 206, 359, 378, 379.

*Sola gratia*, 43, 45, 47, 49, 50, 174, 197, 198, 199, 200, 204, 205, 206, 214, 274, 359, 378, 379.

Solomon, 109

State, the, and Church, *see* Politics.

Supra-lapsarianism, 252, 255, 256, 258, 283, 324, 370, 380.

Synergism, 112, 113, 194, 196, 200, 201, 204, 210, 267, 268, 272, 273, 274, 275, 279, 283, 288, 295, 347, 348, 349, 350, 380.

Theology, crisis, 22, 23-51, 196, 249, 260, 381.
dialectical, 10, 22, 23-51, 166, 201, 202, 392.
history of, 19, 20, 21, 158, 196-214, 272, 349, 386, 389, 390.
liberal; 15, 16, 46, 387, 388.
modern-Protestant; 36, 166, 167, 168, 169, 196, 380.
natural, 18, 53, 124, 125, 126, 127, 176, 182, 183, 184, 185, 190, 193, 194, 298, 299, 302, 304, 309, 312, 313, 323, 324, 330, 331, 332, 380.
19th century, 9, 20, 45, 47, 166, 169, 240, 307, 316, 374, 378, 379, 385.
Reformation, 12, 14, 15, 45, 48, 50, 66, 83, 94, 95, 96, 97, 99, 111, 147, 168, 171-180, 186, 197, 198, 214, 252, 258, 259, 262, 274, 275, 280, 281, 282, 286, 287, 288, 289, 292, 295, 296, 315, 317, 318, 381, 382.
Reformed, 9, 216, 224, 230, 233, 349, 350, 389.
Roman Catholic, 12, 14, 15, 149, 166-195, 196, 197, 198, 199, 203, 250, 251, 252, 318, 349.

Theology and Philosophy, 20, 21, 22, 31, 32, 42, 385-393

Theology of glory, 19, 171, 201, 202, 203.

Theology of the cross, 19, 131, 201, 202, 203, 242, 310, 312, 313, 316.

Theopaschitism, 125-135, 297-327. *See* Jesus Christ, states of.

Thomism, 178, 179, 180, 190, 252.

Time, 152, 153, 154, 155, 157, 158, 165.

*Tohu wabohu*, 58, 59, 311.

Trent, Council of, 174, 178.

Trinity, 20, 387, 390.

Tritheism, 306, 312, 391.

Unbelief, 77, 113-122, 262-274, 278, 279, 287, 288, 290, 293, 294, 295, 322, 364, 371, 374, 380. *See* Election; Sin; Universalism.

Universalism, 138, 211-212, 262-296, 362, 363, 364, 367. *See* Election; Reconciliation.

Vatican Council; 184, 194.
*Vere Deus et vere homo*, 133, 212, 299, 304, 305, 306, 312. *See* Jesus Christ, person of.
Virgin birth, 16, 132, 386, 387, 388.

Will, God's, 56, 57, 62, 64, 70, 82, 86, 88, 95, 99, 100, 103, 137, 139, 220, 221, 227, 245, 248, 289, 310, 312.
Word of God, *see* Scripture.
Wrath, God's, 72, 74, 80, 93, 102, 103, 127, 135, 136, 138, 141, 142, 143, 157, 219, 220, 234, 235, 236, 240, 241, 242, 243, 253, 257, 258, 304, 305, 309, 314, 323, 354, 370, 380. *See* Judgment, God's; No, God's.
Yes, God's, 24-46, 58, 59, 60, 61, 66, 72, 73, 77, 81, 82, 91, 102, 141, 142, 145, 146, 183, 219, 220, 221, 225, 227, 229, 239, 242, 243, 247, 250, 260, 262, 267, 289 378, 381. *See* Love, God's; No, God's.

Zwischen den Zeiten, 16.